BASEBALLISTICS

D1468032

BASEBALLISTICS

**EDITED
BY
BERT
RANDOLPH
SUGAR**

A · THOMAS · DUNNE
BOOK

ST. MARTIN'S PRESS   NEW YORK

Although neither man is around to read this, this book is
dedicated to Jack McClain who co-piloted this venture and
A. Bartlett Giamatti who encouraged it.

BASEBALLISTICS. Copyright © 1990 by Bert Randolph Sugar. All rights reserved. Printed in the United States of America. No part of this book may
be used or reproduced in any manner whatsoever without written permission except in the case of brief quotations embodied in critical articles or
reviews. For information, address St. Martin's Press, 175 Fifth Avenue, New York, N.Y. 10010.

Design by Jaye Zimet

Library of Congress Cataloging-in-Publication Data

Sugar, Bert Randolph.
    Baseballistics edited by Bert Randolph Sugar.
        p. cm.
    "A Thomas Dunne Book."
    ISBN 0-312-03789-9 (pbk.)
    1. Baseball—United States—Records. 2. Baseball—United States—
-Miscellanea.   I. Title.
GV877.S93 1990
796.357-0973-021—dc20   89-27091
                                                       CIP

First Edition
10 9 8 7 6 5 4 3 2 1

CONTENTS

Runs Batted In

Runs Scored

Walks

Strikeouts

Pinch Hits

Extra Base Hits

Stolen Bases

Batting Miscellany

TEAM-BY-TEAM LEADERS
NATIONAL LEAGUE 207

AMERICAN LEAGUE 293

PREFACE

Growing up in the Washington, D.C., area, I was duty bound to root, root, root for the home team—in this instance, the Washington Senators—which was a little like lining up on the side of the undertaker. The Senators might have been one of baseball's most god-awful teams, a threadbare and lackluster group of has-beens, never-wases, and names that were not even household names in their own households. Never inclined to be too severe on pitched balls and whose gloves were often up for adoption, the Senators were utterly dependable losers. Still, I loved them and their ineptitude—charming as it was.

Starting with opening day, which was always an invitation to future disappointments, right through the season, when their few wins, suspended almost like fruit in aspic, would place them exactly where they belonged, in last place, I followed my beloved Senators. This was easy since all one had to do was look at the bottom of the American League standings each and every day in the Journal of Record to see their name written in bold. They were indeed "First in war, first in peace, and last in the American League." Their finishing last—or somewhere close to it—became the longest-running act in baseball.

As each year's performance of the woeful Senators became much like the watering of last year's crops, with the same crop failure, the kids in my neighborhood began to look elsewhere for their baseball fix. Sometimes this took the form of memorizing past glories, which, in the case of the Senators, went almost back to the days of those while-you-get-your-haircut weeklies. Other times, it was just memorizing baseball statistics, past and present, and then framing them into questions to ask of others. These, then, became our primary outlet and just possibly the start of baseball trivia—although I'm sure other kids in other cities were on the same wacky wavelength, doing the same thing.

However, truth to tell, back then we didn't know the word "trivia." All we knew was that every question was framed with one of what Rudyard Kipling had called his "six honest serving men"—all of the questions starting with What, Why, When, How, Where, or Who. We never thought to explain them or give them a name. We just knew what they were, sort of like Louis Armstrong's reply to the question "What is rhythm?" "Man, if you gotta ask, you'll never know."

Collecting these questions soon became a passion, somewhat akin to another prevailing passion of the day, the collecting of baseball trading cards. And pretty soon we had a whole catalogue of them, always at the ready to ask other dandruff-scratchers whenever we ran into them. They were our currency, highly negotiable pieces of information that made us—or so we believed—part of that glorious world of baseball. And even when they were embroidered out of whole cloth, as many were, those who had original copyrights to them stood that much taller in the eyes of his peers, a shining hero, at least for the day the question was first asked.

But soon we discovered girls and cars, in that order, and went away to school. And our mothers did something all mothers everywhere have done since Father Adam first heard the rush of the apple salesmen: they cleaned out our rooms, throwing away all the paraphernalia of our youth, including our baseball cards. Luckily, they couldn't throw away our warehouse of baseball trivia questions, which we transported with us wherever we went.

But while, for most baseball fans at the time, trivia seemed to hold about as much value as bonds issued by the Weimar Republic, we were always able to find other like-minded kids from other neighborhoods in other major league cities who subscribed to the same obsession-cum-religion. And soon our collection of Who's, When's, Where's, How many's, and Why's began to take on a different flavor, a different coloration. Where once they had been filled to the Plimsoll mark with references solely to the Senators (as in: "Who was the last man to hit more home runs than the rest of his team, combined? The answer: Stan Spence, of the 1944 Washington Senators, with 18 of his team's 33), now they took on an ecumenical cast, with questions incorporating cities like New York, Baltimore, Philadelphia, Detroit, and all points north, east, south, and west.

With all applications grudgingly accepted, I now could incorporate into my storehouse of trivia information such questions as "Who is the only pitcher to win more games in the World Series than he had during the regular season?" (Virgil Trucks, 1945 Detroit Tigers); "What pitcher won the most games in a year without pitching a shutout?" (Bullet Joe Bush, 1922 New York Yankees, with 26); "Who was the only left-handed throwing, right-handed hitting player ever to win a batting title?" (Hal Chase, 1919 New York Giants); and "Who was the only man in baseball history to play exactly 1,000 games for a team and have exactly 1,000 base hits?" (Joe Gordon, New York Yankees, 1938–46)

All of a sudden, I had a Turkish bazaar of information at my command. I sallied forth to the local publican's house of refreshment to do battle, where, standing one-legged on the less-than-sober side of the bar, partaking of the kindly spleen of bartenders behind provincial free-lunch counters, I paid my way through seven years of college by winning trivia contest after trivia contest. I also managed to pick up some spare change from less anointed and appointed fellow triviots who were forced to shut up like weak-springed jackknives in the face of such an onslaught—and who came to view me as a widow-and-orphan oppressor with incipient Bright's disease.

However, upon returning back to Washington, I found something as unbelievable as Santa Claus suffering from vertigo: My beloved Senators had succumbed to hibernational ambitions, moving first to Minnesota and then to Dallas. I now had to attach my rooting interest, such as it was, to another team.

The easiest team to root for would have been the New York Yankees, every other kid from the old neighborhood having adopted the Bronx Bombers as "their" team. But I had the same amount of affection for the Yankees as European countries once lavished on flocks of invading Huns. After all, I reasoned, weren't these the same New York Yankees who had always won with dismal monotony and startling variety? What was so exciting about rooting for a team which, as my childhood hero Red Smith once pointed out, was "like rooting for U.S. Steel?" No, I would rather pluck out an offending eye than follow the Yankees. Another team would have to do, thank you. Here a quick note is in order. Yes, as several of my friends and some of my sharp-eyed readers have noted, I did subsequently move to New York, but only for the same reason Willie Sutton robbed banks: "Cause that's where the money is."

In what may have been the greatest act of free association since Professor Rorschach toppled over his ink bottle, I chose the Boston Red Sox as my surrogate team. After all, according to what heresies of reason and silent meditations I could bring to bear on the comparison, weren't the Red Sox, like the Senators before them, so decimated by the mere presence of the Yankees that all that was missing was a note from their mothers explaining their collective absence—for references, see the 1949 pennant race?

Having adopted the Red Sox, I would make my annual pilgrimage to Fenway Park for Opening Day. In the beginning that took the form of a somewhat liquid trip with a group known as the BLOHARDS—Benevolent and Loyal Order of Honorable and Ancient Red Sox Die-Hard Sufferers—an odd collection of New York admen after my own heart. In more recent years, the gathering of the loyal has been put together by George Kimball, the sportswriter for the *Boston Herald.* And no less liquid.

It was at one of those jolly-hops hosted by Kimball, where all Bostonians had been merged into celebrants, that I found myself standing next to one Jack McClain at the Elliott Lounge, our kick-off point for opening day, if you'll excuse the mixed metaphor. Now McClain was a curious piece of goods; a man who possessed unimpeachable courtesy, who had never let success go to his clothing, wearing an outfit that looked like it came off the Goodwill rack. McClain had never met the subject that wouldn't engage and hold his critical fancy, able to converse on several subjects—all at the same time. But what held my attention was his total command of baseball trivia, a well-guarded store of information, all of which he spotted out in a stop-me-if-you've-heard-this-one-before manner.

Now, up to the time I first met McClain, I had always thought that baseball trivia was a quasi-organized mind game, one which hardly took a second thought—the first one covering it all, thank you! All trivia questions were those that begot the traditional one or two answers in return. Or so I thought. However, as I was soon to find out, baseball trivia is dangerous quicksand, its particles constantly shifting. And, in a day and age when more and more baseball statistics are committed to memory and heavy tomes like the MacMillan *Baseball Encyclopedia* and Bill James' monumental book have moved from the door jamb to the living-room table, triviots wanted more than mere baseball shorthand. They wanted the entire mortar of the sport wrapped up in a trivia package—anything else was plain vanilla.

Listening to McClain, I began to feel as bereft as Robinson Crusoe without a boat. All of a sudden baseball trivia took on a new meaning to me. For instance—and here I cease to be the translator and become merely the chronicler as I recapture what I can best remember—"Most home runs by zodiac sign;" "Most consecutive games played at each position;" "Players who pitched and caught in the same game," and on and on and so forth, each delivered in a manner reminiscent of a second assistant to the third assistant D.A. delivering an indictment. No longer was trivia a mere footnote to baseball history, it was baseball history.

But even as I stood there, opening and closing my mouth like a goldfish out of water, it became painfully obvious to me that not only had I missed the point about baseball trivia, but that we were also at the point of missing the Opening Day festivities. And so, the tight knot of revelers, all by now somewhat softened to the magic of the distiller's art, went down the street to "The Fens."

And here, dear reader, if you will but indulge me for a second, I will tell you why I love the game of baseball. Seems that by the time our jolly group fought our way through the traffic surrounding Fenway and into our seats, it was about two minutes before game time, give or take a minute. And then, the large electronic sign that hangs on the famous Green Wall, just at the intersection of left and center, flashed a message that somebody-or-other, whose name escaped me then and still escapes me, was "Caught in traffic and unable to sing the National Anthem." No sooner had the message board gone blank when two little old ladies who looked like Sunday school teachers fully expecting to be hit in the head by an errant spitball the minute they turned their back, got up in the box seats and very quietly began singing something that sounded like, "O say can you see . . ." Like the surface of water broken by a pebble, they were soon joined in by other nearby fans who picked up their sputtering torch and joined in at the second line, "By the dawn's early light . . ." And then, almost in a patriotic wave, that fusion of souls known as Boston Red Sox fans picked up the next line and the next line and the next, standing up, section-by-section, until the entire ballpark rocked with the din and roar of patriotism. As the body assembled concluded, acappella, the last line, "And the home of the brave . . ." the Red Sox ran out of their dugout to take their places on the field. It was extemporaneous, it was wonderful, and it was baseball!

Unfortunately, as memory serves, that was Boston's single shining moment. For soon—very soon—their chances began flowing down like flour out a chute. And even before they were removed for the afternoon in caskets fashioned by Hillerich & Bradsby, we had all repaired back to the Elliot Lounge where the deficiencies of the day might be made up by partaking of the liquids known as tradition. And, not incidentally, to pick up on our game of baseball trivia, the pre-game hors d'oeuvre only serving as a taste for the post-game steady diet of questions, a veritable smorgasbord served in generous portions, with lists of names about as familiar as those in the Riga phone book. All in the name of trivia, of course. Looking back through the fogbanks of memory, I can still remember that game, now long gone; and Jack McClain, also long gone. But for one day, lo those few years back, I was privileged to be in his company at a ballgame and fortunate enough to have become his friend. He supplied many of the lists in this book, hardly cut to any standard pattern, and his painstaking devotion to baseball's traditions and lore are to be seen in the completion of this book, one which he made possible, even though he is no longer around to see the fruits of his efforts.

Others along the way who have aided and abetted in pulling together these baseball trivia questions-cum-lists include some of those found at baseball watering places like Runyon's in New York and Miller's in Chicago and just about anywhere where baseball is spoken. People like Gene Orza, Terry Cashman, Bob Fitzsimmons, Kevin O'Malley, and Richie O'Rourke (Runyon's) and John Carney and Dave Condon (Miller's). In fact, one of the funniest moments I had in compiling these lists occurred at Runyon's. One night I was trying out one of my lists, the list about which major league players played during the most presidential administrations, and had abbreviated it to read: "What twentieth century player played during the most presidential administrations?" While most of those congregated around the bar stood there with as much dignity as the occasion demanded, fuffumping and mumbling, a loud voice from the back called out "Jim Kaat." Turning around to see the identity of the answerer, I found it to be none other than, you guessed it, Jim Kaat!

Also, a special tip of the Sugar hat goes to John Grabowski, a trivia gold mine in and of himself, who spent endless hours updating these lists whenever Nolan Ryan or Mike Schmidt sneezed. To all these people and more, this book is yours. And whatever it is, baseball trivia or baseball list, it sure as hell beats cheering for the Washington Senators, wherever they are.

Bert Randolph Sugar
Chappaqua, New York
June 7, 1989

BATTING

BASE HITS

MOST HITS, BY DECADE

Pre–1900
Cap Anson	3041
Roger Connor	2480
Dan Brouthers	2304
Jim O'Rourke	2303
Bid McPhee	2291
Jimmy Ryan	2152
Hugh Duffy	2146
Monte Ward	2123
Ed McKean	2083
George Van Haltren	2075

1900–1909
Honus Wagner	1850
Sam Crawford	1680
Nap Lajoie	1666
Willie Keeler	1583
Ginger Beaumont	1560
Cy Seymour	1460
Elmer Flick	1441
Fred Clarke	1401
Fred Tenney	1387
Bobby Wallace	1370

1910–1919
Ty Cobb	1951
Tris Speaker	1822
Eddie Collins	1682
Clyde Milan	1556
Joe Jackson	1548
Jake Daubert	1535
Zack Wheat	1516
Frank Baker	1502
Heinie Zimmerman	1481
Ed Konetchy	1473

1920–1929
Rogers Hornsby	2085
Sam Rice	2010
Harry Heilmann	1924
George Sisler	1900
Frankie Frisch	1808
Babe Ruth	1734
Joe Sewell	1698
Charlie Jamieson	1623
Charlie Grimm	1570
George Kelly	1569

1930–1939
Paul Waner	1959
Charlie Gehringer	1865
Jimmie Foxx	1845
Lou Gehrig	1802
Earl Averill	1786
Al Simmons	1700
Ben Chapman	1697
Chuck Klein	1676
Mel Ott	1673
Joe Cronin	1650

1940–1949
Lou Boudreau	1578
Bob Elliott	1563
Dixie Walker	1512
Stan Musial	1432
Bobby Doerr	1407
Tommy Holmes	1402
Luke Appling	1376
Bill Nicholson	1328
Marty Marion	1310
Phil Cavarretta	1304

1950–1959
Richie Ashburn	1875
Nellie Fox	1837
Stan Musial	1771
Alvin Dark	1675
Duke Snider	1605
Gus Bell	1551
Minnie Minoso	1526
Red Schoendienst	1517
Yogi Berra	1499
Gil Hodges	1491

1960–1969
Roberto Clemente	1877
Hank Aaron	1819
Vada Pinson	1776
Maury Wills	1744
Brooks Robinson	1692
Curt Flood	1690
Billy Williams	1651
Willie Mays	1635
Frank Robinson	1603
Ron Santo	1592

1970–1979
Pete Rose	2045
Rod Carew	1787
Al Oliver	1686
Lou Brock	1617
Bobby Bends	1565
Tony Perez	1560
Larry Bowa	1552
Ted Simmons	1550
Amos Otis	1549
Bobby Murcer	1548

1980–89
Robin Yount	1731
Eddie Murray	1642
Willie Wilson	1639
Wade Boggs	1597
Dale Murphy	1553
Harold Baines	1547
Andre Dawson	1535
Alan Trammell	1504
Carney Lansford	1486
Keith Hernandez	1480

EVOLUTION OF SINGLES RECORD

NATIONAL LEAGUE

1900   Willie Keeler, Bklyn.   179
1901   Jesse Burkett, St. L.   180
1927   Lloyd Waner, Pitt.   198

AMERICAN LEAGUE

1901   Nap Lajoie, Phila.   154
1903   Patsy Dougherty, Bost.   161
1904   Willie Keeler, NY   164
1906   Willie Keeler, NY   166
1911   Ty Cobb, Det.   169
1920   George Sisler, St. L.   171
1921   Jack Tobin, St. L.   179
1925   Sam Rice, Wash.   182
1980   Willie Wilson, K.C.   184

BASE HIT LEADERS BY STATE OF BIRTH

Alabama	Hank Aaron	3771
Alaska	Steve Staggs	94
Arizona	Hank Leiber	808
Arkansas	Lou Brock	3023
California	Harry Heilmann	2660
Colorado	Roy Hartzell	1146
Connecticut	Roger Connor	2480
Delaware	Hans Lobert	1252
Florida	Steve Garvey	2599
Georgia	Ty Cobb	4191
Hawaii	Mike Lum	877
Idaho	Harmon Killebrew	2086
Illinois	Red Schoendienst	2449
Indiana	Sam Rice	2987
Iowa	Cap Anson	3041
Kansas	Joe Tinker	1695
Kentucky	Pee Wee Reese	2170
Louisiana	Mel Ott	2876
Maine	George Gore	1612
Maryland	Al Kaline	3007
Massachusetts	Rabbit Maranville	2605
Michigan	Charlie Gehringer	2839
Minnesota	Dave Winfield	2419
Mississippi	Buddy Myer	2131
Missouri	Jake Beckley	2931
Montana	John Lowenstein	881
Nebraska	Sam Crawford	2964
Nevada	Jim Nash	38
New Jersey	Goose Goslin	2735
New Hampshire	Arlie Latham	1833
New Mexico	Vern Stephens	1859
New York	Eddie Collins	3311
North Carolina	Luke Appling	2749
North Dakota	Tim Johnson	283
Ohio	Pete Rose	4256
Oklahoma	Paul Waner	3152
Oregon	Dale Murphy	1820
Pennsylvania	Stan Musial	3630
Rhode Island	Nap Lajoie	3251
South Carolina	Jim Rice	1452
South Dakota	Dave Collins	1297
Tennessee	Vada Pinson	2757
Texas	Tris Speaker	3515
Utah	Duke Sims	580
Vermont	Carlton Fisk	2063
Virginia	Willie Horton	1993
Washington	Ron Santo	2254
West Virginia	Jesse Burkett	2873
Wisconsin	Al Simmons	2927
Wyoming	Rick Sofield	149
District of Columbia	Maury Wills	2134
Puerto Rico	Roberto Clemente	3000
Virgin Islands	Horace Clarke	1230
American Samoa	Tony Solaita	336
Canal Zone	Mike Eden	2

PLAYERS WITH 200 HITS AND 40 HOME RUNS, SAME SEASON

NATIONAL LEAGUE	HITS	HR
Rogers Hornsby, St. L. Cardinals, 1922	250	42
Rogers Hornsby, Chic. Cubs, 1929	229	40
Chuck Klein, Phila. Phillies, 1929	219	43
Chuck Klein, Phila. Phillies, 1930	250	40
Hank Aaron, Milw. Braves, 1963	201	44
Billy Williams, Chic. Cubs, 1970	205	42

AMERICAN LEAGUE	HITS	HR
Babe Ruth, NY Yankees, 1921	204	59
Babe Ruth, NY Yankees, 1923	205	41
Babe Ruth, NY Yankees, 1924	220	46
Lou Gehrig, NY Yankees, 1927	218	47
Lou Gehrig, NY Yankees, 1930	220	41
Lou Gehrig, NY Yankees, 1931	211	46
Jimmie Foxx, Phila. A's, 1932	213	58
Jimmie Foxx, Phila. A's, 1933	204	48
Lou Gehrig, NY Yankees, 1934	210	49
Lou Gehrig, NY Yankees, 1936	205	49
Hal Trosky, Cleve. Indians, 1936	216	42
Joe DiMaggio, NY Yankees, 1937	215	46
Hank Greenberg, Det. Tigers, 1937	200	40
Al Rosen, Cleve. Indians, 1953	201	43
Jim Rice, Bost. Red Sox, 1978	213	46

PLAYERS WITH 200 BASE HITS, LESS THAN 40 EXTRA-BASE HITS (Since 1900)

NATIONAL LEAGUE	HITS	EXTRA BASE HITS
Willie Keeler, Bklyn. Dodgers, 1901	209	33
Milt Stock, St. L. Cardinals, 1920	204	34
Milt Stock, Bklyn. Dodgers, 1925	202	38
Lloyd Waner, Pitt. Pirates, 1927	223	25
Chick Fullis, Phila. Phillies, 1933	200	38
Richie Ashburn, Phila. Phillies, 1953	205	36
Richie Ashburn, Phila. Phillies, 1958	215	39
Maury Wills, L.A. Dodgers, 1962	208	28
Curt Flood, St. L. Cardinals, 1964	211	33
Matty Alou, Pitt. Pirates, 1970	201	30
Ralph Garr, Atl. Braves, 1971	219	39
Dave Cash, Phila. Phillies, 1974	206	39
Tony Gwynn, S.D. Padres, 1984	213	36

AMERICAN LEAGUE	HITS	EXTRA BASE HITS
Johnny Pesky, Bost. Red Sox, 1947	207	35
Nellie Fox, Chic. White Sox, 1954	201	34
Harvey Kuenn, Det. Tigers, 1954	201	39
Cesar Tovar, MN Twins, 1971	204	33
Rod Carew, MN Twins, 1974	218	38

PLAYERS WITH 3,000 HITS

NAME	HITS	DATE OF 3,000	OPPOSING PITCHER
Pete Rose	4256	May 5, 1978	Steve Rogers, Mont.
Ty Cobb	4191	August 19, 1921	Elmer Myers, Bost. (AL)
Hank Aaron	3771	May 17, 1970	Wayne Simpson, Cinn.
Stan Musial	3630	May 13, 1958	Moe Drabowsky, Chic. (NL)
Tris Speaker	3515	May 17, 1925	Tom Zachary, WA
Honus Wagner	3430	June 9, 1914	Erskine Mayer, Phila. (NL)
Carl Yastrzemski	3419	September 12, 1979	Jim Beattie, NY
Eddie Collins	3311	June 3, 1925	Rip Collins, Det.
Willie Mays	3283	August 18, 1970	Mike Wegener, Mont.
Nap Lajoie	3251	September 14, 1914	Rube Foster, Bost. (AL)
Paul Waner	3152	June 19, 1942	Rip Sewell, Pitt.
Rod Carew	3053	August 4, 1985	Frank Viola, MN
Cap Anson	3041	July 18, 1897	Bill Hoffer, Balt.
Lou Brock	3023	August 13, 1979	Dennis Lamp, Chic. (NL)
Al Kaline	3007	September 24, 1974	Dave McNall, Balt.
Roberto Clemente	3000	September 30, 1972	Jon Matlack, NY (NL)

MOST TIMES AT BAT WITHOUT A HIT, SEASON

70	Bob Buhl, Milw.-Chic. (NL), 1962
61	Bill Wight, Chic. (AL), 1950
47	Ron Herbel, S.F. (NL), 1964
46	Karl Drews, St. L. (AL), 1949
41	Ernie Koob, St. L. (AL), 1916
41	Randy Tate, NY (NL), 1975
39	Ed Rakow, Det. (AL), 1964
36	Harry Parker, NY (NL), 1974
34	Steve Stone, S.F. (NL), 1971
33	Ed Lynch, NY (NL), 1982
31	Bob Miller, MN (AL), 1969
31	Don Carman, Phila. (NL), 1986
30	Rick Wise, Phila. (NL), 1966

PLAYERS WITH 200-HIT SEASONS IN EACH LEAGUE

Bill Buckner	1982 Chic. Cubs (NL)
	1985 Bost. Red Sox (AL)
Nap Lajoie	1898 Phila. Nationals (NL)
	1901 Phila. Athletics (AL)
	1904, 1906, 1910 Cleve. Naps (AL)

Al Oliver	1980 TX Rangers (AL)
	1982 Mont. Expos (NL)
George Sisler	1920, 1921, 1922, 1925, 1927 St. L. Browns (AL)
	1929 Bost. Braves (NL)

PLAYERS WITH 200 HITS IN 5 CONSECUTIVE SEASONS

Wade Boggs, Bost. (AL), 1983–89   7 seasons
Charlie Gehringer, Det. (AL), 1933–37   5 seasons
Willie Keeler, Balt. (NL), 1894–98, Bklyn. (NL), 1899–1901   8 seasons
Chuck Klein, Phila. (NL), 1929–33   5 seasons
Al Simmons, Phila. (AL), 1929–32, Chic. (AL), 1933   5 seasons

ROOKIES WITH 200 OR MORE HITS

223 Lloyd Waner, Pitt. NL, 1927	207 Kevin Seitzer, K.C. AL, 1987	203 Earle Combs, NY AL, 1925
217 Tony Oliva, MN AL, 1964	206 Billy Herman, Chic. NL, 1932	201 Roy Johnson, Det. AL, 1929
217 Jimmy Williams, Pitt. NL, 1899	206 Hal Trosky, Cleve. AL, 1934	201 Richie Allen, Phila. NL, 1964
215 Dale Alexander, Det. AL, 1929	206 Joe DiMaggio, NY AL, 1936	200 Dick Wakefield, Det. AL, 1943
209 Johnny Frederick, Bklyn. NL, 1929	205 Johnny Pesky, Bost. AL, 1942	
209 Harvey Kuenn, Det. AL, 1953	205 Vada Pinson, Cinn. NL, 1959*	

*Not a rookie by present standards

TEAMMATES FINISHING ONE-TWO IN BASE HITS (Since 1900)

NATIONAL LEAGUE

1910	Pitt. Pirates	Bobby Byrne (178)	Honus Wagner (178, Tie)
1920	St. L. Cardinals	Rogers Hornsby (218)	Milt Stock (204, Tie)
1927	Pitt. Pirates	Paul Waner (237)	Lloyd Waner (223)
1933	Phila. Phillies	Chuck Klein (223)	Chick Fullis (200)
1952	St. L. Cardinals	Stan Musial (194)	Red Schoendienst (188)
1957	Milw. Braves	Red Schoendienst (200*)	Hank Aaron (198)
1965	Cinn. Reds	Pete Rose (209)	Vada Pinson (204)
1979	St. L. Cardinals	Gary Templeton (211)	Keith Hernandez (210)

AMERICAN LEAGUE

1908	Det. Tigers	Ty Cobb (188)	Sam Crawford (184)
1915	Det. Tigers	Ty Cobb (208)	Sam Crawford (183)
1919	Det. Tigers	Bobby Veach (191)	Ty Cobb (191, Tie)
1923	Cleve. Indians	Charlie Jamieson (222)	Tris Speaker (218)
1927	NY Yankees	Earl Combs (231)	Lou Gehrig (218)
1929	Det. Tigers	Dale Alexander (215)	Charlie Gehringer (215, Tie)
1938	Bost. Red Sox	Joe Vosmik (201)	Doc Cramer (198)
1956	Det. Tigers	Harvey Kuenn (196)	Al Kaline (194)
1960	Chic. White Sox	Minnie Minoso (184)	Nellie Fox (175, Tie)
1965	MN Twins	Tony Oliva (185)	Zoilo Versalles (182)
1982	Milw. Brewers	Robin Yount (210)	Cecil Cooper (205)

*Schoendienst had 122 hits with Braves in '57, 78 with Giants

PLAYERS GETTING 1,000 HITS BEFORE THEIR TWENTY-FIFTH BIRTHDAY

Ty Cobb, Det. (AL), 1911	24 years, 4 months	Freddie Lindstrom, NY (NL), 1930	24 years, 8 months
Mel Ott, NY (NL), 1933	24 years, 5 months	Buddy Lewis, WA (AL), 1941	24 years, 9 months
Al Kaline, Det. (AL), 1959	24 years, 7 months	Robin Yount, Milw. (AL), 1980	24 years, 11 months

PLAYERS WITH 2,500 HITS AND CAREER .300 BATTING AVERAGE, NEVER WON BATTING TITLE (Since 1900)

	HITS	LIFETIME AVERAGE
Eddie Collins	3311	.333
Sam Crawford	2925*	.309
Frankie Frisch	2880	.316
Mel Ott	2876	.304
Sam Rice	2987	.322

*1899 totals not included

PLAYERS WITH 10,000 AT BATS, LESS THAN 3,000 HITS

	AB	HITS
Brooks Robinson (1955–77)	10,654	2,848
Luis Aparicio (1956–73)	10,230	2,677
Rabbit Maranville (1912–33; 1935)	10,078	2,605
Frank Robinson (1956–76)	10,006	2,943

FOREIGN-BORN PLAYERS WITH 2,000 BASE HITS

Rod Carew, Panama	3053	Dave Concepcion, Venezuela	2326	Felipe Alou, Dominican Rep.	2101
Tony Perez, Cuba	2732	Patsy Donovan, Ireland	2249	Cesar Cedeno, Dominican Rep.	2087
Luis Aparicio, Venezuela	2677	Bert Campaneris, Cuba	2249	Tony Taylor, Cuba	2007

PLAYERS WITH 200 HITS, BATTING UNDER .300

PLAYER	HITS	BA
Joe Moore, NY Giants, 1935	201	.295
Maury Wills, L.A. Dodgers, 1962	208	.299
Lou Brock, St. L. Cardinals, 1967	206	.299
Matty Alou, Pitt. Pirates, 1970	201	.297
Ralph Garr, Atl. Braves, 1973	200	.299
Buddy Bell, TX Rangers, 1979	200	.299
Bill Buckner, Bost. Red Sox, 1985	201	.299

BATTING AVERAGE

EVOLUTION OF BATTING AVERAGE RECORD

NATIONAL LEAGUE, PRE–1900

.404   Ross Barnes, Chic. 1876
.407   Cap Anson, Chic. 1879
.421   Cap Anson, Chic. 1887
.438   Hugh Duffy, Bost. 1894

NATIONAL LEAGUE, POST–1900

.381   Honus Wagner, Pitt. 1900
.382   Jesse Burkett, St. L. 1901
.397   Rogers Hornsby, St. L. 1921
.401   Rogers Hornsby, St. L. 1922
.424   Rogers Hornsby, St. L. 1924

AMERICAN LEAGUE

.422   Nap Lajoie, Phila. 1901

HIGHEST BATTING AVERAGE, BY DECADE
(2,000 at bats)

Pre–1900
Willie Keeler	.387
Jesse Burkett	.359
Billy Hamilton	.349
Ed Delahanty	.344
Dan Brouthers	.343
Pete Browning	.343
Fred Clarke	.342
Dave Orr	.342
Jake Stenzel	.339
John McGraw	.336

1900–1909
Honus Wagner	.351
Nap Lajoie	.347
Ty Cobb	.338
Mike Donlin	.338
Willie Keeler	.315
Jesse Burkett	.313
Elmer Flick	.313
Cy Seymour	.311
Ginger Beaumont	.309
Jake Beckley	.309

1910–1919
Ty Cobb	.387
Joe Jackson	.354
Tris Speaker	.344
George Sisler	.331
Eddie Collins	.326
Nap Lajoie	.321
Edd Roush	.314
Sam Crawford	.313
Benny Kauff	.313
Frank Baker	.310
Vin Campbell	.310
Rogers Hornsby	.310
George Stone	.310

1920–1929
Rogers Hornsby	.382
Harry Heilmann	.364
Ty Cobb	.357
Al Simmons	.356
Paul Waner	.356
Babe Ruth	.355
Tris Speaker	.354
George Sisler	.347
Eddie Collins	.346
Bob Fothergill	.342

1930–1939
Bill Terry	.352
Johnny Mize	.346
Lefty O'Doul	.345
Lou Gehrig	.343
Joe DiMaggio	.341
Joe Medwick	.338
Jimmie Foxx	.336
Paul Waner	.336
Charlie Gehringer	.331
Babe Ruth	.331

1940–1949
Ted Williams	.356
Stan Musial	.346
Joe DiMaggio	.325
Barney McCosky	.321
Johnny Pesky	.316
Enos Slaughter	.312
Luke Appling	.311
Dixie Walker	.311
Taffy Wright	.308
George Kell	.305
Joe Medwick	.305

1950–1959
Ted Williams	.336
Stan Musial	.330
Hank Aaron	.323
Willie Mays	.317
Harvey Kuenn	.314
Richie Ashburn	.313
Al Kaline	.311
Mickey Mantle	.311
Jackie Robinson	.311
George Kell	.308
Duke Snider	.308

1960–1969
Roberto Clemente	.328
Matty Alou	.312
Pete Rose	.309
Hank Aaron	.308
Tony Oliva	.308
Frank Robinson	.304
Richie Allen	.300
Willie Mays	.300
Curt Flood	.297
Manny Mota	.297

1970–1979
Rod Carew	.343
Bill Madlock	.320
Dave Parker	.317
Pete Rose	.314
Lyman Bostock	.311
George Brett	.310
Ken Griffey	.310
Jim Rice	.310
Fred Lynn	.309
Ralph Garr	.307

1980–1989 (1,800 AT BATS)
Wade Boggs	.352
Tony Gwynn	.332
Don Mattingly	.323
Kirby Puckett	.323
Rod Carew	.314
George Brett	.311
Pedro Guerrero	.308
Al Oliver	.307
Will Clark	.304
Robin Yount	.303

TOP TEN ROOKIE BATTING AVERAGES, EACH LEAGUE (Min. 100 Games)

NATIONAL LEAGUE

.373 George Watkins, 1930 St. L.
.355 Lloyd Waner, 1927 Pitt.
.354 Kiki Cuyler, 1924 Pitt.
.339 Lonnie Smith, 1980 Phila.
.336 Paul Waner, 1926 Pitt.
.333 Richie Ashburn, 1948 Phila.
.330 Rico Carty, 1964 Milw.
.329 Johnny Mize, 1936 St. L.
.328 John Frederick, 1929 Bklyn.
.322 Alvin Dark, 1948 Bost.

AMERICAN LEAGUE

.408 Joe Jackson, 1911 Cleve.
.349 Wade Boggs, 1982 Bost.
.343 Dale Alexander, 1929 Det.
.343 Jeff Heath, 1938 Cleve.
.342 Earle Combs, 1925 NY
.334 Heinie Manush, 1923 Det.
.334 Charlie Keller, 1939 NY
.331 Mickey Cochrane, 1925 Phila.
.331 Earl Averill, 1929 Cleve.
.331 Johnny Pesky, 1942 Bost.
.331 Fred Lynn, 1975 Bost.

LIFETIME BATTING AVERAGES OF 20-YEAR PLAYERS (Not Including Pitchers)

.367 Ty Cobb (24 years)
.358 Rogers Hornsby (23 years)
.344 Tris Speaker (22 years)
.342 Babe Ruth (22 years)
.339 Nap Lajoie (21 years)
.334 Al Simmons (20 years)
.333 Cap Anson (22 years)
.333 Eddie Collins (25 years)
.333 Paul Waner (20 years)
.331 Stan Musial (22 years)
.329 Honus Wagner (21 years)
.325 Jimmie Foxx (20 years)
.322 Sam Rice (20 years)
.315 Fred Clarke (21 years)
.310 Luke Appling (20 years)
.308 Jake Beckley (20 years)
.305 Hank Aaron (23 years)
.304 Manny Mota (20 years)
.304 Mel Ott (22 years)

.303 Pete Rose (24 years)
.302 Willie Mays (22 years)
.301 Joe Cronin (20 years)
.297 George Davis (20 years)
.297 Gabby Hartnett (20 years)
.297 Joe Judge (20 years)
.297 Al Kaline (22 years)
.296 Doc Cramer (20 years)
.294 Frank Robinson (21 years)
.293 Phil Cavarretta (22 years)
.292 Lave Cross (21 years)
.290 Charlie Grimm (20 years)
.289 Bill Buckner (21 years)
.286 Johnny Cooney (20 years)
.286 Mickey Vernon (20 years)
.285 Max Carey (20 years)
.285 Carl Yastrzemski (23 years)
.282 Willie Stargell (21 years)
.282 Elmer Valo (20 years)

.280 Jimmy Dykes (22 years)
.279 Tony Perez (21 years)
.279 Rusty Staub (22 years)
.278 Deacon McGuire (26 years)
.277 Harry Davis (22 years)
.275 Bill Dahlen (22 years)
.273 Bob O'Farrell (21 years)
.271 Tim McCarver (21 years)
.271 Joe Morgan (22 years)
.270 Willie McCovey (22 years)
.267 Brooks Robinson (23 years)
.267 Bobby Wallace (25 years)
.266 Ron Fairly (21 years)
.263 Jack O'Connor (21 years)
.261 Kid Gleason (22 years)
.259 Luke Sewell (20 years)
.258 Rabbit Maranville (23 years)
.256 Harmon Killebrew (22 years)
.248 Darrell Evans (21 years)

PLAYERS NEVER BATTING BELOW .270 IN CAREER, MINIMUM OF 10 YEARS

SEASONS	NAME	CAREER	LIFETIME AVG.	LOWEST SEASON BA
22	Cap Anson	(1876–97)	.334	.272, 1892
20	Sam Rice	(1915–34)	.322	.293, 1934
15	George Sisler	(1915–22; 1924–30)	.340	.285, 1915
14	Joe Sewell	(1920–33)	.312	.272, 1932
13	Bruce Campbell	(1930–42)	.290	.275, 1941
13	Mickey Cochrane	(1925–37)	.320	.270, 1936
12	Earle Combs	(1924–35)	.325	.282, 1935
12	Bibb Falk	(1920–31)	.314	.285, 1921
12	Bob Fothergill	(1922–33)	.326	.281, 1930
11	Dom DiMaggio	(1940–42; 1946–53)	.298	.283, 1941, 1947
10	Homer Summa	(1920; 1922–30)	.302	.272, 1929

.400 HITTERS AND HOW TEAM FINISHED (Since 1900)

NATIONAL LEAGUE	W/L	PLACE	GAMES BEHIND
Rogers Hornsby, 1922 St. L. Cardinals (.401)	85–69	3	8
Rogers Hornsby, 1924 St. L. Cardinals (.424)	65–89	6	28½
Rogers Hornsby, 1925 St. L. Cardinals (.403)	77–76	4	18
Bill Terry, 1930 NY Giants (.401)	87–67	3	5

AMERICAN LEAGUE	W/L	PLACE	GAMES BEHIND
Napoleon Lajoie, 1901 Phila. Athletics (.422)	74–62	4	9
Ty Cobb, 1911 Det. Tigers (.420)	89–65	2	13½
Joe Jackson, 1911 Cleve. Indians (.408)	80–73	3	22
Ty Cobb, 1912 Det. Tigers (.410)	69–84	6	36½
George Sisler, 1920 St. L. Browns (.407)	76–77	4	21½
George Sisler, 1922 St. L. Browns (.420)	93–61	2	1
Ty Cobb, 1922 Det. Tigers (.401)	79–75	3	15
Harry Heilmann, 1923 Det. Tigers (.403)	83–71	2	16
Ted Williams, 1941 Bost. Red Sox (.406)	84–70	2	17

PLAYERS HITTING .370 SINCE WORLD WAR II

NATIONAL LEAGUE

Stan Musial, 1948 St. L. Cardinals	.376
Tony Gwynn, 1987 S.D. Padres	.370

AMERICAN LEAGUE

Ted Williams, 1957 Bost. Red Sox	.388
Rod Carew, 1977 MN Twins	.388
George Brett, 1980 K.C. Royals	.390

PLAYERS BATTING .300 IN ROOKIE *AND* FINAL SEASONS (Min. Five Years; After 1900)

PLAYER	1ST YEAR	LAST YR
Richie Ashburn	1948, Phila. (NL), .333	1962, NY (NL), .306
Tony Cuccinello	1930, Cinn. (NL), .312	1945, Chic. (AL), .308
Joe Jackson	1911, Cleve. (AL), .408	1920, Chic. (AL), .382
Del Pratt	1912, St. L. (AL), .302	1924, Det. (AL), .303
Ted Williams	1939, Bost. (AL), .327	1960, Bost. (AL), .316

PLAYERS BATTING .300 IN THEIR *ONLY* MAJOR LEAGUE SEASON (Since 1900; Min. 100 Games, 300 AB's)

1901	Irv Waldron, Milw.–WA (AL)	.311
1925	Tex Vache, Bost. (AL)	.313
1931	Buzz Arlett, Phila. (AL)	.313

PLAYERS 40 AND OVER HITTING .300 (50 or More Games)

AVG.	PLAYER	AGE	AVG.	PLAYER	AGE
.388	Cap Anson, 1894 Chic. Cubs	43	.314	Luke Appling, 1948 Chic. White Sox	41
.357	Ty Cobb, 1927 Phila. A's	40	.314	Cap Anson, 1893 Chic. Cubs	42
.349	Sam Rice, 1930 WA Senators	40	.312	Al Nixon, 1927 Phila. Phillies	41
.338	Eddie Collins, 1927 Phila. A's	40	.311	Paul Waner, 1943 Bklyn. Dodgers	40
.335	Cap Anson, 1895 Chic. Cubs	44	.310	Sam Rice, 1931 WA Senators	41
.331	Cap Anson, 1896 Chic. Cubs	45	.310	Birdie Tebbetts, 1950 Bost. Red Sox	40
.330	Stan Musial, 1962 St. L. Cardinals	41	.306	Luke Appling, 1947 Chic. White Sox	40
.328	Ted Williams, 1958 Bost. Red Sox	40	.304	Jim O'Rouke, 1892 NY Giants	40
.325	Jack Saltzgaver, 1945 Pitt. Pirates	40	.304	Bing Miller, 1935 Bost. Red Sox	41
.323	Ty Cobb, 1928 Phila. A's	41	.304	Enos Slaughter, 1958 NY Yankees	42
.323	Sam Rice, 1932 WA Senators	42	.301	Luke Appling, 1949 Chic. White Sox	42
.319	Johnny Cooney, 1941 Bost. Braves	40	.300	Gabby Hartnett, 1941 NY Giants	40
.316	Ted Williams, 1960 Bost. Red Sox	41			

BATTERS HITTING .325 FOR TWO DIFFERENT TEAMS (SINCE 1945)

Rod Carew   MN Twins—1969 (.332), 1970 (.366), 1973 (.350),
                       1974 (.364), 1975 (.359), 1976 (.331), 1977 (.388), 1978 (.333)
                       CA Angels—1980 (.331), 1983 (.339)

Bill Madlock   Chic. Cubs—1975 (.354), 1976 (.339)
                       Pitt. Pirates—1981 (.341)

Mickey Rivers NY Yankees—1977 (.326)
                       TX Rangers—1980 (.333)

Pete Rose   Cinn. Reds—1968 (.335), 1969 (.348), 1973 (.338)
                       Phila. Phillies—1979 (.331), 1981 (.325)

Al Zarilla   St. L. Browns—1948 (.329)
                       Bost. Red Sox—1950 (.325)

HIGHEST SEASON BATTING AVERAGE BY AN AMERICAN LEAGUE RIGHT-HANDED BATTER SINCE JOE DIMAGGIO'S .357 IN 1941

.356 Kirby Puckett, MN 1988	.341 Bobby Avila, Cleve. 1954	.336 Al Rosen, Cleve. 1953
.355 Lou Boudreau, Cleve. 1948	.340 George Kell, Det. 1950	.336 Carney Lansford, Bost. 1981
.353 Harvey Kuenn, Det. 1959	.340 Al Kaline, Det. 1955	.332 Harvey Kuenn, Det. 1956
.353 Paul Molitar, Milw. 1987	.340 Dave Winfield, NY 1984	.332 Hal McRae, K.C. 1976
.343 George Kell, Det. 1949	.339 Kirby Puckett, MN 1989	.332 Kirby Puckett, MN 1987
.343 Alan Trammell, Det. 1987	.336 Carney Lansford, Oak. 1989	.331 Robin Yount, Milw. 1982

BATTING TITLE

CLOSEST BATTING RACES (Since 1900)

SPREAD			AVG.
.0001	1949 American League	George Kell, Det.	.3429
		Ted Williams, Bost.	.3428
.0003	1931 National League	Chick Hafey, St. L.	.3489
		Bill Terry, NY	.3486
.0004	1970 American League	Alex Johnson, CA	.3290
		Carl Yastrzemski, Bost.	.3286
.0006	1935 American League	Buddy Myer, WA	.3490
		Joe Vosmik, Cleve.	.3484
.0009	1982 American League	Willie Wilson, K.C.	.3316
		Robin Yount, Milw.	.3307
.0010	1910 American League	Ty Cobb, Det.	.3851
		Nap Lajoie, Cleve.	.3841
.0012	1976 American League	George Brett, K.C.	.3333
		Hal McRae, K.C.	.3321
.0013	1911 National League	Honus Wagner, Pitt.	.3340
		Doc Miller, Bost.	.3327
.0016	1918 National League	Zack Wheat, Bklyn.	.3349
		Edd Roush, Cinn.	.3333
.0016	1953 American League	Mickey Vernon, WA	.3372
		Al Rosen, Cleve.	.3356
.0017	1928 American League	Goose Goslin, WA	.3794
		Heine Manush, St. L.	.3777
.0022	1930 American League	Al Simmons, Phila.	.3809
		Lou Gehrig, NY	.3787
.0022	1976 National League	Bill Madlock, Chic.	.3385
		Ken Griffey, Cinn.	.3363

TEAMMATES FINISHING ONE-TWO IN BATTING (Since 1900)

NATIONAL LEAGUE

1903	Pitt. Pirates	Honus Wagner (.355)	Fred Clarke (.351)
1923	St. L. Cardinals	Rogers Hornsby (.384)	Jim Bottomley (.371)
1925	St. L. Cardinals	Rogers Hornsby (.403)	Jim Bottomley (.367)
1926	Cinn. Reds	Bubbles Hargrave (.353)	Cuckoo Christenson (.350)
1937	St. L. Cardinals	Joe Medwick (.374)	Johnny Mize (.364)
1954	NY Giants	Willie Mays (.354)	Don Mueller (.342)

AMERICAN LEAGUE

1907	Det. Tigers	Ty Cobb (.350)	Sam Crawford (.323)
1908	Det. Tigers	Ty Cobb (.324)	Sam Crawford (.311)
1919	Det. Tigers	Ty Cobb (.384)	Bobby Veach (.355)
1921	Det. Tigers	Harry Heilmann (.394)	Ty Cobb (.389)
1942	Bost. Red Sox	Ted Williams (.356)	Johnny Pesky (.331)
1958	Bost. Red Sox	Ted Williams (.388)	Pete Runnels (.322)
1959	Det. Tigers	Harvey Kuenn (.353)	Al Kaline (.327)
1961	Det. Tigers	Norm Cash (.361)	Al Kaline (.324)
1976	K.C. Royals	George Brett (.333)	Hal McRae (.332)
1977	MN Twins	Rod Carew (.388)	Lyman Bostock (.336)
1984	NY Yankees	Don Mattingly (.343)	Dave Winfield (.340)

SWITCH-HITTING BATTERS WINNING BATTING CHAMPIONSHIP

Mickey Mantle, NY (AL), 1956	.353	
Willie McGee, St. L. (NL), 1985	.353	
Tim Raines, Mont. (NL), 1986	.334	

Pete Rose, Cinn. (NL),	1968	.335
	1969	.348
	1973	.338
Willie Wilson, K.C. (AL),	1982	.332

CATCHERS WINNING BATTING TITLES

Bubbles Hargrave, Cinn. (NL), 1926	.353 (326 AB, 115 hits)
Ernie Lombardi, Cinn. (NL), 1938	.342 (489 AB, 167 hits)
Ernie Lombardi, Bost. (NL), 1942	.330 (309 AB, 102 hits)

BATTING CHAMPIONS ON LAST-PLACE TEAMS

Larry Doyle, NY (NL), 1915   .320
Richie Ashburn, Phila. (NL), 1958   .350
Tony Gwynn, S.D. (NL), 1987   .370

BATTING-TITLE WINNERS WITHOUT A HOME RUN

1902   Ginger Beaumont, Pitt., (NL)   .357
1918   Zack Wheat, Bklyn., (NL)   .335
1972   Rod Carew, MN, (AL)   .318

BATTING CHAMPIONS DRIVING IN LESS THAN 40 RUNS

	BA	RBI
Richie Ashburn, 1958 Phila. Phillies (NL)	.350	33
Pete Runnels, 1960 Bost. Red Sox (AL)	.320	35
Matty Alou, 1966 Pitt. Pirates (NL)	.342	27

BATTING CHAMPIONS WITH 100 STRIKEOUTS IN YEAR THEY LED LEAGUE

Roberto Clemente, Pitt. (NL), 1967   .357, 103 strikeouts
Dave Parker, Pitt. (NL), 1977   .338, 107 strikeouts

LOWEST BATTING AVERAGES TO LEAD LEAGUE

NATIONAL LEAGUE

.313 Tony Gwynn, S.D. 1988
.320 Larry Doyle, NY 1915
.321 Edd Roush, Cinn. 1919
.323 Bill Madlock, Pitt. 1983
.324 Bill Buckner, Chic. 1980
.325 Dick Groat, Pitt. 1960
.326 Tommy Davis, L.A. 1962
.328 Hank Aaron, Milw. 1956
.329 Jake Daubert, Bklyn. 1914
.329 Roberto Clemente, Pitt. 1965
.330 Ernie Lombardi, Bost. 1942

AMERICAN LEAGUE

.301 Carl Yastrzemski, Bost. 1968
.306 Elmer Flick, Cleve. 1905
.309 Snuffy Stirnweiss, NY 1945
.316 Frank Robinson, Balt. 1966
.318 Rod Carew, MN 1972
.320 Pete Runnels, Bost. 1960
.321 Carl Yastrzemski, Bost. 1963
.321 Tony Oliva, MN 1965
.323 Tony Oliva, MN 1964
.324 Ty Cobb, Det. 1908

HIGHEST BATTING AVERAGES *NOT* LEADING LEAGUE

NATIONAL LEAGUE

.393 Babe Herman, Bklyn. 1930
.386 Chuck Klein, Phila. 1930
.383 Lefty O'Doul, Phila. 1930
.381 Babe Herman, Bklyn. 1929
.380 Rogers Hornsby, Chic. 1929
.379 Freddie Lindstrom, NY 1930
.378 Elmer Flick, Phila. 1901
.375 Zack Wheat, Bklyn. 1924
.373 George Watkins, St. L. 1930
.372 Bill Terry, NY 1929

AMERICAN LEAGUE

.408 Joe Jackson, Cleve. 1911
.401 Ty Cobb, Det. 1922
.395 Joe Jackson, Cleve. 1912
.393 Babe Ruth, NY 1923
.392 Al Simmons, Phila. 1927
.389 Ty Cobb, Det. 1921
.389 Tris Speaker, Cleve. 1925
.388 Tris Speaker, Cleve. 1920
.384 Nap Lajoie, Cleve. 1910
.384 Al Simmons, Phila. 1925

PLAYERS WHO WERE RUNNERS-UP FOR BATTING TITLES IN BOTH LEAGUES

PLAYER	AL		NL	
Mike Donlin	Balt., 1901	.341	Cinn., 1903	.351
			Cinn., 1904	.329
			NY, 1908	.334
Willie Keeler	NY, 1904	.343	Bklyn., 1901	.355
	NY, 1905	.302	Bklyn., 1902	.338
Al Oliver	TX, 1978	.324	Pitt., 1974	.321
Frank Robinson	Balt., 1967	.311	Cinn., 1962	.342

PLAYERS WINNING BATTING TITLE IN YEAR FOLLOWING JOINING NEW CLUB (Since 1900)

NATIONAL LEAGUE

1916	Hal Chase, Cinn. Reds (.339)	Jumped from Federal League
1928	Rogers Hornsby, Bost. Braves (.387)	Traded from NY Giants
1929	Lefty O'Doul, Phila. Phillies (.398)	Traded from NY Giants
1940	Debs Garms, Pitt. Pirates (.355)	Traded from Bost. Braves
1942	Ernie Lombardi, Bost. Braves (.330)	Traded from Cinn. Reds
1966	Matty Alou, Pitt. Pirates (.342)	Traded from S.F. Giants
1982	Al Oliver, Mont. Expos (.331)	Traded from TX Rangers

AMERICAN LEAGUE

1916	Tris Speaker, Cleve. Indians (.386)	Traded from Bost. Red Sox
1966	Frank Robinson, Balt. Orioles (.316)	Traded from Cinn. Reds
1970	Alex Johnson, CA Angels (.329)	Traded from Cinn. Reds
1981	Carney Lansford, Bost. Red Sox (.336)	Traded from CA Angels

BATTING CHAMPIONS CHANGING TEAM SEASON AFTER THEY WON BATTING CHAMPIONSHIP (Since 1900)

NATIONAL LEAGUE

Chuck Klein, 1933 Batting Champion, Phila. Phillies (.368)
    (Traded to Chic. Cubs in off-season for three players and $65,000)
Bill Madlock, 1976 Batting Champion, Chic. Cubs (.339)
    (Traded to S.F. Giants in off-season for Bobby Murcer and two other players)

AMERICAN LEAGUE

Nap Lajoie, 1901 Batting Champion, Phila. Athletics (.422)
    (Sold to Cleve. Indians, June, 1902)
Harvey Kueen, 1959 Batting Champion, Det. Tigers (.353)
    (Traded to Cleve. Indians in off-season for Rocky Colavito)
Pete Runnels, 1962 Batting Champion, Bost. Red Sox (.326)
    (Traded to Houst. Astros in off-season for Roman Mejias)
Rod Carew, 1978 Batting Champion, MN Twins (.333)
    (Traded to CA Angels in off-season for Ken Landreaux and three other players)

BATTING CHAMPIONS WHOSE NEXT SEASON'S AVERAGE DECLINED THE MOST (Since 1900)

NATIONAL LEAGUE	PCT.
Willie McGee, St. L. Cardinals, 1986 (1985 Average, .353; 1986, .256)	−97
Cy Seymour, Cinn. Reds (NY Giants), 1906 (1905 Average, .377; 1906, .286)	−91
Debs Garms, Pitt. Pirates, 1941 (1940 Average, .355; 1941, .264)	−91
Rico Carty, Atl. Braves, 1972* (1970 Average, .366; 1972, .277)	−89
Rogers Hornsby, St. L. Cardinals, 1926 (1925 Average, .403; 1926, .317)	−86
Richie Ashburn, Phila. Phillies, 1959 (1958 Average, .350; 1959, .266)	−84
Lefty O'Doul, Bklyn. Dodgers (NY Giants), 1933 (1932 Average, .368; 1933, .284)	−84

AMERICAN LEAGUE	PCT.
Norm Cash, Det. Tigers, 1962 (1961 Average, .361; 1962, .243)	−118
George Sisler, St. L. Browns, 1924* (1922 Average, .420; 1924, .305)	−115
Goose Goslin, WA Senators, 1929 (1928 Average, .379; 1929, .288)	−91
Lew Fonseca, Cleve. Indians, 1930 (1929 Average, .369; 1930, .279)	−90
Babe Ruth, NY Yankees, 1925 (1924 Average, .378; 1925, .290)	−88
Mickey Vernon, WA Senators, 1947 (1946 Average, .353; 1947, .265)	−88
Dale Alexander, Bost. Red Sox, 1933 (1932 Average, .367 (Det.-Bost.); 1933, .281)	−86

*Missed season after winning batting championship; "Next Season" is first active season after winning title.

LOWEST LIFETIME BATTING AVERAGES FOR PLAYERS LEADING LEAGUE

.268	George "Snuffy" Stirnweiss (1943–52)	Led AL with .309 in 1945
.271	Norm Cash (1958–74)	Led AL with .361 in 1961
.281	Bobby Avila (1949–59)	Led AL with .341 in 1954
.284	Fred Lynn (1974–89)*	Led AL with .333 in 1979
.285	Carl Yastrzemski (1961–83)	Led AL with .321 in 1963, .326 in 1967, and .301 in 1968
.286	Mickey Vernon (1939–43; 1946–60)	Led AL with .353 in 1946; Led AL with .337 in 1953
.286	Dick Groat (1952; 1955–67)	Led NL with .325 in 1960
.288	Alex Johnson (1964–76)	Led AL with .329 in 1970
.289	Bill Buckner (1969–89)*	Led NL with .324 in 1980
.290	Larry Doyle (1907–20)	Led NL with .320 in 1915
.290	Ferris Fain (1947–55)	Led AL with .344 in 1951; Led AL with .327 in 1952
.290	Billy Williams (1959–76)	Led NL with .333 in 1972
.290	Carney Lansford (1978–88)*	Led AL with .336 in 1981
.291	Pete Runnels (1951–64)	Led AL with .320 in 1960; Led AL with .326 in 1962
.291	Sherry Magee (1904–19)	Led NL with .331 in 1910
.291	Hal Chase (1905–19)	Led NL with .339 in 1916

*Active

TWO-TIME BATTING CHAMPIONS WITH LIFETIME AVERAGES BELOW .300

Tommy Davis (1959–76)	.294	Won NL Batting Titles in 1962 & '63
Ferris Fain (1947–55)	.290	Won AL Batting Titles in 1951 & '52
Pete Runnels (1951–64)	.291	Won AL Batting Titles in 1960 & '62
Mickey Vernon (1939–43; 1946–60)	.286	Won AL Batting Titles in 1946 & '53
Carl Yastrzemski (1961–83)	.285	Won AL Batting Titles in 1963, '67 & '68

YEARS IN WHICH BATTING TITLES IN *BOTH* LEAGUES WERE WON BY RIGHT-HANDED BATTERS

	NATIONAL LEAGUE	AMERICAN LEAGUE
1903	Honus Wagner, Pitt.	Nap Lajoie, Cleve.
1904	Honus Wagner, Pitt.	Nap Lajoie, Cleve.
1921	Rogers Hornsby, St. L.	Harry Heilmann, Det.
1923	Rogers Hornsby, St. L.	Harry Heilmann, Det.
1925	Rogers Hornsby, St. L.	Harry Heilmann, Det.
1931	Chick Hafey, St. L.	Al Simmons, Phila.
1938	Ernie Lombardi, Cinn.	Jimmie Foxx, Bost.
1949	Jackie Robinson, Bklyn.	George Kell, Det.
1954	Willie Mays, NY	Bobby Avila, Cleve.
1959	Hank Aaron, Milw.	Harvey Kuenn, Det.
1970	Rico Carty, Atl.	Alex Johnson, CA
1981	Bill Madlock, Pitt.	Carney Lansford, Bost.

HOME RUNS

EVOLUTION OF HOME RUN RECORD

NATIONAL LEAGUE, PRE–1900

1876	George Hall, Phila.	5
1879	Charley Jones, Bost.	9
1883	Buck Ewing, NY	10
1884	Ned Williamson, Chic.	27

POST–1900

1922	Rogers Hornsby, St. L.	42
1929	Chuck Klein, Phila.	43
1930	Hack Wilson, Chic.	56

AMERICAN LEAGUE

1901	Nap Lajoie, Phila.	12
1902	Socks Seybold, Phila.	16
1919	Babe Ruth, Bost.	29
1920	Babe Ruth, NY	54
1921	Babe Ruth, NY	59
1927	Babe Ruth, NY	60
1961	Roger Maris, NY	61

MOST HOME RUNS, BY DECADE

Pre–1900
Roger Connor	136
Sam Thompson	128
Harry Stovey	120
Mike Tiernan	108
Dan Brouthers	106
Jimmy Ryan	100
Hugh Duffy	99
Cap Anson	96
Fred Pfeffer	95
Ed Delahanty	79

1900–1909
Harry Davis	66
Piano Legs Hickman	58
Sam Crawford	57
Buck Freeman	54
Socks Seybold	51
Honus Wagner	51
Nap Lajoie	48
Cy Seymour	43
Jimmy Williams	40
Mike Donlin	39
Hobe Ferris	39

1910–1919
Gavvy Cravath	116
Fred Luderus	83
Frank Baker	76
Frank Schulte	76
Larry Doyle	64
Sherry Magee	61
Heinie Zimmerman	58
Fred Merkle	57
Vic Saier	55
Owen Wilson	52

1920–1929
Babe Ruth	467
Rogers Hornsby	250
Cy Williams	202
Ken Williams	190
Jim Bottomley	146
Lou Gehrig	146
Bob Meusel	146
Harry Heilmann	142
Hack Wilson	137
George Kelly	134

1930–1939
Jimmie Foxx	415
Lou Gehrig	347
Mel Ott	308
Wally Berger	241
Chuck Klein	238
Earl Averill	218
Hank Greenberg	206
Babe Ruth	198
Al Simmons	190
Bob Johnson	186

1940–1949
Ted Williams	234
Johnny Mize	217
Bill Nicholson	211
Rudy York	189
Joe Gordon	181
Joe DiMaggio	180
Vern Stephens	177
Charlie Keller	173
Ralph Kiner	168
Bobby Doerr	164

1950–1959
Duke Snider	326
Gil Hodges	310
Eddie Mathews	299
Mickey Mantle	280
Stan Musial	266
Yogi Berra	256
Willie Mays	250
Ted Kluszewski	239
Gus Zernial	232
Ernie Banks	228

1960–1969
Harmon Killebrew	393
Hank Aaron	375
Willie Mays	350
Frank Robinson	316
Willie McCovey	300
Frank Howard	288
Norm Cash	278
Ernie Banks	269
Mickey Mantle	256
Orlando Cepeda	254

1970–1979
Willie Stargell	296
Reggie Jackson	292
Johnny Bench	290
Bobby Bonds	280
Lee May	270
Dave Kingman	252
Graig Nettles	252
Mike Schmidt	235
Tony Perez	226
Reggie Smith	225

1980–1989
Mike Schmidt	313
Dale Murphy	308
Eddie Murray	274
Dwight Evans	256
Andre Dawson	250
Darrell Evans	230
Tony Armas	225
Lance Parrish	225
Dave Winfield	223
Darryl Strawberry	215

CAREER HOME RUN LEADERS BY ZODIAC SIGN

AQUARIUS (Jan 20–Feb 18) Hank Aaron	755		LEO (July 23–Aug 22) Carl Yastrzemski	452
PISCES (Feb 19–Mar 20) Mel Ott	511		VIRGO (Aug 23–Sept 22) Frank Robinson	586
ARIES (Mar 21–Apr 19) Gil Hodges	370		LIBRA (Sept 23–Oct 23) Mike Schmidt	548
TAURUS (Apr 20–May 20) Willie Mays	660		SCORPIO (Oct 24–Nov 21) Mickey Mantle	536
GEMINI (May 21–June 21) Lou Gehrig	493		SAGITTARIUS (Nov 22–Dec 21) Dave Kingman	442
CANCER (June 22–July 22) Harmon Killebrew	573		CAPRICORN (Dec 22–Jan 19) Willie McCovey	521

ALL-TIME HOME RUN LEADERS BY LETTER OF ALPHABET

A	Hank Aaron	755	J	Reggie Jackson	530	S	Mike Schmidt	548
B	Ernie Banks	512	K	Harmon Killebrew	573	T	Frank Thomas	286
C	Orlando Cepeda	379	L	Greg Luzinski	307	U	Willie Upshaw	88
D	Joe DiMaggio	361	M	Willie Mays	660	V	Mickey Vernon	172
E	Darrell Evans	403	N	Graig Nettles	390	W	Ted Williams	521
F	Jimmie Foxx	534	O	Mel Ott	511	Y	Carl Yastrzemski	452
G	Lou Gehrig	493	P	Tony Perez	377	Z	Gus Zernial	237
H	Frank Howard	382	Q	Joe Quinn	30			
I	Monte Irvin	99	R	Babe Ruth	714			

HOME RUN LEADERS BY STATE OF BIRTH

State	Player	HR		State	Player	HR
Alabama	Hank Aaron	755		New Jersey	Goose Goslin	248
Alaska	Steve Staggs	2		New Hampshire	Red Rolfe	69
Arizona	Hank Leiber	101		New Mexico	Ralph Kiner	369
Arkansas	Brooks Robinson	268		New York	Lou Gehrig	493
California	Ted Williams	521		North Carolina	Jim Ray Hart	170
Colorado	Johnny Frederick	85		North Dakota	Ken Hunt	33
Connecticut	Dick McAuliffe	197		Ohio	Mike Schmidt	548
Delaware	Dave May	96		Oklahoma	Mickey Mantle	536
Florida	Boog Powell	339		Oregon	Dave Kingman	442
Georgia	Johnny Mize	359		Pennsylvania	Reggie Jackson	563
Hawaii	Mike Lum	90		Rhode Island	Gabby Hartnett	236
Idaho	Harmon Killebrew	573		South Carolina	Jim Rice	379
Illinois	Greg Luzinski	307		South Dakota	Dave Collins	32
Indiana	Gil Hodges	370		Tennessee	Vada Pinson	256
Iowa	Ken Henderson	122		Texas	Frank Robinson	586
Kansas	Bob Horner	218		Utah	Duke Sims	100
Kentucky	Gus Bell	206		Vermont	Carlton Fisk	336
Louisiana	Mel Ott	511		Virginia	Willie Horton	325
Maine	Del Bissonette	65		Washington	Ron Santo	342
Maryland	Babe Ruth	714		West Virginia	George Brett	255
Massachusetts	Richie Hebner	203		Wisconsin	Al Simmons	307
Michigan	John Mayberry	255		Wyoming	Rick Scofield	9
Minnesota	Dave Winfield	357				
Mississippi	George Scott	271		District of Columbia	Don Money	176
Missouri	Yogi Berra	358		Puerto Rico	Orlando Cepeda	379
Montana	John Lowenstein	116		Virgin Islands	Ellie Hendricks	62
Nevada	Jim Nash	4		American Samoa	Tony Solaita	50

MOST CAREER HOME RUNS FOR ONE CLUB

733	Hank Aaron	Braves	536	Mickey Mantle	Yankees	493	Eddie Mathews	Braves
659	Babe Ruth	Yankees	521	Ted Williams	Red Sox	475	Stan Musial	Cardinals
646	Willie Mays	Giants	512	Ernie Banks	Cubs		Willie Stargell	Pirates
559	Harmon Killebrew	Twins	511	Mel Ott	Giants	469	Willie McCovey	Giants
548	Mike Schmidt	Phillies	493	Lou Gehrig	Yankees	452	Carl Yastrzemski	Red Sox

MOST CAREER HOME RUNS, BY POSITION

		BY POSITION	TOTAL
1B	Lou Gehrig	493	493
2B	Joe Morgan	265	268
SS	Ernie Banks	293	512
3B	Mike Schmidt	509	548
LF	Hank Aaron	661	755
CF	Willie Mays	643	660
RF	Babe Ruth	692	714
C	Johnny Bench	324	389
P	Wes Ferrell	37	38

MOST LIFETIME HOME RUNS, NEVER LED LEAGUE IN A SEASON

475	Stan Musial	379	Tony Perez	358	Yogi Berra
426	Billy Williams	377	Norm Cash	357	Dave Winfield
399	Al Kaline	370	Gil Hodges	354	Lee May

MOST INSIDE-THE-PARK HOME RUNS (SINCE 1898)

Sam Crawford (1899–1917)	51	Sam Rice (1915–34)	21
Tommy Leach (1898–1918)	48	Kiki Cuyler (1920–37)	16
Ty Cobb (1905–28)	47	Ben Chapman (1930–48)	15
Edd Roush (1913–29; 1931)	29	Tris Speaker (1907–28)	14
Rabbit Maranville (1912–35)	22	Honus Wagner (1897–1917)	14

PLAYERS HITTING 40 OR MORE HOME RUNS IN SEASON WITH 10 OR MORE LETTERS IN LAST NAME

Roy Campanella, Bklyn. (NL)	41, 1953
Ted Kluszewski, Cinn. (NL)	40, 1953
	49, 1954
	47, 1955
Rico Petrocelli, Bost. (AL)	40, 1969
Carl Yastrzemski, Bost. (AL)	44, 1967
	40, 1969
	40, 1970

MOST HOME RUNS BY MONTH

MONTH	HR		MONTH	HR	
April	11	Willie Stargell, 1971	Aug.	18	Rudy York, 1937
		Graig Nettles, 1974	Sept.	17	Babe Ruth, 1927
		Mike Schmidt, 1976	Oct.	4	Ned Williamson, 1884
May	16	Mickey Mantle, 1956			John Milligan, 1889
June	15	Babe Ruth, 1930			Gus Zernial, 1950
		Bob Johnson, 1934			Mike Schmidt, 1980
		Roger Maris, 1961			George Brett, 1985
		Pedro Guerrero, 1985			Ron Kittle, 1985
July	15	Joe DiMaggio, 1937			Dave Parker, 1985
		Hank Greenberg, 1938			Wally Joyner, 1987
		Joe Adcock, 1956			

MOST HOME RUNS IN SEASON, BY POSITION

1B	Hank Greenberg	58	1938	Det. Tigers
2B	Rogers Hornsby	42	1922	St. L. Cardinals
	Davey Johnson	42	1973	Atl. Braves
SS	Ernie Banks	47	1958	Chic. Cubs
3B	Mike Schmidt	48	1980	Phila. Phillies
LF	Ralph Kiner	54	1949	Pitt. Pirates
CF	Hack Wilson	56	1930	Chic. Cubs
RF	Roger Maris	61	1961	NY Yankees
C	Roy Campanella	41	1953	Bklyn. Dodgers
P	Wes Ferrell	9	1931	Cleve. Indians

PLAYERS LEADING LEAGUE IN HOME RUNS PLAYING FOR DIFFERENT TEAMS

Sam Crawford	Cinn. (NL), 1901 (16) Det. (AL), 1908 (7), 1914 (8)	Johnny Mize	St. L. (NL), 1939 (28), 1940 (43) NY (NL), 1947 (51-T), 1948 (40-T)
Jimmie Foxx	Phila. (AL), 1932 (58), 1933 (48), 1935 (36) Bost. (AL), 1939 (35)	Babe Ruth	Bost. (AL), 1918 (11), 1919 (29) NY (AL), 1920 (54), 1921 (59), 1923 (41), 1924 (46), 1926 (47), 1927 (60), 1928 (54), 1929 (46), 1930 (49), 1931 (46)
Reggie Jackson	Oak. (AL), 1973 (32), 1975 (36) NY (AL), 1980 (41) CA (AL), 1982 (39)	Cy Williams	Chic. (NL), 1916 (12) Phila. (NL), 1920 (15), 1923 (41)
Dave Kingman	Chic. (NL), 1979 (48) NY (NL), 1982 (37)		

PLAYERS HITTING 100 HOME RUNS OVER TWO CONSECUTIVE SEASONS

Jimmie Foxx	1932 and 1933, Phila. A's (58 and 48)	106
Ralph Kiner	1949 and 1950, Pitt. Pirates (54 and 49)	103
Babe Ruth	1920 and 1921, NY Yankees (54 and 59)	113
	1927 and 1928, NY Yankees (60 and 54)	114
Roger Maris	1960 and 1961, NY Yankees (39 and 61)	100

PLAYERS WITH FIRST 20-HOME RUN SEASON AFTER 35TH BIRTHDAY

Cy Williams	26 HR's, Phila. (NL)	1922 (35 on Dec. 21, 1921)
Charlie Gehringer	20 HR's, Det. (AL)	1938 (35 on May 11, 1938)
Luke Easter	28 HR's, Cleve. (AL)	1950 (36 on Aug. 4, 1950)
Mickey Vernon	20 HR's, WA (AL)	1954 (36 on Apr. 22, 1954)
John Lowenstein	24 HR's, Balt. (AL)	1982 (35 on Jan. 27, 1982)
Frank White	20 HR's, K.C. (AL)	1985 (35 on Sept. 4, 1985)*
Buddy Bell	20 HR's, Cinn. (NL)	1986 (35 on Aug. 27, 1986)

*20th HR came Sept. 15, 1985

SHORTSTOPS WITH SEVEN CONSECUTIVE 20-HOMER SEASONS

Ernie Banks, Chic. Cubs   1955–44
   1956–28
   1957–43*
   1958–47
   1959–45
   1960–41
   1961–29†

Cal Ripken, Balt. Orioles   1982–28
   1983–27
   1984–27
   1985–26
   1986–25
   1987–27
   1988–23
   1989–21

*Played 58 games at 3rd base
†Played 23 games in outfield, 76 at first

PLAYERS HITTING FOUR HOME RUNS IN ONE GAME—PITCHERS OFF WHOM HIT

NATIONAL LEAGUE

PITCHERS

Bobby Lowe, Bost., May 30, 1894   Icebox Chamberlain (4)—Cinn.
Ed Delahanty, Phila., July 13, 1896   Adonis Bill Terry (4)—Chic.
Chuck Klein, Phila., July 10, 1936   Jim Weaver, Mage Brown (2), Bill Swift—Pitt.
Gil Hodges, Bklyn., August 31, 1950   Warren Spahn, Normie Roy, Bob Hall, Johnny Antonelli—Bost.
Joe Adcock, Milw., July 31, 1954   Don Newcombe, Erv Palica, Pete Wojey, Johnny Podres—Bklyn.
Willie Mays, S.F., April 30, 1961   Lew Burdette (2), Seth Morehead, Don McMahon—Milw.
Mike Schmidt, Phila., April 17, 1976   Rich Reuschel (2), Paul Reuschel, Darold Knowles—Chic.
Bob Horner, Atl., July 6, 1986   Andy McGaffigan (3), Jeff Reardon—Mont.

AMERICAN LEAGUE

Lou Gehrig, NY, June 3, 1932   George Earnshaw (3), Roy Mahaffey—Phila.
Pat Seerey, Chic., July 18, 1948   Carl Scheib (4), Bob Savage, Lou Brissie—Phila.
Rocky Colavito, Cleve., June 10, 1959   Jerry Walker (2), Arnie Portocarrero, Ernie Johnson—Balt.

PLAYERS WITH THREE HOME RUNS IN ONE GAME, LESS THAN 10 IN SEASON (Since 1900)

NATIONAL LEAGUE	IN SEASON	AMERICAN LEAGUE	IN SEASON
Hal Lee, Bost., 1934	8	Mickey Cochrane, Phila., 1925	6
Babe Ruth, Bost., 1935	6	Merv Connors, Chic., 1938	6
Clyde McCullough, Chic., 1942	5	Billy Glynn, Cleve., 1954	5
Jim Tobin, Bost., 1942	6	Preston Ward, K.C., 1958	6
Tommy Brown, Bklyn., 1950	8	Don Leppert, WA, 1963	6
Del Wilber, Phila., 1951	8	Joe Lahoud, Bost., 1969	9
Jim Pendleton, Milw., 1953	7	Fred Patek, CA, 1980	5
Bob Thurman, Cinn., 1956	8	Juan Beniquez, Balt., 1986	6
Roman Mejias, Pitt., 1958	5		
Gene Oliver, Atl., 1966	8		
Mike Lum, Atl., 1970	7		
George Mitterwald, Chic., 1974	7		
Pete Rose, Cinn., 1978	7		

PLAYERS IN ORGANIZED BALL HITTING 60 HOMERS IN SEASON

1925	Tony Lazzeri, Salt Lake City, PCL (AAA)	60	1954	Bob Lennon, Nashville, Southern Assoc. (AA)	64
1926	John Clabaugh, Tyler, East TX (D)	62	1954	Joe Bauman, Roswell, Longhorn (C)	72
1927	Babe Ruth, NY, American League	60	1956	Ken Guettler, Shreveport, TX League (AA)	62
1930	Joe Hauser, Balt., International League (AAA)	63	1956	Dick Stuart, Lincoln, Western League (A)	66
1933	Joe Hauser, Minneapolis, Amer. Assoc. (AAA)	69	1956	Frosty Kennedy, Plainview, Southwestern (B)	60
1948	Bob Crues, Amarillo, W. TX-NM League (C)	69	1961	Roger Maris, NY, American League	61

ROOKIES HITTING 30 OR MORE HOME RUNS

49	Mark McGwire, Oak. (AL), 1987	34	Walt Dropo, Bost. (AL), 1950	31	Jim Hart, S.F. (NL), 1964
38	Wally Berger, Bost. (NL), 1930	33	Jimmie Hall, MN (AL), 1963	30	Bob Allison, WA (AL), 1959
38	Frank Robinson, Cinn. (NL), 1956	33	Jose Canseco, Oak. (AL), 1986	30	Willie Montanez, Phila. (NL), 1971
37	Al Rosen, Cleve. (AL), 1950	33	Earl Williams, Atl. (NL), 1971	30	Pete Incaviglia, TX (AL), 1986
35	Hal Trosky, Cleve. (AL), 1934	32	Tony Oliva, MN (AL), 1964	30	Matt Nokes, Det. (AL), 1987
35	Rudy York, Det. (AL), 1937	31	Ted Williams, Bost. (AL), 1939		

PLAYERS HITTING 49 HOME RUNS IN SEASON, NEVER HITTING 50

NATIONAL LEAGUE

Ted Kluszewski, Cinn., 1954
Andre Dawson, Chic., 1987

AMERICAN LEAGUE

Lou Gehrig, NY, 1934
Lou Gehrig, NY, 1936
Harmon Killebrew, MN, 1964
Frank Robinson, Balt., 1966
Harmon Killebrew, MN, 1969
Mark McGwire, Oak., 1987

MOST CONSECUTIVE YEARS HITTING GRAND SLAMS

9	Willie McCovey	1964–72
7	Gil Hodges	1949–55
	Vern Stephens	1944–50
6	Lou Gehrig	1927–32
	Eddie Murray	1981–86
	Willie Stargell	1969–74

MOST HOME RUNS BY AGE

TEENS		TWENTIES		THIRTIES		FORTIES	
Tony Conigliaro	24	Jimmie Foxx	376	Babe Ruth	434	Carl Yastrzemski	49
Mel Ott	19	Eddie Mathews	370	Hank Aaron	371	Stan Musial	46
Phil Cavarreta	14	Mickey Mantle	361	Willie Mays	348	Ted Williams	44
Mickey Mantle	13	Hank Aaron	342	Willie Stargell	276	Hank Aaron	42
						Reggie Jackson	32

GRAND-SLAM HOME RUNS HIT BY TEENAGERS

Scott Stratton (Louisville, AA), May 27, 1889	19 yrs., 7 mos.
George S. Davis (Cleve., NL), May 30, 1890	19 yrs., 9 mos.
Eddie Onslow (Det., AL), August 22, 1912	19 yrs., 6 mos.
Phil Cavarretta (Chic., NL), May 16, 1936	19 yrs., 10 mos.
Al Kaline (Det., AL), June 11, 1954	19 yrs., 6 mos.
Harmon Killebrew (WA, AL), June 11, 1954	19 yrs., 11 mos.
Vada Pinson (Cinn., NL), April 18, 1958	19 yrs., 8 mos.
Tony Conigliaro (Bost., AL), June 3, 1964	19 yrs., 5 mos.

OLDEST PLAYERS TO HIT GRAND SLAMS

Cap Anson Chic., (NL), August 1, 1894   42 yrs., 3 mos.
Honus Wagner Pitt., (NL), July 29, 1915   41 yrs., 5 mos.
Minnie Minoso WA, (AL), July 24, 1963   40 yrs., 8 mos.
Stan Musial St. L., (NL), June 23, 1961   40 yrs., 7 mos.

Hank Aaron Atl., (NL), June 4, 1974   40 yrs., 3 mos.
Darrell Evans Det., (AL), September 5, 1987   40 yrs., 3 mos.
Hank Aaron Atl., (NL), April 26, 1974   40 yrs., 2 mos.
Mickey Vernon Cleve., (AL), April 25, 1958   40 yrs., 0 mos.

MOST CAREER HOME RUNS BY PLAYERS HITTING HOME RUN ON FIRST PITCH IN MAJORS

185   Gary Gaetti (MN Twins), Sept. 20, 1981
79   Bert Campaneris (K.C. A's), July 23, 1964
69   Clyde Vollmer (Cinn. Reds), May 31, 1942
38   Brant Alyea (WA Senators), September 12, 1965
21   Chuck Tanner (Milw. Braves), April 12, 1955
12   George Vico (Det. Tigers), April 20, 1948

3   Clise Dudley (Bklyn. Dodgers), April 27, 1929
3   Jay Bell (Cleve. Indians), September 29, 1986
1   Eddie Morgan (St. L. Cardinals), April 14, 1936
1   Bill Lefebvre (Bost. Red Sox), June 10, 1938
1   Don Rose (CA Angels), May 24, 1972

PLAYERS HITTING HOME RUNS IN FIRST PLATE APPEARANCE IN THE MAJORS AND NEVER HITTING ANOTHER

Dan Bankhead, Bklyn. Dodgers, 1947
Cuno Barragan, Chic. Cubs, 1961
Andre David, MN Twins, 1984
Bill Lefebvre, L.A. Dodgers, 1965

Dave Machemer, CA Angels, 1978
Hack Miller, Det. Tigers, 1944
Ed Morgan, St. L. Cardinals, 1936
Bill Roman, Det. Tigers, 1964

Don Rose, CA Angels, 1972
Jose Sosa, Houst. Astros, 1975
Hoyt Wilhelm, NY Giants, 1952

MOST AT BATS, NO HOME RUNS

Bill Holbert (1876–88)   2335
Tom Oliver (1930–33)   1931
Irv Hall (1943–46)   1904
Pat Deasley (1881–88)   1466

Tommy Bond (1876–84)   1441
Roxy Walters (1915–25)   1426
Paul Cook (1884–91)   1364
Don Sutton (1966–89)   1354

Joe McGinnity (1899–1908)   1297
Waite Hoyt (1918–38)   1287

MOST CONSECUTIVE AT BATS WITHOUT A HOME RUN

3347	Tommy Thevenow	Sept. 22, 1926–End of Career, 1938
3278	Eddie Foster	April 20, 1916–End of Career, 1923
3246	Al Bridwell	Start of Career, 1905–April 30, 1913
3186	Terry Turner	July 16, 1906–June 30, 1914 (1)*
3104	Sparky Adams	July 26, 1925–June 30, 1931
3021	Jack McCarthy	June 28, 1899–End of Career, 1907
2701	Lee Tannehill	Sept. 2, 1903–July 31, 1910
2663	Roger "Doc" Cramer	Sept. 8, 1935 (1)–May 21, 1940
2617	Donie Bush	Aug. 29, 1915–Aug. 21, 1920
2568	Mike Tresh	May 19, 1940–April 20, 1948
2480	Bill Bergen	June 3, 1901–Sept. 6, 1909 (2)
2426	Joe Sugden	May 31, 1895–End of Career, 1912
2423	Emil Verban	Start of Career, 1944–Sept. 6, 1948 (1)*
2401	Everett Scott	August 1, 1914–April 26, 1920

*First game of a double-header

LOWEST BATTING AVERAGE FOR HOME RUN LEADERS

BA	PLAYER	HR	BA	PLAYER	HR
.204	Dave Kingman, NY Mets, (NL) 1982	37	.244	Gorman Thomas, Milw. Brewers, (AL) 1979	45
.232	Gavvy Cravath, Phila. Phillies, (NL) 1918	8	.245	Gorman Thomas, Milw. Brewers, (AL) 1982	39
.241	Fred Odwell, Cinn. Reds, (NL) 1905	9	.247	Tim Jordan, Bklyn. Dodgers, (NL) 1908	12
.242	Harmon Killebrew, MN Twins, (AL) 1959	42	.247	Ralph Kiner, Pitt. Pirates, (NL) 1946	23
.243	Harmon Killebrew, MN Twins, (AL) 1962	48	.248	Darrell Evans, Det. Tigers, (AL) 1985	40
.244	Wally Pipp, NY Yankees, (AL) 1917	9	.249	Mike Schmidt, Phila. Phillies, (NL) 1975	38
.244	Ralph Kiner, Pitt. Pirates, (NL) 1952	37			

REVERSE 30-30 CLUB—PLAYERS WITH 30 HOME RUNS, 30 ERRORS, SAME SEASON

NATIONAL LEAGUE	HR	ERRORS
Rogers Hornsby, St. L., 1922	42	30
Rogers Hornsby, St. L., 1924	39	34
Ernie Banks, Chic., 1958	47	32
Tony Perez, Cinn., 1969	37	32
Tony Perez, Cinn., 1970	40	35
Davey Johnson, Atl., 1973	43	30
Pedro Guerrero, L.A., 1983	32	30

AMERICAN LEAGUE	HR	ERRORS
Harmon Killebrew, WA, 1959	42	30

PLAYERS INCREASING THEIR HOME RUN PRODUCTION IN SEVEN CONSECUTIVE SEASONS

Jimmy Piersall	1950 Bost. (AL)	0			1949 WA (AL)	18
	1952 Bost. (AL)	1			1950 WA-Chic. (AL)	21
	1953 Bost. (AL)	3			1951 Chic. (AL)	29
	1954 Bost. (AL)	8		John Shelby	1981 Balt. (AL)	0
	1955 Bost. (AL)	13			1982 Balt. (AL)	1
	1956 Bost. (AL)	14			1983 Balt. (AL)	5
	1957 Bost. (AL)	19			1984 Balt. (AL)	6
Tim McCarver	1960 St. L. (NL)	0			1985 Balt. (AL)	7
	1961 St. L. (NL)	1			1986 Balt. (AL)	11
	1963 St. L. (NL)	4			1987 L.A. (NL)	22
	1964 St. L. (NL)	9		Cy Williams	1917 Chic. (NL)	5
	1965 St. L. (NL)	11			1918 Phila. (NL)	6
	1966 St. L. (NL)	12			1919 Phila. (NL)	9
	1967 St. L. (NL)	14			1920 Phila. (NL)	15
Eddie Robinson	1942 Cleve. (AL)	0			1921 Phila. (NL)	18
	1946 Cleve. (AL)	3			1922 Phila. (NL)	26
	1947 Cleve. (AL)	14			1923 Phila. (NL)	41
	1948 Cleve. (AL)	16				

MOST HOME RUNS BY SWITCH-HITTER, CAREER

Mickey Mantle (1951–68)	536	Ken Singleton (1970–84)	246	Ripper Collins (1931–38; 1941)	135
Eddie Murray (1977–88)*	353	Pete Rose (1963–86)	160	Ken Henderson (1965–80)	122
Reggie Smith (1966–82)	314	Roy White (1965–79)	160	Frankie Frisch (1919–37)	105
Ted Simmons (1968–88)*	248	Tom Tresh (1961–69)	153	Roy Cullenbine (1938–47)	101

*Active

100 HOME RUNS, BOTH LEAGUES

PLAYER	NL	AL
Bobby Bonds	191	135
Darrell Evans*	273	119
Frank Howard	123	259
Lee May	228	123
Frank Robinson	324	262
Reggie Smith	146	149

*Active

MOST HOME RUNS HIT IN ONE BALLPARK, CAREER

Mel Ott	323	Polo Grounds		Lou Gehrig	251	Yankee Stadium
Ernie Banks	290	Wrigley Field		Ted Williams	248	Fenway Park
Mickey Mantle	266	Yankee Stadium		Carl Yastrzemski	237	Fenway Park
Mike Schmidt	265	Veterans Stadium		Billy Williams	231	Wrigley Field
Babe Ruth	259	Yankee Stadium		Ron Santo	212	Wrigley Field

PLAYERS HITTING AT LEAST HALF OF THEIR TEAM'S HOME RUNS (Since 1900)

NATIONAL LEAGUE

Shad Barry, Phila., 1902	3 of team's 5 total HR
Jimmy Sheckard, Bklyn., 1903	9 of team's 15 total HR
Homer Smoot, St. L., 1903	4 of team's 8 total HR
Harry Lumley, Bklyn., 1904	9 of team's 15 total HR
Sherry Magee, Phila., 1906	6 of team's 12 total HR
Harry Lumley, Bklyn., 1907	9 of team's 18 total HR
Dick Hoblitzell, Cinn., 1911	11 of team's 21 total HR
Ed Konetchy, St. L., 1913	7 of team's 14 total HR*
Cy Williams, Phila., 1927	30 of team's 57 total HR
Wally Berger, Bost., 1930	38 of team's 66 total HR
Wally Berger, Bost., 1931	19 of team's 34 total HR
Wally Berger, Bost., 1933	27 of team's 54 total HR
Bill Nicholson, Chic., 1943	29 of team's 52 total HR

AMERICAN LEAGUE

Erve Beck, Cleve., 1901	6 of team's 12 total HR
Joe Judge, WA, 1917	2 of team's 4 total HR
Babe Ruth, Bost., 1918	11 of team's 15 total HR
Tilly Walker, Phila., 1918	11 of team's 22 total HR
Smoky Joe Wood, Cleve., 1918	5 of team's 9 total HR
Babe Ruth, Bost., 1919	29 of team's 33 total HR
Goose Goslin, WA, 1924	12 of team's 22 total HR
Jimmie Foxx, Bost., 1938	50 of team's 98 total HR
Stan Spence, WA, 1944	18 of team's 33 total HR
Sam Chapman, Phila., 1946	20 of team's 40 total HR

*Konetchy also accomplished feat in 1915 with Pitt. of Federal League, hitting 10 of team's 20 total HR

SHORTSTOPS LEADING LEAGUE IN HOME RUNS

1945	Vern Stephens, St. L. (AL)	24
1958	Ernie Banks, Chic. (NL)	47
1959	Ernie Banks, Chic. (NL)	41

FOREIGN-BORN PLAYERS WITH 40 HOME RUNS IN SEASON

Tony Perez, Cuba | 40 home runs, Cinn. (NL), 1970
Ben Oglivie, Panama | 41 home runs, Milw. (AL), 1980
Tony Armas, Venezuela | 43 home runs, Bost. (AL), 1984
George Bell, Dominican Republic | 47 home runs, Tor. (AL), 1987
Jose Canseco, Cuba | 40 home runs, Oak. (AL), 1988

BATTERS HITTING HOME RUNS IN 20 CONSECUTIVE SEASONS

24	Ty Cobb	1905–1928	21	Ron Fairly	1958–1978
23	Hank Aaron	1954–1976		Reggie Jackson	1967–1987
	Rusty Staub	1963–1985		Frank Robinson	1956–1976
	Carl Yastrzemski	1961–1983		Babe Ruth	1915–1935
22	Al Kaline	1953–1974	20	Mel Ott	1927–1946
	Willie Mays	1951–52; 1954–73			
	Willie McCovey	1959–1980			
	Stan Musial	1941–44; 1946–63			
	Tony Perez	1965–1986			
	Brooks Robinson	1956–1977			

CAREER HOME RUNS BY BATTERS HITTING FOUR HOMERS IN ONE GAME

660	Willie Mays	April 30, 1961	370	Gil Hodges	August 31, 1950	100	Ed Delahanty	July 13, 1896
548	Mike Schmidt	April 17, 1976	336	Joe Adcock	July 31, 1954	86	Pat Seerey	July 18, 1948
493	Lou Gehrig	June 3, 1932	300	Chuck Klein	July 10, 1936	70	Bobby Lowe	May 30, 1894
374	Rocky Colavito	June 10, 1959	218	Bob Horner	July 6, 1986			

PLAYERS WITH 100 HOME RUNS FOR THREE DIFFERENT TEAMS

Darrell Evans	Atl. (NL), 1969–76, 1989	131	Reggie Jackson	K.C.-Oak. (AL), 1967–75	269
	S.F. (NL), 1976–83	142		NY (AL), 1977–81	144
	Det. (AL), 1984–88	141		CA (AL), 1982–86	123

PLAYERS WITH 40 HOME RUN SEASONS BEFORE 25TH BIRTHDAY

		HR	AGE
Hank Aaron	Milw. (NL), 1957	44	23
Richie Allen	Phila. (NL), 1966	40	24
Ernie Banks	Chic. (NL), 1955	44	24
Joe DiMaggio	NY (AL), 1937	46	22
Jimmie Foxx	Phila. (AL), 1932	58	24*
Lou Gehrig	NY (AL), 1927	47	24
Reggie Jackson	Oak. (AL), 1969	47	23
Harmon Killebrew	WA (AL), 1959	42	23
Ralph Kiner	Pitt. (NL), 1947	51	24*
Chuck Klein	Phila. (NL), 1929	43	24*
Mickey Mantle	NY (AL), 1956	52	24*
Eddie Mathews	Bost. (NL), 1953	47	21
Willie Mays	NY (NL), 1954	41	23
	NY (NL), 1955	51	24
Mark McGwire	Oak. (AL), 1987	49	23
Mel Ott	NY (NL), 1929	42	20
Hal Trosky	Cleve. (AL), 1936	42	23

*Turned 25 during season

RUNS BATTED IN

EVOLUTION OF RBI RECORD

NATIONAL LEAGUE, PRE–1900

1876	Deacon White, Chic.	60
1879	Charley Jones, Bost.	62
	John O'Rourke, Bost.	62
1881	Cap Anson, Chic.	82
1885	Cap Anson, Chic.	114
1886	Cap Anson, Chic.	147
1887	Sam Thompson, Det.	165

NATIONAL LEAGUE, POST–1900

1900	Elmer Flick, Phila.	110
1901	Honus Wagner, Pitt.	126
1913	Gaavy Cravath, Phila.	128
1922	Rogers Hornsby, St. L.	152
1929	Hack Wilson, Chic.	159
1930	Hack Wilson, Chic.	190

AMERICAN LEAGUE

1901	Nap Lajoie, Phila.	125
1911	Ty Cobb, Det.	144
1921	Babe Ruth, NY	170
1927	Lou Gehrig, NY	175
1931	Lou Gehrig, NY	184

MOST RUNS BATTED IN, BY DECADE

Pre–1900
Cap Anson	1715
Sam Thompson	1296
Hugh Duffy	1215
Ed Delahanty	1133
Jake Beckley	1077
Roger Connor	1077
Ed McKean	1069
Dan Brouthers	1056
Billy Nash	976
Jimmy Ryan	944

1900–1909
Honus Wagner	956
Sam Crawford	808
Nap Lajoie	793
Harry Davis	688
Cy Seymour	685
Jimmy Williams	678
Bobby Wallace	638
Harry Steinfeldt	610
Bill Dahlen	597
Piano Legs Hickman	590

1910–1919
Ty Cobb	852
Frank Baker	819
Heinie Zimmerman	769
Sherry Magee	752
Tris Speaker	750
Duffy Lewis	718
Sam Crawford	697
Ed Konetchy	687
Eddie Collins	682
Gavvy Cravath	665

1920–1929
Babe Ruth	1330
Rogers Hornsby	1153
Harry Heilmann	1131
Bob Meusel	1005
George Kelly	923
Jim Bottomley	885
Ken Williams	860
George Sisler	827
Goose Goslin	821
Joe Sewell	817

1930–1939
Jimmie Foxx	1403
Lou Gehrig	1360
Mel Ott	1135
Al Simmons	1081
Earl Averill	1046
Joe Cronin	1036
Charlie Gehringer	1003
Chuck Klein	979
Bill Dickey	937
Wally Berger	893

1940–1949
Bob Elliott	903
Ted Williams	893
Bobby Doerr	887
Rudy York	854
Bill Nicholson	835
Vern Stephens	824
Joe DiMaggio	786
Dixie Walker	759
Johnny Mize	744
Joe Gordon	710

1950–1959
Duke Snider	1031
Gil Hodges	1001
Yogi Berra	997
Stan Musial	972
Del Ennis	925
Jackie Jensen	863
Mickey Mantle	841
Ted Kluszewski	823
Gus Bell	817
Larry Doby	816

1960–1969
Hank Aaron	1107
Harmon Killebrew	1013
Frank Robinson	1011
Willie Mays	1003
Ron Santo	937
Ernie Banks	925
Orlando Cepeda	896
Roberto Clemente	862
Billy Williams	853
Brooks Robinson	836

1970–1979
Johnny Bench	1013
Tony Perez	954
Lee May	936
Reggie Jackson	922
Willie Stargell	906
Rusty Staub	860
Bobby Bonds	856
Carl Yastrzemski	846
Bobby Murcer	840
Bob Watson	832

1980–1989
Eddie Murray	996
Dale Murphy	929
Mike Schmidt	929
Dwight Evans	900
Dave Winfield	899
Andre Dawson	895
Jim Rice	868
George Brett	851
Harold Baines	835
Robin Yount	821

TEAMMATES FINISHING ONE-TWO IN RBI
(Since 1900)

NATIONAL LEAGUE

1900	Phila. Phillies	Elmer Flick (110)	Ed Delahanty (109)
1902	Pitt. Pirates	Honus Wagner (91)	Tommy Leach (85)
1904	NY Giants	Bill Dahlen (80)	Sam Mertes (78)
1914	Phila. Phillies	Sherry Magee (103)	Gavvy Cravath (100)
1932	Phila. Phillies	Don Hurst (143)	Chuck Klein (137)
1960	Milw. Braves	Hank Aaron (126)	Eddie Mathews (124)
1965	Cinn. Reds	Deron Johnson (130)	Frank Robinson (113)
1970	Cinn. Reds	Johnny Bench (148)	Tony Perez (129)—Tie
1976	Cinn. Reds	George Foster (121)	Joe Morgan (111)

AMERICAN LEAGUE

1905	Phila. Athletics	Harry Davis (83)	Lave Cross (77)
1908	Det. Tigers	Ty Cobb (108)	Sam Crawford (80)
1909	Det. Tigers	Ty Cobb (107)	Sam Crawford (97)
1910	Det. Tigers	Sam Crawford (120)	Ty Cobb (91)
1913	Phila. Athletics	Home Run Baker (126)	Stuffy McInnis (90)—Tie
1915	Det. Tigers	Bobby Veach (112)	Sam Crawford (112)—Tie
1917	Det. Tigers	Bobby Veach (103)	Ty Cobb (102)—Tie
1927	NY Yankees	Lou Gehrig (175)	Babe Ruth (164)
1928	NY Yankees	Lou Gehrig (142)	Babe Ruth (142)—Tie
1931	NY Yankees	Lou Gehrig (184)	Babe Ruth (163)
1932	Phila. A's	Jimmie Foxx (169)	Al Simmons (151)—Tie
1940	Det. Tigers	Hank Greenberg (150)	Rudy York (134)
1949	Bost. Red Sox	Vern Stephens (159)	Ted Williams (159)—Tie
1950	Bost. Red Sox	Vern Stephens (144)	Walt Dropo (144)—Tie
1980	Milw. Brewers	Cecil Cooper (122)	Ben Oglivie (118)—Tie
1984	Bost. Red Sox	Tony Armas (123)	Jim Rice (122)

LARGEST DIFFERENTIAL BETWEEN LEAGUE RBI LEADER AND RUNNER UP (Since 1900)

NATIONAL LEAGUE

1937	Joe Medwick (154)	Frank Demaree (115)	39
1910	Sherry Magee (123)	Mike Mitchell (88)	35
1913	Gavvy Cravath (128)	Heinie Zimmerman (95)	33
1915	Gavvy Cravath (115)	Sherry Magee (87)	28
1943	Bill Nicholson (128)	Bob Elliott (101)	27
1957	Hank Aaron (132)	Del Ennis (105)	27

AMERICAN LEAGUE

1935	Hank Greenberg (170)	Lou Gehrig (119)	51
1913	Home Run Baker (126)	Stuffy McInnis and Duffy Lewis (90)	36
1921	Babe Ruth (171)	Harry Heilmann (139)	32
1926	Babe Ruth (145)	George Burns and Tony Lazzeri (114)	31
1953	Al Rosen (145)	Mickey Vernon (115)	30
1910	Sam Crawford (120)	Ty Cobb (91)	29
1911	Ty Cobb (144)	Sam Crawford and Home Run Baker (115)	29
1922	Ken Williams (155)	Bobby Veach (126)	29
1938	Jimmie Foxx (175)	Hank Greenberg (146)	29
1908	Ty Cobb (108)	Sam Crawford (80)	28

PLAYERS DRIVING IN 100 RUNS IN FIRST TWO SEASONS IN MAJORS (Since 1900)

Al Simmons, Phila. (AL)	1924 (102) and 1925 (129)
Glenn Wright, Pitt. (NL)	1924 (111) and 1925 (121)
Tony Lazzeri, NY (AL)	1926 (114) and 1927 (102)
Pinky Whitney, Phila. (NL)	1928 (103) and 1929 (115)
Dale Alexander, Det. (AL)	1929 (137) and 1930 (135)
Joe DiMaggio, NY (AL)	1936 (125) and 1937 (167)
Ted Williams, Bost. (AL)	1939 (145) and 1940 (113)
Ray Jablonski, St. L. (NL)	1953 (112) and 1954 (104)
Wally Joyner, CA (AL)	1986 (100) and 1987 (117)

CATCHERS WITH 100 RBI AND 100 RUNS SCORED, SAME SEASON

		RBI	RUNS
1932	Mickey Cochrane, Phila. (AL)	112	118
1950	Yogi Berra, NY (AL)	124	116
1953	Roy Campanella, Bklyn. (NL)	142	103
1974	Johnny Bench, Cinn. (NL)	129	108
1977	Carlton Fisk, Bost. (AL)	102	106
1979	Darrell Porter, K.C. (AL)	112	101

CATCHERS HITTING .300, WITH 30 HR AND 100 RBI IN A SEASON

	HR	RBI		HR	RBI
Gabby Hartnett (1930)	37	122	Roy Campanella (1951)	33	108
Rudy York (1938)	33	127 (116 at C, 15 at others)	Roy Campanella (1953)	41	142
Walker Cooper (1947)	35	122	Joe Torre (1966)	36	101 (114 at C, 36 at others)

PLAYERS WITH OVER 40 HOMERS, UNDER 100 RBI, SEASON

NATIONAL LEAGUE	HR	RBI	AMERICAN LEAGUE	HR	RBI
Duke Snider, Bklyn., 1957	40	92	Mickey Mantle, NY, 1958	42	97
Hank Aaron, Atl., 1969	44	97	Mickey Mantle, NY, 1960	40	94
Hank Aaron, Atl., 1973	40	96	Harmon Killebrew, MN, 1963	45	96
Davey Johnson, Atl., 1973	43	99	Rico Petrocelli, Bost., 1969	40	97

OVER 100 RBI, FEWEST HOME RUNS, SEASON

NATIONAL LEAGUE	RBI	HR	AMERICAN LEAGUE	RBI	HR
Pie Traynor, Pitt., 1928	124	3	Larry Gardner, Cleve., 1920	118	3
Pie Traynor, Pitt., 1931	103	2	Larry Gardner, Cleve., 1921	115	3
Ross Youngs, NY, 1921	102	3	Joe Sewell, Cleve., 1923	109	3
			Joe Sheely, Chic., 1924	103	3
			Billy Rogell, Det., 1934	100	3

MOST LIFETIME RBI, NEVER LED LEAGUE IN SEASON

Willie Mays (1951–52; 1954–73)	1,903	Harry Heilmann (1914; 1916–32)	1,551
Tony Perez (1964–86)	1,652	Billy Williams (1959–76)	1,475
Al Kaline (1953–74)	1,583	Rusty Staub (1963–85)	1,466
Jake Beckley (1888–1907)	1,575	Eddie Mathews (1952–68)	1,453

PLAYERS WITH 1,000 CAREER RBI, NEVER DRIVING IN 100 RUNS IN SEASON

Pete Rose (1963–86)	1314	Jimmy Dykes (1918–39)	1071	Joe Judge (1915–34)	1037
Tommy Corcoran (1890–1907)	1135	Willie Davis (1960–79)	1053	Dusty Baker (1968–86)	1013
Charlie Grimm (1916; 1918–36)	1078	Ron Fairly (1958–78)	1044	Amos Otis (1967–84)	1007
Jose Cruz (1970–88)	1077	Bobby Murcer (1965–83)	1043		

PLAYERS DRIVING IN 130 TEAMMATES DURING SEASON

	TEAMMATES	HR	RBI
Hank Greenberg, Det. (AL), 1937	143	40	183
Lou Gehrig, NY (AL), 1935	138	46	184
Ty Cobb, Det. (AL), 1911	136	8	144
Hank Greenberg, Det. (AL), 1935	134	36	170
Hack Wilson, Chic. (NL), 1930	134	56	190
Lou Gehrig, NY (AL), 1930	133	41	174
Chuck Klein, Phila. (NL), 1930	130	40	170

PLAYERS DRIVING IN 100 RBI, BOTH LEAGUES (Post 1900)

Richie Allen	National League	1966 Phila. Phillies	110
		1970 St. L. Cardinals	101
	American League	1972 Chic. White Sox	113
Bobby Bonds	National League	1971 S.F. Giants	102
	American League	1977 CA Angels	115
Sam Crawford	National League	1901 Cinn. Reds	104
	American League	1910 Det. Tigers	120
		1911 Det. Tigers	115
		1912 Det. Tigers	109
		1914 Det. Tigers	104
		1915 Det. Tigers	112
Jeff Burroughs	American League	1974 TX Rangers	118
	National League	1977 Atl. Braves	114
Frank Howard	National League	1962 L.A. Dodgers	119
	American League	1968 WA Senators	106
		1969 WA Senators	111
		1970 WA Senators	126
Lee May	National League	1969 Cinn. Reds	110
		1973 Houst. Astros	105
	American League	1976 Balt. Orioles	109
Tony Perez	National League	1967 Cinn. Reds	102
		1969 Cinn. Reds	122
		1970 Cinn. Reds	129
		1973 Cinn. Reds	101
		1974 Cinn. Reds	101
		1975 Cinn. Reds	109
	American League	1980 Bost. Red Sox	105
Frank Robinson	National League	1959 Cinn. Reds	125
		1961 Cinn. Reds	124
		1962 Cinn. Reds	136
		1965 Cinn. Reds	113
	American League	1966 Balt. Orioles	122
		1969 Balt. Orioles	100
Ken Singleton	National League	1973 Mont. Expos	103
	American League	1979 Balt. Orioles	111
		1980 Balt. Orioles	104
Rusty Staub	National League	1975 NY Mets	105
	American League	1977 Det. Tigers	101
		1978 Det. Tigers	121
Dick Stuart	National League	1961 Pitt. Pirates	117
	American League	1963 Bost. Red Sox	118
		1964 Bost. Red Sox	114
Richie Zisk	National League	1974 Pitt. Pirates	100
	American League	1977 Chic. White Sox	101

PLAYERS WITH MORE RBI THAN GAMES PLAYED (Min. 100 Games)

NATIONAL LEAGUE		RBI	GAMES
+35	Hack Wilson, Chic., 1930	190	155
+14	Chuck Klein, Phila., 1930	170	156
+9	Hack Wilson, Chic., 1929	159	150
+5	Rogers Hornsby, St. L., 1925	143	138
+1	Mel Ott, NY, 1929	151	150

AMERICAN LEAGUE		RBI	GAMES
+29	Lou Gehrig, NY, 1931	184	155
+29	Hank Greenberg, Det., 1937	183	154
+27	Al Simmons, Phila., 1930	165	138
+26	Jimmie Foxx, Bost., 1938	175	149
+20	Lou Gehrig, NY, 1927	175	155
+20	Lou Gehrig, NY, 1930	174	154
+19	Babe Ruth, NY, 1921	171	152
+19	Babe Ruth, NY, 1929	154	135
+18	Babe Ruth, NY, 1931	163	145
+18	Hank Greenberg, Det., 1935	170	152
+16	Joe DiMaggio, NY, 1937	167	151
+15	Jimmie Foxx, Phila., 1932	169	154
+14	Al Simmons, Phila., 1929	157	143
+14	Jimmie Foxx, Phila., 1933	163	149
+13	Babe Ruth, NY, 1927	164	151
+11	Lou Gehrig, NY, 1934	165	154
+11	Hal Trosky, Cleve., 1936	162	151
+8	Babe Ruth, NY, 1930	153	145
+8	Walt Dropo, Bost., 1950	144	136
+6	Joe DiMaggio, NY, 1939	126	120
+4	Babe Ruth, NY, 1932	137	133
+4	Vern Stephens, Bost., 1949	159	155
+4	Ted Williams, Bost., 1949	159	155
+3	Ken Williams, St. L., 1925	105	102
+3	Jimmie Foxx, Phila., 1930	156	153
+2	Ken Williams, St. L., 1922	155	153
+2	Al Simmons, Phila., 1927	108	106
+2	Lou Gehrig, NY, 1937	159	157
+2	Hank Greenberg, Det., 1940	150	148
+2	Joe DiMaggio, NY, 1948	155	153
+1	Joe DiMaggio, NY, 1940	133	132
+1	George Brett, K.C., 1980	118	117

BATTERS DRIVING IN 20 PERCENT OF THEIR TEAM'S RUNS

22.75%	Nate Colbert, S.D. Padres, (NL) 1972	111 of 488
22.61%	Wally Berger, Bost. Braves, (NL) 1935	130 of 575
21.25%	Ernie Banks, Chic. Cubs, (NL) 1959	143 of 673
20.41%	Jim Gentile, Balt. Orioles, (AL) 1961	141 of 691
20.27%	Bill Buckner, Chic. Cubs, (NL) 1981	75 of 370
20.25%	Bill Nicholson, Chic. Cubs, (NL) 1943	128 of 632
20.23%	Frank Howard, WA Senators, (AL) 1968	106 of 524
20.18%	Babe Ruth, Bost. Red Sox, (AL) 1919	114 of 565
20.13%	Frank Howard, WA Senators, (AL) 1970	126 of 626

LOWEST BATTING AVERAGE FOR 100 RBI SEASON

	RBI	AVG.		RBI	AVG.
Tony Armas, Bost. (AL), 1983	107	.218	Gorman Thomas, Milw. (AL), 1979	123	.244
Roy Sievers, WA (AL), 1954	102	.232	Ben Oglivie, Milw. (AL), 1982	102	.244
Carlton Fisk, Chic. (AL), 1985	107	.238	Bob Allison, MN (AL), 1961	105	.245
Gorman Thomas, Milw. (AL), 1980	105	.239	Gorman Thomas, Milw. (AL), 1982	112	.245
Jose Canseco, Oak. (AL), 1986	117	.240	Ralph Kiner, Pitt. (NL), 1946	109	.247
Ron Cey, L.A. (NL), 1977	110	.241	Eddie Robinson, Phila. (AL), 1953	102	.247
Harmon Killebrew, MN (AL), 1959	105	.242	Jim Wynn, Houst. (NL), 1967	107	.249
Harmon Killebrew, MN (AL), 1962	126	.243	Nate Colbert, S.D. (NL), 1972	111	.250
Sal Bando, Oak. (AL), 1974	103	.243			

PLAYERS DRIVING IN 100 RUNS IN SEASON, THREE DIFFERENT TEAMS

Richie Allen	Phila. Phillies (NL), 1966	110		WA–St. L. Browns (AL), 1930	138
	St. L. Cardinals (NL), 1970	101		St. L. Browns (AL), 1931	105
	Chic. White Sox (AL), 1972	113		1932	104
Dan Brouthers	Det. (NL), 1887	101		Det. Tigers (AL), 1934	100
	Bost. (NL), 1889	118		1935	109
	Bost. (PL), 1890	108		1936	125
	Bklyn. (NL), 1892	124	Lee May	Cinn. Reds (NL), 1969	110
	Balt. (NL), 1894	128		Houst. Astros (NL), 1973	105
Orlando Cepeda	S.F. Giants (NL), 1959	105		Balt. Orioles (AL), 1976	109
	1961	142	Al Simmons	Phila. Athletics (AL), 1924	102
	1962	114		1925	129
	St. L. Cardinals (NL), 1967	111		1926	109
	Atl. Braves (NL), 1970	111		1927	108
Rocky Colavito	Cleve. Indians (AL), 1958	113		1928	107
	1959	111		1929	157
	Det. Tigers (AL), 1961	140		1930	165
	1962	112		1931	128
	K.C. A's (AL), 1964	102		1932	151
	Cleve. Indians, (AL), 1965	108		Chic. White Sox (AL), 1933	119
Rogers Hornsby	St. L. Cardinals (NL), 1921	126		1934	104
	1922	152		Det. Tigers (AL), 1936	112
	1925	143	Vic Wertz	Det. Tigers (AL), 1949	133
	NY Giants (NL), 1927	125		1950	123
	Chic. Cubs (NL), 1929	149		Cleve. Indians (AL), 1956	106
Goose Goslin	WA Senators (AL), 1924	129		1957	105
	1925	113		Bost. Red Sox (AL), 1960	103
	1926	108			
	1927	120			
	1928	102			

PLAYERS ON LAST-PLACE TEAMS LEADING LEAGUE IN RBI

Wally Berger, Bost. (NL), 1935
Roy Sievers, WA (AL), 1957
Frank Howard, WA (AL), 1970
Andre Dawson, Chic. (NL), 1987

PLAYERS DRIVING IN 95 OR MORE RUNS IN SEASON THREE TIMES, NEVER DRIVING IN 100

Donn Clendenon (1961–72)	96 RBI, 1965
	98 RBI, 1966
	97 RBI, 1970
Kevin McReynolds (1983–89)	96 RBI, 1986
	95 RBI, 1987
	99 RBI, 1988
Arky Vaughan (1932–43; 1947–48)	97 RBI, 1933
	99 RBI, 1935
	95 RBI, 1940

RUNS SCORED

EVOLUTION OF RUNS SCORED RECORD

NATIONAL LEAGUE, PRE–1900

1876	Ross Barnes, Chic.	126
1886	King Kelly, Chic.	155
1894	Billy Hamilton, Phila.	192

POST–1900

1900	Roy Thomas, Phila.	132
1901	Jesse Burkett, St. L.	142
1925	Kiki Cuyler, Pitt.	144
1929	Rogers Hornsby, Chic.	156
1930	Chuck Klein, Phila.	158

AMERICAN LEAGUE

1901	Nap Lajoie, Phila.	145
1911	Ty Cobb, Det.	147
1920	Babe Ruth, NY	158
1921	Babe Ruth, NY	177

MOST RUNS SCORED, BY DECADE

Pre–1900
Cap Anson	1719
Bid McPhee	1684
Roger Connor	1621
Dan Brouthers	1523
Tom Brown	1521
Billy Hamilton	1520
Harry Stovey	1494
Arlie Latham	1477
Hugh Duffy	1468
Jim O'Rourke	1445

1900–1909
Honus Wagner	1013
Fred Clarke	884
Harry Hooper	868
Roy Thomas	864
Ginger Beaumont	836
Tommy Leach	828
Sam Crawford	815
Jimmy Sheckard	807
Nap Lajoie	806
Fielder Jones	803

1910–1919
Ty Cobb	1050
Sam Rice	1001
Eddie Collins	991
Tris Speaker	966
Donie Bush	958
Joe Jackson	765
Clyde Milan	758
Larry Doyle	745
Frank Baker	733
Max Carey	727
Jake Daubert	727

1920–1929
Babe Ruth	1365
Rogers Hornsby	1195
Frankie Frisch	992
Harry Heilmann	962
Lu Blue	896
George Sisler	894
Charlie Jamieson	868
Ty Cobb	830
Tris Speaker	830
Max Carey	818

1930–1939
Lou Gehrig	1257
Jimmie Foxx	1244
Charlie Gehringer	1179
Earl Averill	1102
Mel Ott	1095
Ben Chapman	1009
Paul Waner	973
Chuck Klein	955
Al Simmons	930
Joe Cronin	885

1940–1949
Ted Williams	951
Stan Musial	815
Bob Elliott	803
Bobby Doerr	764
Lou Boudreau	758
Bill Nicholson	743
Dom DiMaggio	721
Vern Stephens	708
Dixie Walker	704
Joe DiMaggio	684

1950–1959
Mickey Mantle	994
Duke Snider	970
Richie Ashburn	952
Stan Musial	948
Nellie Fox	902
Minnie Minoso	898
Eddie Yost	898
Gil Hodges	890
Alvin Dark	860
Yogi Berra	848

1960–1969
Hank Aaron	1091
Willie Mays	1050
Frank Robinson	1013
Roberto Clemente	916
Vada Pinson	885
Maury Wills	874
Harmon Killebrew	864
Billy Williams	861
Ron Santo	816
Al Kaline	811

1970–1979
Pete Rose	1068
Bobby Bonds	1020
Joe Morgan	1005
Amos Otis	861
Carl Yastrzemski	845
Lou Brock	843
Rod Carew	837
Reggie Jackson	833
Bobby Murcer	816
Johnny Bench	792

1980–1989
Keith Hernandez	1122
Robin Yount	957
Dwight Evans	956
Dale Murphy	938
Tim Raines	866
Eddie Murray	858
Willie Wilson	845
Mike Schmidt	832
Wade Boggs	823
Alan Trammell	815

PLAYERS SCORING MORE THAN ONE RUN PER GAME, SEASON (Minimum 100 Games)

NATIONAL LEAGUE		RUNS	GAMES	
Chuck Klein	Phila., 1930	158	150	+ 8

AMERICAN LEAGUE				
Babe Ruth	NY, 1921	177	152	+25
Babe Ruth	NY, 1920	158	142	+16
Nap Lajoie	Phila., 1901	145	131	+14
Al Simmons	Phila., 1930	152	138	+14
Lou Gehrig	NY, 1936	167	155	+12
Babe Ruth	NY, 1928	163	154	+ 9
Lou Gehrig	NY, 1932	163	155	+ 8
Babe Ruth	NY, 1927	158	151	+ 7
Babe Ruth	NY, 1930	150	145	+ 5
Babe Ruth	NY, 1931	149	145	+ 4
Rickey Henderson	NY, 1985	146	143	+ 3
Ty Cobb	Det., 1911	147	146	+ 1

PLAYERS SCORING 1,000 RUNS IN CAREER, NEVER SCORING 100 IN SEASON

Brooks Robinson (1955–77)	1232		Steve Garvey (1969–87)	1143
Graig Nettles (1967–88)	1193		Jimmy Dykes (1918–39)	1108
Al Oliver (1968–85)	1189		Ted Simmons (1968–88)*	1074
Bert Campaneris (1964–81; 1983)	1181		Bob Elliott (1939–53)	1064
Bill Buckner (1969–89)*	1173		Jose Cruz (1970–88)*	1036
Buddy Bell (1972–89)*	1150			

*Active

WALKS

EVOLUTION OF BATTERS' WALKS RECORD

NATIONAL LEAGUE, PRE–1900

1876	Ross Barnes, Chic.	20
1877	Jim O'Rourke, Bost.	20
1879	Charley Jones, Bost.	29
1881	John Clapp, Cleve.	35
1883	Tom York, Cleve.	37
1884	George Gore, Chic.	61
1885	Ned Williamson, Chic.	75
1886	George Gore, Chic.	102
1890	Cap Anson, Chic.	113
1892	John Crooks, St. L.	136

POST–1900

1911	Jimmy Sheckard, Chic.	147
1945	Eddie Stanky, Bklyn.	148
1969	Jim Wynn, Houst.	148

AMERICAN LEAGUE

1901	Dummy Hoy, Chic.	86
1902	Topsy Hartsel, Phila.	87
1905	Topsy Hartsel, Phila.	121
1920	Babe Ruth, NY	148
1923	Babe Ruth, NY	170

PLAYERS WITH 2,000 HITS, 1,000 WALKS, and 300 HOME RUNS

PLAYER	HITS	WALKS	HR
Hank Aaron	3771	1402	755
Stan Musial	3630	1599	475
Carl Yastrzemski	3419	1845	452
Willie Mays	3283	1463	660
Al Kaline	3007	1277	399
Frank Robinson	2943	1420	586
Rogers Hornsby	2930	1038	301
Mel Ott	2876	1708	511
Babe Ruth	2873	2056	714
Lou Gehrig	2721	1508	493
Billy Williams	2711	1045	426
Ted Williams	2654	2019	521
Jimmie Foxx	2646	1452	534
Reggie Jackson	2584	1375	563
Mickey Mantle	2415	1734	536
Eddie Mathews	2315	1444	512
Dwight Evans	2262	1270	336
Ron Santo	2254	1108	342
Mike Schmidt	2234	1507	548
Graig Nettles	2225	1088	390
Darrell Evans	2223	1605	414
Willie McCovey	2211	1345	521
Harmon Killebrew	2086	1559	573

LED LEAGUE IN BASE HITS AND WALKS, SAME SEASON

PLAYER	HITS	WALKS
Rogers Hornsby, St. L. (NL), 1924	227	89
Richie Ashburn, Phila. (NL), 1958	215	97
Carl Yastrzemski, Bost. (AL), 1963	183	95
Wade Boggs, Bost. (AL), 1988	214	125

BATTERS WITH 200 BASE HITS AND 100 WALKS IN SEASON (Since 1900)

		HITS	WALKS
Wade Boggs	1986 Bost. Red Sox	207	105
	1987 Bost. Red Sox	200	105
	1988 Bost. Red Sox	214	125
	1989 Bost. Red Sox	205	107
Ty Cobb	1915 Det. Tigers	208	118
Woody English	1930 Chic. Cubs	214	100
Jimmie Foxx	1932 Phila. A's	213	116
Lou Gehrig	1927 NY Yankees	218	109
	1930 NY Yankees	220	101
	1931 NY Yankees	211	117
	1932 NY Yankees	208	138
	1934 NY Yankees	210	109
	1936 NY Yankees	205	130
	1937 NY Yankees	200	127
Stan Musial	1949 St. L. Cardinals	207	107
	1953 St. L. Cardinals	200	105
Babe Ruth	1923 NY Yankees	205	170
	1924 NY Yankees	200	142
Hack Wilson	1930 Chic. Cubs	208	105

BATTERS WITH MORE WALKS THAN HITS, SEASON (Minimum 100 Walks)

Year	Player	WALKS	HITS	Year	Player	WALKS	HITS
1926	Max Bishop, Phila. A's	116	106	1956	Eddie Yost, WA Senators	151	119
1927	Max Bishop, Phila. A's	105	103	1962	Mickey Mantle, NY Yankees	122	121
1929	Max Bishop, Phila. A's	128	110	1968	Mickey Mantle, NY Yankees	106	103
1930	Max Bishop, Phila. A's	128	111	1969	Jim Wynn, Houst. Astros	148	133
1932	Max Bishop, Phila. A's	110	104	1974	Gene Tenace, Oak. A's	110	102
1945	Eddie Stanky, Bklyn. Dodgers	148	143	1975	Jim Wynn, L.A. Dodgers	110	102
1946	Eddie Stanky, Bklyn. Dodgers	137	132	1977	Gene Tenace, S.D. Padres	125	102
1947	Eddie Joost, Phila. A's	114	111	1978	Gene Tenace, S.D. Padres	101	90
1947	Hank Greenberg, Pitt. Pirates	104	100	1985	Toby Harrah, TX Rangers	113	107
1949	Eddie Joost, Phila. A's	149	138	1987	Jack Clark, St. L. Cardinals	136	120
1951	Wes Westrum, NY Giants	104	79				

PLAYERS WITH 40 HOME RUNS—WITH MORE HOMERS THAN WALKS

	HOME RUNS	WALKS
Tony Armas, Bost. Red Sox (AL), 1984	43	32
George Bell, Tor. Blue Jays (AL), 1987	47	39
Hal Trosky, Cleve. Indians (AL), 1936	42	36
Orlando Cepeda, S.F. Giants (NL), 1961	46	39
Andre Dawson, Chic. Cubs (NL), 1987	49	32
Dave Kingman, Chic. Cubs (NL), 1979	48	45

PLAYERS WITH 90 WALKS IN EACH OF FIRST TWO SEASONS

Alvin Davis, Seattle (AL)	1984 (97 walks)	1985 (90 walks)
Ferris Fain, Phila. (AL)	1947 (95 walks)	1948 (113 walks)
Roy Thomas, Phila. (NL)	1899 (115 walks)	1900 (115 walks)
Ted Williams, Bost. (AL)	1939 (107 walks)	1940 (96 walks)

STRIKEOUTS

BATTERS WITH MORE CAREER STRIKEOUTS THAN HITS (1,000 base hits, minimum)

	HITS	STRIKEOUTS
Reggie Jackson	2584	2597
Dave Kingman	1575	1816
Gorman Thomas	1051	1339

500 AT BATS, LESS THAN 10 STRIKEOUTS, SEASON (Since 1910 for NL, 1913 for AL)

			AB	STRIKEOUTS				AB	STRIKEOUTS
1921	Stuffy McInnis, Bost. (AL)		584	9	1929	Mickey Cochrane, Phila. (AL)		514	8
1922	Stuffy McInnis, Cleve. (AL)		537	5	1929	Sam Rice, WA (AL)		616	9
1922	Charlie Hollocher, Chic. (NL)		592	5	1929	Pie Traynor, Pitt. (NL)		540	7
1923	Eddie Collins, Chic. (AL)		505	8	1931	Freddy Leach, NY (NL)		515	9
1924	Stuffy McInnis, Bost. (NL)		581	6	1932	Joe Sewell, NY (AL)		503	3
1925	Joe Sewell, Cleve. (AL)		608	4	1933	Joe Sewell, NY (AL)		524	4
1926	Joe Sewell, Cleve. (AL)		578	7	1933	Lloyd Waner, Pitt. (NL)		500	8
1926	Homer Summa, Cleve. (AL)		581	9	1945	Tommy Holmes, Bost. (NL)		636	9
1927	Joe Sewell, Cleve. (AL)		569	7	1947	Emil Verban, Phila. (NL)		540	8
1927	Tris Speaker, WA (AL)		523	8	1948	Lou Boudreau, Cleve. (AL)		560	9
1928	Joe Sewell, Cleve. (AL)		588	9	1952	Dale Mitchell, Cleve. (AL)		511	9
1929	Joe Sewell, Cleve. (AL)		578	4					

Strikeout records first began for National League in 1910; 1913 for American League

200 HITS, 100 STRIKEOUTS IN SEASON

		HITS	STRIKEOUTS			HITS	STRIKEOUTS
1937	Hank Greenberg, Det. Tigers	200	101	1971	Lou Brock, St. L. Cardinals	200	107
1963	Bill White, St. L. Cardinals	200	100	1977	Dave Parker, Pitt. Pirates	215	107
1964	Richie Allen, Phila. Phillies	201	138	1977	Ron LeFlore, Det. Tigers	212	121
1964	Lou Brock, Chic. Cubs-St. L. Cards	200	127	1977	Jim Rice, Bost. Red Sox	206	120
1966	Roberto Clemente, Pitt. Pirates	202	109	1978	Jim Rice, Bost. Red Sox	213	126
1967	Lou Brock, St. L. Cardinals	206	109	1984	Ryne Sandberg, Chic. Cubs	200	101
1967	Roberto Clemente, Pitt. Pirates	209	103	1987	Alan Trammell, Det. Tigers	205	105
1970	Bobby Bonds, S.F. Giants	200	189				

PLAYERS WHO HAD AT LEAST 10 MORE HOME RUNS THAN STRIKEOUTS, SEASON

		RUNS	STRIKEOUTS
Tommy Holmes	Bost. Braves, 1945	28	9
Lou Gehrig	NY Yankees, 1934	49	31
Joe DiMaggio	NY Yankees, 1941	30	13
Yogi Berra	NY Yankees, 1950	28	12
Ted Kluszewski	Cinn. Reds, 1954	49	35

PLAYERS HITTING 40 HOME RUNS IN SEASON, LESS THAN 50 STRIKEOUTS

NATIONAL LEAGUE	RUNS	STRIKEOUTS	AMERICAN LEAGUE	RUNS	STRIKEOUTS
Mel Ott, NY, 1929	42	38	Lou Gehrig, NY 1934	49	31
Johnny Mize, St. L., 1940	43	49	Lou Gehrig, NY 1936	49	46
Johnny Mize, NY, 1947	51	42	Joe DiMaggio, NY 1937	46	37
Johnny Mize, NY, 1948	40	37	Ted Williams, Bost. 1949	43	48
Ted Kluszewski, Cinn., 1953	40	34	Al Rosen, Cleve., 1953	43	48
Ted Kluszewski, Cinn., 1954	49	35			
Ted Kluszewski, Cinn., 1955	47	40			
Hank Aaron, Atl., 1969	44	47			

PLAYERS WITH 100 MORE STRIKEOUTS THAN RBI, SEASON

		STRIKEOUTS	RBI
111	Bobby Bonds, S.F. (NL), 1970	189	78
106	Rob Deer, Milw. (AL), 1987	186	80
105	Dave Nicholson, Chic. (AL), 1963	175	70
102	Ron LeFlore, Det. (AL), 1975	139	37

PINCH HITS

PINCH-HITTING—HIGHEST BATTING AVERAGE, SEASON (Min. 25 At Bats)

NATIONAL LEAGUE

.486	Ed Kranepool, NY, 1974	17 for 35
.465	Frenchy Bordagaray, St. L., 1938	20 for 43
.452	Jose Pagan, Pitt., 1969	19 for 42
.433	Milt Thompson, Atl., 1985	13 for 30
.425	Candy Maldonado, S.F., 1986	17 for 40
.419	Richie Ashburn, NY, 1962	13 for 31
.419	Bob Bowman, Phila., 1958	13 for 31
.415	Merritt Ranew, Chic., 1963	17 for 41
.412	Kurt Bevacqua, S.D., 1983	14 for 34
.409	Dave Philley, Phila., 1958	18 for 44

AMERICAN LEAGUE

.467	Smead Jolley, Chic., 1931	14 for 30
.462	Gates Brown, Det., 1968	18 for 39
.457	Rick Miller, Bost., 1983	16 for 35
.452	Elmer Valo, K.C., 1955	14 for 31
.433	Randy Bush, MN, 1986	13 for 30
.433	Ted Easterly, Cleve.-Chic., 1912	13 for 30
.429	Don Dillard, Cleve., 1961	15 for 35
.429	Joe Cronin, Bost., 1943	18 for 42
.419	Dick Williams, Balt., 1962	13 for 31
.412	Bob Hansen, Milw., 1974	14 for 34

EXTRA BASE HITS

EVOLUTION OF TOTAL BASES RECORD

NATIONAL LEAGUE, PRE–1900

1876	Ross Barnes, Chic.	190
1879	Paul Hines, Providence	197
1883	Dan Brouthers, Buffalo	243
1884	Abner Dalrymple, Chic.	263
1886	Dan Brouthers, Det.	284
1887	Sam Thompson, Det.	311
1893	Ed Delahanty, Phila.	347
1894	Hugh Duffy, Bost.	372

POST–1900

1921	Rogers Hornsby, St. L.	378
1922	Rogers Hornsby, St. L.	450

AMERICAN LEAGUE

1901	Nap Lajoie, Phila.	345
1911	Ty Cobb, Det.	367
1920	George Sisler, St. L.	399
1921	Babe Ruth, NY	457

PLAYERS WITH 100 EXTRA BASE HITS IN SEASON

		DOUBLES	TRIPLES	HOME RUNS
119	Babe Ruth, NY Yankees, 1921	44	16	59
117	Lou Gehrig, NY Yankees, 1927	52	18	47
107	Chuck Klein, Phila. Phillies, 1930	59	8	40
103	Chuck Klein, Phila. Phillies, 1932	50	15	38
103	Hank Greenberg, Det. Tigers, 1937	49	14	40
103	Stan Musial, St. L. Cardinals, 1948	46	18	39
102	Rogers Hornsby, St. L. Cardinals, 1922	46	14	42
100	Lou Gehrig, NY Yankees, 1930	42	17	41
100	Jimmie Foxx, Phila. Athletics, 1932	33	9	58

400 TOTAL BASES, SEASON

NATIONAL LEAGUE

Rogers Hornsby, St. L., 1922	450
Rogers Hornsby, Chic., 1929	410
Chuck Klein, Phila., 1929	405
Chuck Klein, Phila., 1930	445
Hack Wilson, Chic., 1930	423
Babe Herman, Bklyn., 1930	416
Chuck Klein, Phila., 1932	420
Joe Medwick, St. L., 1937	406
Stan Musial, St. L., 1948	429
Hank Aaron, Milw., 1959	400

AMERICAN LEAGUE

Babe Ruth, NY, 1921	457
Lou Gehrig, NY, 1927	447
Babe Ruth, NY, 1927	417
Lou Gehrig, NY, 1930	419
Lou Gehrig, NY, 1931	410
Jimmie Foxx, Phila., 1932	438
Jimmie Foxx, Phila., 1933	403
Lou Gehrig, NY, 1934	409
Hal Trosky, Cleve., 1936	405
Joe DiMaggio, NY, 1937	418
Jim Rice, Bost., 1978	406

EVOLUTION OF DOUBLES RECORD

NATIONAL LEAGUE, PRE–1900

1876	Ross Barnes, Chic.	21
	Paul Hines, Chic.	21
	Dick Higham, Hartford	21
1878	Dick Higham, Providence	22
1879	Charlie Eden, Cleve.	31
1882	King Kelly, Chic.	37
1883	Ned Williamson, Chic.	49
1894	Hugh Duffy, Bost.	51
1899	Ed Delahanty, Phila.	55

POST–1900

1932	Paul Waner, Pitt.	62
1936	Joe Medwick, St. L.	64

AMERICAN LEAGUE

1901	Nap Lajoie, Phila.	48
1904	Nap Lajoie, Cleve.	50
1910	Nap Lajoie, Cleve.	53
1912	Tris Speaker, Bost.	53
1923	Tris Speaker, Cleve.	59
1926	George Burns, Cleve.	64
1931	Earl Webb, Bost.	67

40 HOME RUNS, 40 DOUBLES, SAME SEASON

NATIONAL LEAGUE

	RUNS	DOUBLES
Rogers Hornsby, St. L., 1922	42	46
Rogers Hornsby, Chic., 1929	40	47
Chuck Klein, Phila., 1929	43	45
Chuck Klein, Phila., 1930	40	59
Willie Stargell, Pitt., 1973	44	43

AMERICAN LEAGUE

	RUNS	DOUBLES
Babe Ruth, NY, 1921	59	44
Babe Ruth, NY, 1923	41	45
Lou Gehrig, NY, 1927	47	52
Lou Gehrig, NY, 1930	41	42
Lou Gehrig, NY 1934	49	40
Hank Greenberg, Det., 1935	36	46
Hal Trosky, Cleve., 1936	42	45
Hank Greenberg, Det., 1937	40	49
Hank Greenberg, Det., 1940	41	50

EVOLUTION OF TRIPLES RECORD

NATIONAL LEAGUE, PRE–1900

1876	Ross Barnes, Chic.	14
1879	Buttercup Dickerson, Cinn.	14
1880	Harry Stovey, Worcester	14
1882	Roger Connor, Troy	18
1884	Buck Ewing, NY	20
1886	Roger Conner, NY	20
1887	Sam Thompson, Det.	23
1890	Long John Reilly, Cinn.	26
1893	Perry Werden, St. L.	29
1894	Heinie Reitz, Balt.	31

POST–1900

1912	Owen Wilson, Pitt.	36

AMERICAN LEAGUE

1901	Jimmy Williams, Balt.	21
1902	Jimmy Williams, Balt.	21
1903	Sam Crawford, Det.	25
1912	Joe Jackson, Cleve.	26

PLAYERS LEADING LEAGUE IN TRIPLES *AND* HOME RUNS, SAME SEASON

	TRIPLES	HOME RUNS
Harry Lumley, Bklyn. (NL), 1904	18	9
Jim Bottomley, St. L. (NL), 1928	20	31 (Tie)
Mickey Mantle, NY (AL), 1955	11 (Tie)	37
Willie Mays, NY (NL), 1955	15 (Tie)	51
Jim Rice, Bost. (AL), 1978	15	46

PLAYERS HITTING 20 HOME RUNS, 20 TRIPLES AND 20 DOUBLES, SAME SEASON

NATIONAL LEAGUE	DOUBLES	TRIPLES	HOME RUNS
Wildfire Schulte, Chic., 1911	30	21	21
Jim Bottomley, St. L., 1928	42	20	31
Willie Mays, NY, 1957	26	20	35

AMERICAN LEAGUE	DOUBLES	TRIPLES	HOME RUNS
Jeff Heath, Cleve., 1941	32	20	24
George Brett, K.C., 1979	42	20	23

PLAYERS LEADING LEAGUE IN DOUBLES, TRIPLES AND HOME RUNS DURING CAREER (Since 1900)

Jim Bottomley
Doubles, 1925 (44), 1926 (40)
Triples, 1928 (20)
Home Runs, 1928 (31)

Ty Cobb
Doubles, 1908 (36), 1911 (47), 1917 (44)
Triples, 1908 (20), 1911 (24), 1917 (24), 1918 (14)
Home Runs, 1909 (9)

Sam Crawford
Doubles, 1909 (35)
Triples, 1902 (23), 1903 (25), 1910 (19), 1913 (23), 1914 (26), 1915 (19)
Home Runs, 1908 (7)

Lou Gehrig
Doubles, 1927 (52)
Triples, 1926 (20)
Home Runs, 1931 (46), 1934 (49), 1936 (49)

Rogers Hornsby
Doubles, 1920 (44), 1921 (44), 1922 (46)
Triples, 1917 (17), 1921 (18)
Home Runs, 1922 (42), 1925 (39)

Johnny Mize
Doubles, 1941 (39)
Home Runs, 1938 (16)
Home Runs, 1939 (28), 1940 (43), 1947 (51, Tie), 1948 (40, Tie)

PLAYERS SINCE WORLD WAR II WITH 100 DOUBLES, TRIPLES, HOME RUNS AND STOLEN BASES

	DOUBLES	TRIPLES	HOME RUNS	STOLEN BASES
George Brett (1973–89)*	472	117	243	161
Lou Brock (1961–79)	486	141	149	938
Willie Davis (1960–79)	395	138	182	398
Willie Mays (1951–73)	523	140	660	338
Vada Pinson (1958–75)	485	127	256	305
Pete Rose (1963–86)	746	135	160	198
Mickey Vernon (1939–60)	490	120	172	137
Robin Yount (1974–89)*	443	100	195	204

*Active

200 HITS IN SEASON, FEWEST EXTRA BASE HITS (Since 1900)

NATIONAL LEAGUE

25 Lloyd Waner, Pitt., 1927
29 Maury Wills, L.A., 1962
30 Matty Alou, Pitt., 1970
33 Willie Keller, Bklyn., 1901
33 Curt Flood, St. L., 1964
34 Milt Stock, St. L., 1920
36 Richie Ashburn, Phila., 1953
36 Tony Gwynn, S.D., 1984
38 Milt Stock, Bklyn., 1925
38 Chick Fullis, Phila., 1933
38 Tony Gwynn, S.D., 1989
39 Richie Ashburn, Phila., 1958
39 Ralph Garr, Atl., 1971
39 Dave Cash, Phila., 1974

AMERICAN LEAGUE

33 Cesar Tovar, MN, 1971
34 Nellie Fox, Chic., 1954
35 Johnny Pesky, Bost., 1947
38 Rod Carew, MN, 1974
39 Harvey Kuenn, Det., 1954

STOLEN BASES

EVOLUTION OF STOLEN BASE RECORD

NATIONAL LEAGUE, PRE–1900

1886	Ed Andrews, Phila.	57
1887	Monte Ward, NY	111
1889	Billy Hamilton, Phila.	111
1891	Billy Hamilton, Phila.	111

POST–1900

1900	George Van Haltren, NY	45
1901	Honus Wagner, Pitt.	49
1903	Jimmy Sheckard, Bklyn.	67
	Frank Chance, Chic.	67
1910	Bob Bescher, Cinn.	70
1911	Bob Bescher, Cinn.	80
1962	Maury Wills, L.A.	104
1974	Lou Brock, St. L.	118

AMERICAN LEAGUE

1901	Frank Isbell, Chic.	52
1909	Ty Cobb, Det.	76
1910	Eddie Collins, Phila.	81
1911	Ty Cobb, Det.	83
1912	Clyde Milan, WA	88
1915	Ty Cobb, Det.	96
1980	Rickey Henderson, Oak.	100
1982	Rickey Henderson, Oak.	130

MOST STOLEN BASES, BY DECADE

Pre–1900
Billy Hamilton	889
Arlie Latham	678
Tom Brown	627
Hugh Duffy	571
Dummy Hoy	559
Bid McPhee	528
Monte Ward	504
George Van Haltren	494
Mike Griffin	473
Tommy McCarthy	467

1900–1909
Honus Wagner	487
Frank Chance	361
Sam Mertes	305
Jimmy Sheckard	295
Elmer Flick	279
Jimmy Slagle	251
Frank Isbell	250
Fred Clarke	239
Wid Conroy	239
Fielder Jones	239

1910–1919
Ty Cobb	577
Eddie Collins	489
Clyde Milan	434
Max Carey	392
Bob Bescher	364
Tris Speaker	336
Donie Bush	322
George Burns	293
Buck Herzog	286
Burt Shotton	286

1920–1929
Max Carey	346
Frankie Frisch	310
Sam Rice	254
George Sisler	214
Kiki Cuyler	210
Eddie Collins	178
Johnny Mostil	175
Bucky Harris	166
Cliff Heathcote	145
Jack Smith	144

1930–1939
Ben Chapman	269
Bill Werber	176
Lyn Lary	158
Gee Walker	158
Pepper Martin	136
Kiki Cuyler	118
Roy Johnson	115
Charlie Gehringer	101
Pete Fox	100
Stan Hack	100

1940–1949
George Case	285
Snuffy Stirnweiss	130
Wally Moses	126
Johnny Hopp	117
Pee Wee Reese	108
Mickey Vernon	108
Joe Kuhel	93
Luke Appling	91
Bob Dillinger	90
Jackie Robinson	88

1950–1959
Willie Mays	179
Minnie Minoso	167
Richie Ashburn	158
Jim Rivera	150
Luis Aparicio	134
Jackie Jensen	134
Jim Gilliam	132
Pee Wee Reese	124
Billy Bruton	121
Jackie Robinson	109

1960–1969
Maury Wills	535
Lou Brock	387
Luis Aparicio	342
Bert Campaneris	292
Willie Davis	240
Tommy Harper	208
Hank Aaron	204
Vada Pinson	202
Don Buford	161
Tony Taylor	157

1970–1979
Lou Brock	551
Joe Morgan	488
Cesar Cedeno	427
Bobby Bonds	380
Davey Lopes	375
Fred Patek	344
Bert Campaneris	336
Billy North	324
Ron Leflore	294
Amos Otis	294

1980–1989
Rickey Henderson	838
Tim Raines	583
Vince Coleman	472
Willie Wilson	451
Ozzie Smith	364
Steve Sax	333
Lonnie Smith	331
Mookie Wilson	319
Brett Butler	307
Dave Collins	284

TEAMMATES COMBINING FOR 125 STOLEN BASES

166	1985 St. L. Cardinals	Vince Coleman	110		138	1988 St. L. Cardinals	Vince Coleman	81
		Willie McGee	56				Ozzie Smith	57
159	1980 Mont. Expos	Ron LeFlore	96		137	1913 WA Senators	Clyde Milan	75
		Rodney Scott	63				Danny Moeller	62
158	1982 Oak. A's	Rickey Henderson	130		136	1962 L.A. Dodgers	Maury Wills	104
		Davey Lopes	28				Willie Davis	32
152	1987 St. L. Cardinals	Vince Coleman	109		131	1915 Det. Tigers	Ty Cobb	96
		Ozzie Smith	43				Donie Bush	35
148	1974 St. L. Cardinals	Lou Brock	118		129	1909 Det. Tigers	Ty Cobb	76
		Bake McBride	30				Donie Bush	53
141	1983 Oak. A's	Rickey Henderson	108		129	1976 Oak. A's	Bill North	75
		Mike Davis	33				Bert Campaneris	54
138	1986 St. L. Cardinals	Vince Coleman	107		126	1980 Oak. A's	Rickey Henderson	100
		Ozzie Smith	31				Dwayne Murphy	26

PLAYERS STEALING 30 BASES FOR 10 CONSECUTIVE SEASONS

SEASONS

14	Lou Brock (1964–77)
12	Ty Cobb (1907–18)
11	Honus Wagner (1899–1909)
11	Willie Wilson (1978–88)
11	Rickey Henderson (1979–89)
10	Bert Campaneris (1965–74)

PLAYERS LEADING IN STOLEN BASES AND TOTAL BASES, SAME SEASON

		STOLEN BASES	TOTAL BASES
Ty Cobb	1907, Det. Tigers	49	286
	1909, Det. Tigers	76	296
	1911, Det. Tigers	83	367
	1915, Det. Tigers	96	274
	1917, Det. Tigers	55	336
Chuck Klein	1932, Phila. Phillies	20	420
George Stirnweiss	1945, NY Yankees	33	301
Honus Wagner	1904, Pitt. Pirates	53	255
	1907, Pitt. Pirates	61	264
	1908, Pitt. Pirates	53	308

200 HOME RUNS, 200 STOLEN BASES, LIFETIME

	RUNS	STOLEN BASES
Hank Aaron (1954–76)	755	240
Don Baylor (1970–88)*	338	285
Bobby Bonds (1968–81)	332	461
Reggie Jackson (1967–87)	563	228
Willie Mays (1951–52; 1954–73)	660	338
Joe Morgan (1963–84)	268	689
Vida Pinson (1958–75)	256	305
Frank Robinson (1956–76)	586	204
Jimmy Wynn (1963–77)	291	225

*Active

PLAYERS WITH 400 HOME RUNS AND 10 STEALS OF HOME

Lou Gehrig	493	15
Babe Ruth	714	10

200 HITS, 20 HOME RUNS, 20 STOLEN BASES, SEASON

	HITS	HR	STOLEN BASES
Babe Herman, Bklyn. (NL), 1929	217	21	21
Chuck Klein, Phila. (NL), 1932	226	38	20
Willie Mays, S.F. (NL), 1958	208	29	31
Vada Pinson, Cinn. (NL), 1959	205	20	21
Hank Aaron, Milw. (NL), 1963	201	44	31
Vada Pinson, Cinn. (NL), 1963	204	22	27
Vada Pinson, Cinn. (NL), 1965	205	22	21
Bobby Bonds, S.F. (NL), 1970	200	26	48

PLAYERS WITH 10 DOUBLES, TRIPLES, HOME RUNS AND STEALS EACH OF FIRST THREE SEASONS IN MAJORS

		DOUBLES	TRIPLES	HR	STEALS
Ben Chapman	1930 NY Yankees	31	10	10	14
	1931 NY Yankees	28	11	17	61
	1932 NY Yankees	41	15	10	38
Juan Samuel	1984 Phila. Phillies	36	19	15	72
	1985 Phila. Phillies	31	13	19	53
	1986 Phila. Phillies	36	12	16	42
	1987 Phila. Phillies	37	15	28	35

PLAYERS STEALING SECOND, THIRD AND HOME IN INNING (Since 1900)

NATIONAL LEAGUE

Honus Wagner, Pitt., September 25, 1907
Hans Lobert, Cinn., September 27, 1908
Honus Wagner, Pitt., May 2, 1909
Dode Paskert, Cinn., May 23, 1910
Wilbur Good, Chic., August 18, 1915
Jim Johnstone, Bklyn., September 22, 1916
Greasy Neale, Cinn., August 15, 1919
Max Carey, Pitt., August 13, 1923
Max Carey, Pitt., May 26, 1925
Harvey Hendrick, Bklyn., June 12, 1928
Pete Rose, Phila., May 11, 1980
Dusty Baker, S.F., June 27, 1984

AMERICAN LEAGUE

Dave Fultz, Phila., September 4, 1902
Wild Bill Donovan, Det., May 7, 1906
Bill Coughlin, Det., June 4, 1906
Ty Cobb, Det., July 22, 1909
Ty Cobb, Det., July 12, 1911
Ty Cobb, Det., July 4, 1912
Joe Jackson, Cleve., August 11, 1912
Eddie Collins, Phila., September 22, 1912
Eddie Ainsmith, WA, June 26, 1913
Red Faber, Chic., July 14, 1915
Don Moeller, WA, July 19, 1915
Fritz Maisel, NY, August 17, 1915
Buck Weaver, Chic., September 6, 1919
Bobby Roth, WA, May 31, 1920
Bob Meusel, NY, May 16, 1927
Jack Tavener, Det., July 10, 1927
Jack Tavener, Det., July 25, 1928
Don Kolloway, Chic., June 28, 1941
Rod Carew, MN, May 18, 1969
Dave Nelson, TX, August 30, 1974
Paul Molitor, Milw., July 26, 1987

STEALS OF HOME BY PITCHERS (Since 1900)

NATIONAL LEAGUE

July 15, 1902	John Menafee, Chic.	vs. Bklyn.
August 8, 1903	Joe McGinnity, NY	vs. Bklyn.
April 29, 1904	Joe McGinnity, NY	vs. Bost.
September 12, 1911	Christy Mathewson, NY	vs. Bost.
May 22, 1912	Leon Ames, NY	vs. Bklyn.
June 28, 1912	Christy Mathewson, NY	vs. Bost.
July 22, 1913	Slim Sallee, NY	vs. St. L.
April 16, 1916	Sherry Smith, Bklyn.	vs. NY
June 23, 1916	Tom Seaton, Chic.	vs. Cinn.
July 26, 1918	Bob Steele, NY	vs. St. L.
August 9, 1919	Jim Vaughn, Chic.	vs. NY
September 3, 1919	Dutch Reuther, Cinn.	vs. Chic.
July 27, 1920	Jesse Barnes, NY	vs. St. L.
May 4, 1921	Dutch Reuther, Bklyn.	vs. NY
September 23, 1943	Johnny Vander Meer, Cinn.	vs. NY
April 20, 1946	Bucky Walters, Cinn.	vs. Pitt.
May 26, 1955	Don Newcombe, Bklyn.	vs. Pitt.
September 1, 1963	Curt Simmons, St. L.	vs. Phila.
July 29, 1988	Rick Sutcliffe, Chic.	vs. Phila.

AMERICAN LEAGUE

August 2, 1904	Frank Owen, Chic.	vs. WA
May 7, 1906	Bill Donovan, Det.	vs. Cleve.
April 27, 1908	Frank Owen, Chic.	vs. St. L.
June 13, 1908	Ed Walsh, Chic.	vs. NY
June 2, 1909	Ed Walsh, Chic.	vs. St. L.
August 30, 1909	Eddie Plank, Phila.	vs. Chic.
August 27, 1910	Jack Warhop, NY	vs. Chic.
July 12, 1912	Jack Warhop, NY	vs. St. L.
July 14, 1915	Urban Faber, Chic.	vs. Phila.
August 7, 1916	Reb Russell, Chic.	vs. Bost.
August 24, 1918	Babe Ruth, Bost.	vs. St. L.
July 8, 1921	Dickie Kerr, Chic.	vs. NY
April 23, 1923	Urban Faber, Chic.	vs. St. L.
August 15, 1923	George Mogridge, WA	vs. Chic.
September 17, 1944	Joe Haynes, Chic.	vs. St. L.
August 29, 1947	Fred Hutchinson, Det.	vs. St. L.
June 2, 1950	Harry Dorish, St. L.	vs. WA

MOST STOLEN BASES, SEASON—CATCHER

36 John Wathan, K.C. (AL), 1982	24 Ray Schalk, Chic. (AL), 1914	19 Ed Sweeney, NY (AL), 1914
30 Ray Schalk, Chic. (AL), 1916	23 Johnny Kling, Chic. (NL), 1902	19 Roger Bresnahan, Chic. (NL), 1915
28 John Wathan*, K.C. (AL), 1983	23 Johnny Kling, Chic. (NL), 1903	19 Ray Schalk, Chic. (AL), 1917
25 Roger Bresnahan*, NY (NL), 1906	21 Benito Santiago, S.D. (NL), 1987	17 Eddie Ainsmith, WA (AL), 1913
25 John Stearns, NY (NL), 1978	20 Red Dooin, Phila. (NL), 1908	17 Carlton Fisk, Chic. (AL), 1982

*Caught in majority of games played in during season

MOST STOLEN BASES, LIFETIME—CATCHER

176 Ray Schalk (1912–29)	105 John Wathan (1976–85)*	86 Jimmie Wilson (1923–40)
140 Roger Bresnahan (1900–15)*	96 Billy Sullivan (1899–1914)	84 Ivy Wingo (1911–29)
131 Red Dooin (1902–16)	94 Wally Schang (1913–31)	66 John Roseboro (1957–70)
121 Johnny Kling (1900–13)	91 John Stearns (1975–84)	
117 Carlton Fisk (1969–89)	86 Eddie Ainsmith (1910–24)	

*Caught in majority of games played in during career

PLAYERS WITH 50 STOLEN BASES, 100 RBI, SEASON

	STOLEN BASES	RBI		STOLEN BASES	RBI
Sam Mertes, NY (NL), 1905	52	108	George Sisler, St. L. (AL), 1922	51	105
Honus Wagner, Pitt. (NL), 1905	57	101	Ben Chapman, NY (AL), 1931	61	122
Honus Wagner, Pitt. (NL), 1908	53	108	Cesar Cedeno, Houst. (NL), 1974	57	102
Ty Cobb, Det. (AL), 1909	76	115	Joe Morgan, Cinn. (NL), 1976	60	111
Ty Cobb, Det. (AL), 1911	83	144	Eric Davis, Cinn. (NL), 1987	50	100
Ty Cobb, Det. (AL), 1917	55	102			

BATTING MISCELLANY

MOST TIMES LEADING LEAGUE IN OFFENSIVE CATEGORY

NATIONAL LEAGUE

Base Hits — Pete Rose, 7
(1965, 1968, 1970, 1972, 1973, 1976, 1981)

Singles — Ginger Beaumont, 4
(1902, 1903, 1904, 1907)
Lloyd Waner, 4
(1927, 1928, 1929, 1931)
Richie Ashburn, 4
(1951, 1953, 1957, 1958)
Maury Wills, 4
(1961, 1962, 1965, 1967)

Doubles — Stan Musial, 8
(1943, 1944, 1946, 1948, 1949, 1952, 1953, 1954)

Triples — Stan Musial, 5
(1943, 1946, 1948, 1949, 1951)

Home Runs — Mike Schmidt, 8
(1974, 1975, 1976, 1980, 1981, 1983, 1984, 1986)

Total Bases — Hank Aaron, 8
(1956, 1957, 1959, 1960, 1961, 1963, 1967, 1969)

Slugging Pct. — Rogers Hornsby, 9
(1917, 1920, 1921, 1922, 1923, 1924, 1925, 1928, 1929)

Batting Avg. — Honus Wagner, 8
(1900, 1903, 1904, 1906, 1907, 1908, 1909, 1911)

Runs — Rogers Hornsby, 5
(1921, 1922, 1924, 1927, 1929)
Stan Musial, 5
(1946, 1948, 1951, 1952, 1954)

AMERICAN LEAGUE

Ty Cobb, 8
(1907, 1908, 1909, 1911, 1912, 1915, 1917, 1919)
Nellie Fox, 8
(1952, 1954, 1955, 1956, 1957, 1958, 1959, 1960)

Tris Speaker, 8
(1912, 1914, 1916, 1918, 1920, 1921, 1922, 1923)
Sam Crawford, 5
(1903, 1910, 1913, 1914, 1915)
Babe Ruth, 12
(1918, 1919, 1920, 1921, 1923, 1924, 1926, 1927, 1928, 1929, 1930, 1931)
Ty Cobb, 6
(1907, 1908, 1909, 1911, 1915, 1917)
Babe Ruth, 6
(1919, 1921, 1923, 1924, 1926, 1928)
Ted Williams, 6
(1939, 1942, 1946, 1947, 1949, 1951)
Babe Ruth, 13
(1918, 1919, 1920, 1921, 1922, 1923, 1924, 1926, 1927, 1928, 1929, 1930, 1931)
Ty Cobb, 12
(1907, 1908, 1909, 1910, 1911, 1912, 1913, 1914, 1915, 1917, 1918, 1919)
Babe Ruth, 8
(1919, 1920, 1921, 1923, 1924, 1926, 1927, 1928)

MOST TIMES LEADING LEAGUE IN OFFENSIVE CATEGORY (continued)

	NATIONAL LEAGUE	AMERICAN LEAGUE
RBI	Honus Wagner, 4 (1901, 1902, 1908, 1909) Rogers Hornsby, 4 (1920, 1921, 1922, 1925) Hank Aaron, 4 (1957, 1960, 1963, 1966) Mike Schmidt, 4 (1980, 1981, 1984, 1986)	Babe Ruth, 6 (1919, 1920, 1921, 1923, 1926, 1928)
Bases on Balls	Roy Thomas, 7 (1900, 1901, 1902, 1903, 1904, 1906, 1907)	Babe Ruth, 11 (1920, 1921, 1923, 1924, 1926, 1927, 1928, 1930, 1931, 1932, 1933)
Times Striking Out	Vince DiMaggio, 6 (1937, 1938, 1942, 1943, 1944, 1945)	Jimmie Foxx, 7 (1929, 1930, 1931, 1933, 1935, 1936, 1941)
Stolen Bases	Max Carey, 10 (1913, 1915, 1916, 1917, 1918, 1920, 1922, 1923, 1924, 1925)	Luis Apparicio, 9 (1956, 1957, 1958, 1959, 1960, 1961, 1962, 1963, 1964)

MOST CONSECUTIVE YEARS LEADING LEAGUE IN AN OFFENSIVE CATEGORY (Since 1900)

	NATIONAL LEAGUE	AMERICAN LEAGUE
Batting Avg.	Rogers Hornsby, 6 1920–25	Ty Cobb, 9 1907–15
Slugging Pct.	Rogers Hornsby, 6 1920–25	Babe Ruth, 7 1918–24
Runs	Chuck Klein, 3 1930–32 Duke Snider, 3 1953–55 Pete Rose, 3 1974–76	Ty Cobb, 3 1909–11 Eddie Collins, 3 1912–14 Babe Ruth, 3 (2 times) 1919–21; 1926–28 Ted Williams, 3 1940–42 Mickey Mantle, 3 1956–58
Hits	Ginger Beaumont, 3 1902–04 Rogers Hornsby, 3 1920–22 Frank McCormick, 3 1938–40	Ty Cobb, 3 1907–09 Tony Oliva, 3 1964–66
Singles	Ginger Beaumont, 3 1902–04 Lloyd Waner, 3 1927–29	Nellie Fox, 7 1954–58
Doubles	Honus Wagner, 4 1906–09	Tris Speaker, 4 1920–23
Triples	Garry Templeton, 3 1977–79	Elmer Flick, 3 1905–07 Sam Crawford, 3 1913–15 Zoilo Versalles, 3 1963–65
Home Runs	Ralph Kiner, 7 1946–52	Babe Ruth, 6 1926–31
Total Bases	Honus Wagner, 4 1906–09 Chuck Klein, 4 1930–33	Ty Cobb, 3 1907–09 Jim Rice, 3 1977–79
RBI	Rogers Hornsby, 3 1920–22 Joe Medwick, 3 1936–38 George Foster, 3 1976–78	Ty Cobb, 3 1907–09 Babe Ruth, 3 1919–21

MOST CONSECUTIVE YEARS LEADING LEAGUE IN AN OFFENSIVE CATEGORY (Since 1900) (continued)

	NATIONAL LEAGUE	AMERICAN LEAGUE
Walks	George Burns, 3 1919–21 Mel Ott, 3 1931–33 Arky Vaughan, 3 1934–36 Eddie Mathews, 3 1961–63 Ron Santo, 3 1966–68 Mike Schmidt, 3 1981–83	Babe Ruth, 4 1930–33 Ted Williams, 4 1946–49
Strikeouts	Hack Wilson, 4 1927–30 Vince DiMaggio, 4 1942–45	Reggie Jackson, 4 1968–71
Stolen Bases	Maury Wills, 6 1960–65	Luis Aparicio, 9 1956–64

PLAYERS LEADING IN ALL TRIPLE CROWN CATEGORIES, BUT *NOT* IN SAME YEAR*

Henry Aaron	Batting: 1956, 1959 Home Runs: 1957, 1963 (Tie), 1966, 1967 Runs Batted In: 1957, 1960, 1963, 1966
Dan Brouthers	Batting: 1882, 1883, 1889, 1891, 1892 Home Runs: 1881, 1886 Runs Batted In: 1892
Ed Delahanty	Batting: 1899 Home Runs: 1893 Runs Batted In: 1893, 1896, 1899
Joe DiMaggio	Batting: 1939, 1940 Home Runs: 1937, 1948 Runs Batted In: 1941, 1948
Johnny Mize	Batting: 1939 Home Runs: 1939, 1940, 1947 (Tie), 1948 (Tie) Runs Batted In: 1940, 1942, 1947
Babe Ruth	Batting: 1924 Home Runs: 1918 (Tie), 1919, 1920, 1921, 1923, 1924, 1926, 1927, 1928, 1929, 1930, 1931 (Tie) Runs Batted In: 1919, 1920, 1921, 1923, 1926, 1928 (Tie)

*Includes only players who never won triple crown

HIGHEST OFFENSIVE CAREER TOTALS BY PLAYERS WHO NEVER LED LEAGUE

	NATIONAL LEAGUE	AMERICAN LEAGUE
Base Hits	Lou Brock, 3023	Eddie Collins, 3311
Singles	Hank Aaron, 3648	Carl Yastrzemski, 2262
Doubles	Willie Mays, 523	Al Simmons, 534
Triples	Rabbit Maranville, 177	Tris Speaker, 223
Home Runs	Stan Musial, 475	Al Kaline, 399
Total Bases	Pete Rose, 5752	Reggie Jackson, 4834
Batting Average	Riggs Stephenson, .336	Joe Jackson, .356
Slugging Percentage	Richie Allen, .526	Al Simmons, .541
Runs	Eddie Mathews, 1491	Tris Speaker, 1881
RBI	Willie Mays, 1903	Al Kaline, 1584
Bases on Balls	Pete Rose, 1566	Tris Speaker, 1381
Strikeouts	Tony Perez, 1660	Carl Yastrzemski, 1393
Stolen Bases	Cesar Cedeno, 550	Tris Speaker, 433

CAREER OFFENSIVE LEADERS BY PLAYERS UNDER SIX FEET TALL

Games Played	3,562, Pete Rose (5' 11")		Total Bases	6,066, Willie Mays (5' 10½")
Times At Bat	14,053, Pete Rose (5' 11")		Runs	2,165, Pete Rose (5' 11")
Base Hits	4,256, Pete Rose (5' 11")		RBI	1,903, Willie Mays (5' 10½")
Singles	3,115, Pete Rose (5' 11")		Bases or Balls	1,865, Joe Morgan (5' 7")
Doubles	793, Tris Speaker (5' 11½")		Strikeouts	1,730, Lou Brock (5' 11½")
Triples	252, Honus Wagner (5' 11")		Batting Average	.358, Rogers Hornsby (5' 11")
Home Runs	660, Willie Mays (5' 10½")		Slugging Percentage	.577, Rogers Hornsby (5' 11")
Extra Base Hits	1,323, Willie Mays (5' 10½")		Stolen Bases	938, Lou Brock (5' 11½")

LARGEST MARGIN BETWEEN LEAGUE LEADERS AND RUNNERS-UP

CATEGORY		LEADER	RUNNER-UP	YEAR	MARGIN
Batting Average	AL	Nap Lajoie, Phila. (.422)	Mike Donlin, Balt. (.340)	1901	.082
	NL	Rogers Hornsby, St. L. (.424)	Zack Wheat, Bklyn. (.375)	1924	.049
Hits	AL	Nap Lajoie, Phila. (229)	John Anderson, Milw. (190)	1901	39
	NL	Stan Musial, St. L. (228)	Dixie Walker, Bklyn. (184)	1946	44
Doubles	AL	Nap Lajoie, Cleve. (51)	Ty Cobb, Det. (36)	1910	15
	NL	Honus Wagner, Pitt. (44)	Sam Mertes, NY (28)	1904	16
Triples	AL	Dale Mitchell, Cleve. (23)	Bob Dillinger, St. L. (13)	1949	10
	NL	Owen Wilson, Pitt. (36)	Honus Wagner, Pitt. (20)	1912	16
Home Runs	AL	Babe Ruth, NY (54)	George Sisler, St. L. (19)	1920	35
	NL	Cy Williams, Phila. (41)	Jack Fournier, Bklyn. (22)	1923	19
Runs Scored	AL	Babe Ruth, NY (177)	Jack Tobin, St. L. (132)	1921	45
	NL	Tommy Leach, Pitt. (126)	Fred Charles, Pitt. (97)	1909	29
RBI	AL	Hank Greenberg, Det. (170)	Lou Gehrig, NY (119)	1935	51
	NL	Joe Medwick, St. L. (154)	Frank Demaree, Chic. (115)	1937	39
Total Bases	AL	Babe Ruth, NY (457)	Harry Heilmann, Det. (365)	1921	92
	NL	Rogers Hornsby, St. L. (450)	Irish Meusel, NY (314)	1922	136
Slugging Average	AL	Babe Ruth, NY (.846)	Harry Heilmann, Det. (.606)	1921	.240
	NL	Rogers Hornsby, St. L. (.756)	Kiki Cuyler, Pitt. (.593)	1925	.163
Stolen Bases	AL	Rickey Henderson, Oak. (130)	Damaso Garcia, Tor. (54)	1982	76
	NL	Maury Wills, L.A. (104)	Willie Davis, L.A. (32)	1962	72
Walks	AL	Babe Ruth, NY (170)	Joe Sewell, Cleve. (98)	1923	72
	NL	Jimmy Sheckard, Chic. (147)	Johnny Bates, Cinn. (103)	1911	44

EVOLUTION OF SLUGGING PERCENTAGE RECORD

NATIONAL LEAGUE, PRE–1900

1876	Ross Barnes, Chic.	.556
1883	Dan Brouthers, Buffalo	.572
1886	Dan Brouthers, Det.	.581
1893	Ed Delahanty, Phila.	.583
1894	Hugh Duffy, Bost.	.690

POST–1900

1922	Rogers Hornsby, St. L.	.722
1925	Rogers Hornsby, St. L.	.756

AMERICAN LEAGUE

1901	Nap Lajoie, Phila.	.630
1919	Babe Ruth, Bost.	.657
1920	Babe Ruth, NY	.847

MOST TIMES AWARDED FIRST BASE ON CATCHER'S INTERFERENCE OR OBSTRUCTION

Pete Rose (1963–86)   29
Dale Berra (1977–87)   18
Julian Javier (1960–72)   18
Bob Stinson (1969–80)   16
Hector Torres (1968–77)   12

Richie Hebner (1968–85)   11
Chris Short (1959–73)   11
Chris Chambliss (1971–86)   9
Pat Corrales (1964–87)   9
George Hendrick (1971–87)   9

PITCHING

SHUTOUTS

EVOLUTION OF SHUTOUT RECORD

NATIONAL LEAGUE, PRE–1900

1876	George Bradley, St. L.	16

NATIONAL LEAGUE, POST–1900

1900	Clark Griffith, Chic.	4
	Noodles Hahn, Cinn.	4
	Kid Nichols, Bost.	4
	Cy Young, St. L.	4
1901	Jack Chesbro, Pitt.	6
	Al Orth, Phila.	6
	Vic Willis, Bost.	6
1902	Jack Chesbro, Pitt.	8
	Christy Mathewson, NY	8
	Jack Taylor, Chic.	8
1904	Joe McGinnity, NY	9
1906	Mordecai Brown, Chic.	10
1908	Christy Mathewson, NY	12
1915	Grover Cleve. Alexander, Phila.	12
1916	Grover Cleve. Alexander, Phila..	16

AMERICAN LEAGUE

1901	Clark Griffith, Chic.	5
	Cy Young, Bost.	5
1902	Addie Joss, Cleve.	5
1903	Cy Young, Bost.	7
1904	Cy Young, Bost.	10
1906	Ed Walsh, Chic.	10
1908	Ed Walsh, Chic.	11
1910	Jack Coombs, Phila.	13

20 OR MORE WINS WITH NO SHUTOUTS

26	Joe Bush, NY (AL), 1922	26–7
24	Ron Bryant, S.F. (NL), 1973	24–12
	Alvin Crowder, WA (AL), 1933	24–15
23	Christy Mathewson, NY (NL), 1912	23–12
22	Tex Hughson, Bost. (AL), 1942	22–6
	Lefty Williams, Chic. (AL), 1920	22–14
	Earl Wilson, Det. (AL), 1967	22–11
21	Mordecai Brown, Chic. (NL), 1911	21–12
	Russ Ford, NY (AL), 1911	21–11
	Lefty Gomez, NY (AL), 1931	21–9
	George Mullin, Det. (AL), 1905	21–21
	Willie Sherdel, St. L. (NL), 1928	21–10
20	Dave Boswell, MN (AL), 1969	20–12
	Alex Kellner, Phila. (AL), 1949	20–12
	Bobo Newsom, St. L. (AL), 1938	20–16
	Luis Tiant, Bost. (AL), 1973	20–13
	Rube Walberg, Phila. (AL), 1931	20–12

PITCHERS LEADING LEAGUE IN WINS, WITH NO SHUTOUTS

Alvin Crowder, WA (AL), 1933   24 wins
Tex Hughson, Bost. (AL), 1942   22 wins
Bob Lemon, Cleve. (AL), 1955   18 wins (Tie)
Earl Wilson, Det. (AL), 1967   22 wins
Ron Bryant, S.F. (NL), 1973   24 wins

MOST CAREER STARTS, NO SHUTOUTS

			W/L
128	Roy Mahaffey	(1926–27; 1930–36)	67–49
119	Al Nipper	(1983–88)	44–47
117	Roger Erickson	(1978–83)	35–53
99	Bob Miller	(1957; 1959–74)	69–81
99	Chris Knapp	(1975–80)	36–32
95	Eddie Solomon	(1973–82)	36–42

MOST LIFETIME SHUTOUTS, NEVER LED LEAGUE IN CATEGORY FOR SEASON

Rube Waddell (1897; 1899–1910)	50	Chief Bender (1903–17; 1925)	41
Ferguson Jenkins (1965–83)	49	Claude Osteen (1957; 1959–75)	40
Doc White (1901–13)	46	Ed Reulbach (1905–17)	40
Phil Niekro (1964–87)	45	Mel Stottlemyre (1964–74)	40
Catfish Hunter (1965–79)	42	Mickey Welch (1880–92)	40

PITCHED SHUTOUTS IN FIRST TWO STARTS IN MAJORS

Albert Spalding, Chic. (NL)	1876	Joe Doyle, NY (AL)	1906	Al Worthington, NY (NL)	1953
John Ward, Providence (NL)	1878	Johnny Marcum, Phila. (AL)	1933	Karl Spooner, Bklyn. (NL)	1954
Jim Hughes, Balt. (NL)	1898	Dave "Boo" Ferriss, Bost. (AL)	1945	Tom Phoebus, Balt. (AL)	1966

MOST HITS ALLOWED BY PITCHER PITCHING SHUTOUT

14 Larry Cheney, Chic. (NL), Sept. 14, 1913	12 Leon Cadore, Bklyn. (NL), Sept. 4, 1920
14 Milt Gaston, WA (AL), July 10, 1928	12 George Smith, Phila. (NL), Aug. 12, 1921
13 Scott Stratton, Louisville (NL), Sept. 19, 1893	12 Milt Gaston, St. L. (AL), Sept. 12, 1926
13 Ned Garvin, Chic. (NL), Sept. 22, 1899	12 Garland Buckeye, Cleve. (AL), Sept. 16, 1926
13 Bill Lee, Chic. (NL), Sept. 17, 1938	12 Hal Schumacher, NY (NL), July 19, 1934
12 Nixey Callahan, Chic. (NL), April 30, 1899	12 Fritz Ostermueller, Pitt. (NL), May 17, 1947
12 Pol Perritt, NY (NL), Sept. 14, 1917	12 Bob Friend, Pitt. (NL), Sept. 24, 1959
12 Rube Benton, NY (NL), Aug. 28, 1920	12 Stan Bahnsen, Chic. (AL), June 21, 1973

HIGHEST PERCENTAGE OF SHUTOUTS TO GAMES STARTED, LIFETIME

	GAMES STARTED	SHUTOUTS	PCT.
Ed Walsh (1904–17)	315	57	18.10
Smokey Joe Wood (1908–20)	158	28	17.72
Addie Joss (1902–10)	260	46	17.69
Mordecai "Three Finger" Brown (1903–16)	332	57	17.17
Walter Johnson (1907–27)	666	110	16.52
Grover Cleve. Alexander (1911–30)	598	90	15.05
Lefty Leifield (1905–20)	217	32	14.75
Rube Waddell (1897–1910)	340	50	14.71
Christy Mathewson (1900–16)	552	80	14.49
Spud Chandler (1937–47)	184	26	14.13
Nap Rucker (1907–16)	273	38	13.92
Mort Cooper (1938–49)	239	33	13.81
Ed Reulbach (1905–17)	299	40	13.38
Babe Adams (1906–07; 1909–26)	355	47	13.24
Eddie Plank (1901–17)	527	69	13.09
Sam Leever (1898–1910)	299	39	13.04

WINS

MOST VICTORIES, BY DECADE

Pre–1900
Pud Galvin	361
Tim Keefe	344
John Clarkson	326
Mickey Welch	311
Hoss Radbourn	308
Kid Nichols	297
Tony Mullane	285
Cy Young	265
Jim McCormick	264
Gus Weyhing	258

1900–1909
Christy Mathewson	236
Cy Young	232
Joe McGinnity	219
Jack Chesbro	192
Eddie Plank	187
Vic Willis	187
Rube Waddell	181
Sam Leever	166
Jack Powell	160
George Mullin	157

1910–1919
Walter Johnson	264
Grover Alexander	208
Eddie Cicotte	162
Hippo Vaughn	156
Slim Sallee	148
Rube Marquard	144
Eddie Plank	140
Christy Mathewson	137
Claude Hendrix	134
Hooks Dauss	125

1920–1929
Burleigh Grimes	190
Eppa Rixey	166
Grover Alexander	165
Herb Pennock	162
Waite Hoyt	161
Urban Shocker	156
Eddie Rommel	154
Jesse Haines	153
George Uhle	152
Red Faber	149

1930–1939
Lefty Grove	199
Carl Hubbell	188
Red Ruffing	175
Wes Ferrell	170
Lefty Gomez	165
Mel Harder	158
Larry French	156
Tommy Bridges	150
Paul Derringer	148
Dizzy Dean	147

1940–1949
Hal Newhouser	170
Bob Feller	137
Rip Sewell	133
Dizzy Trout	129
Dutch Leonard	122
Bucky Walters	122
Mort Cooper	114
Claude Passeau	111
Kirby Higbe	105
Bobo Newsom	105

1950–1959
Warren Spahn	202
Robin Roberts	199
Early Wynn	188
Billy Pierce	155
Bob Lemon	150
Mike Garcia	128
Lew Burdette	126
Don Newcombe	126
Whitey Ford	121
Johnny Antonelli	116

1960–1969
Juan Marichal	191
Bob Gibson	164
Don Drysdale	158
Jim Bunning	150
Jim Kaat	142
Larry Jackson	141
Sandy Koufax	137
Jim Maloney	134
Milt Pappas	131
Camilo Pascual	127

1970–1979
Jim Palmer	186
Gaylord Perry	184
Steve Carlton	178
Ferguson Jenkins	178
Tom Seaver	178
Catfish Hunter	169
Don Sutton	166
Phil Niekro	164
Vida Blue	155
Nolan Ryan	155

1980–1989
Jack Morris	162
Dave Steib	143
Bob Welch	137
Charlie Hough	128
Fernando Valenzuela	128
Bert Blyleven	123
Nolan Ryan	122
Jim Clancy	119
Frank Viola	117
Mike Scott	114

MOST WINS BY LETTER OF THE ALPHABET

A	Grover Cleve. Alexander	373	J	Walter Johnson	416	S	Warren Spahn	363
B	Bert Blyleven	271	K	Tim Keefe	344*	T	Luis Tiant	229
C	Steve Carlton	329	L	Ted Lyons	260	U	George Uhle	200
D	Paul Derringer	223	M	Christy Mathewson	373	V	Dazzy Vance	197
E	Howard Ehmke	166	N	Kid Nichols	360*	W	Mickey Welch	311*
F	Bob Feller	266	O	Al Orth	202*	Y	Cy Young	511
G	Pud Galvin	361*	P	Gaylord Perry	314	Z	Tom Zachary	186
H	Carl Hubbell	253	Q	Jack Quinn	247			
I	Bert Inks	27*	R	Charles "Hoss" Radbourn	308*			

*Includes pre-1900 wins; if post-1900 wins only, then Lefty Grove (300), Ham Iburg (11), Jim Kaat (283), Phil Niekro (318), Claude Osteen (196), Nolan Ryan (289), and Early Wynn (300)

MOST CAREER VICTORIES BY ZODIAC SIGN

AQUARIUS (Jan. 20–Feb. 18)	Nolan Ryan	289
PISCES (Feb. 19–Mar. 20)	Grover C. Alexander	373
ARIES (Mar. 21–Apr. 19)	Cy Young	511
TAURUS (Apr. 20–May 20)	Warren Spahn	363
GEMINI (May 21–June 21)	Tommy John	288
CANCER (June 22–July 22)	John Clarkson	327
LEO (July 23–Aug. 22)	Christy Mathewson	373
VIRGO (Aug. 22–Sept. 22)	Kid Nichols	361
LIBRA (Sept. 23–Oct. 23)	Robin Roberts	286
SCORPIO (Oct. 24–Nov. 21)	Walter Johnson	416
SAGITTARIUS (Nov. 22–Dec. 21)	Old Hoss Radbourn	308
CAPRICORN (Dec. 22–Jan. 19)	Pud Galvin	361

MOST VICTORIES BY STATE OF BIRTH

State	Pitcher	Wins		State	Pitcher	Wins
Alabama	Don Sutton	324		Nevada	Jim Nash	68
Alaska	N/A			New Jersey	Don Newcombe	149
Arizona	John Denny	123		New Hampshire	Mike Flanagan	155
Arkansas	Lon Warneke	193		New Mexico	Wade Blasingame	46
California	Tom Seaver	311		New York	Warren Spahn	363
Colorado	Goose Gossage	110		North Carolina	Gaylord Perry	314
Connecticut	Red Donahue	167		North Dakota	Lynn Nelson	33
Delaware	Vic Willis	247		Ohio	Cy Young	511
Florida	Steve Carlton	329		Oklahoma	Allie Reynolds	182
Georgia	Nap Rucker	134		Oregon	Mickey Lolich	217
Hawaii	Charlie Hough	174		Pennsylvania	Christy Mathewson	373
Idaho	Larry Jackson	194		Rhode Island	Tom Lovett	88
Illinois	Robin Roberts	286		South Carolina	Bobo Newsom	211
Indiana	Tommy John	288		South Dakota	Floyd Bannister	129
Iowa	Bob Feller	266		Tennessee	Bob Caruthers	218
Kansas	Walter Johnson	416		Texas	Nolan Ryan	289
Kentucky	Gus Weyhing	264		Utah	Bruce Hurst	85
Louisiana	Ted Lyons	260		Vermont	Ray Fisher	100
Maine	Bob Stanley	115		Virginia	Eppa Rixey	266
Maryland	Lefty Grove	300		Washington	Gerry Staley	134
Massachusetts	Tim Keefe	344		West Virginia	Wilbur Cooper	216
Michigan	Jim Kaat	283		Wisconsin	Kid Nichols	360
Minnesota	Jerry Koosman	222		Wyoming	Dick Ellsworth	115
Mississippi	Guy Bush	176				
Missouri	Pud Galvin	361		District of Columbia	Doc White	190
Montana	Dave McNally	184		Puerto Rico	Juan Pizarro	131
Nebraska	Grover Cleveland Alexander	373		Virgin Islands	Al McBean	67

MOST WINS BY COUNTRY, PITCHERS BORN OUTSIDE U.S.

Country	Pitcher	Wins		Country	Pitcher	Wins
Canada	Ferguson Jenkins	284		Nicaragua	Dennis Martinez	153
Cuba	Luis Tiant	229		Norway	Jimmy Wiggs	3
Czechoslovakia	Joe Hovlik	2		Panama	Juan Berenguer	46
Dominican Republic	Juan Marichal	243		Poland	Moe Drabowsky	88
England	Danny Cox	56		Russia	Rube Schauer	10
France	Charlie Lea	62		Scotland	Jim McCormick	264
Germany	Charlie Getzein	145		Spain	Bryan Oelkers	3
Holland	Bert Blyleven	271		Sweden	Eric Erickson	34
Ireland	Tommy Bond	193		Switzerland	Otto Hess	70
Italy	Marino Pieretti	30		Venezuela	Luis Leal	51
Japan	Masanori Murakami	5		Wales	Ted Lewis	94
Mexico	Fernando Valenzuela	128				

PITCHERS WITH FIVE CONSECUTIVE 20-WIN SEASONS (Since 1900)

Cy Young, St. L. (NL), Cleve. (AL)	1900–04	Carl Hubbell, NY (NL)	1933–37
Christy Mathewson, NY (NL)	1903–14	Robin Roberts, Phila. (NL)	1950–55
Three Finger Brown, Chic. (NL)	1906–11	Warren Spahn, Milw. (NL)	1956–61
Walter Johnson, WA (AL)	1910–19	Ferguson Jenkins, Chic. (NL)	1967–72
Grover Cleve. Alexander, Phila. (NL)	1913–17	Jim "Catfish" Hunter, Oak. (AL), NY (AL)	1971–75
Lefty Grove, Phila. (AL)	1927–33		

100-GAME WINNERS, BOTH LEAGUES

	NATIONAL LEAGUE	AMERICAN LEAGUE	TOTAL
Jim Bunning	106 (1964–71)	118 (1955–63)	224
Ferguson Jenkins	169 (1965–73; 1981)	115 (1974–81)	284
Gaylord Perry	175 (1962–71; 1978–79)	139 (1972–77; 1980; 1983)	314
Nolan Ryan	135 (1966–71; 1980–88)	154 (1972–79, 1989)	289
Cy Young	289 (1890–1900; 1911)	222 (1901–11)	511

PITCHERS WITH 500 CAREER DECISIONS

		W/L			W/L
Cy Young (1890–1911)	824	511–313	Nolan Ryan (1966–89)	552	289–263
Walter Johnson (1907–27)	695	416–279	Early Wynn (1939–44; 1946–63)	544	300–244
Warren Spahn (1942; 1946–65)	608	363–245	Robin Roberts (1948–66)	531	286–245
Phil Niekro (1964–87)	592	318–274	Jim Kaat (1959–83)	520	283–237
Grover C. Alexander (1911–30)	581	373–208	Tommy John (1963–74; 1976–89)	519	288–231
Don Sutton (1966–88)	580	324–256	Eppa Rixey (1912–33)	517	266–251
Gaylord Perry (1962–83)	579	314–265	Mickey Welch (1880–92)	518	311–207
Steve Carlton (1965–87)	572	329–243	Ferguson Jenkins (1965–83)	510	284–226
Tim Keefe (1880–93)	569	344–225	John Clarkson (1882; 1884–94)	503	326–177
Kid Nichols (1890–1901; 1904–06)	563	360–203	Jack Powell (1897–1912)	501	246–255
Christy Mathewson (1900–16)	561	373–188			

MOST WINS, MAJOR LEAGUES AND MINORS COMBINED

		MAJORS	MINORS			MAJORS	MINORS
526	Cy Young	511	15	355	Joe Martina	6	349
482	Joe McGinnity	247	235	353	Steve Carlton	329	24
444	Kid Nichols	360	84	350	Bobo Newsom	211	139
418	Grover Alexander	373	45	348	Don Sutton	324	24
416	Walter Johnson	416	0	348	Bill Thomas	0	348
415	Warren Spahn	363	52	347	Jack Quinn	247	100
412	Lefty Grove	300	112	343	Tim Keefe	343	0
398	Christy Mathewson	373	25	342	Burleigh Grimes	270	72
369	Gaylord Perry	314	55	341	Stan Coveleski	214	133
366	Early Wynn	300	66	336	August Weyhing	262	74
361	Pud Galvin	361	0	332	Red Faber	254	78
361	Phil Niekro	318	43	332	Dazzy Vance	197	135
360	Tony Freitas	25	335	331	Alex McColl	4	327

PITCHERS WITH 100 MORE CAREER WINS THAN LOSSES

		W/L			W/L			W/L
Cy Young	198	511–313	Walter Johnson	137	416–279	Jim Palmer	116	268–152
Christy Mathewson	185	373–188	Whitey Ford	130	236–106	Bob Caruthers	116	217–101
Grover Alexander	165	373–208	Eddie Plank	124	305–181	Tom Seaver	106	311–205
Lefty Grove	159	300–141	Tim Keefe	118	342–224	Bob Feller	104	266–162
Kid Nichols	153	361–208	Warren Spahn	118	363–245	Juan Marichal	101	243–142
John Clarkson	151	327–176	Old Hoss Radbourn	117	308–191	Clark Griffith	100	240–140

MOST LIFETIME WINS, NEVER LED LEAGUE IN SEASON

Pud Galvin (1879–92)	361	Tommy John (1963–74; 1976–89)	288	Jack Quinn (1909–33)	247
Eddie Plank (1901–17)	327	Tony Mullane (1881–94)	285	Vic Willis (1898–1910)	247
Don Sutton (1966–88)	324	Gus Weyhing (1887–1901)	264	Jack Powell (1897–1912)	246
Mickey Welch (1880–92)	311	Bert Blyleven (1970–88)	254		
Nolan Ryan (1966–88)	273	Red Faber (1914–33)	254		

PITCHERS WINNING 200 GAMES, NEVER WINNING 20 GAMES IN SEASON

Jerry Reuss (1969–89)   220–191
Milt Pappas (1957–73)   209–164

PLAYERS WITH 100 WINS, 500 HITS

Walter Johnson (1907–27)   416   549
Jack Stivetts (1889–99)   207   592
Smokey Joe Wood (1908–22)   116   553

VICTORIES IN MOST CONSECUTIVE SEASONS

24 seasons	Don Sutton (1966–89)		21 seasons	Walter Johnson (1907–27)
23 seasons	Jim Kaat (1960–82)			Joe Niekro (1967–87)
	Phil Niekro (1965–87)			Eppa Rixey (1912–33)*
22 seasons	Steve Carlton (1966–87)			Red Ruffing (1925–47)*
	Gaylord Perry (1962–83)		20 seasons	Red Faber (1914–33)
	Nolan Ryan (1968–89)			Lindy McDaniel (1956–75)
	Early Wynn (1941–63)*			Tom Seaver (1967–86)
	Cy Young (1890–1911)			Warren Spahn (1946–65)

*Includes time in service

MOST CAREER WINS BY PITCHERS 6′ 6″ OR MORE

164	John Candelaria (6′ 7″), 1975–89	167–107*		117	Rick Sutcliffe (6′ 7″), 1976–89	133–103*
146	Ron Reed (6′ 6″), 1966–84	146–140		107	J. R. Richard (6′ 8″), 1971–80	107–71
137	Fred Toney (6′ 6″), 1911–23	137–102		100	Mike Witt (6′ 7″), 1981–89	109–104*
120	Bob Veale (6′ 6″), 1962–74	120–95				

*Active

MOST VICTORIES BY PITCHERS UNDER SIX FEET TALL

361	Pud Galvin (5' 8")*	239	Mordecai "Three Finger" Brown (5' 10")
360	Kid Nichols (5' 10½")*	236	Whitey Ford (5' 10")
344	Tim Keefe (5' 10½")*	229	Will White (5' 9½")*
327	Eddie Plank (5' 11½")	228	George Mullin (5' 11")
326	John Clarkson (5' 10")*	221	Hooks Dauss (5' 10½")
311	Mickey Welch (5' 8")*	218	Bob Caruthers (5' 7")*
308	Old Hoss Radbourn (5' 9")*	218	Earl Whitehill (5' 9½")
285	Tony Mullane (5' 10½")*	217	Freddie Fitzsimmons (5' 11")
270	Burleigh Grimes (5' 10")	216	Wilbur Cooper (5' 11½")
264	Jim McCormick (5' 10")*	215	Stan Coveleski (5' 11")
264	Gus Weyhing (5' 10")*	211	Billy Pierce (5' 10")
260	Ted Lyons (5' 11")	208	Carl Mays (5' 11½")
247	Joe McGinnity (5' 11")	208	Eddie Cicotte (5' 9")
240	Clark Griffith (5' 6½")*	201	Charlie Root (5' 10½")

*19th Century pitchers

PITCHERS WINNING 20 GAMES IN SEASON SPLIT BETWEEN TWO TEAMS

1902	Joe McGinnity, Balt.(AL)–NY(NL)	21–18
	Balt. (AL)	13–10
	NY (NL)	8–8
1903	Robert Wicker, St. L.–Chic.(NL)	20–9
	St. L. (NL)	0–0
	Chic. (NL)	20–9
1904	Patsy Flaherty, Chic.(AL)–Pitt.(NL)	20–11
	Chic. (AL)	1–2
	Pitt. (NL)	19–9
1906	John Taylor, St. L.–Chic.(NL)	20–12
	St. L. (NL)	8–9
	Chic. (NL)	12–3
1939	Bobo Newsom, St. L.–Det.(AL)	20–11
	St. L. (AL)	3–1
	Det. (AL)	17–10
1945	Red Barrett, Bost.–St. L.(NL)	23–12
	Bost. (NL)	2–3
	St. L. (NL)	21–9
1945	Hank Borowy, NY(AL)–Chic.(NL)	21–7
	NY (AL)	10–5
	Chic. (NL)	11–2
1953	Virgil Trucks, St. L.–Chic.(AL)	20–10
	St. L.(AL)	5–4
	Chic. (AL)	15–6
1977	Tom Seaver, NY–Cinn.(NL)	21–6
	NY (NL)	7–3
	Cinn. (NL)	14–3
1984	Rick Sutcliffe, Cleve.(AL)–Chic.(NL)	20–6
	Cleve. (AL)	4–5
	Chic. (NL)	16–1

OLDEST PITCHERS TO WIN 20 GAMES FOR THE FIRST TIME (SINCE 1900)

AGE		WINS		AGE		WINS
37	Allie Reynolds, NY, (AL), 1952	20		34	Sal Maglie, NY, (NL), 1951	23
36	Curt Davis, St. L., (NL), 1939	22		34	Earl Whitehill, WA, (AL), 1933	22
36	Rip Sewell, Pitt., (NL), 1943	22		34	Whit Wyatt, Bklyn., (NL), 1941	22
36	Preacher Roe, Bklyn., (NL), 1951	22		34	Slim Sallee, Cinn., (NL), 1919	21
36	Spud Chandler, NY, (AL), 1943	20		34	Sam Jones, S.F., (NL), 1959	21
35	Thorton Lee, Chic., (AL), 1941	22		34	Joe Niekro, Houst., (NL), 1979	21
35	Murray Dickson, Pitt., (NL), 1951	20		34	Jim Turner, Bost., (NL), 1937	20
35	Dick Donovan, Cleve., (AL), 1962	20		34	Tommy John, L.A., (NL), 1977	20

YOUNGEST PITCHERS TO WIN 20 GAMES (Since 1900)

AGE		WINS		AGE		WINS
20 yrs., 10 mos.	Bob Feller, Cleve., (AL), 1939	24		21 yrs., 8 mos.	Wes Ferrell, Cleve., (AL), 1929	21
20 yrs., 10 mos.	Dwight Gooden, NY, (NL), 1985	24		21 yrs., 9 mos.	Ralph Branca, Bklyn., (NL), 1947	21
21 yrs., 4 mos.	Al Mamaux, Pitt., (NL), 1915	21		21 yrs., 11 mos.	Rube Marquard, NY, (NL), 1911	24
21 yrs., 7 mos.	Babe Ruth, Bost., (AL), 1916	23				

ROOKIES WINNING 20 GAMES (Since 1900)

NATIONAL LEAGUE

Christy Mathewson, NY, 1901	20–17
Henry Schmidt, Bklyn., 1903	21–13
Jake Weimer, Chic., 1903	21–9
Irv Young, Bost., 1905	20–21
George McQuillan, Phila., 1908	23–17
King Cole, Chic., 1910	20–4
Grover C. Alexander, Phila., 1911	28–13
Larry Cheney, Chic., 1912	26–10
Jeff Pfeffer, Bklyn., 1914	23–12
Lou Fette, Bost., 1937	20–10
Cliff Melton, NY, 1937	20–9
Jim Turner, Bost., 1937	20–11
Johnny Beazley, St. L., 1942	21–6
Bill Voiselle, NY, 1944	21–16
Larry Jansen, NY, 1947	21–5
Harvey Haddix, St. L., 1953	20–9
Tom Browning, Cinn., 1985	20–9

AMERICAN LEAGUE

Roscoe Miller, Det., 1901	23–13
Roy Patterson, Chic., 1901	20–16
Ed Summers, Det., 1908	24–12
Russ Ford, NY, 1910	26–6
Vean Gregg, Cleve., 1911	23–7
Reb Russell, Chic., 1913	21–17
Scott Perry, Phila., 1918	21–19
Wes Ferrell, Cleve., 1929	21–10
Monte Weaver, WA, 1932	22–10
Dave "Boo" Ferriss, Bost., 1945	21–10
Gene Bearden, Cleve., 1948	20–7
Alex Kellner, Phila., 1949	20–12
Bob Grim, NY, 1954	20–6

PITCHERS WINNING 20 GAMES IN ROOKIE YEAR, LESS THAN 20 BALANCE OF CAREER

1901	Roscoe Miller Det. (AL)	23–13	Career (1901–04) 39–46
1903	Henry Schmidt Bklyn. (NL)	21–13	Career (1903) 21–13
1942	Johnny Beazley St. L. (NL)	21–6	Career (1941–42; 1946–49) 31–12

20-GAME WINNERS WHO DIDN'T WIN 20 GAMES DURING REST OF THEIR CAREER (Since 1900)

Roscoe Miller, 23 wins, 1901 Det. Tigers   16 rest of career
Henry Schmidt, 21 wins, 1903 Bklyn. Dodgers   0 rest of career
Buck O'Brien, 20 wins, 1912 Bost. Red Sox   9 rest of career
Bill James, 26 wins, 1914 Bost. Braves   11 rest of career
George McConnell, 25 wins, 1915 Chic. Feds   16 rest of career
Johnny Beazley, 21 wins, 1942 St. L. Cardinals   11 rest of career

ROOKIE PITCHERS WITH 20 WINS, 200 STRIKEOUTS

1901	Christy Mathewson, NY Giants (NL)	20–17	221
1910	Russ Ford, NY Yankees (AL)	26–6	209
1911	Grover Cleve. Alexander, Phila. Phillies (NL)	28–13	227

DOUBLE WIN FIGURES IN ONLY BIG LEAGUE SEASON

21	Henry Schmidt, Bklyn. (1903) 21–13
19	Fred Smith, Toledo (1890) 19–13
19	Parke Swartzel, K.C. (1889) 19–27
17	John Keefe, Syracuse (1890) 17–24
12	Max Fiske, Chic. (1914) 12–9
12	Joe Hart, St. L. (1890) 12–8
12	Doc Landis, Phila., Balt. (1882) 12–28
12	Erv Lange, Chic. (1914) 12–10
12	Perry Werden, St. L. (1884) 12–1
11	Joe Borden, Bost. (1876) 11–12
11	Ham Iburg, Phila. (1902) 11–18
11	Jumping Jack Jones, Det., Phila. (1883) 11–7
10	George Cobb, Balt. (1892) 10–37
10	Charlie Gagus, WA (1884) 10–9

PITCHERS WINNING 20 GAMES IN THEIR LAST SEASON IN MAJORS

Henry Schmidt, Bklyn. Dodgers (NL), 1903   21–13
Eddie Cicotte, Chic. White Sox (AL), 1920   21–10

Lefty Williams, Chic. White Sox (AL), 1920   22–14
Sandy Koufax, L.A. Dodgers (NL), 1966   27–9

PITCHERS WINNING 10 MORE GAMES THAN SECOND-LEADING WINNER IN LEAGUE

1904   Jack Chesbro, NY (AL)   44   (Runner-up, Cy Young, 30)
1908   Ed Walsh, Chic. (AL)   40   (Runners-up, Ed Summers and Addie Joss, 24)
1913   Walter Johnson, WA (AL)   36   (Runners-up, Chief Bender, Rip Russell, Cy Falkenberg, 21)
1915   Grover C. Alexander, Phila. (NL)   31   (Runners-up, Dick Rudolph, Al Mamaux, Erskine Mayer, 21)
1952   Robin Roberts, Phila. (NL)   28   (Runner-up, Sal Maglie, 18)

PITCHERS ON LOSING TEAMS LEADING LEAGUE IN VICTORIES (Since 1900)

NATIONAL LEAGUE

Grover C. Alexander, 27–15, 1914 Phila. Phillies (74–80)
Grover C. Alexander, 27–14, 1920 Chic. Cubs (75–79)
Dazzy Vance, 22–9, 1925 Bklyn. Dodgers (68–85)
Jumbo Elliott, 19–14 (Tie), 1931 Phila. Phillies (66–88)
Heine Meine, 19–13 (Tie), 1931 Pitt. Pirates (75–79)
Ewell Blackwell, 22–8, 1947 Cinn. Reds (73–81)
Warren Spahn, 21–14, 1949 Bost. Braves (75–79)
Robin Roberts, 23–15, 1954 Phila. Phillies (75–79)
Larry Jackson, 24–11, 1964 Chic. Cubs (76–86)
Bob Gibson, 23–7, 1970 St. L. Cardinals (76–86)
Steve Carlton, 27–10, 1972 Phila. Phillies (59–97)
Randy Jones, 22–14, 1976 S.D. Padres (73–89)
Phil Niekro, 21–20, 1979 Atl. Braves (66–94)
Fernando Valenzuela, 21–11, 1986 L.A. Dodgers (73–89)
Rick Suttcliffe, 18–10, 1987 Chic. Cubs (76–85)

AMERICAN LEAGUE

Walter Johnson, 25–20, 1916 WA Senators (76–77)
Eddie Rommel, 27–13, 1922 Phila. Athletics (65–89)
Ted Lyons, 22–14, 1927 Chic. White Sox (70–83)
Bob Feller, 25–13, 1941 Cleve. Indians (75–79)
Bob Feller, 26–15, 1946 Cleve. Indians (68–86)
Jim Perry, 18–10, 1960 Cleve. Indians (76–78)
Gaylord Perry, 24–16, 1972 Cleve. Indians (72–84)
Wilbur Wood, 24–20, 1973 Chic. White Sox (77–85)

PITCHERS WINNING 20 GAMES ON LAST-PLACE TEAMS

NATIONAL LEAGUE

Noodles Hahn, 22–19, 1901 Cinn. Redlegs
Steve Carlton, 27–10, 1972 Phila. Phillies
Phil Niekro, 21–20, 1979 Atl. Braves

AMERICAN LEAGUE

Scott Perry, 21–19, 1918 Phila. Athletics
Howard Ehmke, 20–17, 1923 Bost. Red Sox
Hollis Thurston, 20–14, 1924 Chic. White Sox
Ned Garver, 20–12, 1951 St. L. Browns
Nolan Ryan, 22–16, 1974 CA Angels

PITCHERS WINNING GREATEST PERCENTAGE OF THEIR TEAM'S WINS IN SEASON

PCT.

45.8	Steve Carlton, Phila. Phillies (NL), 1972 27–10	Team, 59–97
45.5	Ed Walsh, Chic. White Sox (AL), 1908 40–15	Team, 88–64
44.6	Jack Chesbro, NY Highlanders (AL), 1904 41–13	Team, 92–59
42.3	Noodles Hahn, Cinn. Redlegs (NL), 1901 22–19	Team, 52–87
41.8	Cy Young, Bost. Pilgrims (AL), 1901 33–10	Team, 79–57
41.7	Joe Bush, Phila. Athletics (AL), 1916 15–22	Team, 36–117
41.6	Cy Young, Bost. Pilgrims (AL), 1902 32–11	Team, 77–60
41.5	Eddie Rommel, Phila. Athletics (AL), 1922 27–13	Team, 65–89
40.9	Walter Johnson, WA Senators (AL), 1910 27–17	Team, 66–85
40.4	Scott Perry, Phila. Athletics (AL), 1918 21–19	Team, 52–76
40.3	Red Faber, Chic. White Sox (AL), 1921 25–15	Team, 62–92

20-GAME WINNERS WITH WORST LIFETIME WINNING PERCENTAGES (Since 1900)

		LIFETIME	20-WIN SEASON(S)			LIFETIME	20-WIN SEASON(S)
Scott Perry	41–68	.376	1918	Bob Harmon	103–133	.436	1911
Irv Young	62–94	.397	1905	Al Schulz	48–61	.440	1915
Pete Schneider	57–86	.399	1917	Vern Kennedy	104–132	.441	1936
Ben Cantwell	76–108	.413	1933	Patsy Flaherty	66–83	.443	1904
Joe Oeschger	83–116	.417	1921	Bob Groom	121–150	.446	1912
Tom Hughes	128–172	.427	1903	Oscar Jones	45–56	.446	1903
Willie Sudhoff	102–135	.430	1903	Randy Jones	100–123	.448	1975 & 1976
Roger Wolff	52–69	.430	1945	Ned Garver	129–157	.451	1951
Frank Allen	50–66	.431	1915	George McConnell	42–51	.452	1915
Otto Hess	69–90	.434	1906	Chick Fraser	176–212	.454	1901

"PURE" 20-GAME WINNERS (PITCHERS WITH 20 MORE WINS THAN LOSSES, Since 1900)

NATIONAL LEAGUE	W/L		AMERICAN LEAGUE	W/L
Joe McGinnity, Bklyn., 1900	29–9		Cy Young, Bost., 1901	33–10
Jack Chesbro, Pitt., 1902	28–6		Cy Young, Bost., 1902	32–11
Joe McGinnity, NY, 1904	35–8		Jack Chesbro, NY, 1904	41–12
Christy Mathewson, NY, 1904	33–12		Ed Walsh, Chic., 1908	40–15
Christy Mathewson, NY, 1905	31–8		George Mullin, Det., 1909	29–8
"Three Finger" Brown, Chic., 1906	26–6		Jack Coombs, Phila., 1910	31–9
"Three Finger" Brown, Chic., 1908	29–9		Russ Ford, NY, 1910	26–6
Christy Mathewson, NY, 1908	37–11		Smokey Joe Wood, Bost., 1912	34–5
Grover C. Alexander, Phila., 1914	31–10		Walter Johnson, WA, 1912	32–12
Grover C. Alexander, Phila., 1916	33–12		Eddie Plank, Phila., 1912	26–6
Dazzy Vance, Bklyn., 1923	28–6		Walter Johnson, WA, 1913	36–7
Dizzy Dean, St. L., 1934	30–7		Eddie Cicotte, Chic., 1919	29–7
Carl Hubbell, NY, 1935	26–6		Lefty Grove, Phila., 1930	28–5
Robin Roberts, Phila., 1951	28–7		Lefty Grove, Phila., 1931	31–4
Don Newcombe, Bklyn., 1955	27–7		Lefty Gomez, NY, 1934	26–5
Sandy Koufax, L.A., 1962	25–5		Hal Newhouser, Det., 1944	29–9
Dwight Gooden, NY, 1985	24–4		Whitey Ford, NY, 1961	25–4
			Denny McLain, Det., 1968	31–6
			Ron Guidry, NY, 1978	25–3
			Roger Clemens, Bost., 1986	24–4

PITCHERS BEATING EVERY ONE OF THE EXISTING 26 MAJOR LEAGUE TEAMS

Doyle Alexander	National League	L.A., 1971
		Atl., 1980, 1986–87
		S.F., 1981
	American League	Balt., 1972–76
		NY, 1976, 1982–83
		TX, 1977–79
		Tor., 1983–86
		Det., 1987–88
Tommy John	National League	L.A., 1972–74; 1976–78*
	American League	Cleve., 1963–64
		Chic., 1965–71
		NY, 1979–82; 1986–88
		CA, 1982–85
		Oak., 1985
Gaylord Perry	National League	S.F., 1962–71
		S.D., 1978–79
		Atl., 1981
	American League	Cleve., 1972–75
		TX, 1975–77; 1980
		NY, 1980
		Seattle, 1982–83
		K.C., 1983

Nolan Ryan	National League	NY, 1966; 1968–71
		Houst., 1980–88
	American League	CA, 1972–79
		TX, 1989
Don Sutton	National League	L.A., 1966–80; 1988
		Houst., 1981–82
	American League	Milw., 1982–84
		Oak., 1985
		CA, 1985–87
Mike Torrez	National League	St. L., 1967–71
		Mont., 1971–74
		NY, 1984
	American League	Balt., 1975
		Oak., 1976–77; 1984
		NY, 1977
		Bost., 1978–82
Rick Wise	National League	Phila., 1964–71
		St. L., 1972–73
		S.D., 1981–82
	American League	Bost., 1974–77
		Cleve., 1978–79

*John also beat the L.A. Dodgers in the second game of the 1981 World Series to complete his cycle

NATIONAL LEAGUE LEFTIES SINCE WORLD WAR II WINNING 20 GAMES TWICE

Johnny Antonelli	1954 NY Giants (21)		Howie Pollet	1946 St. L. Cardinals (21)
	1956 NY Giants (20)			1949 St. L. Cardinals (20)
Steve Carlton	1971 St. L. Cardinals (20)		Warren Spahn	1947 Bost. Braves (21)
	1972 Phila. Phillies (27)			1949 Bost. Braves (21)
	1976 Phila. Phillies (20)			1950 Bost. Braves (21)
	1977 Phila. Phillies (23)			1951 Bost. Braves (22)
	1980 Phila. Phillies (24)			1953 Milw. Braves (23)
	1982 Phila. Phillies (23)			1954 Milw. Braves (21)
Randy Jones	1975 S.D. Padres (20)			1956 Milw. Braves (20)
	1976 S.D. Padres (22)			1957 Milw. Braves (21)
Sandy Koufax	1963 L.A. Dodgers (25)			1958 Milw. Braves (22)
	1965 L.A. Dodgers (26)			1959 Milw. Braves (21)
	1966 L.A. Dodgers (27)			1960 Milw. Braves (21)
Claude Osteen	1969 L.A. Dodgers (20)			1961 Milw. Braves (21)
	1972 L.A. Dodgers (20)			1963 Milw. Braves (23)

PITCHERS WITH 20-GAME SEASONS AFTER AGE 40

	AGE		W/L
Grover Cleve. Alexander	40	1927 St. L. Cardinals (NL)	21–10
Phil Niekro	40	1979 Atl. Braves (NL)	21–20
Gaylord Perry	40	1978 S.D. Padres (NL)	21–6
Warren Spahn	40	1961 Milw. Braves (NL)	21–15
	42	1963 Milw. Braves (NL)	23–7
Cy Young	40	1907 Bost. Red Sox (AL)	22–15
	41	1908 Bost. Red Sox (AL)	21–11

PITCHERS LEADING BOTH LEAGUES IN WINS (Since 1900)

Jack Chesbro	NL—1902 Pitt. Pirates, 28–6		Gaylord Perry	NL—1970 S.F. Giants, 23–13 (Tie)
	AL—1904 NY Yankees, 41–13			1978 S.D. Padres, 21–6
Ferguson Jenkins	NL—1971 Chic. Cubs, 24–13			AL—1972 Cleve. Indians, 24–16 (Tie)
	AL—1974 TX Rangers, 25–12 (Tie)			

"20/20" PITCHERS—PITCHERS WITH 20 WINS, 20 LOSSES, SAME SEASON

NATIONAL LEAGUE

Joe McGinnity, 1903 NY   31–20
Irv Young, 1906 Bost.   20–21
Phil Niekro, 1979 Atl.   21–20

AMERICAN LEAGUE

Joe McGinnity, 1901 Balt.   26–21
Bill Dineen, 1902 Bost.   21–21
George Mullin, 1905 Det.   21–20
George Mullin, 1907 Det.   20–20
Jim Scott, 1913 Chic.   20–20
Walter Johnson, 1916 WA   25–20
Wilbur Wood, 1973 Chic.   24–20

LOSSES

EVOLUTION OF PITCHERS' LOSSES RECORD

NATIONAL LEAGUE, PRE–1900

1876	Jim Devlin, Louisville	35
1879	George Bradley, Troy	40
	Jim McCormick, Cleve.	40
1880	Will White, Cinn.	42
1883	John Coleman, Phila.	48

NATIONAL LEAGUE, POST–1900

1900	Bill Carrick, NY	21
1901	Dummy Taylor, NY	27
1905	Vic Willis, Bost.	29

AMERICAN LEAGUE

1901	Pete Dowling, Milw.-Cleve.	26
1904	Jack Townsend, WA	26
1909	Bob Groom, WA	26

MOST LOSSES, BY DECADE

Pre–1900
Pud Galvin	310
Gus Weyhing	227
Tim Keefe	225
Tony Mullane	215
Jim McCormick	214
Mickey Welch	207
Jim Whitney	207
Adonis Terry	195
Hoss Radbourn	191
John Clarkson	177

1900–1909
Vic Willis	171
Jack Powell	164
Cy Young	145
Bill Dineen	143
Al Orth	142
Rube Waddell	141
Harry Howell	138
Chick Fraser	135
Long Tom Hughes	135
George Mullin	134

1910–1919
Walter Johnson	143
Bob Groom	124
Bob Harmon	122
Eddie Cicotte	121
Red Ames	117
Slim Sallee	114
Hippo Vaughn	109
Claude Hendrix	105
Lefty Tyler	105
Ray Caldwell	104

1920–1929
Dolf Luque	146
Eppa Rixey	142
Howard Ehmke	137
Slim Harriss	135
Burleigh Grimes	130
Jimmy Ring	128
George Uhle	124
Tom Zachary	122
Jesse Haines	119
Sam Jones	118

1930–1939
Paul Derringer	137
Larry French	134
Mel Harder	123
Bump Hadley	119
Wes Ferrell	115
Ted Lyons	115
Ed Brandt	112
Danny MacFayden	111
Earl Whitehill	107
Willis Hudlin	106

1940–1949
Dutch Leonard	123
Bobo Newsom	120
Dizzy Trout	119
Hal Newhouser	118
Sid Hudson	100
Johnny Vander Meer	92
Early Wynn	92
Bucky Walters	90
Ken Raffensberger	89
Jim Tobin	88

1950–1959
Robin Roberts	149
Warren Spahn	149
Bob Friend	127
Murry Dickson	124
Bob Rush	123
Billy Pierce	121
Early Wynn	119
Ned Garver	117
Chuck Stobbs	113
Alex Kellner	100

1960–1969
Jack Fisher	133
Dick Ellsworth	132
Larry Jackson	132
Don Drysdale	126
Claude Osteen	121
Jim Kaat	119
Jim Bunning	118
Don Cardwell	111
Ken Johnson	105
Bob Gibson	105

1970–1979
Phil Niekro	151
Nolan Ryan	146
Gaylord Perry	133
Ferguson Jenkins	130
Bert Blyleven	128
Jerry Koosman	127
Steve Carlton	126
Wilbur Wood	123
Mickey Lolich	117
Rick Wise	117

1980–1989
Jim Clancy	126
Frank Tanana	122
Jack Morris	119
Bob Knepper	118
Charlie Hough	114
Rich Dotson	109
Floyd Bannister	109
Dave Steib	109
Nolan Ryan	104
Bert Blyleven	103
Fernando Valenzuela	103

PITCHERS WITH 7 OR MORE CONSECUTIVE LOSING SEASONS

10	Bill Bailey (1908–12, 14–15, 18, 21–22)		7	Jesse Jefferson (1975–81)
10	Ron Kline (1952, 55–63)		7	Howie Judson (1948–54)
9	Milt Gaston (1926–34)		7	Dick Littlefield (1952–58)
8	Pete Broberg (1971–78)		7	Skip Lockwood (1969–75)
8	Jack Fisher (1961–68)		7	Duane Pillette (1949–55)
8	Bill Hart (1886–87, 92, 95–98, 01)		7	Eric Rasmussen (1976–80, 82–83)
8	Ken Raffensberger (1940–41, 43–48)		7	Buck Ross (1936–42)
8	Charlie Robertson (1919, 22–28)		7	Jack Russell (1926–32)
8	Socks Seibold (1916–17, 19, 29–33)		7	Herm Wehmeier (1949–55)
7	Boom Boom Beck (1928, 33–34, 39–42)		7	Bob Weiland (1929–35)
7	Bert Cunningham (1887–91, 95–96)		7	Carlton Willey (1959–65)
7	Bill Dietrich (1933–39)			

PITCHERS WITH 150 CAREER WINS—MORE LOSSES THAN WINS

Jack Powell (1897–1912)	246–255	Bill Dineen (1898–1909)	171–177
Bobo Newsom (1929–53)	211–222	Pink Hawley (1892–1901)	168–177
Bob Friend (1951–66)	197–230	Red Donahue (1893; 1895–1906)	167–173
Jim Whitney (1881–90)	192–207	Ted Breitenstein (1891–1901)	166–170
Tom Zachary (1918–36)	186–191	Bump Hadley (1926–41)	161–165
Chick Fraser (1896–1909)	177–212	Mark Baldwin (1887–1893)	154–165
Murray Dickson (1939–43; 1946–59)	172–181		

PITCHERS ON WINNING TEAMS LEADING LEAGUE IN LOSSES (Since 1900)

NATIONAL LEAGUE

Dick Rudolph, 22–19 (T), 1915 Bost. Braves (83–69)
Dolf Luque, 13–23, 1922 Cinn. Reds (86–68)
Wilbur Cooper, 17–19, 1923 Pitt. Pirates (87–67)
Charlie Root, 18–17 (T), 1926 Chic. Cubs (82–72)
Rip Sewell, 14–17, 1941 Pitt. Pirates (81–73)
Ron Kline, 13–16, 1958 Pitt. Pirates (84–70)
Bob Friend, 8–19, 1959 Pitt. Pirates (78–76)
Phil Niekro, 15–18, 1980 Atl. Braves (81–80)

AMERICAN LEAGUE

Bill Dineen, 21–21, 1902 Bost. Pilgrims (77–60)
Herman Pillette, 14–19 (T), 1923 Det. Tigers (83–71)
Hal Newhouser, 17–17, 1947 Det. Tigers (85–69)
Brian Kingman, 8–20, 1980 Oak. A's (83–79)
Bert Blyleven, 10–17, 1988 MN Twins (91–71)

PITCHERS WINNING 20 GAMES IN ROOKIE YEAR, LOSING 20 GAMES IN SECOND YEAR

1901   Roscoe Miller, Det. (AL)—23–13   1902—7–20

1949   Alex Kellner, Phila. (AL)—20–12   1950—8–20

300-GAME WINNERS WITH LESS THAN 200 LOSSES

	LOSSES	WINS
Lefty Grove (1925–41)	141	300
John Clarkson (1882; 1884–94)	176	327
Eddie Plank (1901–17)	181	305
Christy Mathewson (1900–16)	188	373
Old Hoss Radbourn (1880–91)	191	308

EARNED RUN AVERAGE

BEST EARNED RUN AVERAGE, BY DECADE (1,000 innings)

Pre–1900
Jim Devlin	1.89
Monte Ward	2.10
Tommy Bond	2.25
Will White	2.28
Larry Corcoran	2.36
Terry Larkin	2.43
Jim McCormick	2.43
George Bradley	2.50
Tim Keefe	2.62
Charlie Ferguson	2.67
Hoss Radbourn	2.67

1900–1909
Three Finger Brown	1.63
Ed Walsh	1.68
Ed Reulbach	1.72
Addie Joss	1.87
Christy Mathewson	1.97
Rube Waddell	2.11
Cy Young	2.12
Orval Overall	2.13
Frank Smith	2.19
Lefty Leifield	2.20
Doc White	2.20

1910–1919
Walter Johnson	1.59
Joe Wood	1.97
Ed Walsh	1.98
Grover Alexander	2.09
Carl Mays	2.15
Babe Ruth	2.19
Jeff Pfeffer	2.20
Dutch Leonard	2.23
Eddie Plank	2.25
Eddie Cicotte	2.27

1920–1929
Grover Alexander	3.04
Lefty Grove	3.09
Dolf Luque	3.09
Dazzy Vance	3.10
Stan Coveleski	3.20
Eppa Rixey	3.24
Urban Shocker	3.33
Red Faber	3.34
Walter Johnson	3.34
Wilbur Cooper	3.36

1930–1939
Carl Hubbell	2.70
Lefty Grove	2.91
Dizzy Dean	2.97
Bill Lee	3.21
Lefty Gomez	3.23
Lon Warneke	3.23
Hal Schumacher	3.38
Larry French	3.42
Van Lingle Mungo	3.42
Curt Davis	3.50
Paul Derringer	3.50
Charlie Root	3.50

1940–1949
Spud Chandler	2.67
Max Lanier	2.68
Harry Brecheen	2.74
Hal Newhouser	2.84
Bob Feller	2.90
Mort Cooper	2.91
Tex Hughson	2.94
Claude Passeau	2.94
Bucky Walters	2.97
Howie Pollet	2.99

1950–1959
Whitey Ford	2.66
Hoyt Wilhelm	2.79
Warren Spahn	2.92
Billy Pierce	3.06
Allie Reynolds	3.07
Eddie Lopat	3.12
Bob Buhl	3.14
Johnny Antonelli	3.18
Sal Maglie	3.19
Early Wynn	3.28

1960–1969
Hoyt Wilhelm	2.16
Sandy Koufax	2.36
Juan Marichal	2.57
Bob Gibson	2.74
Mike Cuellar	2.76
Dean Chance	2.77
Tommy John	2.81
Don Drysdale	2.83
Whitey Ford	2.83
Joe Horlen	2.83
Bob Veale	2.83

1970–1979
Jim Palmer	2.58
Tom Seaver	2.61
Bert Blyleven	2.88
Rollie Fingers	2.89
Gaylord Perry	2.92
Andy Messersmith	2.93
Frank Tanana	2.93
Jon Matlack	2.97
Mike Marshall	2.98
Don Wilson	3.01

1980–1989
Dwight Gooden	2.64
Orel Hershiser	2.69
Roger Clemens	3.07
Dave Righetti	3.08
Dave Dravecky	3.13
John Tudor	3.13
Nolan Ryan	3.14
Fernando Valenzuela	3.19
Bob Welch	3.21
Sid Fernandez	3.22

TEAMMATES FINISHING 1-2 IN ERA (Since 1900)

NATIONAL LEAGUE

1901	Pitt. Pirates	Jesse Tannehill (2.18)	Deacon Phillippe (2.22)
1906	Chic. Cubs	Three Finger Brown (1.04)	Jack Pfiester (1.56)*
1907	Chic. Cubs	Jack Pfiester (1.15)	Carl Lundgren (1.17)*
1912	NY Giants	Jeff Tesreau (1.96)	Christy Mathewson (2.12)
1918	Chic. Cubs	Hippo Vaughn (1.74)	Lefty Tyler (2.00)
1919	Chic. Cubs	Grover C. Alexander (1.72)	Hippo Vaughn (1.79)
1923	Cinn. Reds	Dolf Luque (1.93)	Eppa Rixey (2.80)
1925	Cinn. Reds	Dolf Luque (2.63)	Eppa Rixey (2.88)
1931	NY Giants	Bill Walker (2.26)	Carl Hubbell (2.66)
1935	Pitt. Pirates	Cy Blanton (2.58)	Bill Swift (2.70)
1942	St. L. Cardinals	Mort Cooper (1.78)	Johnny Beazley (2.13)
1943	St. L. Cardinals	Howie Pollet (1.75)	Max Lanier (1.90)*
1944	Cinn. Reds	Ed Heusser (2.38)	Bucky Walters (2.40)
1945	Chic. Cubs	Hank Borowy (2.13)	Claude Passeau (2.46)
1956	Milw. Braves	Lew Burdette (2.70)	Warren Spahn (2.78)
1957	Bklyn. Dodgers	Johnny Podres (2.66)	Don Drysdale (2.69)
1959	S.F. Giants	Sam Jones (2.83)	Stu Miller (2.84)
1964	L.A. Dodgers	Sandy Koufax (1.74)	Don Drysdale (2.18)
1974	Atl. Braves	Buzz Capra (2.28)	Phil Niekro (2.38)
1981	Houst. Astros	Nolan Ryan (1.69)	Bob Knepper (2.18)

AMERICAN LEAGUE

1914	Bost. Red Sox	Dutch Leonard (1.01)	Rube Foster (1.65)
1924	WA Senators	Walter Johnson (2.72)	Tom Zachary (2.75)
1927	NY Yankees	Waite Hoyt (2.63)	Urban Shocker (2.84)
1933	Cleve. Indians	Monte Pearson (2.33)	Mel Harder (2.95)
1943	NY Yankees	Spud Chandler (1.64)	Ernie Bonham (2.27)
1944	Det. Tigers	Dizzy Trout (2.12)	Hal Newhouser (2.22)
1945	Det. Tigers	Hal Newhouser (1.81)	Al Benton (2.02)
1948	Cleve. Indians	Gene Bearden (2.43)	Bob Lemon (2.82)
1957	NY Yankees	Bobby Shantz (2.45)	Tom Studivant (2.54)
1963	Chic. White Sox	Gary Peters (2.33)	Juan Pizzaro (2.39)
1966	Chic. White Sox	Gary Peters (1.98)	Joel Horlen (2.43)
1967	Chic. White Sox	Joel Horlen (2.06)	Gary Peters (2.28)
1968	Cleve. Indians	Luis Tiant (1.60)	Sam McDowell (1.81)
1979	NY Yankees	Ron Guidry (2.78)	Tommy John (2.97)

*3rd teammate third in ERA

PITCHERS WITH 3,000 INNINGS PITCHED AND LESS THAN 3.00 ERA

	INNINGS	ERA		INNINGS	ERA
Walter Johnson	4,195	2.37	Juan Marichal	3,506	2.89
Grover C. Alexander	4,622	2.56	Bob Gibson	3,885	2.91
Whitey Ford	3,171	2.74	Carl Mays	3,022	2.92
Jim Palmer	3.947	2.86	Don Drysdale	3,432	2.95
Tom Seaver	4,782	2.86	Carl Hubbell	3,591	2.98
Stanley Coveleski	3,071	2.88	Lefty Grove	3,940	2.98
Wilbur Cooper	3,482	2.89			

PITCHERS LEADING LEAGUE IN ERA AFTER 40TH BIRTHDAY

		ERA	AGE
1942	Ted Lyons, Chic. (AL)	2.10	42
1947	Spud Chandler, NY (AL)	2.46	40
1987	Nolan Ryan, Houst. (NL)	2.76	40

PITCHERS LEADING LEAGUE IN ERA WITH LOSING RECORDS (Since 1900)

NATIONAL LEAGUE	ERA	W/L
Rube Waddell, 1900 Pitt. Pirates	2.37	8–13
Dolf Luque, 1925 Cinn. Reds	2.63	16–18
Dave Koslo, 1949 NY Giants	2.50	11–14
Stu Miller, 1958 S.F. Giants	2.47	6–9
Nolan Ryan, 1987 Houst. Astros	2.76	8–16
Joe Magrane, 1988 St. L. Cardinals	2.18	5–9

AMERICAN LEAGUE	ERA	W/L
Ed Siever, 1902 Det. Tigers	1.91	8–11
Ed Walsh, 1910 Chic. White Sox	1.27	18–20
Stan Coveleski, 1923 Cleve. Indians	2.76	13–14

20-GAME WINNERS WITH 4.00 ERA

Bobo Newsom, 5.08, 20–16, 1938 St. L. Browns (AL)
Vern Kennedy, 4.63, 21–9, 1936 Chic. White Sox (AL)
George Earnshaw, 4.44, 22–13, Phila. Athletics (AL)
Lefty Gomez, 4.21, 24–7, 1932 NY Yankees (AL)
Wes Ferrell, 4.19, 20–15, 1936 Bost. Red Sox (AL)

Jim Merritt, 4.08, 20–12, 1970 Cinn. Reds (NL)
Monte Weaver, 4.08, 22–10, 1932 WA Senators (AL)
Lew Burdette, 4.07, 21–15, 1959 Milwaukee Braves (NL)
George Uhle, 4.07, 22–16, 1922 Cleve. Indians (AL)
Billy Hoeft, 4.06, 20–14, 1956 Det. Tigers (AL)

20-GAME LOSERS WITH ERA BELOW 2.00

Ed Walsh, 1.27, 18–20, 1910 Chic. White Sox (AL)
Kaiser Wilhelm, 1.87, 16–22, 1908 Bklyn. Dodgers (NL)
Walter Johnson, 1.89, 25–20, 1916 WA Senators (AL)

Jim Scott, 1.90, 20–20, 1913 Chic. White Sox (AL)
Harry Howell, 1.98, 15–22, 1905 St. L. Browns (AL)

STRIKEOUTS

EVOLUTION OF STRIKEOUT RECORD

NATIONAL LEAGUE, PRE–1900

1876	Jim Devlin, Louisville	122
1877	Tommy Bond, Bost.	170
1878	Tommy Bond, Bost.	182
1879	Monte Ward, Providence	239
1880	Larry Corcoran, Chic.	268
1883	Jim Whitney, Bost.	345
1884	Old Hoss Radbourne, Prov.	441

NATIONAL LEAGUE, POST–1900

1900	Rube Waddell, Pitt.	130
1901	Noodles Hahn, Cinn.	239
1903	Christy Mathewson, NY	267
1961	Sandy Koufax, L.A.	269
1963	Sandy Koufax, L.A.	306
1965	Sandy Koufax, L.A.	382

AMERICAN LEAGUE

1901	Cy Young, Bost.	158
1902	Rube Waddell, Phila.	21
1903	Rube Waddell, Phila.	30
1904	Rube Waddell, Phila.	34
1973	Nolan Ryan, CA	383

MOST STRIKEOUTS, BY DECADE

Pre–1900
Tim Keefe	2533
John Clarkson	2015
Amos Rusie	1951
Mickey Welch	1850
Hoss Radbourn	1830
Tony Mullane	1812
Pud Galvin	1799
Jim McCormick	1704
Charlie Buffinton	1700
Gus Weyhing	1648

1900–1909
Rube Waddell	2251
Christy Mathewson	1794
Cy Young	1570
Eddie Plank	1342
Vic Willis	1304
Wild Bill Donovan	1293
Jack Chesbro	1237
Jack Powell	1209
Long Tom Hughes	1115
Doc White	1105

1910–1919
Walter Johnson	2219
Grover Alexander	1540
Hippo Vaughn	1253
Rube Marquard	1141
Eddie Cicotte	1104
Bob Groom	1028
Claude Hendrix	1020
Lefty Tyler	938
Larry Cheney	926
Willie Mitchell	913

1920–1929
Dazzy Vance	1464
Burleigh Grimes	1018
Dolf Luque	904
Walter Johnson	895
Lefty Grove	837
Howard Ehmke	824
George Uhle	808
Red Faber	804
Bob Shawkey	788
Urban Shocker	749

1930–1939
Lefty Gomez	1337
Lefty Grove	1313
Carl Hubbell	1282
Red Ruffing	1260
Tommy Bridges	1207
Dizzy Dean	1136
Van Lingle Mungo	1022
Paul Derringer	1018
Bump Hadley	1006
Bobo Newsom	963

1940–1949
Hal Newhouser	1579
Bob Feller	1396
Bobo Newsom	1070
Johnny Vander Meer	972
Dizzy Trout	930
Kirby Higbe	853
Allie Reynolds	791
Dutch Leonard	779
Mort Cooper	772
Virgil Trucks	760

1950–1959
Early Wynn	1544
Robin Roberts	1516
Billy Pierce	1487
Warren Spahn	1464
Harvey Haddix	1093
Bob Rush	1072
Johnny Antonelli	1026
Mike Garcia	1000
Sam Jones	994
Bob Turley	983

1960–1969
Bob Gibson	2071
Jim Bunning	2019
Don Drysdale	1910
Sandy Koufax	1910
Juan Marichal	1840
Sam McDowell	1663
Jim Maloney	1585
Jim Kaat	1435
Bob Veale	1428
Camilo Pascual	1391

1970–1979
Nolan Ryan	2678
Tom Seaver	2304
Steve Carlton	2097
Bert Blyleven	2082
Gaylord Perry	1907
Phil Niekro	1866
Ferguson Jenkins	1841
Don Sutton	1767
Vida Blue	1600
Jerry Koosman	1587

1980–1989
Nolan Ryan	2167
Fernando Valenzuela	1644
Jack Morris	1630
Bert Blylevan	1480
Bob Welch	1457
Steve Carlton	1453
Dave Stieb	1380
Charlie Hough	1364
Mario Soto	1360
Floyd Bannister	1356

MEMBERS OF THE SAME PITCHING STAFF FINISHING ONE-TWO IN STRIKEOUTS, SAME SEASON (Since 1900)

NATIONAL LEAGUE

1903	NY Giants	Christy Mathewson (267)	Joe McGinnity (171)
1905	NY Giants	Christy Mathewson (206)	Red Ames (198)
1920	Chic. Cubs	Grover C. Alexander (173)	Hippo Vaughn (131)
1924	Bklyn. Dodgers	Dazzy Vance (262)	Burleigh Grimes (135)
1960	L.A. Dodgers	Don Drysdale (246)	Sandy Koufax (197)
1961	L.A. Dodgers	Sandy Koufax (269)	Stan Williams (205)
1962	L.A. Dodgers	Don Drysdale (232)	Sandy Koufax (216)
1987	Houst. Astros	Nolan Ryan (270)	Mike Scott (233)

AMERICAN LEAGUE

1918	WA Senators	Walter Johnson (162)	Jim Shaw (129)
1919	WA Senators	Walter Johnson (147)	Jim Shaw (128)
1927	Phila. Athletics	Lefty Grove (174)	Rube Walberg (136)
1929	Phila. Athletics	Lefty Grove (170)	George Earnshaw (149)
1930	Phila. Athletics	Lefty Grove (209)	George Earnshaw (193)
1931	Phila. Athletics	Lefty Grove (175)	George Earnshaw (152)
1935	Det. Tigers	Tommy Bridges (163)	Schoolboy Rowe (140)
1944	Det. Tigers	Hal Newhouser (187)	Dizzy Trout (144)
1948	Cleve. Indians	Bob Feller (164)	Bob Lemon (147)
1949	Det. Tigers	Virgil Trucks (153)	Hal Newhouser (144)
1953	Chic. White Sox	Billy Pierce (186)	Virgil Trucks (149)*
1976	CA Angels	Nolan Ryan (327)	Frank Tanana (261)

*Trucks also pitched 16 games with St. L.

PITCHERS LEADING LEAGUE WITH 100 MORE STRIKEOUTS THAN RUNNER-UP IN CATEGORY

NATIONAL LEAGUE

Dazzy Vance   1924 Bklyn. Dodgers—262 strikeouts
   Runner Up: Burleigh Grimes—135 strikeouts
Sandy Koufax   1965 L.A. Dodgers—382 strikeouts
   Runner Up: Bob Veale, 276 strikeouts
J. R. Richard   1979 Houst. Astros—313 strikeouts
   Runner Up: Steve Carlton, 213 strikeouts

AMERICAN LEAGUE

Rube Waddell   1903 Phila. Athletics—302 strikeouts
   Runner Up: Wild Bill Donovan, 187 strikeouts
Rube Waddell   1904 Phila. Athletics—349 strikeouts
   Runner Up: Jack Chesbro, 239 strikeouts
Nolan Ryan   1973 CA Angels—383 strikeouts
   Runner Up: Bert Blyleven, 258 strikeouts
Nolan Ryan   1974 CA Angels—367 strikeouts
   Runner Up: Bert Blyleven, 249 strikeouts

PITCHERS WITH 3,000 STRIKEOUTS, NEVER LEADING LEAGUE

Don Sutton (1966–88)   3,574
Bert Blyleven (1970–88)   3,564*
Gaylord Perry (1962–83)   3,534

*Active

PITCHERS STRIKING OUT 1,000 BATTERS BEFORE 24TH BIRTHDAY

Bob Feller   1233   24th birthday, Nov. 3, 1942
Bert Blyleven   1194   24th birthday, Apr. 6, 1975
Dwight Gooden   1067   24th birthday, Nov. 16, 1988

MOST TIMES 10 OR MORE STRIKEOUTS IN A GAME

199	Nolan Ryan	72	Bob Gibson	53	Walter Johnson
98	Sandy Koufax	70	Rube Waddell	50	Mickey Lolich
82	Steve Carlton	70	Tom Seaver		
74	Sam McDowell	54	Bob Feller		

PITCHERS AVERAGING 10 STRIKEOUTS PER NINE INNINGS, SEASON

NATIONAL LEAGUE	AVERAGE	STRIKEOUTS	INNINGS
Nolan Ryan, Houst. Astros, 1987	11.48	270	212
Dwight Gooden, NY Mets, 1984	11.39	276	218
Sandy Koufax, L.A. Dodgers, 1962	10.57	216	184
Sandy Koufax, L.A. Dodgers, 1965	10.23	382	336
Sandy Koufax, L.A. Dodgers, 1959	10.18	173	153
Sandy Koufax, L.A. Dodgers, 1960	10.13	197	175
Mike Scott, Houst. Astros, 1986	10.00	306	275
AMERICAN LEAGUE			
Nolan Ryan, TX Rangers, 1989	11.33	301	239
Sam McDowell, Cleve. Indians, 1965	10.71	325	273
Nolan Ryan, CA Angels, 1973	10.57	383	326
Sam McDowell, Cleve. Indians, 1966	10.44	225	194
Nolan Ryan, CA Angels, 1972	10.43	329	284

PITCHERS WITH A COMBINED TOTAL OF 500 STRIKEOUTS AND WALKS IN A SEASON (Since 1900)

		STRIKEOUTS	WALKS	TOTAL
1946	Bob Feller, Cleve. (AL)	348	153	501
1973	Nolan Ryan, CA (AL)	383	162	545
1974	Nolan Ryan, CA (AL)	367	202	569
1976	Nolan Ryan, CA (AL)	327	183	510
1977	Nolan Ryan, CA (AL)	341	204	545

PITCHERS STRIKING OUT THE SIDE ON NINE PITCHES (Since 1900)

NATIONAL LEAGUE

Pat Ragan, Bklyn. Dodgers	October 5, 1914
Hod Eller, Cinn. Reds	August 21, 1917
Joe Oeschger, Bost. Braves	September 8, 1921
Dazzy Vance, Bklyn. Dodgers	September 14, 1924
Sandy Koufax, L.A. Dodgers	June 30, 1962
Sandy Koufax, L.A. Dodgers	April 18, 1964
Bob Bruce, Houst. Astros	April 19, 1964
Nolan Ryan, NY Mets	April 19, 1968
Bob Gibson, St. L. Cardinals	May 12, 1969
Lynn McGlothen, St. L. Cardinals	August 19, 1975
Bruce Sutter, Chic. Cubs	September 8, 1977

AMERICAN LEAGUE

Rube Waddell, Phila. Athletics	July 1, 1902
Sloppy Thurston, Chic. White Sox	August 22, 1923
Lefty Grove, Phila. A's	August 23, 1928
Lefty Grove, Phila. A's	September 27, 1928
Jim Bunning, Det. Tigers	August 2, 1959
Al Downing, NY Yankees	August 11, 1967
Nolan Ryan, CA Angels	July 9, 1972
Ron Guidry, NY Yankees	August 7, 1984

PITCHERS WITH 200 STRIKEOUTS, LESS THAN 50 WALKS, SEASON

NATIONAL LEAGUE	STRIKEOUTS	WALKS
Christy Mathewson, 1908 NY Giants	259	42
Jim Bunning, 1964 Phila. Phillies	219	46
Juan Marichal, 1965 S.F. Giants	240	46
Juan Marichal, 1966 S.F. Giants	222	36
Gaylord Perry, 1966 S.F. Giants	201	40
Juan Marichal, 1968 S.F. Giants	218	46
Tom Seaver, 1968 NY Mets	205	48
Ferguson Jenkins, 1971 Chic. Cubs	263	37

AMERICAN LEAGUE	STRIKEOUTS	WALKS
Cy Young, 1904 Bost. Pilgrims	203	29
Walter Johnson, 1913 WA Senators	243	38
Jim Kaat, 1967 MN Twins	211	42
Ferguson Jenkins, 1974 TX Rangers	225	45

ROOKIE PITCHERS STRIKING OUT 200 BATTERS (Since 1900)

NATIONAL LEAGUE	
Tom Hughes, 1901 Chic. Cubs	225
Christy Mathewson, 1901 NY Giants	221
Grover C. Alexander, 1911 Phila. Phillies	227
Don Sutton, 1966 L.A. Dodgers	209
Gary Nolan, 1967 Cinn. Reds	206
Tom Griffin, 1969 Houst. Astros	200
John Montesufsco, 1975 S.F. Giants	215
Dwight Gooden, 1984 NY Mets	276

AMERICAN LEAGUE	
Russ Ford, 1910 NY Highlanders	209
Herb Score, 1955 Cleve. Indians	245
Bob Johnson, 1970 K.C. Royals	200
Mark Langston, 1984 Seattle Mariners	204

ROOKIES LEADING THE LEAGUE IN STRIKEOUTS (Since 1900)

NATIONAL LEAGUE	
Dazzy Vance, 1922 Bklyn. Dodgers	134
Dizzy Dean, 1932 St. L. Cardinals	191
Bill Voiselle, 1944 NY Giants	161
Sam Jones, 1955 Chic. Cubs	198
Jack Sanford, 1957 S.F. Giants	188
Fernando Valenzuela, 1981 L.A. Dodgers	180
Dwight Gooden, 1984 NY Mets	276

AMERICAN LEAGUE	
Lefty Grove, 1925 Phila. A's	116
Allie Reynolds, 1943 Cleve. Indians	151
Herb Score, 1955 Cleve. Indians	245
Mark Langston, 1984 Seattle Mariners	204

PITCHERS LEADING LEAGUE IN STRIKEOUTS, TEN OR MORE YEARS APART

Nolan Ryan   1972 CA Angels (AL)
                    1987, 1988 Houst. Astros (NL)

Walter Johnson   1910 WA Senators (AL)
                    1924 WA Senators (AL)

Steve Carlton   1972 Phila. Phillies (NL)
                  1982, 1983 Phila. Phillies (NL)

Bob Feller   1938 Cleve. Indians (AL)
               1948 Cleve. Indians (AL)

WALKS

PITCHERS WALKING LESS THAN A BATTER EVERY NINE INNINGS, SEASON (Since 1900)

	WALKS	INNINGS	PCT.
Babe Adams, 1920 Pitt. (NL)	18	264	.068
Christy Mathewson, 1913 NY (NL)	21	306	.069
Christy Mathewson, 1914 NY (NL)	23	312	.074
Cy Young, 1904 Bost. (AL)	29	380	.076
Red Lucas, 1933 Cinn. (NL)	18	220	.082
Babe Adams, 1919 Pitt. (NL)	23	263	.087
Slim Sallee, 1919 Cinn. (NL)	20	228	.087
Cy Young, 1906 Bost. (AL)	25	288	.087
Cy Young, 1905 Bost. (AL)	30	321	.093
Deacon Phillippe, 1902 Pitt. (NL)	26	272	.096
Addie Joss, 1908 Cleve. (AL)	30	325	.092
Grover Cleveland Alexander, 1923 Chic. (NL)	30	305	.098

HIGHEST PERCENTAGE OF WALKS TO INNINGS PITCHED, SEASON

	WALKS	INNINGS	PCT.		WALKS	INNINGS	PCT.
Tommy Byrne, 1949 NY (AL)	179	196	.913	Bump Hadley, 1932 Chic.-St. L. (AL)	171	248	.689
Sam Jones, 1955 Chic. (NL)	185	242	.764	Bobo Newsom, 1937 WA-Bost. (AL)	167	275	.607
Bob Feller, 1938 Cleve. (AL)	208	278	.748	Nolan Ryan, 1974 CA (AL)	202	333	.607
Bob Turley, 1954 Balt. (AL)	181	247	.732	John Wycoff, 1915 Phila. (AL)	165	276	.598
Bob Turley, 1955 NY (AL)	177	247	.716	Bobo Newsom, 1938 St. L. (AL)	192	330	.582

LOW-HIT GAMES

PITCHERS LOSING NO-HIT GAMES

May 9, 1901	Earl Moore (Cleve.) vs. White Sox
	(Allows two hits and four runs in tenth to lose 4–2)
April 15, 1909	Leon (Red) Ames (NY Giants) vs. Bklyn.
	(Allows hit in tenth by Whitey Alperman and loses 3–0 in 13)
August 30, 1910	Long Tom Hughes (NY Yankees) vs. Cleve.
	(Allows hit in tenth by Harry Niles and loses 5–0 in 11)
May 14, 1914	Death Valley Jim Scott (Chic. White Sox) vs. WA
	(Allows hit in tenth by Chick Gandil and loses 1–0)
May 2, 1917	James (Hippo) Vaughn (Chic. Cubs) vs. Cinn.
	(Allows two hits in tenth and loses 1–0)
September 18, 1934	Louis (Bobo) Newsom (St. L. Browns) vs. Bost.
	(Allows hit in tenth by Roy Johnson and loses 2–1)
May 26, 1956	Johnny Klippstein (7 innings), Hersh Freeman (1 inning) and Joe Black (1 inning), Cinn. vs. Milw.
	(Black allows single to Hank Aaron and Reds lose 2–1)
May 26, 1959	Harvey Haddix (Pitt.) vs. Milw.
	(After 12 innings of Perfect Game, Felix Mantilla reaches first on Don Hoak's error and scores on Joe Adcock's double as Haddix loses, 1–0)
April 23, 1964	Ken Johnson (Houst.) vs. Cinn.
	(Johnson loses in two Astro errors in ninth, 1–0)
June 14, 1965	Jim Maloney (Cinn.) vs. NY Mets
	(Loses on Johnny Lewis' 11th-inning homer, 1–0)
April 30, 1967	Steve Barber (8⅔ innings) and Stu Miller (⅓ inning), Balt. Orioles vs. Det.
	(Det. scores two runs in the ninth on a wild pitch and error to win, 2–1)

PITCHED NO-HITTER IN FIRST MAJOR LEAGUE START

Ted Breitenstein, St. L. (AA), October 4, 1891 vs. Louisville, 8–0
Charles "Bumpus" Jones, Cinn. (NL), October 15, 1892 vs. Pitt. 7–1
Alva "Bobo" Holloman, St. L. (AL), May 6, 1953 vs. Phila., 6–0

PITCHED ONE-HITTER IN MAJOR LEAGUE DEBUT

Addie Joss, Cleve. Indians (AL), April 26, 1902
Mike Fornieles, WA Senators (AL), September 2, 1952
Juan Marichal, S.F. Giants (NL), July 19, 1960
Bill Rohr, Bost. Red Sox (AL), April 14, 1967
Jimmy Jones, S.D. Padres (NL), September 21, 1986

LAST OUTS IN PERFECT GAMES

June 12, 1880	John Richmond, Worcerster (NL), 1–0 v. Cleve. Last out: Second baseman George Creamer
June 17, 1880	John M. Ward, Providence (NL), 5–0 v. Buffalo Last out: Pitcher Pud Galvin
May 5, 1904	Cy Young, Bost. (AL), 3–0 v. Phila. Last out: Pitcher Rube Waddell, fly out to center
October 2, 1908	Addie Joss, Cleve. (AL), 1–0 v. Chic. Last out: Pinch-hitter John Anderson, ground out to third
June 23, 1917	Ernie Shore, Bost. (AL), 4–0 v. WA Last out: Pinch-hitter Mike Menosky, pop out to second
April 30, 1922	Charley Robertson, Chic. (AL), 2–0 v. Det. Last out: Pinch-hitter John Bassler, fly out to left
October 8, 1956	Don Larsen, NY (AL), 2–0 v. Bklyn. Last out: Pinch-hitter Dale Mitchell, strikeout
May 26, 1959	Harvey Haddix, Pitt. (NL), 0–1 v. Milw. Last batter: First baseman Joe Adcock (double)
June 21, 1964	Jim Bunning, Phila. (NL), 6–0 v. NY Last out: Pinch-hitter John Stephenson, strikeout
September 9, 1965	Sandy Koufax, L.A. (NL), 1–0 v. Chic. Last Batter: Pinch-hitter Harvey Kuenn, strikeout
May 8, 1968	Jim "Catfish" Hunter, Oak. (AL), 4–0 v. MN Last batter: Pinch-hitter Rich Reese, strikeout
May 15, 1981	Len Barker, Cleve. (AL), 3–0 v. Tor. Last batter: Pinch-hitter Ernie Whitt, fly out to center
September 30, 1984	Mike Witt, CA Angels (AL), 1–0 v. TX Last batter: Marv Foley, ground out to 2nd
September 16, 1988	Tom Browning, Cinn. Reds (NL), 1–0 v. L.A. Last batter: Tracy Woodson, strikeout

PERFECT GAME PITCHERS, LIFETIME WINS

Cy Young (1890–1911)	511	Mike Witt (1981–89)	109*
Jim Bunning (1955–71)	224	Don Larsen (1953–67)	81
Catfish Hunter (1965–79)	224	Tom Browning (1984–89)	78*
Sandy Koufax (1955–66)	165	John Richmond (1879–86)	75
Monte Ward (1878–84)	161	Len Barker (1976–87)	74
Addie Joss (1902–10)	160	Ernie Shore (1912; 1914–17; 1919–20)	65
Harvey Haddix (1952–65)	136	Charlie Robertson (1919; 1922–28)	49

*Active

26-MAN PERFECT GAMES

Hooks Wiltse, NY (NL) vs. Phila., July 4, 1908 Spoiler, George McQuillan, HBP
Tommy Bridges, Det. (AL) vs. WA, August 5, 1932 Spoiler, Dave Harris, singled
Billy Pierce, Chic. (AL) vs. WA, June 28, 1958 Spoiler, Ed FitzGerald, doubled
Milt Wilcox, Det. (AL) vs. Chic., April 15, 1983 Spoiler, Jerry Hairston, singled
Milt Pappas, Chic. (NL) vs. S.D., Sept. 2, 1972 Spoiler, Larry Stahl, walked
Ron Robinson, Cinn. (NL) vs. Mont., May 2, 1988 Spoiler, Wallace Johnson, singled
Dave Stieb, Tor. (AL) vs. NY, August 4, 1989 Broke-up by Roberto Kelly, doubled

MOST WALKS GIVEN UP BY NO-HIT PITCHERS

11 Blue Moon Odom (9), Francisco Barrios (2), Chic. White Sox, July 28, 1976
10 Jim Maloney, Cinn. Reds, August 19, 1965
    Steve Barber (10), Stu Miller (0), Balt. Orioles, April 30, 1967
 9 John Klippstein (7), Hersh Freeman (0), Joe Black (2), Cinn. Reds, May 26, 1956
 8 Amos Rusie, NY Giants, July 31, 1891
    Johnny Vander Meer, Cinn. Reds, June 15, 1938
    Cliff Chambers, Pitt. Pirates, May 6, 1951
    Dock Ellis, Pitt. Pirates, June 12, 1970
    Nolan Ryan, CA Angels, September 28, 1974
 7 Bobo Newsom, St. L. Browns, September 18, 1934
    Sam Jones, Chic. Cubs, May 12, 1955
    Burt Hooten, Chic. Cubs, April 16, 1972
    Bill Stoneman, Mont. Expos, October 2, 1972
    Joe Cowley, Chic. White Sox, September 19, 1986

PITCHERS PITCHING NO-HITTERS IN 20-LOSS SEASON

Joe Bush   1916, Phila. A's, 15–22 (Aug. 26 vs. Cleve.)
Sad Sam Jones   1955, Chic. Cubs, 14–20 (May 12 vs. Pitt.)
Harry McIntire   1906, Bklyn. Dodgers, 12–21 (Aug. 1 vs. Pitt.)*
Bobo Newsom   1934, St. L. Browns, 16–20 (Sept. 18 vs. Bost.)*
Nap Rucker   1908, Bklyn. Dodgers, 18–20 (Sept. 5 vs. Bost.)

*Lost in extra innings

PITCHERS HITTING HOME RUNS IN GAME IN WHICH THEY PITCHED NO-HITTER

Wes Ferrell, Cleve. Indians   April 29, 1931   Off Sam Gray, St. L.
Jim Tobin, Bost. Braves   April 27, 1944   Off Fritz Ostermueller, Bklyn.
Earl Wilson, Bost. Red Sox   June 26, 1962   Off Bo Belinsky, L.A.
Rick Wise, Phila. Phillies   June 23, 1971(2)   Off Ross Grimsley and Clay Carroll, Cinn.

PITCHERS THROWING NO-HITTERS IN CONSECUTIVE SEASONS

Steve Busby, K.C., 1973–74
Sandy Koufax, L.A., 1962–65
Nolan Ryan, CA, 1973–75
Warren Spahn, Milw., 1960–61

NO-HIT PITCHERS GOING WINLESS FOLLOWING SEASON

1905	Weldon Henley, Phila. (AL)	1944	Clyde Shoun, Cinn. (NL)
1906	Mal Eason, Bklyn. (NL)*	1946	Ed Head, Bklyn. (NL)*
1907	Jeff Pfeffer, Bost. (NL)	1953	Bobo Holloman, St. L. (AL)†
1910	Tom Hughes, NY (AL)	1956	Mel Parnell, Bost. (AL)*
	Addie Joss, Cleve. (AL)*	1957	Bob Keegan, Chic. (AL)
1917	Ernie Koob, St. L. (AL)	1969	Jim Maloney, Cinn. (NL)
	Ernie Shore, Bost. (AL)	1986	Joe Cowley, Chic. (AL)
1940	Tex Carleton, Bklyn. (NL)*		

*Last Major League Season
†Only Major League Season

BACK-TO-BACK ONE-HIT GAMES (Since 1900)

Rube Marquard, NY (NL)   August 28—September 1, 1911
Lon Warneke, Chic. (NL)   April 17—April 22, 1934
Mort Cooper, St. L. (NL)   May 31—June 4, 1943
Whitey Ford, NY (AL)   September 2—September 7, 1955
Sam McDowell, Cleve. (AL)   April 25—May 1, 1966
Dave Steib, Tor. (AL)   September 24—October 1, 1988

SAVES/ RELIEFS

EVOLUTION OF SAVES RECORD (Since 1900)

NATIONAL LEAGUE

4	1900	Frank Kitson, Bklyn.
5	1904	Joe McGinnity, NY
6	1905	Claude Elliott, Bost.
	1906	George Ferguson, NY
	1908	Mordecai "Three Finger" Brown, Chic.
7	1909	Mordecai "Three Finger" Brown, Chic.
	1910	Mordecai "Three Finger" Brown, Chic.
13	1911	Mordecai "Three Finger" Brown, Chic.
15	1931	Jack Quinn, Phila.
	1945	Ace Adams, NY
	1945	Andy Karl, Phila.
18	1947	Hugh Casey, Bklyn.
22	1950	Jim Konstanty, Phila.
24	1954	Jim Hughes, Bklyn.
26	1959	Lindy McDaniel, St. L.
28	1962	Roy Face, Pitt.
31	1965	Ted Abernathy, Chic.
35	1970	Wayne Granger, Cinn.
37	1972	Clay Carroll, Cinn.
	1978	Rollie Fingers, S.D.
	1979	Bruce Sutter, Chic.
45	1984	Bruce Sutter, St. L.

AMERICAN LEAGUE

3	1901	Bill Hoffer, Cleve.
	1902	Jack Powell, St. L.
4	1905	Rube Waddell, Phila.
	1907	Bill Dineen, Bost.-St. L.
	1907	Long Tom Hughes, WA
	1907	Ed Walsh, Chic.
6	1908	Ed Walsh, Chic.
8	1909	Frank Arellanes, Bost.
10	1912	Ed Walsh, Chic.
12	1913	Chief Bender, Phila.
15	1924	Firpo Marberry, WA
	1925	Firpo Marberry, WA
22	1926	Firpo Marberry, WA
27	1949	Joe Page, NY
	1953	Ellis Kinder, Bost.
29	1961	Luis Arroyo, NY
	1964	Dick Radatz, Bost.
	1965	Ron Kline, WA
32	1966	Jack Aker, K.C.
34	1970	Ron Perranoski, MN
35	1972	Sparky Lyle, NY
38	1973	John Hiller, Det.
45	1983	Dan Quisenberry, K.C.
46	1986	Dave Righetti, NY

MOST GAMES WON BY RELIEF PITCHER, SEASON

NATIONAL LEAGUE

18	Elroy Face, Pitt., 1959	18–1
16	Jim Konstanty, Phila., 1950	16–7
16	Ron Perranoski, L.A., 1963	16–3
15	Mace Brown, Pitt., 1938	15–9
15	Mike Marshall, L.A., 1974	15–12
15	Dale Murray, Mont., 1975	15–8
15	Hoyt Wilhelm, NY, 1952	15–3

AMERICAN LEAGUE

17	John Hiller, Det., 1974	17–14
17	Bill Campbell, MN, 1976	17–5
16	Tom Johnson, MN, 1977	16–7
16	Dick Radatz, Bost., 1964	16–9
15	Luis Arroyo, NY, 1961	15–5
15	Eddie Fisher, Chic., 1965	15–7
15	Dick Radatz, Bost., 1963	15–6

MOST CAREER GAMES WON BY RELIEF PITCHER

123	Hoyt Wilhelm (1952–72)		104	Goose Gossage (1972–89)		94	Gene Garber (1969–87)
119	Lindy McDaniel (1955–75)		99	Sparky Lyle (1967–82)		94	Kent Tekulve (1974–89)
107	Rollie Fingers (1968–85)		96	Elroy Face (1953–69)		92	Mike Marshall (1967–81)

TEAMS WITH TWO PITCHERS WITH 20 SAVES

1965	Chic. White Sox (AL)	1983	S.F. Giants (NL)	1986	NY Mets (NL)
	Eddie Fisher 24		Greg Minton 22		Roger McDowell 22
	Hoyt Wilhelm 20		Gary Lavelle 20		Jesse Orosco 21

PITCHERS HAVING 20-VICTORY SEASONS *AND* 20-SAVE SEASONS

Dennis Eckersley	20 wins, Bost. (AL), 1978	45 saves, Oak. (AL), 1988
Jim "Mudcat" Grant	21 wins, MN (AL), 1965	24 saves, Oak.-Pitt., 1970
Ellis Kinder	23 wins, Bost. (AL), 1949	27 saves, Bost., 1953
Johnny Sain	20 wins, Bost. (NL), 1946	22 saves, NY (AL), 1954
	21 wins, Bost. (NL), 1947	
	24 wins, Bost. (NL), 1948	
	20 wins, Bost. (NL), 1950	
Wilbur Wood	22 wins, Chic. (AL), 1971	21 saves, Chic. (AL), 1970
	24 wins, Chic. (AL), 1972	
	24 wins, Chic. (AL), 1973	
	20 wins, Chic. (AL), 1974	

PITCHERS WITH 15 SAVES AND 15 WINS IN RELIEF, SAME SEASON

		WINS	SAVES
1950	Jim Konstanty, Phila. (NL)	16	22
1961	Luis Arroyo, NY (AL)	15	29
1963	Dick Radatz, Bost. (AL)	15	25
1963	Ron Perranoski, L.A. (NL)	16	21
1964	Dick Radatz, Bost. (AL)	16	29
1965	Eddie Fisher, Chic. (AL)	15	24
1974	Mike Marshall, L.A. (NL)	15	21
1976	Bill Campbell, MN (AL)	17	20
1977	Tom Johnson, MN (AL)	16	15

PITCHING MISCELLANY

BEST WINNING PERCENTAGE, BY DECADE (100 decisions)

Pre–1900
Bill Hoffer	.693
Bob Caruthers	.692
Dave Foutz	.690
Kid Nichols	.669
Larry Corcoran	.663
Ted Lewis	.650
John Clarkson	.648
Lady Baldwin	.640
Clark Griffith	.640
Cy Young	.640

1900–1909
Ed Reulbach	.719
Sam Leever	.695
Three Finger Brown	.689
Christy Mathewson	.678
Jack Pfiester	.637
Hooks Wiltse	.637
Ed Walsh	.636
Joe McGinnity	.633
Jesse Tannehill	.633
Deacon Phillippe	.631

1910–1919
Joe Wood	.680
Grover Alexander	.675
Chief Bender	.663
Babe Ruth	.659
Eddie Plank	.657
Walter Johnson	.649
Doc Crandall	.643
Christy Mathewson	.643
Jack Coombs	.623
Jeff Tesreau	.623

1920–1929
Ray Kremer	.660
Carl Mays	.638
Urban Shocker	.627
Freddie Fitzsimmons	.626
Lefty Grove	.626
Dazzy Vance	.620
Art Nehf	.615
Waite Hoyt	.612
Grover Alexander	.611
Stan Coveleski	.599

1930–1939
Lefty Grove	.724
Johnny Allen	.706
Firpo Marberry	.686
Lefty Gomez	.650
Dizzy Dean	.648
Carl Hubbell	.644
Red Ruffing	.641
Monte Pearson	.634
Lon Warneke	.629
Hal Schumacher	.603

1940–1949
Spud Chandler	.714
Tex Hughson	.640
Harry Brecheen	.638
Howie Pollet	.629
Mort Cooper	.626
Bob Feller	.626
Max Lanier	.621
Schoolboy Rowe	.619
Warren Spahn	.613
Rip Sewell	.605

1950–1959
Whitey Ford	.708
Allie Reynolds	.669
Eddie Lopat	.667
Sal Maglie	.663
Vic Raschi	.643
Don Newcombe	.633
Bob Buhl	.618
Bob Lemon	.615
Early Wynn	.612
Warren Spahn	.607

1960–1969
Sandy Koufax	.695
Juan Marichal	.685
Whitey Ford	.673
Denny McLain	.667
Jim Maloney	.626
Dave McNally	.621
Bob Gibson	.610
Ray Culp	.596
Bob Purkey	.593
Dick Hall	.582

1970–1979
Don Gullett	.686
John Candelaria	.648
Pedro Borbon	.647
Jim Palmer	.644
Tom Seaver	.638
Catfish Hunter	.624
Frank Tanana	.619
Tommy John	.613
Gary Nolan	.612
Clay Carroll	.610

1980–1989
(90 decisions)
Dwight Gooden	.719
Roger Clemens	.679
Ted Higuera	.639
Ron Darling	.613
John Tudor	.612
Ron Guidry	.607
Orel Hershiser	.605
Dennis Rasmussen	.605
Jimmy Key	.602
Tom Browning	.600

MOST TIMES LEADING LEAGUE IN PITCHING CATEGORY

	NATIONAL LEAGUE	AMERICAN LEAGUE
Games Pitched	Joe McGinnity, 6 (1900, 1903, 1904, 1905, 1906, 1907)	Firpo Marberry, 6 (1924, 1925, 1926, 1928, 1929, 1932)
Complete Games	Warren Spahn, 9 (1949, 1951, 1957, 1958, 1959, 1960, 1961, 1962, 1963)	Walter Johnson, 6 (1910, 1911, 1913, 1914, 1915, 1916)
Innings Pitched	Grover C. Alexander, 7 (1911, 1912, 1914, 1915, 1916, 1917, 1920)	Walter Johnson, 5 (1910, 1913, 1914, 1915, 1916) Bob Feller, 5 (1939, 1940, 1941, 1946, 1947)
Games Won	Warren Spahn, 8 (1949, 1950, 1953, 1957, 1958, 1959, 1960, 1961)	Walter Johnson, 6 (1913, 1914, 1915, 1916, 1918, 1924)
Games Lost	Phil Niekro, 4 (1977, 1978, 1979, 1980)	Bob Newsom, 4 (1934, 1935, 1941, 1945) Pedro Ramos, 4 (1958, 1959, 1960, 1961)
Won-Lost Pct.	Tom Seaver, 4 (1969, 1975, 1979, 1981)	Lefty Grove, 5 (1929, 1930, 1931, 1933, 1939)
ERA	Christy Mathewson, 5 (1905, 1908, 1909, 1911, 1913)	Lefty Grove, 9 (1926, 1929, 1930, 1931, 1932, 1935, 1936, 1938, 1939)
	Grover C. Alexander, 5 (1915, 1916, 1917, 1919, 1920) Sandy Koufax, 5 (1962, 1963, 1964, 1965, 1966)	
Strikeouts	Dazzy Vance, 7 (1922, 1923, 1924, 1925, 1926, 1927, 1928)	Walter Johnson, 12 (1910, 1912, 1913, 1914, 1915, 1916, 1917, 1918, 1919, 1921, 1923, 1924)
Shutouts	Grover C. Alexander, 7 (1911, 1913, 1915, 1916, 1917, 1919, 1921)	Walter Johnson, 7 (1911, 1913, 1914, 1915, 1918, 1919, 1924)
Saves	Bruce Sutter, 5 (1979, 1980, 1981, 1982, 1984)	Firpo Marberry, 5 (1924, 1925, 1926, 1929, 1932) Dan Quisenberry, 5 (1980, 1982, 1983, 1984, 1985)

MOST CONSECUTIVE YEARS LEADING LEAGUE IN A PITCHING CATEGORY (Since 1900)

	NATIONAL LEAGUE	AMERICAN LEAGUE
Winning Pct.	Ed Reulbach, 3 1906–08	Lefty Grove, 3 1929–31
ERA	Sandy Koufax, 5 1962–66	Lefty Grove, 4 1929–32
Shutouts	Grover C. Alexander, 3 1915–17	Walter Johnson, 3 1913–15
Strikeouts	Dazzy Vance, 7 1922–28	Walter Johnson, 8 1912–19
Saves	Three Finger Brown, 4 1908–11 Bruce Sutter, 4 1979–82	Dan Quisenberry, 4 1982–85

HIGHEST CAREER PITCHING TOTALS BY PITCHERS WHO NEVER LED LEAGUE

	AMERICAN LEAGUE	NATIONAL LEAGUE
Games Pitched	Tom Burgmeier, 745*	Gene Garber, 827
Complete Games	Eddie Plank, 395	Eppa Rixey, 290
Innings Pitched	Eddie Plank, 4269.1	Don Sutton, 4075
Games Won	Red Faber, 254	Don Sutton, 247
Games Lost	Walter Johnson, 279	Warren Spahn, 245
Winning Percentage (Min. 100 Wins)	Bob Lemon, .618	Three Finger Brown, .649
ERA	Eddie Plank, 2.34	Orval Overall, 2.24
Strikeouts	Luis Tiant, 2384*	Don Sutton, 2939
Shutouts	Rube Waddell, 47	Phil Niekro, 43
Saves	Ron Davis, 130*	Gene Garber, 192*

*Others have had higher totals and not led league with totals *split* between the two leagues—i.e. Lindy McDaniel in games pitched, Gaylord Perry in strikeouts, and Hoyt Wilhelm in saves.

CAREER PITCHING LEADERS BY PLAYERS UNDER SIX FEET TALL

Games Pitched	931, Gene Garber, 5′ 10″
Games Won	361, Pud Galvin, 5′ 8″
Games Lost	310, Pud Galvin, 5′ 8″
Winning Percentage (Min. 150 wins)	.692, Bob Caruthers, 5′ 7″
ERA (Min. 100 wins)	2.06, Three Finger Brown, 5′ 10″
Complete Games	639, Pud Galvin, 5′ 8″
Innings Pitched	5941, Pud Galvin, 5′ 8″
Games Started	682, Pud Galvin, 5′ 8″
Strikeouts	2,533, Tim Keefe, 5′ 10½″
Shutouts	69, Eddie Plank, 5′ 11½″
Walks	1,566, Gus Weyhing, 5′ 10″
Saves	218, Gene Garber, 5′ 10″

PITCHING'S "TRIPLE CROWN" WINNERS (Led League in Wins, ERA and Strikeouts, Same Season; Since 1900)

NATIONAL LEAGUE	WINS	ERA	STRIKEOUTS	AMERICAN LEAGUE	WINS	ERA	STRIKEOUTS
Christy Mathewson, NY, 1905	31	1.27	206	Cy Young, Bost., 1901	33	1.62	158
Christy Mathewson, NY, 1908	37	1.43	259	Rube Waddell, Phila., 1905	26	1.48	287
Grover C. Alexander, Phila., 1915	31	1.22	241	Walter Johnson, WA, 1913	36	1.09	243
Grover C. Alexander, Phila., 1916	33	1.55	167	Walter Johnson, WA, 1918	23	1.27	162
Grover C. Alexander, Phila., 1917	30	1.86	201	Walter Johnson, WA, 1924	23	2.72	158
James "Hippo" Vaughn, Chic., 1918	22	1.74	148	Lefty Grove, Phila., 1930	28	2.54	209
Grover C. Alexander, Chic., 1920	27	1.91	173	Lefty Grove, Phila., 1931	31	2.06	175
Dazzy Vance, Bklyn., 1924	28	2.16	262	Lefty Gomez, NY, 1934	26	2.33	158
Bucky Walters, Cinn., 1939	27	2.29	137	Lefty Gomez, NY, 1937	21	2.33	194
Sandy Koufax, L.A., 1963	25	1.88	306	Hal Newhouser, Det., 1945	25	1.81	212
Sandy Koufax, L.A., 1965	26	2.04	382				
Sandy Koufax, L.A., 1966	27	1.73	317				
Steve Carlton, Phila., 1972	27	1.97	310				
Dwight Gooden, NY, 1985	24	1.53	268				

MOST HOME RUNS GIVEN UP, SEASON

Bert Blyleven, 1986 Cleve.-MN (AL)	50 in 272 inns.	Robin Roberts, 1957 Phila. (NL)	40 in 250 inns.
Robin Roberts, 1956 Phila. (NL)	46 in 297 inns.	Ralph Terry, 1962 NY (AL)	40 in 299 inns.
Pedro Ramos, 1957 WA (AL)	43 in 231 inns.	Orlando Pena, 1964 K.C. (AL)	40 in 219 inns.
Denny McLain, 1966 Det. (AL)	42 in 264 inns.	Phil Niekro, 1979 Atl. (NL)	40 in 230 inns.
Robin Roberts, 1955 Phila. (NL)	41 in 305 inns.	Ferguson Jenkins, 1979 TX (AL)	40 in 259 inns.
Phil Niekro, 1979 Atl. (NL)	41 in 342 inns.	Jack Morris, 1986 Det. (AL)	40 in 267 inns.

PITCHERS WITH 2,000 INNINGS PITCHED, NO GRAND SLAMS

4535.1 Charles "Old Hoss" Radbourn (1880–91)
4505.1 Eddie Plank (1901–17)
4275.2 Jim McCormick (1878–87)
3948   Jim Palmer (1965–1984)
3558.1 Herb Pennock (1912–34)
2967   Dazzy Vance (1915, 1918–35)
2074.2 Joaquin Andujar (1976–88)

20-GAME WINNERS BATTING .300, SAME SEASON (Since 1900)

NATIONAL LEAGUE	WINS	BA	AMERICAN LEAGUE	WINS	BA
Jesse Tannehill, Pitt., 1900	20	.336	Clark Griffith, Chic., 1901	24	.303
Brickyard Kennedy, Bklyn., 1900	20	.301	Cy Young, Bost., 1903	28	.321
Claude Hendrix, Pitt., 1912	23	.322	Ed Killian, Det., 1907	25	.320
Burleigh Grimes, Bklyn., 1920	23	.306	Jack Coombs, Phila., 1911	29	.319
Wilbur Cooper, Pitt., 1924	20	.346	Babe Ruth, Bost., 1917	24	.325
Pete Donahue, Cinn., 1926	20	.311	Carl Mays, NY, 1921	27	.343
Burleigh Grimes, Pitt., 1928	25	.321	Joe Bush, NY, 1922	26	.326
Bucky Walters, Cinn., 1939	27	.325	George Uhle, Cleve., 1923	26	.361
Curt Davis, St. L., 1939	22	.381	Joe Shaute, Cleve., 1924	20	.318
Johnny Sain, Bost., 1947	21	.346	Walter Johnson, WA, 1925	20	.433
Don Newcombe, Bklyn., 1955	20	.359	Ted Lyons, Chic., 1930	22	.311
Warren Spahn, Milw., 1958	22	.333	Wes Ferrell, Cleve., 1931	22	.319
Don Drysdale, L.A., 1965	23	.300	Schoolboy Rowe, Det., 1934	24	.303
Bob Gibson, St. L., 1970	23	.303	Wes Ferrell, Bost., 1935	25	.347
			Red Ruffing, NY, 1939	21	.307
			Ned Garver, St. L., 1951	20	.305
			Catfish Hunter, Oak., 1971	21	.350

CY YOUNG WINNERS WITH HIGHER BATTING AVERAGES THAN THAT YEAR'S LEADER IN MOST HOME RUNS

NATIONAL LEAGUE

1970 Bob Gibson, St. L. Cardinals—.303
(Home Run Leader: Johnny Bench, Cinn.—.293)
1982 Steve Carlton, Phila. Phillies—.218
(Home Run Leader: Dave Kingman, NY—.204)

AMERICAN LEAGUE

1959 Early Wynn, Chic. White Sox—.244
(Home Run Leader: Harmon Killebrew, MN (Tie)—.242)

PITCHERS WITH TWO SEASONS OF 1.000 BATTING AVERAGES (Since 1900)

Nick Altrock	1924 WA Senators	1 game, 1-for-1	Al Schroll	1958 Bost. Red Sox	5 games, 1-for-1
	1929 WA Senators	1 game, 1-for-1		1960 Chic. Cubs	2 games, 1-for-1
Clark Griffith	1913 WA Senators	1 game, 1-for-1	Lefty Weinert	1919 Phila. Phillies	1 game, 2-for-2
	1914 WA Senators	1 game, 1-for-1		1921 Phila. Phillies	8 games, 1-for-1
John Morris	1969 Seattle Pilots	6 games, 1-for-1			
	1974 S.F. Pilots	17 games, 1-for-1			

EVOLUTION OF COMPLETE GAMES RECORD

NATIONAL LEAGUE, PRE–1900

1876	Jim Devlin, Louisville	66
1879	Will White, Cinn.	75

POST–1900

1900	Pink Hawley, NY	34
1901	Noodles Hahn, Cinn.	41
1902	Vic Willis, Bost.	45

AMERICAN LEAGUE

1901	Joe McGinnity, Balt.	39
1902	Cy Young, Bost.	41
1904	Jack Chesbro, NY	48

PITCHERS STARTING 20 GAMES IN 20 CONSECUTIVE SEASONS

Don Sutton   22 1966–1987
Phil Niekro   21 1967–1987
Tom Seaver   20 1967–1986
Cy Young   20 1891–1910

EVOLUTION OF MOST GAMES PITCHED RECORD

NATIONAL LEAGUE, PRE–1900

68 Jim Devlin, Louisville, 1876
76 Will White, Cinn., 1879
76 Pud Galvin, Buffalo, 1883
    Old Hoss Radbourn, Providence, 1883

NATIONAL LEAGUE, POST–1900

45 Bill Carrick, NY, 1900
    Joe McGinnity, Bklyn., 1900
45 Wild Bill Donovan, Bklyn., 1901
    Jack Powell, St. L., 1901
    Dummy Taylor, NY, 1901
51 Vic Willis, Bost., 1902
55 Joe McGinnity, NY, 1903
56 Christy Mathewson, NY, 1908
56 Hugh Mulcahy, Phila., 1937
61 Ace Adams, NY, 1942
70 Ace Adams, NY, 1943
74 Jim Konstanty, Phila., 1950
74 Bob Miller, L.A., 1964
84 Ted Abernathy, Chic., 1965
90 Wayne Granger, Cinn., 1969
92 Mike Marshall, Mont., 1973
106 Mike Marshall, L.A., 1974

AMERICAN LEAGUE

48 Joe McGinnity, Balt., 1901
55 Jack Chesbro, NY, 1904
56 Ed Walsh, Chic., 1907
66 Ed Walsh, Chic., 1908
69 Ellis Kinder, Bost., 1953
70 Mike Fornieles, Bost., 1960
71 Stu Miller, Balt., 1963
81 John Wyatt, K.C., 1964
82 Eddie Fisher, Chic., 1965
88 Wilbur Wood, Chic., 1968
90 Mike Marshall, MN, 1979

EVOLUTION OF INNINGS PITCHED RECORD

NATIONAL LEAGUE, PRE–1900

1876 Jim Devlin, Louisville   622
1879 Will White, Cinn.   680

NATIONAL LEAGUE, POST–1900

1900 Joe McGinnity, Bklyn.   347
1901 Noodles Hahn, Cinn.   375.1
1902 Vic Willis, Bost.   410
1903 Joe McGinnity, NY   434

AMERICAN LEAGUE

1901 Joe McGinnity, Balt.   382
1902 Cy Young, Bost.   384.2
1904 Jack Chesbro, NY   454.2
1908 Ed Walsh, Chic.   464

LAST LEGAL SPITBALL PITCHERS

NATIONAL LEAGUE

Bill Doak (1912–29)
Phil Douglas (1912–22)
Dana Fillingim (1915–25)
Ray Fisher (1910–20)
Marvin Goodwin (1916–25)
Burleigh Grimes (1916–34)
Claude Hendrix (1911–20)
Clarence Mitchell (1911–32)*
Dick Rudolph (1910–27)

AMERICAN LEAGUE

Yancey "Doc" Ayers (1913–21)
Ray Caldwell (1910–21)
Stan Coveleski (1912–28)
Urban Faber (1914–33)
Hub Leonard (1913–25)*
Jack Quinn (1909–33)
Allan Russell (1915–25)
Urban Shocker (1916–28)
Allan Sothoron (1914–26)

*Left-hander

LEFT-HANDED PITCHERS APPEARING IN MORE THAN 700 GAMES

Sparky Lyle (1967–82)   899
Jim Kaat (1959–83)   898
Tug McGraw (1965–84)   824
Darold Knowles (1965–80)   765
Tommy John (1963–74; 1976–89)   760

Warren Spahn (1942; 1946–65)   750
Tom Burgmeier (1968–84)   745
Gary Lavelle (1974–87)   745
Steve Carlton (1965–87)   737
Ron Perranoski (1961–73)   737

HALL OF FAME

HALL OF FAMERS BY TEAM

AMERICAN LEAGUE

BALTIMORE (ST. LOUIS) (17)
1939 George Sisler
1942 Rogers Hornsby
1946 Jesse Burkett
    Rube Waddell
1953 Bobby Wallace
    Dizzy Dean
1964 Heinie Manush
1968 Goose Goslin
1971 Satchel Paige
1974 Jim Bottomley
1976 Robin Roberts
1982 Frank Robinson
1983 Brooks Robinson
    George Kell
1984 Rick Ferrell
    Luis Aparicio
1985 Hoyt Wilhelm
1990 Jim Palmer

BOSTON (23)
1936 Babe Ruth
1937 Tris Speaker
    Cy Young
1945 Jimmy Collins
1946 Jesse Burkett
    Jack Chesbro
1947 Lefty Grove
1948 Herb Pennock
1951 Jimmie Foxx
1953 Al Simmons
1956 Joe Cronin
1964 Heinie Manush
1966 Ted Williams
1967 Red Ruffing
1969 Waite Hoyt
1970 Lou Boudreau
1971 Harry Hooper
1983 George Kell
    Juan Marichal
1984 Luis Aparicio
    Rick Ferrell
1986 Bobby Doerr
1989 Carl Yastrzemski

CALIFORNIA (2)
1982 Frank Robinson
1985 Hoyt Wilhelm

CHICAGO (18)
1939 Eddie Collins
1946 Johnny Evers
    Clark Griffith
    Ed Walsh
1953 Al Simmons
    Chief Bender
1955 Ted Lyons
    Ray Schalk

1962 Edd Roush
1964 Luke Appling
    Red Faber
1967 Red Ruffing
1971 Harry Hooper
1972 Early Wynn
1974 Jocko Conlan
1983 George Kell
1984 Luis Aparicio
1985 Hoyt Wilhelm

CLEVELAND (18)
1937 Nap Lajoie
    Tris Speaker
    Cy Young
1962 Bob Feller
1963 Elmer Flick
    Sam Rice
1969 Stan Coveleski
1970 Lou Boudreau
1971 Satchel Paige
1972 Early Wynn
1975 Earl Averill
    Ralph Kiner
1976 Bob Lemon
1977 Al Lopez
    Joe Sewell
1978 Addie Joss
1982 Frank Robinson
1985 Hoyt Wilhelm

DETROIT (16)
1936 Ty Cobb
1945 Hughie Jennings
1947 Mickey Cochrane
1949 Charlie Gehringer
1952 Harry Heilmann
1953 Al Simmons
1956 Hank Greenberg
1957 Sam Crawford
1964 Heinie Manush
1968 Goose Goslin
1969 Waite Hoyt
1975 Earl Averill
    Bucky Harris
1978 Eddie Mathews
1980 Al Kaline
1983 George Kell

KANSAS CITY (2)
1971 Satchel Paige
1984 Harmon Killebrew

MILWAUKEE (SEATTLE) (1)
1984 Henry Aaron

MINNESOTA (WASHINGTON) (16)
1936 Walter Johnson
1937 Tris Speaker
1939 George Sisler

1945 Ed Delahanty
1946 Clark Griffith
1953 Al Simmons
1956 Joe Cronin
1963 Sam Rice
1964 Heinie Manush
1968 Goose Goslin
1969 Stanley Coveleski
1972 Lefty Gomez
    Early Wynn
1975 Bucky Harris
1984 Harmon Killebrew
    Rick Ferrell

NEW YORK (MILWAUKEE, BALTIMORE) (31)
1936 Babe Ruth
1937 John McGraw
1939 Willie Keeler
    Lou Gehrig
1945 Hugh Duffy
    Wilbert Robinson
1946 Frank Chance
    Jack Chesbro
    Clark Griffith
    Joe McGinnity
1948 Herb Pennock
1952 Paul Waner
1954 Bill Dickey
1955 Home Run Baker
    Joe DiMaggio
    Dazzy Vance
1962 Bill McKechnie
1964 Burleigh Grimes
1967 Branch Rickey
    Red Ruffing
1969 Stan Coveleski
    Waite Hoyt
1970 Earle Combs
1971 Joe Kelley
1972 Yogi Berra
    Lefty Gomez
1974 Mickey Mantle
    Whitey Ford
1977 Joe Sewell
1981 Johnny Mize
1985 Enos Slaughter
1987 Catfish Hunter

OAKLAND (PHILADELPHIA, KANSAS CITY) (24)
1936 Ty Cobb
1937 Tris Speaker
    Nap Lajoie
1939 Eddie Collins
1945 Jimmy Collins
1946 Eddie Plank
    Rube Waddell

1947 Mickey Cochrane
    Lefty Grove
1948 Herb Pennock
1951 Jimmie Foxx
1953 Chief Bender
    Al Simmons
1955 Home Run Baker
1959 Zack Wheat
1969 Stan Coveleski
    Waite Hoyt
1971 Satchel Paige
1983 George Kell
1985 Enos Slaughter
1986 Willie McCovey
1987 Catfish Hunter
1990 Joe Morgan

NATIONAL LEAGUE

ATLANTA (BOSTON, MILWAUKEE) (38)
1936 Babe Ruth
1937 George Wright
    Cy Young
1939 Old Hoss Radbourne
    George Sisler
1942 Rogers Hornsby
1945 Dan Brouthers
    Jimmy Collins
    Hugh Duffy
    King Kelly
    Jim O'Rourke
1946 Johnny Evers
    Tommy McCarthy
    Ed Walsh
1949 Kid Nichols
1952 Paul Waner
1953 Al Simmons
1954 Rabbit Maranville
1961 Billy Hamilton
1962 Bill McKechnie
1963 John Clarkson
1964 Burleigh Grimes
1966 Casey Stengel
1967 Lloyd Waner
1968 Joe Medwick
1971 Dave Bancroft
    Joe Kelley
    Rube Marquard
1973 Warren Spahn
1975 Earl Averill
    Billy Herman
1977 Al Lopez
1978 Eddie Mathews
1982 Henry Aaron
1985 Enos Slaughter
    Hoyt Wilhelm
1986 Ernie Lombardi
1989 Red Schoendienst

HALL OF FAMERS BY TEAM (continued)

CHICAGO (32)
1938	Grover C. Alexander
1939	Cap Anson
	Al Spalding
1942	Rogers Hornsby
1945	Roger Bresnahan
	Hugh Duffy
	King Kelly
1946	Frank Chance
	Johnny Evers
	Clark Griffith
	Joe Tinker
	Rube Waddell
1949	Mordecai Brown
1951	Jimmie Foxx
1953	Dizzy Dean
1954	Rabbit Maranville
1955	Gabby Hartnett
1963	John Clarkson
1964	Burleigh Grimes
1968	Kiki Cuyler
1973	Monte Irvin
	George Kelly
1975	Billy Herman
	Ralph Kiner
1976	Fred Lindstrom
	Robin Roberts
1977	Ernie Banks
1979	Hack Wilson
1980	Chuck Klein
1985	Lou Brock
	Hoyt Wilhelm
1986	Billy Williams

CINCINNATI (29)
1936	Christy Mathewson
1939	Candy Cummings
	Old Hoss Radbourn
1945	King Kelly
1946	Clark Griffith
	Joe Tinker
1949	Mordecai Brown
1952	Harry Heilmann
1953	Al Simmons
1955	Dazzy Vance
1957	Sam Crawford
1962	Bill McKechnie
	Edd Roush
1963	Eppa Rixey
1964	Miller Huggins
1967	Lloyd Waner
1968	Kiki Cuyler
1970	Jesse Haines
1971	Jake Beckley
	Chick Hafey
	Joe Kelley
	Rube Marquard
1973	George Kelly
1974	Jim Bottomley
1977	Amos Rusie

1982	Frank Robinson
1986	Ernie Lombardi
1989	Johnny Bench
1990	Joe Morgan

HOUSTON (3)
1976	Robin Roberts
1978	Eddie Mathews
1990	Joe Morgan

LOS ANGELES (BROOKLYN) (37)
1939	Willie Keeler
1945	Dan Brouthers
	Hughie Jennings
1946	Tommy McCarthy
	Joe McGinnity
1952	Paul Waner
1954	Rabbit Maranville
1955	Dazzy Vance
1959	Zack Wheat
1961	Max Carey
1962	Jackie Robinson
1964	Burleigh Grimes
	Heinie Manush
	John M. Ward
1966	Casey Stengel
1967	Lloyd Waner
1968	Kiki Cuyler
	Joe Medwick
1969	Roy Campanella
	Waite Hoyt
1971	Dave Bancroft
	Joe Kelley
	Rube Marquard
1972	Sandy Koufax
1973	George Kelly
1975	Billy Herman
1977	Al Lopez
1979	Hack Wilson
1980	Duke Snider
1982	Frank Robinson
1983	Juan Marichal
1984	Don Drysdale
	Pee Wee Reese
1985	Arky Vaughan
	Hoyt Wilhelm
1986	Ernie Lombardi

MONTREAL (0)

NEW YORK (4)
1972	Yogi Berra
1973	Warren Spahn
1979	Willie Mays
1980	Duke Snider

PHILADELPHIA (24)
1937	Nap Lajoie
1938	Grover C. Alexander

1945	Dan Brouthers
	Ed Delahanty
	Hugh Duffy
	Hughie Jennings
1946	Johnny Evers
	Tommy McCarthy
1949	Kid Nichols
1951	Jimmie Foxx
1953	Chief Bender
1961	Billy Hamilton
1963	Elmer Flick
	Eppa Rixey
1964	Tim Keefe
1966	Casey Stengel
1967	Lloyd Waner
1971	Dave Bancroft
1974	Sam Thompson
1976	Roger Connor
	Robin Roberts
1979	Hack Wilson
1980	Chuck Klein
1990	Joe Morgan

PITTSBURGH (31)
1936	Honus Wagner
1937	Connie Mack
1945	Fred Clarke
1946	Jack Chesbro
	Rube Waddell
1948	Pie Traynor
1952	Paul Waner
1954	Rabbit Maranville
1955	Dazzy Vance
1956	Joe Cronin
	Hank Greenberg
1961	Max Carey
1962	Bill McKechnie
1964	Burleigh Grimes
	Heinie Manush
1965	Pud Galvin
1966	Casey Stengel
1967	Lloyd Waner
1968	Kiki Cuyler
1969	Hoyt Wilhelm
1971	Jake Beckley
	Joe Kelley
1973	Roberto Clemente
	George Kelly
1975	Billy Herman
	Ralph Kiner
1976	Fred Lindstrom
1977	Al Lopez
1980	Chuck Klein
1985	Arky Vaughan
1988	Willie Stargell

ST. LOUIS (31)
1937	John McGraw
	Cy Young
1938	Grover C. Alexander

1942	Rogers Hornsby
1945	Roger Bresnahan
	Wilbert Robinson
1946	Jesse Burkett
1947	Frankie Frisch
1949	Mordecai Brown
	Kid Nichols
1953	Dizzy Dean
	Bobby Wallace
1954	Rabbit Maranville
1955	Dazzy Vance
1964	Burleigh Grimes
	Miller Huggins
1965	Pud Galvin
1968	Joe Medwick
1969	Stan Musial
1970	Jesse Haines
1971	Jake Beckley
	Chick Hafey
1974	Jim Bottomley
1976	Roger Connor
1981	Bob Gibson
	Johnny Mize
1983	Walter Alston
1985	Lou Brock
	Enos Slaughter
	Hoyt Wilhelm
1989	Red Schoendienst

SAN DIEGO (1)
1986	Willie McCovey

SAN FRANCISCO (NEW YORK) (46)
1936	Christy Mathewson
1937	John McGraw
1939	Buck Ewing
	Willie Keeler
1942	Rogers Hornsby
1945	Roger Bresnahan
	Dan Brouthers
	George Kelly
	Jim O'Rourke
1946	Jesse Burkett
	Joe McGinnity
1947	Frankie Frisch
	Carl Hubbell
1951	Mel Ott
1954	Bill Terry
1955	Gabby Hartnett
	Ray Schalk
1962	Bill McKechnie
1964	Burleigh Grimes
	Tim Keefe
	John M. Ward
1966	Casey Stengel
1968	Joe Medwick
1969	Waite Hoyt
1971	Jake Beckley
	Rube Marquard

HALL OF FAMERS BY TEAM (continued)

SAN FRANCISCO (CONT.)

1971	Dave Bancroft
1972	Ross Youngs
1973	George Kelly
1973	Monte Irvin
	Warren Spahn
	Mickey Welch
1976	Roger Connor
	Fred Lindstrom
1977	Amos Rusie
1979	Willie Mays
	Hack Wilson

1980	Duke Snider
1981	Johnny Mize
1982	Travis Jackson
1983	Juan Marichal
1985	Hoyt Wilhelm
1986	Ernie Lombardi
	Willie McCovey
1989	Red Schoendienst
1990	Joe Morgan

PLAYERS ELECTED TO HALL OF FAME IN FIRST YEAR OF ELIGIBILITY

Ty Cobb	1936	Ted Williams	1966	Al Kaline	1980	Willie Stargell	1988
Babe Ruth	1936	Stan Musial	1969	Bob Gibson	1981	Johnny Bench	1989
Honus Wagner	1936	Sandy Koufax	1972	Hank Aaron	1982	Carl Yastrzemski	1989
Christy Mathewson	1936	Warren Spahn	1973	Frank Robinson	1982	Joe Morgan	1990
Walter Johnson	1936	Mickey Mantle	1974	Brooks Robinson	1983	Jim Palmer	1990
Bob Feller	1962	Ernie Banks	1977	Lou Brock	1985		
Jackie Robinson	1962	Willie Mays	1979	Willie McCovey	1986		

PLAYERS RECEIVING VOTES IN FIRST HALL OF FAME BALLOTING (1936) STILL NOT IN THE HALL

Hal Chase, 1B
Lew Criger, C
Joe Jackson, OF

FIRST MEN ELECTED TO HALL OF FAME FROM EACH POSITION

1st Base	George Sisler, 1939
	Cap Anson, 1939
2nd Base	Nap Lajoie, 1937
3rd Base	Jimmy Collins, 1945
Shortstop	Honus Wagner, 1936
Left Field	Fred Clarke, 1945
Center Field	Ty Cobb, 1936
Right Field	Babe Ruth, 1936
Catcher	Roger Bresnahan, 1945
	King Kelly, 1945
Pitcher	Walter Johnson, 1936
	Christy Mathewson, 1936
Left-Handed Pitcher	Eddie Plank, 1946
	Rube Waddell, 1946
Relief Pitcher	Hoyt Wilhelm, 1985

HALL OF FAMERS WITH LIFETIME BATTING AVERAGES BELOW .265 (Non-Pitchers)

Luis Aparicio, SS	.262	1956–73	Elected 1984
Harmon Killebrew, 1B-3B	.256	1954–75	Elected 1984
Rabbit Maranville, SS-2B	.258	1912–35	Elected 1954
Ray Schalk, C	.253	1912–29	Elected 1955
Joe Tinker, SS	.263	1902–16	Elected 1946

TEAMS WITH MOST FUTURE HALL OF FAME PLAYERS

1923 NY Giants—Kelly, Frisch, Jackson, Bancroft, Youngs, Terry, Wilson, Stengel
1930 NY Yankees—Gehrig, Ruth, Combs, Dickey, Ruffing, Pennock, Gomez, Hoyt
1931 NY Yankees—Gehrig, Sewell, Ruth, Combs, Dickey, Ruffing, Gomez, Pennock
1933 NY Yankees—Gehrig, Sewell, Ruth, Combs, Dickey, Ruffing, Gomez, Pennock

INFIELDS WITH FOUR FUTURE HALL OF FAMERS

1925 NY Giants	1926 NY Giants	1927 NY Giants
1B—Bill Terry	1B—George Kelly	1B—Bill Terry
2B—George Kelly	2B—Frank Frisch	2B—Rogers Hornsby
3B—Fred Lindstrom	3B—Fred Lindstrom	3B—Fred Lindstrom
SS—Travis Jackson	SS—Travis Jackson	SS—Travis Jackson

HALL OF FAMERS WHO BATTED RIGHT, THREW LEFT

Sandy Koufax
Eppa Rixey
Rube Waddell

LEADING PITCHING MARKS BY THOSE ELIGIBLE FOR HALL OF FAME BUT NOT IN

Most Games Pitched	Lindy McDaniel (1955–75)	987
Most Games Started	Jim Kaat (1959–83)	625
Most Complete Games	Tony Mullane (1881–94)	469
Most Innings Pitched	Tony Mullane (1881–94)	4540.1
Most Bases on Balls Allowed	Bobo Newsom (1929–53)	1732
Most Strikeouts	Jim Bunning (1955–71)	2855
Most Shutouts	Vic Willis (1898–1910)	50
Most Games Won	Tony Mullane (1881–94)	285
Most Games Lost	Jack Powell (1897–1912)	255
Most Saves	Elroy Face (1953–69)	193
Lowest ERA	Orval Overall (1905–10, 1913)	2.24

LEADING BATTING MARKS BY THOSE ELIGIBLE FOR HALL OF FAME BUT NOT IN

Most Games Played	Vada Pinson (1958–75)	2469
Most At Bats	Vada Pinson (1958–75)	9645
Most Base Hits	Vada Pinson (1958–75)	2757
Most Doubles	Mickey Vernon (1939–60)	490
Most Triples	Bid McPhee (1882–99)	189
Most Home Runs	Frank Howard (1958–73)	382
Most Runs Scored	Bid McPhee (1882–99)	1684
Most Runs Batted In	George Davis (1890–1909)	1435
Most Bases on Balls	Eddie Yost (1944, 1946–62)	1614
Most Strikeouts	Bobby Bonds (1968–81)	1757
Most Stolen Bases	Maury Wills (1959–72)	586
Highest Lifetime Batting Average	Joe Jackson (1908–20)	.356
Highest Lifetime Slugging Average	Richie Allen (1963–77)	.534

MOST HITS BY PLAYERS ELIGIBLE FOR HALL OF FAME BUT NOT IN

2757	Vada Pinson (1958–75)	2663	Nellie Fox (1947–65)	2561	Willie Davis (1960–76; 1979)
2705	Doc Cramer (1929–48)	2644	Lave Cross (1887–1907)	2536	George Van Haltren (1887–1903)
2688	George Davis (1890–1909)	2574	Richie Ashburn (1948–62)	2529	Jimmy Ryan (1885–1903)

MOST WINS BY PITCHERS ELIGIBLE FOR HALL OF FAME BUT NOT IN

285	Tony Mullane (1881–94)	247	Vic Willis (1898–1910)	231	Charles Buffinton (1882–92)
264	Jim McCormick (1878–87)	247	Jack Quinn (1909–33)	229	Will White (1877–86)
264	Gus Weyhing (1887–1901)	246	Jack Powell (1897–1912)	228	George Mullin (1902–15)

MOST HOME RUNS BY PLAYERS ELIGIBLE FOR HALL OF FAME BUT NOT IN

382	Frank Howard	370	Gil Hodges	339	Boog Powell
379	Orlando Cepeda	354	Lee May	336	Joe Adcock
377	Norm Cash	351	Dick Allen	332	Bobby Bonds
374	Rocky Colavito	342	Ron Santo	325	Willie Horton

HALL OF FAME INDUCTEES RECEIVING 90% OF VOTE

98.2	Ty Cobb, 1936 (226 ballots cast)	93.8	Bob Feller, 1962 (160 ballots cast)
97.8	Hank Aaron, 1982 (415 ballots cast)	93.4	Ted Williams, 1966 (302 ballots cast)
96.4	Johnny Bench, 1989 (431 ballots cast)	93.2	Stan Musial, 1969 (340 ballots cast)
95.1	Babe Ruth, 1936 (226 ballots cast)	92.7	Roberto Clemente, 1973 (424 ballots cast)
95.1	Honus Wagner, 1936 (226 ballots cast)	92.5	Jim Palmer, 1990 (444 ballots cast)
94.6	Willie Mays, 1979 (432 ballots cast)	91.2	Brooks Robinson, 1983 (374 ballots cast)
94.6	Carl Yastrzemski, 1989 (423 ballots cast)	90.7	Christy Mathewson, 1936 (226 ballots cast)

FOREIGN-BORN HALL OF FAMERS (BORN OUTSIDE CONTINENTAL U.S.)

Luis Aparacio	Selected 1984	Maracaibo, Venezuela
Henry Chadwick	Selected 1938	Exeter, England
Roberto Clemente	Selected 1973	Carolina, Puerto Rico
Tom Connolly	Selected 1953	Manchester, England
Martin DiHigo	Selected 1977	Matanzae, Cuba
Juan Marichal	Selected 1983	Laguna Verde, Dominican Republic
Harry Wright	Selected 1937	Sheffield, England

AWARDS

CLOSEST VOTES FOR MVP

NATIONAL LEAGUE			TOTAL VOTES
1979	TIE	Willie Stargell, Pitt.	216
		Keith Hernandez, St. L.	216
1944	1 Vote	Marty Marion, St. L.	190
		Bill Nicholson, Chic.	189
1937	2 Votes	Joe Medwick, St. L.	70
		Gabby Hartnett, Chic.	68
1911	4 Votes	Wildfire Schulte, Chic.	29
		Christy Mathewson, NY	25
1912	5 Votes	Larry Doyle, NY	48
		Honus Wagner, Pitt.	43
1955	5 Votes	Roy Campanella, Bklyn.	226
		Duke Snider, Bklyn.	221

AMERICAN LEAGUE			TOTAL VOTES
1947	1 Vote	Joe DiMaggio, NY	202
		Ted Williams, Bost.	201
1928	2 Votes	Mickey Cochrane, Phila.	53
		Heinie Manush, St. L.	51
1934	2 Votes	Mickey Cochrane, Det.	67
		Charlie Gehringer, Det.	65
1960	3 Votes	Roger Maris, NY	225
		Mickey Mantle, NY	222
1925	4 Votes	Roger Peckinpaugh, WA	45
		Al Simmons, Phila.	41
1937	4 Votes	Charlie Gehringer, Det.	78
		Joe DiMaggio, NY	74
1944	4 Votes	Hal Newhouser, Det.	236
		Dizzy Trout, Det.	232
1961	4 Votes	Roger Maris, NY	202
		Mickey Mantle, NY	198

UNANIMOUS MVP SELECTIONS

NATIONAL LEAGUE

1936	Carl Hubbell, Pitcher, NY Giants
1967	Orlando Cepeda, First Baseman, St. L. Cardinals
1980	Mike Schmidt, Third Baseman, Phila. Phillies

AMERICAN LEAGUE

1911	Ty Cobb, Outfielder, Det. Tigers
1923	Babe Ruth, Outfielder, NY Yankees
1935	Hank Greenberg, First Baseman, Det. Tigers
1953	Al Rosen, Third Baseman, Cleve. Indians
1956	Mickey Mantle, Outfielder, NY Yankees
1966	Frank Robinson, Outfielder, Balt. Orioles
1968	Denny McLain, Pitcher, Det. Tigers
1973	Reggie Jackson, Outfielder, Oak. A's
1988	Jose Canseco, Outfielder, Oak. A's

WON MVP AWARD IN CONSECUTIVE YEARS, BY POSITION

1B	Jimmie Foxx, Phila. (AL), 1932–33
2B	Joe Morgan, Cinn. (NL), 1975–76
SS	Ernie Banks, Chic. (NL), 1959–60
3B	Mike Schmidt, Phila. (NL), 1980–81
OF	Mickey Mantle, NY (AL), 1956–57

OF	Roger Maris, NY (AL), 1960–61
OF	Dale Murphy, Atl. (NL), 1982–83
C	Yogi Berra, NY (AL), 1954–55
P	Hal Newhouser, Det. (AL), 1944–45

TEAMMATES FINISHING ONE-TWO IN MVP BALLOTING

NATIONAL LEAGUE

1914	Johnny Evers (2B), Rabbit Maranville (SS), Bill James (P)*	Bost. Braves
1941	Dolf Camilli (1B), Pete Reiser (OF), Whit Wyatt (P)*	Bklyn. Dodgers
1942	Mort Cooper (P), Enos Slaughter (OF)	St. L. Cardinals
1943	Stan Musial (OF), Mort Cooper (P)	St. L. Cardinals
1955	Roy Campanella (C), Duke Snider (OF)	Bklyn. Dodgers
1956	Don Newcombe (P), Sal Maglie (P)	Bklyn. Dodgers
1960	Dick Groat (SS), Don Hoak (3B)	Pitt. Pirates
1967	Orlando Cepeda (1B), Tim McCarver (C)	St. L. Cardinals
1976	Joe Morgan (2B), George Foster (OF)	Cinn. Reds
1989	Kevin Mitchell (OF), Will Clark (1B)	S.F. Giants

AMERICAN LEAGUE

1934	Mickey Cochrane (C), Charlie Gehringer (2B)	Det. Tigers
1944	Hal Newhouser (P), Dizzy Trout (P)	Det. Tigers
1945	Hal Newhouser (P), Eddie Mayo (2B)	Det. Tigers
1956	Mickey Mantle (OF), Yogi Berra (C)	NY Yankees
1959	Nellie Fox (2B), Luis Aparicio (SS), Early Wynn (P)*	Chic. White Sox
1960	Roger Maris (OF), Mickey Mantle (OF)	NY Yankees
1961	Roger Maris (OF), Mickey Mantle (OF)	NY Yankees
1962	Mickey Mantle (OF), Bobby Richardson (2B)	NY Yankees
1965	Zoilo Versalles (SS), Tony Oliva (OF)	MN Twins
1966	Frank Robinson (OF), Brooks Robinson (3B), Boog Powell (1B)*	Balt. Orioles
1968	Denny McLain (P), Bill Freehan (C)	Det. Tigers
1971	Vida Blue (P), Sal Bando (3B)	Oak. A's
1983	Cal Ripkin (SS), Eddie Murray (1B)	Balt. Orioles

*Teammates finishing 1-2-3 in voting

TRIPLE CROWN WINNERS NOT WINNING MVP

NATIONAL LEAGUE

1912   Heinie Zimmerman, Chic. Cubs
       (Winner: Larry Doyle, NY Giants)
1933   Chuck Klein, Phila. Phillies
       (Winner: Carl Hubbell, NY Giants)

AMERICAN LEAGUE

1934   Lou Gehrig, NY Yankees
       (Winner: Mickey Cochrane, Det. Tigers)
1942   Ted Williams, Bost. Red Sox
       (Winner: Joe Gordon, NY Yankees)
1947   Ted Williams, Bost. Red Sox
       (Winner: Joe DiMaggio, NY Yankees)

MVPs ON NON-WINNING TEAMS

		TEAM RECORD
1952	Hank Sauer, Chic. (NL)	77-77
1958	Ernie Banks, Chic. (NL)	72-82
1959	Ernie Banks, Chic. (NL)	74-80
1987	Andre Dawson, Chic. (NL)	76-85

MVPS NOT *BATTING* .300, HITTING 30 HOME RUNS *OR* DRIVING IN 100 RUNS (Excluding Pitchers)

NATIONAL LEAGUE

1914 Johnny Evers, Bost.
1926 Bob O'Farrell, St. L.
1944 Marty Marion, St. L.
1962 Maury Wills, L.A.
1988 Kirk Gibson, L.A.

AMERICAN LEAGUE

1925 Roger Peckinpaugh, WA
1928 Mickey Cochrane, Phila.
1951 Yogi Berra, NY
1963 Elston Howard, NY
1965 Zoilo Versalles, MN

PITCHERS WINNING MVP AWARDS

NATIONAL LEAGUE

Dazzy Vance, Bklyn., 1924**
Carl Hubbell, NY, 1933
Dizzy Dean, St. L., 1934
Carl Hubbell, NY, 1936
Bucky Walters, Cinn., 1939
Mort Cooper, St. L., 1942
Jim Konstanty, Phila., 1950
Don Newcombe, Bklyn., 1956
Sandy Koufax, L.A., 1963
Bob Gibson, St. L., 1968

AMERICAN LEAGUE

Walter Johnson, WA, 1912*
Walter Johnson, WA, 1924**
Lefty Grove, Phila., 1931
Spud Chandler, NY, 1943
Hal Newhouser, Det., 1944
Hal Newhouser, Det., 1945
Bobby Shantz, Phila., 1952
Denny McLain, Det., 1968
Vida Blue, Oak., 1971
Rollie Fingers, Milw., 1981
Willie Hernandez, Det., 1984
Roger Clemens, Bost., 1986

*Chalmers Award
**League Award

PLAYERS WINNING MVP FIRST SEASON IN LEAGUE

NATIONAL LEAGUE

1988 Kirk Gibson, L.A.

AMERICAN LEAGUE

1966 Frank Robinson, Balt.
1972 Richie Allen, Chic.
1975 Fred Lynn, Bost.
1984 Willie Hernandez, Det.

MOST MVPs ON ONE TEAM (Past, Present, and Future)

6 1928 Phila. Athletics	**6** 1933 St. L. Cardinals	**5** 1951 NY Yankees
Ty Cobb, 1911	Dazzy Vance, 1924	Joe DiMaggio, 1939, 1941, 1947
Tris Speaker, 1912	Rogers Hornsby, 1925, 1929	Phil Rizzuto, 1950
Eddie Collins, 1914	Frankie Frisch, 1931	Yogi Berra, 1951, 1953, 1954
Mickey Cochrane, 1928, 1934	Bob O'Farrell, 1926	Mickey Mantle, 1956, 1957, 1962
Lefty Grove, 1931	Dizzy Dean, 1934	Jackie Jensen, 1958
Jimmie Foxx, 1932, 1933, 1938	Joe Medwick, 1937	

PLAYERS WINNING MVP AWARD WITH TWO DIFFERENT TEAMS

Mickey Cochrane	1928 Phila. (AL)	Rogers Hornsby	1925 St. L. (NL)
	1934 Det. (AL)		1929 Chic. (NL)
Jimmie Foxx	1932, 1933 Phila. (AL)	Frank Robinson	1961 Cinn. (NL)
	1938 Bost. (AL)		1966 Balt. (AL)

PITCHERS WINNING 25 GAMES, *NOT* WINNING CY YOUNG AWARD

1963	Juan Marichal, S.F. (NL)	25–8
	(Winner: Sandy Koufax, 25–5)	
1966	Juan Marichal, S.F. (NL)	25–6
	(Winner: Sandy Koufax, 27–9)	
1966	Jim Kaat, MN (AL)	25–13
	(Winner: Sandy Koufax, 27–9)	
1968	Juan Marichal, S.F. (NL)	26–9
	(Winner: Bob Gibson, 22–9)	
1971	Mickey Lolich, Det. (AL)	25–14
	(Winner: Vida Blue, 24–8)	

CY YOUNG WINNERS NOT IN TOP 10 IN LEAGUE IN ERA

LaMarr Hoyt, Chic. White Sox, 1933	Jim Lonborg, Bost. Red Sox, 1967	Mike McCormick, S.F. Giants, 1967
3.66, 17th in American League	3.16, 18th in American League	2.85, 16th in National League

RELIEF PITCHERS WINNING CY YOUNG AWARD

1974 Mike Marshall, L.A. (NL)
1977 Sparky Lyle, NY (AL)

1979 Bruce Sutter, Chic. (NL)
1981 Rollie Fingers, Milw. (AL)

1984 Willie Hernandez, Det. (AL)
1987 Steve Bedrosian, Phila. (NL)

CY YOUNG WINNERS INCREASING THEIR VICTORIES FOLLOWING SEASON

Warren Spahn—Cy Young winner, 1957, Milw. Braves, 21–11 1958 record, 22–11
Sandy Koufax—Cy Young winner, 1965, L.A. Dodgers, 26–8 1966 Record, 27–9
Mike Cuellar—Cy Young winner, 1969, Balt. Orioles, 23–11 1970 Record, 24–8
Steve Bedrosian—Cy Young winner, 1987, Phila. Phillies, 5–3 1988 Record, 6–6

ROOKIE OF YEAR WINNERS ON TEAM OTHER THAN THE ONE THEY FIRST PLAYED ON

Tommie Agee, 1966 American League Rookie of the Year, Chic. White Sox (First came up for 5 games with Cleve., 1962)
Alfredo Griffin, 1979 American League co-winner, Rookie of the Year, Tor. Blue Jays (First came up for 12 games with Cleve., 1976)
Lou Piniella, 1969 American League Rookie of the Year, K.C. Royals (First came up for 4 games with Balt., 1964)

RELIEF PITCHERS WINNING ROOKIE OF YEAR AWARD

1952 Joe Black, Bklyn., (NL)
1980 Steve Howe, LA, (NL)
1986 Todd Worrell, St. L., (NL)
1976 Butch Metzger, SD, (NL) (Tie)

MANAGERS

WINNINGEST MANAGERS, BY LETTER OF THE ALPHABET

A	Walter Alston (1954–76)	2040–1613
B	Lou Boudreau (1942–50; 1952–57; 1960)	1162–1224
C	Fred Clarke (1897–1915)	1602–1179
D	Leo Durocher (1939–46; 1948–55; 1966–73)	2010–1710
E	Buck Ewing (1890; 1895–1900)	489–395
F	Frankie Frisch (1933–38; 1940–46; 1949–51)	1137–1078
G	Clark Griffith (1901–20)	1491–1367
H	Bucky Harris (1924–43; 1947–48; 1950–56)	2159–2219
I	Arthur Irwin (1889; 1891–92; 1894–96; 1898–99)	405–408
J	Hughie Jennings (1907–1920)	1131–972
K	Bill Killefer (1921–25; 1930–33)	523–623
L	Al Lopez (1951–65; 1968–69)	1422–1026
M	Connie Mack (1894–96; 1901–50)	3776–4025
N	Johnny Neun (1946–48)	125–143
O	Steve O'Neill (1935–37; 1943–48; 1950–54)	1039–819
P	Roger Peckinpaugh (1914; 1928–33; 1941)	499–489
Q	Frank Quilici (1972–75)	280–287
R	Wilbert Robinson (1902; 1914–1931)	1397–1395
S	Casey Stengel (1934–36; 1938–43; 1949–60; 1962–65)	1926–1867
T	Chuck Tanner (1970–88)	1352–1381
U	Bob Unglaub (1907)	8–20
V	Bill Virdon (1972–84)	995–921
W	Dick Williams (1967–69; 1971–88)	1571–1451
Y	Cy Young (1907)	3–4
Z	Don Zimmer (1972–73; 1976–82; 1988)	790–755

MANAGERS WINNING 1,000 GAMES WITH ONE FRANCHISE

Connie Mack, Phila. (AL), 1901–50	3,637
John McGraw, NY (NL), 1902–32	2,658
Walter Alston, Bklyn.-L.A. (NL), 1954–76	2,040
Fred Clarke, Louisville-Pitt. (NL), 1897–1915	1,602
Earl Weaver, Balt. (AL), 1968–82; 1985–86	1,480
Joe McCarthy, NY (AL), 1931–46	1,460
Wilbert Robinson, Bklyn. (NL), 1914–31	1,375
Bucky Harris, WA (AL), 1924–28; 1935–42; 1950–54	1,336
Cap Anson, Chic. (NL), 1879–97	1,288
Casey Stengel, NY (AL), 1949–60	1,149
Hughie Jennings, Det. (AL), 1907–20	1,131
Danny Murtaugh, Pitt. (NL), 1957–64; 1967; 1970–71; 1973–76	1,115
Miller Huggins, NY (AL), 1918–29	1,067
Red Schoendienst, St. L. (NL), 1965–76; 1980	1,028
Tommy Lasorda, L.A. (NL), 1976–88	1,099
Frank Selee, Bost. (NL), 1890–1901	1,004

MANAGERS WITH MOST CAREER VICTORIES FOR EACH FRANCHISE (Since 1900)

NATIONAL LEAGUE

Atl.	Lum Harris (1968–72)	379–473	.445
Bost.	George Stallings (1913–20)	579–597	.492
Bklyn.	Wilbert Robinson (1914–31)	1375–1351	.504
Chic.	Charlie Grimm (1932–38; 1944–49; 1960)	946–784	.547
Cinn.	Sparky Anderson (1970–78)	863–586	.596
Houst.	Bill Virdon (1975–82)	544–522	.510
L.A.	Walter Alston (1958–76)	1673–1355	.552
Milw.	Fred Haney (1956–59)	341–231	.596
Mont.	Gene Mauch (1969–75)	499–627	.443
NY (Mets)	Davey Johnson (1984–88)	575–395	.593
NY (Giants)	John McGraw (1902–32)	2658–1823	.593
Phila.	Gene Mauch (1960–68)	645–684	.485
Pitt.	Fred Clarke (1900–15)	1422–969	.595
St. L.	Red Schoendienst (1965–76; 1980)	1028–944	.521
S.D.	Dick Williams (1982–85)	337–311	.520
S.F.	Herman Franks (1965–68)	377–280	.574

AMERICAN LEAGUE

Balt.	Earl Weaver (1968–82; 1985–86)	1480–1060	.583
Bost.	Joe Cronin (1935–47)	1071–916	.539
CA	Bill Rigney (1965–69)	625–737	.459
Chic.	Jimmy Dykes (1934–46)	899–938	.489
Cleve.	Lou Boudreau (1942–50)	728–649	.529
Det.	Hughie Jennings (1907–20)	1131–972	.538
K.C. (Royals)	Whitey Herzog (1975–79)	410–304	.574
K.C. (A's)	Harry Craft (1957–59)	162–196	.452
Milw.	George Bamberger (1978–80; 1985–86)	377–351	.518
MN	Sam Mele (1961–67)	518–427	.548
NY	Joe McCarthy (1931–46)	1460–867	.627
Oak.	Dick Williams (1971–73)	288–190	.602
Phila.	Connie Mack (1901–50)	3627–3891	.482
Seattle (Mariners)	Darrell Johnson (1977–80)	226–362	.384
Seattle (Pilots)	Joe Schultz (1969)	64–98	.395
St. L.	Jimmy McAleer (1902–09)	551–632	.466
TX	Bobby Valentine (1985–88)	368–408	.468
Tor.	Bobby Cox (1982–85)	355–292	.549
WA	Bucky Harris (1924–28; 1935–42; 1950–54)	1336–1408	.487
WA (Expansion Team)	Gil Hodges (1963–67)	321–445	.419

MANAGERS WITH LOWER WON-LOST PERCENTAGES THAN THEIR LIFETIME BATTING AVERAGES AS PLAYERS

NAME	MANAGERIAL W/L PCT.	LIFETIME BA
Luke Appling	10–30, K.C. (AL), 1967, .250	.310
Joe Battin	4–19, Pitt. (AA), C-P (U) 1883–84, .174	.218
Tommy Bond	5–22, Worcester (NL), 1882, .185	.236
Jim Bottomley	21–58, St. L. (AL), 1937, .266	.310
Roger Connor	9–37, St. L. (NL), 1896, .196	.318
Lave Cross	8–30, Cleve. (NL), 1899, .211	.292
Dude Esterbrook	2–8, Louisville (NL), 1889, .200	.261
Charlie Gould	9–56, Cinn. (NL), 1876, .138	.258
Mike Griffin	1–3, Bklyn. (NL), 1898, .250	.299
Sandy Griffin	4–13, WA (AA), 1891, .235	.275
Bill Hallman	13–46, St. L. (NL), 1897, .220	.272
Mel Harder	0–1, Cleve. (AL), 1961, .000	.165
Guy Hecker	23–113, Pitt. (NL), 1890, .169	.284
Roy Johnson	0–1, Chic. (NL), 1944, .000	.296
Malachi Kittredge	1–16, WA (AL), 1904, .059	.219
Arlie Latham	0–2, St. L. (NL), 1896, .000	.269
Jeff Newman	2–8, Oak. (AL), 1986, .200	.224
Lip Pike	3–11, Cinn. (NL), 1877, .214	.304
Blondie Purcell	13–68, Phila. (NL), 1883, .160	.267
Joe Quinn	25–131, St. L. (NL), 1895; Cleve. (NL), 1899, .160	.261
Dave Rowe	44–126, K.C. (NL), 1886, K.C. (AA), 1888, .259	.263
Jack Rowe	36–96, Buffalo (P), 1890, .273	.286
Ken Silvestri	0–3, Atl. (NL), 1967, .000	.217
Heinie Smith	5–27, NY (NL), 1902, .156	.238
Chick Stahl	5–13, Bost. (AL), 1906, .278	.307
George Van Haltren	5–16, Balt. (AA), 1891, Balt. (NL), 1892, .238	.316
Honus Wagner	1–4, Pitt. (NL), 1917, .200	.329
Chicken Wolf	15–51, Louisville (AA), 1889, .227	.290
Rudy York	0–1, Bost. (AL), 1959, .000	.275

MEN WHO PLAYED IN 2,000 GAMES, MANAGED IN 2,000 GAMES

	PLAYED	MANAGED
Cap Anson	2276 (1876–97)	2296 (1879–98)
Fred Clarke	2245 (1894–1915)	2822 (1897–1915)
Joe Cronin	2124 (1926–45)	2315 (1933–47)
Jimmy Dykes	2282 (1918–39)	2960 (1934–46, 1951–54, 1958–61)
Frankie Frisch	2311 (1919–37)	2245 (1933–38, 1940–46, 1949–51)
Charlie Grimm	2164 (1916, 1918–36)	2370 (1932–38, 1944–49, 1952–56, 1960)

MANAGERS OF TEAMS IN ALL FOUR DIVISIONS

Dick Williams	American League East	Bost. (1967–69)
	American League West	Oak. (1971–73)
		CA (1974–76)
		Seattle (1986–88)
	National League East	Mont. (1977–81)
	National League West	S.D. (1982–85)

Don Zimmer	American League East	Bost. (1976–80)
	American League West	TX (1981–82)
	National League East	Chic. (1988–89)
	National League West	S.D. (1972–73)

MANAGERS MANAGING 100-LOSS TEAMS AFTER 1,000TH CAREER VICTORY

Lou Boudreau, K.C., 1956
Leo Durocher, Chic. (NL), 1966
Jimmy Dykes, Balt., 1954
Ned Hanlon, Bklyn., 1905
Ralph Houk, Det., 1975
Connie Mack, Phila. (AL), 1915, 1916, 1919, 1920, 1943, 1946
Bill McKechnie, Bost. (NL), 1935
Casey Stengel, NY (NL), 1962, 1963, 1964
Chuck Tanner, Pitt., 1985

FORMER PITCHERS WINNING PENNANTS AS MANAGERS (Since 1900)

Clark Griffith—Chic. (AL), 1901
Eddie Dyer—St. L. (NL), 1946
Fred Hutchinson—Cinn. (NL), 1961
Tommy Lasorda—L.A. (NL), 1977, 78, 81, 88
Bob Lemon—NY (AL), 1978, 81
Dallas Green—Phila. (NL), 1980

MANAGERS OF WORLD SERIES TEAMS TAKING OVER IN MIDSEASON

1932   Charlie Grimm, Chic. Cubs (NL), 37–20 (Replaced Rogers Hornsby)
1938   Gabby Hartnett, Chic. Cubs (NL), 44–27 (Replaced Charlie Grimm)
1947   Burt Shotton, Bklyn. Dodgers (NL), 93–60 (Replaced Clyde Sukeforth)
1978   Bob Lemon, NY Yankees (AL), 48–20 (Replaced Dick Howser)
1981   Bob Lemon, NY Yankees (AL), 13–15 (Replaced Gene Michael)
1982   Harvey Kuenn, Milw. Brewers (AL), 72–43 (Replaced Buck Rodgers)
1983   Paul Owens, Phila. Phillies (NL), 47–30 (Replaced Pat Corrales)

MANAGERS REPLACED WHILE TEAM WAS IN FIRST PLACE

1947   Clyde Sukeforth, Bklyn. Dodgers 1–0
(Replaced by Burt Shotton, 93–60)

1983   Pat Corrales, Phila. Phillies, 43–42
(Replaced by Paul Owens, 47–30)

MANAGERS WITH LEAST NUMBER OF LIFETIME WINS TO WIN WORLD SERIES

Dallas Green, 169 wins—Phila. Phillies, 1980*
Jake Stahl, 263 wins—1912 Bost. Red Sox
Tom Kelly, 268 wins—MN Twins, 1987*
Ed Barrow, 310 wins—1918 Bost. Red Sox
Pants Rowland, 339 wins—1917 Chic. White Sox
Gabby Street, 368 wins—1931 St. L. Cardinals
Johnny Keane, 398 wins—1964 St. L. Cardinals

Mickey Cochrane, 413 wins—1935 Det. Tigers
Bob Lemon, 432 wins—1978 NY Yankees
Joe Altobelli, 437 wins—1983 Balt. Orioles
Eddie Dyer, 446 wins—1946 St. L. Cardinals
Jimmy Collins, 464 wins—1903 Bost. Red Sox
Davey Johnson, 488 wins—1986 NY Mets*
Bill Carrigan, 489 wins—1915, 1916 Bost. Red Sox

*Active

MANAGERS WITH MOST WINS NEVER TO MANAGE A WORLD SERIES TEAM (Since 1903)

	WINS	SEASONS		WINS	SEASONS
Gene Mauch	1901	26	Birdie Tebbetts	781	11
Jimmy Dykes	1407	21	Lee Fohl	713	11
Clark Griffith	1334	18	Dave Bristol	658	11
Bill Rigney	1239	18	Harry Walker	630	9
Bill Virdon	995	13	Bobby Cox	621	8
Paul Richards	923	12	Danny Ozark	618	8
Don Zimmer	790	11	Herman Franks	605	7

MOST TIMES MANAGED THE SAME CLUB

Billy Martin	NY Yankees	5	1975–78, 1979, 1983, 1985, 1988
Danny Murtaugh	Pitt. Pirates	4	1957–64, 1967, 1970–71, 1973–76
Bucky Harris	WA Senators	3	1924–28, 1935–42, 1950–54
Charlie Grimm	Chic. Cubs	3	1932–38, 1944–49, 1960

BEST WINNING PERCENTAGE FOR FIRST FIVE FULL YEARS OF MANAGING

Frank Chance (Chic. Cubs, 1906–10)	530–235	.693
Al Lopez (Cleve. Indians, 1951–55)	482–288	.626
Earl Weaver (Balt. Orioles, 1969–73)	495–303	.620
John McGraw (Balt. (NL), 1899; Balt. (AL), 1900; NY (NL), 1903–05)	449–277	.618
Davey Johnson (NY Mets, 1984–88)	488–320	.604
Hughie Jennings (Det. Tigers, 1907–11)	455–308	.596
Leo Durocher (Bklyn. Dodgers, 1939–43)	457–310	.596
Sparky Anderson (Cinn. Reds, 1970–74)	473–329	.590
Fielder Jones (Chic. White Sox, 1904–07; St. L. Terriers (FL), 1915)	447–313	.588
Joe McCarthy (Chic. Cubs, 1926–29; NY Yankees, 1931)	450–316	.587
Pat Moran (Phila. Phillies, 1915–18; Cinn. Reds, 1919)	419–301	.582

MANAGERS NEVER EXPERIENCING A LOSING SEASON (Minimum two seasons)

WINNING SEASONS	MANAGER	YEARS	W/L	PCT.
24	Joe McCarthy	(1926–46; 1948–50)	2136–1335	.614
14	Steve O'Neill	(1935–37; 1943–48; 1950–54)	1039–819	.559
6	Davey Johnson	(1984–89)	575–395	.593
5	Eddie Dyer	(1946–50)	446–325	.578
4	Tom Kelly	(1986–89)	268–241	.527
3	Bill Joyce	(1896–98)	177–122	.592
3	Ossie Vitt	(1938–40)	262–198	.570
3	Harvey Kuenn	(1975; 1982–83)	160–118	.576
3	Dallas Green	(1979–81)	169–130	.565
3	Tom Trebelhorn	(1986–88)	184–146	.558
2	Bill Reccius	(1882–83)	36–28	.563
2	Eddie Collins	(1925–26)	160–147	.521
2	Dick Sisler	(1964–65)	121–94	.563

CAREER ONE-GAME MANAGERS

Roy Johnson, Chic. Cubs (NL), 1944   1–0
Clyde Sukeforth, Bklyn. Dodgers (NL), 1947   1–0
Bill Burwell, Pitt. Pirates (NL), 1947   1–0
Rudy York, Bost. Red Sox (AL), 1959   0–1

Jo Jo White, Cleve. Indians (AL), 1960   1–0
Andy Cohen, Phila. Phillies (NL), 1960   1–0
Mel Harder, Cleve. Indians (AL), 1961   0–1
Ted Turner, Atl. Braves (NL), 1977   0–1

MANAGERS MANAGING IN CIVILIAN CLOTHES

Judge Emil Fuchs (1929 Bost., NL)
Connie Mack (1894–96, Pitt., NL; 1901–50, Phila., AL)
Burt Shotton (1928–33, Phila., NL; 1934, Cinn., NL; 1947–48, 1949–50 Bklyn., NL)
George Stallings (1897–99, Phila., NL; 1901 Det., AL; 1909–10, NY, AL; 1913–20, Bost., NL)

MANAGERS WHO WERE LAWYERS

Emil Fuchs (Bost., NL 1929)
Miller Huggins (St. L., NL, 1913–17; NY, AL, 1918–29)
Hughie Jennings (Det., AL, 1907–20)
Tony LaRusso (Chic., AL, 1979–86; Oak., AL, 1986–88)
Branch Rickey (St. L., AL, 1913–15; St. L., NL, 1919–25)
Monte Ward (NY, NL, 1884, 1893–94; Bklyn., P, 1890; Bklyn., NL, 1891–92)

FIELDING

MOST CAREER GAMES PLAYED, BY POSITION

1st Base	Jake Beckley, 1888–1907	2377
	Mickey Vernon, 1939–60	2237
	Lou Gehrig, 1923–39	2136
	Charlie Grimm, 1916, 1918–36	2129
	Joe Judge, 1915–34	2080
2nd Base	Eddie Collins, 1906–30	2650
	Joe Morgan, 1963–84	2527
	Nellie Fox, 1947–65	2527
	Charlie Gehringer, 1924–42	2205
	Bid McPhee, 1882–99	2125
3rd Base	Brooks Robinson, 1955–77	2870
	Graig Nettles, 1967–88	2412
	Eddie Mathews, 1952–68	2181
	Ron Santo, 1960–74	2130
	Buddy Bell, 1972–88	2098
Shortstop	Luis Aparicio, 1956–73	2581
	Larry Bowa, 1970–85	2222
	Luke Appling, 1930–50	2218
	Dave Concepcion, 1970–88	2178
	Rabbit Maranville, 1912–33; 1935	2154
Left Field	Zack Wheat, 1909–27	2341
	Fred Clarke, 1894–15	2184
	Lou Brock, 1961–79	2163
	Ted Williams, 1939–42; 1946–60	1984
	Goose Goslin, 1921–38	1948
Center Field	Willie Mays, 1951–52; 1954–73	2829
	Tris Speaker, 1907–28	2693
	Willie Davis, 1960–79	2238
	Ty Cobb, 1905–28	2210
	Doc Cramer, 1929–48	2031
Right Field	Roberto Clemente, 1955–72	2302
	Paul Waner, 1926–45	2256
	Harry Hooper, 1909–25	2190
	Hank Aaron, 1954–76	2171
	Mel Ott, 1926–47	2167
Catcher	Bob Boone, 1972–89	2185
	Jim Sundberg, 1974–89	1927
	Al Lopez, 1928–47	1918
	Rick Ferrell, 1929–47	1805
	Gabby Hartnett, 1922–41	1790
	Ted Simmons, 1968–88	1772
Starting Pitcher	Cy Young, 1890–1911	818
	Don Sutton, 1966–88	756
	Phil Niekro, 1964–87	716
	Steve Carlton, 1965–87	709
	Gaylord Perry, 1962–83	690
Relief Pitcher	Kent Tekulve, 1974–89	1050
	Hoyt Wilhelm, 1952–72	1018
	Lindy McDaniels, 1955–75	913
	Rollie Fingers, 1968–85	907
	Sparky Lyle, 1967–82	899
	Gene Garber, 1969–88	922

MOST CONSECUTIVE GAMES PLAYED AT EACH POSITION

NATIONAL LEAGUE

1B	652	Frank McCormick	Reds (1938–42)
2B	443	Dave Cash	Pirates-Phillies (1973–76)
3B	364	Ron Santo	Cubs (1964–66)
SS	584	Roy McMillan	Reds (1951–55)
OF	897	Billy Williams	Cubs (1963–69)
C	217	Ray Mueller	Reds (1943–44)
P	13	Mike Marshall	Dodgers (1974)

AMERICAN LEAGUE

1B	885	Lou Gehrig	Yankees (1925–30)
2B	798	Nellie Fox	White Sox (1955–60)
3B	576	Eddie Yost	Senators (1951–55)
SS	1307	Everett Scott	Red Sox-Yanks (1916–25)
OF	511	Clyde Milan	Senators (1910–13)
C	312	Frankie Hayes	Browns-A's-Indians (1943–46)
P	8	Ben Flowers	Red Sox (1953)

PLAYERS WHO PLAYED 1,000 OR MORE GAMES AT TWO POSITIONS

Ernie Banks	1,125	shortstop
	1,259	first base
Rod Carew	1,130	second base
	1,184	first base
Babe Ruth	1,054	left field
	1,133	right field

UNASSISTED TRIPLE PLAYS

PLAYER EXECUTING	POSITION	TEAM	DATE	INNING	BATTER, TEAM
Neal Ball	SS	Cleve., AL	July 19, 1909	2nd	Amby McConnell, Bost.

Ball speared McConnell's line drive, came down on second to double up Heinie Wagner and tagged out Jake Stahl coming from first.

Bill Wambsganss	2B	Cleve., AL	October 10, 1920	5th	Clarence Mitchell, Bklyn.

"Wamby" caught Clarence Mitchell's liner, stepped on second to retire Pete Kilduff and wheeled around to tag Otto Miller coming down from first.

George Burns	1B	Bost., AL	September 14, 1923	2nd	Frank Brower, Cleve.

Burns took Brower's line drive, reached out and tagged Walter Lutzke, who had been on first base, and then rushed down to second to tag base before base runner Joe Stephenson could return.

Ernie Padgett	SS	Bost., NL	October 6, 1923	4th	Walter Holke, Phila.

Padgett took Holke's line drive, tagged second to retire Cotton Tierney, and then tagged out Cliff Lee who was coming into second.

Glenn Wright	SS	Pitt., NL	May 7, 1925	9th	Jim Bottomley, St. L.

Wright snared Bottomley's liner, touched second to retire Jim Cooney, and then tagged out Rogers Hornsby on his way into second.

Jim Cooney	SS	Chic., NL	May 30, 1927	4th	Paul Waner, Pitt.

Cooney grabbed Waner's line drive, doubled Lloyd Waner off second, and then tagged out Clyde Barnhart, coming down from first.

Johnny Neun	1B	Det., AL	May 31, 1927	9th	Homer Summa, Cleve.

Neun snared Summa's liner and tagged first to double up Charlie Jamieson, then raced down toward second to tag out base runner Glenn Myatt before he could return to second, ending the game.

Ron Hansen	SS	WA, AL	July 29, 1968	1st	Joe Azcue, Cleve.

Azcue's liner grabbed by Hansen who stepped on second, doubling up Dave Nelson and then tagged out Russ Snyder, barreling down from first.

CATCHERS CATCHING MOST NO-HITTERS

4 Ray Schalk (1912–29)
 James Scott, Chic. (AL), 1914
 Joseph Benz, Chic. (AL), 1914
 Eddie Cicotte, Chic. (AL), 1917
 Charlie Robertson, Chic. (AL), 1922*
3 Lou Criger (1896–1910; 1912)
 Cy Young, Bost. (AL), 1904*
 Bill Dineen, Bost. (AL), 1905
 Cy Young, Bost. (AL), 1908
3 Bill Carrigan (1906–16)
 Joe Wood, Bost. (AL), 1911
 Rube Foster, Bost. (AL), 1916
 Dutch Leonard, Bost. (AL), 1916
3 Val Picinich (1916–33)
 Joe Bush, Phila. (AL), 1916
 Walter Johnson, WA (AL), 1920
 Howard Ehmke, Bost. (AL), 1923
3 Luke Sewell (1921–39; 1942)
 Wes Ferrell, Cleve. (AL), 1931
 Vern Kennedy, Chic. (AL), 1935
 Bill Dietrich, Chic. (AL), 1937
3 Jim Hegan (1941–42; 1946–60)
 Don Black, Cleve. (AL), 1947
 Bob Lemon, Cleve. (AL), 1948
 Bob Feller, Cleve. (AL), 1951

3 Yogi Berra (1946–63; 1965)
 Allie Reynolds, NY (AL), 1951
 Allie Reynolds, NY (AL), 1951
 Don Larsen, NY (AL), 1956*
3 Roy Campanella (1948–57)
 Carl Erskine, Bklyn. (NL), 1952
 Carl Erskine, Bklyn. (NL), 1956
 Sal Maglie, Bklyn. (NL), 1956
3 Del Crandall (1949–66)
 Jim Wilson, Milw. (NL), 1954
 Lew Burdette, Milw. (NL), 1960
 Warren Spahn, Milw. (NL), 1960
3 Johnny Edwards (1961–74)
 Jim Maloney, Cinn. (NL), 1965
 Jim Maloney, Cinn. (NL), 1965
 George Culver, Cinn. (NL), 1968
3 Jeff Torborg (1964–73)
 Sandy Koufax, L.A. (NL), 1965*
 Bill Singer, L.A. (NL), 1970
 Nolan Ryan, CA (AL), 1973
3 Alan Ashby (1973–88)
 Ken Forsch, Houst. (NL), 1979
 Nolan Ryan, Houst. (NL), 1981
 Mike Scott, Houst. (NL), 1986

*Perfect Game

RELATIVES

FATHER-SON COMBINATION WITH 250 CAREER HOME RUNS

Gus Bell (1950–64)	206		Earl Averill, Sr. (1929–41)	238 homers
Buddy Bell (1972–88)	201		Earl Averill, Jr. (1956–63)	44
	407 homers			282 homers
Yogi Berra (1946–65)	358		Dolf Camilli (1933–45)	239
Dale Berra (1977–87)	49		Doug Camilli (1960–69)	18
	407 homers			257 homers
Bobby Bonds (1968–81)	332		Ray Boone (1948–60)	151
Barry Bonds (1986–89)	84		Bob Boone (1972–89)	105
	416 homers			256 homers

BROTHER BATTERIES

Will and Deacon White—Bost. 1877; Cinn. 1878–79
Ed and Bill Dugan—Richmond 1884
Pete and Fred Wood—Buffalo 1885
Dick and Bill Conway—Balt. 1886
John and Buck Ewing—NY 1890; NY 1891
Mike and John O'Neill—St. L. 1902–03
Tom and Homer Thompson—NY 1912
George and Fred Tyler—Bost. 1914

Milt and Alex Gaston—Bost. 1929
Wes and Rick Ferrell—Bost. 1934–37; WA 1937–38
Mort and Walker Cooper—St. L. 1940–45; NY 1947
Elmer and Johnny Riddle—Cinn. 1941; 1944–45
Bobby and Billy Shantz—Phila. 1954; K.C. 1955; NY 1960
Jim and Ed Bailey—Cinn. 1959
Larry and Norm Sherry—L.A. 1959–62

TWINS PLAYING MAJOR LEAGUE BASEBALL

Cliburn, Stan, catcher, CA (AL), 1980
       Stu, pitcher, CA (AL) 1984–85
Edwards, Marshall, outfielder, Milw. (AL), 1981–83
       Mike, infielder, Pitt. (NL), 1977 Oak. (AL), 1978–80
Grimes, Ray, first baseman, Bost. (AL), 1920 Chic. (NL), 1921–24 Phila. (NL), 1926
       Roy, second baseman, NY (NL), 1920
Hunter, Bill, outfielder, Cleve. (AL), 1912
       George, outfielder-pitcher, Bklyn. (NL), 1909–10
Jonnard, Bubber, catcher, Chic. (AL), 1920 Pitt. (NL), 1922 Phila. (NL), 1926–27, 1935 St. L. (NL), 1929
       Claude, pitcher, NY (NL), 1921–24 St. L. (AL), 1926 Chic. (NL), 1929
O'Brien, Eddie, shortstop-outfielder-pitcher, Pitt. (NL), 1953–58
       Johnny, infielder-pitcher, Pitt. (NL), 1953–58 St. L. (NL), 1958 Milw. (NL), 1959
Reccius, John, outfielder-pitcher, Louisville (AA), 1882–83
       Phil, infielder-outfielder-pitcher, Louisville (AA), 1882–87 Cleve. (AA), 1887–1888 Rochester (AA), 1890
Shannon, Joe, outfielder-second baseman, Bost. (NL), 1915
       Red, infielder, Bost. (NL), 1915 Phila. (AL), 1917–19 Bost. (AL), 1919 WA (AL), 1920 Phila. (AL), 1920–21 Chic. (NL), 1926

HALL OF FAMERS WHOSE SONS PLAYED IN THE MAJORS

FATHER	SON		FATHER	SON	
Earl Averill	Earl Averill		Connie Mack	Earle Mack	
Yogi Berra	Dale Berra		Jim O'Rourke	Jim O'Rourke	
Eddie Collins	Eddie Collins		George Sisler	Dave Sisler	Dick Sisler
Fred Lindstrom	Charlie Lindstrom		Ed Walsh	Ed Walsh	

PLAYERS WHO HAD TWO SONS WHO PLAYED IN THE MAJORS

Jimmy Cooney (1890–92), father of Johnny (1921–44) and Jimmy (1917, 1919, 1924–28) Cooney
Larry Gilbert (1914–15), father of Charlie (1940–43, 1946–47) and Tookie (1950, 1953) Gilbert
Sam Hairston (1951), father of Jerry (1973–88) and John (1969) Hairston
George Sisler (1915–22; 1923–30), father of Dave (1956–62) and Dick (1946–53) Sisler
Dixie Walker (1909–12), father of Dixie (1931, 1933–49) and Harry (1940–43, 1946–55) Walker

RELATIVES WHO PLAYED BOTH IN THE MAJORS AND IN JAPAN

Hector and Tommy Cruz (brothers)
Adrian and Wayne Garrett (brothers)
Marty and Matt Keough (father-son)

BROTHER DOUBLE-PLAY COMBINATIONS

1945	Wes and Granny Hamner, Phillies	
1956	Eddie and Johnny O'Brien, Pirates	
1987–88	Bill and Cal Ripken, Orioles	

MOST HOME RUNS, BROTHERS

Hank (755) and Tommie (13) Aaron	768		Graig (390) and Jim (16) Nettles	406
Joe (361), Vince (125) and Dom (87) DiMaggio	573		Richie (351), Hank (6), and Ron (1) Allen	358
Ken (282) and Clete (162) Boyer	444		Bob (288) and Roy (58) Johnson	346
Lee (354) and Carlos (90) May	444			

PITCHING BROTHERS WINNING 20 GAMES IN SAME SEASON

1970	Jim Perry, MN (AL)	24–12
	Gaylord Perry, S.F. (NL)	23–13

1979	Phil Niekro, Atl. (NL)	21–20
	Joe Niekro, Houst. (NL)	21–11

BROTHERS OF HALL OF FAMERS WHO PLAYED 10 OR MORE SEASONS IN MAJORS (Since 1900)

Jim Delehanty, Brother of Ed, 11 seasons (1901–12)
Dom DiMaggio, Brother of Joe, 11 seasons (1940–42; 1946–53)
Vince DiMaggio, Brother of Joe, 10 seasons (1937–46)
Wes Ferrell, Brother of Rick, 15 seasons (1927–41)
Luke Sewell, Brother of Joe, 20 seasons (1921–42)
Lloyd Waner, Brother of Paul, 18 seasons (1927–42; 1944–45)
Paul Waner, Brother of Lloyd, 20 seasons (1926–45)

FATHER-SON TANDEMS BOTH PLAYING FOR SAME MANAGER

Eddie Collins, Sr.   1906–14; 1927–30 Phila. A's—Manager, Connie Mack
Eddie Collins, Jr.   1939, 1941–42 Phila. A's—Manager, Connie Mack
Earle Brucker, Sr.   1937–40, 1943 Phila. A's—Manager, Connie Mack
Earle Brucker, Jr.   1948 Phila. A's—Manager, Connie Mack
Sam Hairston   1951 Chic. White Sox—Manager, Paul Richards
Jerry Hairston   1976 Chic. White Sox—Manager, Paul Richards

SONS WHO PLAYED FOR THEIR FATHERS

Earle Mack, for Connie (1910–11, 1914)—Phila. A's
Dale Berra, for Yogi (1984–85)—NY Yankees
Cal Ripken, for Cal (1985, 1987–88)—Balt. Orioles
Billy Ripken, for Cal (1987–88)—Balt. Orioles

BEST WON-LOST PERCENTAGE FOR PITCHING BROTHERS

BROTHERS	WIN/LOSS	PERCENT	BROTHERS	WIN/LOSS	PERCENT
Kelly (George-Ren)	1–0	1.000	Johnson (Chet-Earl)	49–32	.556
Hovlik (Hick-Joe)	4–1	.800	Pfeffer (Big Jeff-Jeff)	189–152	.554
Mathewson (Christy-Henry)	373–189	.664	Perry (Gaylord-Jim)	529–439	.546
Corcoran (Larry-Mike)	177–91	.660	McDaniel (Lindy-Von)	148–124	.544
Hughes (Jim-Mickey)	122–69	.639	Gumbert (Ad-Billy)	129–109	.542
Dean (Dizzy-Paul)	200–117	.631	O'Toole (Denny-Jim)	98–84	.538
Clarkson (Dad-John-Walter)	383–232	.623	Galvin (Lou-Pud)	361–312	.536
Radbourne (George-Old Hoss)	309–193	.616	Romo (Enrique-Vicente)	76–66	.535
Coveleski (Harry-Stan)	296–197	.600	Forsch (Bob-Ken)	278–244	.533
Gregg (Dave-Vean)	91–63	.591	Reuschel (Paul-Rick)	227–199	.533
Ferry (Cy-Jack)	10–7	.588	Niekro (Joe-Phil)	538–477	.530
Wiltse (Hooks-Snake)	169–121	.583	Weyhing (Gus-John)	267–240	.527
Pipgras (Ed-George)	102–74	.580	Lary (Al-Frank)	128–117	.522
White (Deacon-Will)	229–166	.580	Fowler (Art-Jesse)	55–52	.514
Ford (Gene-Russ)	98–72	.576	Kilroy (Matt-Mike)	142–137	.509
Mayer (Erskine-Sam)	91–70	.565	Barnes (Jesse-Virgil)	214–208	.507
Morrison (Johnny-Phil)	103–80	.563	Pascual (Camilo-Carlos)	175–171	.506
Camnitz (Harry-Howie)	134–106	.558	Foreman (Brownie-Frank)	108–106	.505
Gettinger (Charlie-Tom)	15–12	.556	Olivo (Chi Chi-Diomedes)	12–12	.500

BROTHERS WITH MOST TOTAL CAREER WINS, COMBINED

539 Niekro
  Phil (1964–87) 318
  Joe (1967–87) 221
529 Perry
  Gaylord (1962–83) 314
  Jim (1959–75) 215
383 Clarkson
  John (1882–94) 326
  Dad (1891–96) 39
  Walter (1904–08) 18
373 Mathewson
  Christy (1900–16) 373
  Henry (1906–07) 0
361 Galvin
  Pud (1879–92) 361
  Lou (1884) 0
296 Coveleski
  Stan (1912–28) 215
  Harry (1907–18) 81

278 Forsche
  Bob (1974–89) 168
  Ken (1970–84) 114
214 Barnes
  Jesse (1905–27) 153
  Virgil (1919–28) 61
210 Reuschel
  Rick (1972–89) 211
  Paul (1975–79) 16
200 Dean
  Dizzy (1930–47) 150
  Paul (1934–43) 50
189 Pfeffer
  Jeff (1911–24) 158
  Big Jeff (1905–11) 31

PITCHING BROTHERS FACING EACH OTHER, REGULAR SEASON

1896 Frank Foreman—Cinn. (NL) versus Brownie Foreman—Pitt. (NL)*
1916 Stan Coveleski—Cleve. (AL) versus Harry Coveleski—Det. (AL)*
1923 Virgil Barnes—NY (NL) versus Jesse Barnes—Bost. (NL)
1927 Virgil Barnes—NY (NL) versus Jesse Barnes—Bklyn. (NL)
1968 Phil Niekro—Atl. (NL) versus Joe Niekro—Chic. (NL)
1973 Gaylord Perry—Cleve. (AL) versus Jim Perry—Det. (AL)
1974 Bob Forsch—St. L. (NL) versus Ken Forsch—Houst. (NL)
1979 Tom Underwood—Tor. (AL) versus Pat Underwood—Det. (AL)
1986 Greg Maddux—Chic. (NL) versus Mike Maddux—Phila. (NL)
1988 Greg Maddux—Chic. (NL) versus Mike Maddux—Phila. (NL)

*Same game, but not same time

MOST CAREER VICTORIES BY FATHER-SON COMBINATION (Since 1900)

258 Trout, Dizzy (170) Steve (88)
224 Bagby, Jim, Sr. (127) Jim, Jr. (97)
205 Walsh, Ed, Sr. (194) Ed, Jr. (11)
194 Coleman, Joe, Sr. (52) Joe, Jr. (142)
157 Lee, Thorton (117) Don (40)

124 Grimsley, Ross, Sr. (0) Ross, Jr. (124)
115 Wood, Smoky Joe (115) Joe, Jr. (0)
 73 Krausse, Lew, Sr. (5) Lew, Jr. (68)
 72 Pillette, Herman (34) Duane (38)
 47 Queen, Mel, Sr. (27) Mel, Jr. (20)

WORLD SERIES

PLAYERS BATTING .500 OR OVER IN WORLD SERIES (Min. 10 at Bats)

	HITS	AB	PERCENT	GAMES
Babe Ruth, NY Yankees, 1928	10	16	.625	4
Hank Gowdy, Bost. Braves, 1914	6	11	.545	4
Lou Gehrig, NY Yankees, 1928	6	11	.545	4
Johnny Bench, Cinn. Reds, 1976	8	15	.533	4
Lou Gehrig, NY Yankees, 1932	9	17	.529	4
Thurman Munson, NY Yankees*, 1976	9	17	.529	4
Larry McLean, NY Giants*, 1913	6	12	.500	5
Dave Robertson, NY Giants*, 1917	11	22	.500	6
Mark Koenig, NY Yankees, 1927	9	18	.500	4
Pepper Martin, St. L. Cardinals, 1931	12	24	.500	7
Joe Gordon, NY Yankees, 1941	7	14	.500	5
Billy Martin, NY Yankees, 1953	12	24	.500	6
Vic Wertz, Cleve. Indians*, 1954	8	16	.500	4
Phil Garner, Pitt., 1979	12	24	.500	7

*Losing team

PLAYERS ON WORLD CHAMPIONSHIP TEAMS IN BOTH LEAGUES

	NATIONAL LEAGUE	AMERICAN LEAGUE
Doug Bair	1982 St. L. Cardinals	1984 Det. Tigers
Terry Crowley	1975 Cinn. Reds	1970 Balt. Orioles
Mike Cuellar	1964 St. L. Cardinals (DNP)	1970 Balt. Orioles
Vic Davalillo	1971 Pitt. Pirates	1973 Oak. A's
Murray Dickson	1942, '46 St. L. Cardinals	1958 NY Yankees
Leo Durocher	1934 St. L. Cardinals	1928 NY Yankees
Lonnie Frey	1940 Cinn. Reds	1947 NY Yankees
Billy Gardner	1954 NY Giants (DNP)	1961 NY Yankees
Kirk Gibson	1988 L.A. Dodgers	1984 Det. Tigers
Don Gullett	1975, '76 Cinn. Reds	1977 NY Yankees
Mule Haas	1925 Pitt. Pirates (DNP)	1929, '30 Phila. A's
Johnny Hopp	1942, '44 St. L. Cardinals	1950, '51 NY Yankees
Jay Johnstone	1981 L.A. Dodgers	1978 NY Yankees
Ed Mathews	1957 Milw. Braves	1968 Det. Tigers
Dal Maxvill	1964, '67 St. L. Cardinals	1972 (DNP), '74 Oak. A's
Roger Maris	1967 St. L. Cardinals	1961, '62 NY Yankees
Stuffy McInnis	1925 Pitt. Pirates	1911, '13 Phila. A's, 1918 Bost. Red Sox
Don McMahon	1957 Milw. Braves	1968 Det. Tigers
Dave Parker	1989 Oak. A's	1979 Pitt. Pirates
Merv Rettenmund	1975 Cinn. Reds	1970 Balt. Orioles
Paul Richards	1933 NY Giants (DNP)	1945 Det. Tigers
"Dutch" Ruether	1919 Cinn. Reds	1927 NY Yankees (DNP)
Rosy Ryan	1921 (DNP) '23 NY Giants	1928 NY Yankees (DNP)
Enos Slaughter	1942, '44 St. L. Cardinals	1956, '58 NY Yankees
Lonnie Smith	1980 Phila. Phillies, 1982 St. L. Cardinals	1985 K.C. Royals
Dave Stewart	1989 Oak. A's	1981 LA Dodgers
Gene Tenace	1982 St. L. Cardinals	1972, '73, '74 Oak. A's
Dick Tracewski	1963, '65 L.A. Dodgers	1968 Det. Tigers
Bob Welch	1989 Oak. A's	1981 LA Dodgers

HIGHEST SLUGGING AVERAGE FOR PITCHERS IN WORLD SERIES

PITCHER	G	AB	R	H	2B	3B	HR	RBI	BAT.	SLUG.
Orel Hershiser	2	3	1	3	2	0	0	1	1.000*	1.667*
Jack Bentley	10	12	1	5	1	0	1	2	.417	.750
Dutch Ruether	7	11	2	4	1	2*	0	4	.364	.818
Ken Holtzman	8	12	4*	4	3*	0	1	1	.333	.833
Jack Coombs	6	24	1	8	1	0	0	4	.333	.375
Dizzy Dean	6	15	3	5	2	0	0	1	.333	.467
Mike Moore	2	3	1	1	1	0	0	2	.333	.667
Burleigh Grimes	9	19	1	6	0	0	0	2	.316	.316
Johnny Podres	7	16	2	5	1	0	0	1	.313	.375
Allie Reynolds	15	26	2	8	1	0	0	2	.308	.346
Ch. Mathewson	11	32	2	9*	0	0	0	1	.281	.281
Red Ruffing	14	34	1	6	1	0	0	4	.176	.206
Bob Gibson	9	28	4*	4	0	0	2*	3	.143	.357
Dave McNally	9	16	2	2	0	0	2*	6*	.125	.500
Whitey Ford	22*	49*	4*	4	0	0	0	3	.082	.082

*Leader in category

WORLD SERIES-ENDING HITS

1924 Earl McNeeley's single over Freddie Lindstrom's head in 12th inning of 7th game wins for the Washington Senators over the New York Giants, 4 games to 3.

1929 Double by Bing Miller in ninth inning of 5th game drives in Al Simmons with winning run as Philadelphia A's beat Chicago Cubs, 4 games to 1.

1935 Goose Goslin's single drives in Charlie Gehringer of the Tigers for winning run as Detroit beats the Cubs, 4 games to 2.

1953 Billy Martin's 12th hit of the Series, a single, drives in Hank Bauer with the Series-ending run as the Yankees beat the Dodgers, 4 games to 2.

1960 Bill Mazeroski's lead-off homer in the bottom of the ninth of the Seventh game wins the Series for the Pittsburgh Pirates over the New York Yankees, 4 games to 3.

PITCHERS IN WORLD SERIES AFTER 300th VICTORY

	WINS		WINS
Cy Young, 1903 Bost. (AL)	378	Walter Johnson, 1924 WA (AL)	396
Christy Mathewson, 1912 NY (NL)	312	Grover Cleveland Alexander, 1926 St. L. (NL)	327
Christy Mathewson, 1913 NY (NL)	337	Grover Cleveland Alexander, 1928 St. L. (NL)	364
Walter Johnson, 1924 WA (AL)	376	Steve Carlton, 1983 Phila. (NL)	300

PLAYERS ON WORLD SERIES TEAMS IN THREE DECADES

Yogi Berra	1947, '49 NY Yankees 1950, '51, '52, '53, '55, '56, '57, '58 NY Yankees 1960, '61, '63 NY Yankees	Jim Palmer	1966, '69 Balt. Orioles 1970, '71, '79 Balt. Orioles 1983 Balt. Orioles
Bill Dickey	1928 NY Yankees (DNP) 1932, '36, '37, '38, '39 NY Yankees 1941, '42, '43 NY Yankees	Herb Pennock	1913 (DNP), '14 Phila. Athletics 1923, '26, '27, '28 (DNP) NY Yankees 1932 NY Yankees
Joe DiMaggio	1936, '37, '38, '39 NY Yankees 1941, '42, '47, '49 NY Yankees 1950, '51 NY Yankees	Billy Pierce	1945 Det. Tigers (DNP) 1959 Chic. White Sox 1962 S.F. Giants
Leo Durocher	1928 NY Yankees 1934 St. L. Cardinals 1941 Bklyn. Dodgers (DNP)	Babe Ruth	1915, '16, '18 Bost. Red Sox 1921, '22, '23, '26, '27, '28 NY Yankees 1932 NY Yankees
Willie Mays	1951, '54 NY Giants 1962 S.F. Giants 1973 NY Mets	Wally Schang	1913, '14 Phila. A's; 1918 Bost. Red Sox 1921, '22, '23 NY Yankees 1930 Phila. A's (DNP)
Tug McGraw	1969 NY Mets (DNP) 1973 NY Mets 1980 Phila. Phillies	Jimmy Wilson	1928 St. L. Cardinals 1930, '31 St. L. Cardinals 1940 Cinn. Reds

PLAYER-MANAGERS OF WORLD SERIES-WINNING TEAMS

1903	Jimmy Collins, Bost. (AL)	1916	Bill Carrigan, Bost. (AL)
1906	Fielder Jones, Chic. (AL)	1920	Tris Speaker, Cleve. (AL)
1907	Frank Chance, Chic. (NL)	1924	Bucky Harris, WA (AL)
1908	Frank Chance, Chic. (NL)	1926	Rogers Hornsby, St. L. (NL)
1909	Fred Clarke, Pitt. (NL)	1933	Bill Terry, NY (NL)
1912	Jake Stahl, Bost. (AL)	1934	Frankie Frisch, St. L. (NL)
1915	Bill Carrigan, Bost. (AL)	1948	Lou Boudreau, Cleve. (AL)

LEADERS IN OFFENSIVE CATEGORIES BY PLAYERS WHO NEVER APPEARED IN WORLD SERIES (Since 1903)

GAMES	Ernie Banks, 2528	EXTRA-BASE HITS	Ernie Banks, 1009
BASE HITS	Rod Carew, 3053	RUNS BATTED IN	Ernie Banks, 1636
RUNS	Rod Carew, 1424	WALKS	Eddie Yost, 1614
SINGLES	Rod Carew, 2404	STRIKEOUTS	Dave Kingman, 1816
DOUBLES	Harry Heilmann, 542	SLUGGING PERCENT	Harry Heilmann, .520 (Min. 4000 TB's)
TRIPLES	Harry Heilmann, 151		
HOME RUNS	Ernie Banks, 512	BATTING AVERAGE	Lefty O'Doul, .349 (Min. 10 Yrs.)
GRAND SLAMS	Dave Kingman, 16	.300 SEASONS	Luke Appling, 14
PINCH HIT HR'S	Jose Morales, 12	STOLEN BASES	Tim Raines, 585
TOTAL BASES	Ernie Banks, 4706		

PLAYED MOST YEARS WITHOUT A WORLD SERIES APPEARANCE (Since 1903)

24 years   Phil Niekro, pitcher (1964–87)
22 years   Gaylord Perry, pitcher (1962–83)
21 years   Ted Lyons, pitcher (1923–42; 1946)
             Lindy McDaniel, pitcher (1955–75)
20 years   Luke Appling, shortstop (1930–50)
             Johnny Cooney, outfielder (1921–30; 1935–44)
             Mel Harder, pitcher (1928–47)
             Dutch Leonard, pitcher (1933–36; 1938–53)
             Elmer Valo, outfielder (1940–43; 1946–61)
             Mickey Vernon, first baseman (1939–43; 1946–60)

19 years   Ernie Banks, shortstop (1953–71)
             Rube Bressler, outfielder-pitcher (1914–32)
             Rod Carew, infielder (1967–85)
             Jose Cruz, outfielder (1970–88)
             Gene Garber, pitcher (1969–70; 1972–88)
             Ferguson Jenkins, pitcher (1965–83)
             Al Lopez, catcher (1928; 1930–47)
             Tony Taylor, second baseman (1958–76)
             Cy Williams, outfielder (1912–30)

MOST GAMES, NEVER APPEARED IN WORLD SERIES (Since 1903)

Ernie Banks (1953–71)   2528
Billy Williams (1959–76)   2488
Rod Carew (1967–85)   2469
Luke Appling (1930–50)   2422
Mickey Vernon (1939–60)   2409
Buddy Bell (1972–89)   2405

Chris Speier (1971–89)   2260
Jose Cruz (1970–88)   2353
Ron Santo (1960–74)   2243
Joe Torre (1960–77)   2209
Tony Taylor (1958–76)   2195
Toby Harrah (1969–86)   2155

MOST HOME RUNS, NEVER APPEARED IN WORLD SERIES (Since 1903)

Ernie Banks (1953–71)   512
Dave Kingman (1971–86)   442
Billy Williams (1959–76)   426
Rocky Colavito (1955–68)   374
Ralph Kiner (1946–55)   369

Dale Murphy (1976–89)   354
Richie Allen (1963–77)   351
Ron Santo (1960–74)   342
Bobby Bonds (1968–81)   332
Roy Sievers (1949–65)   318

HIGHEST LIFETIME BATTING AVERAGE, NEVER APPEARED IN WORLD SERIES (Min. 10 Years, Since 1903)

George Sisler (1915–22; 1924–30)	.340	Bibb Falk (1920–31)	.314
Rod Carew (1967–85)	.328	Cecil Travis (1933–41; 1945–47)	.314
Nap Lajoie (1903–16)	.328*	Jack Fournier (1912–18; 1920–27)	.313
Babe Herman (1926–37; 1945)	.324	Baby Doll Jacobson (1915; 1917; 1919–27)	.311
Ken Williams (1915–29)	.319	Rip Radcliff (1934–43)	.311

*Average from 1903 on

MOST HITS, NEVER APPEARING IN WORLD SERIES (Since 1903)

Rod Carew (1967–85)	3,053	Buddy Bell (1972–88)	2,499
George Sisler (1915–22; 1924–30)	2,812	Mickey Vernon (1939–60)	2,495
Luke Appling (1930–50)	2,749	Joe Torre (1960–77)	2,342
Billy Williams (1959–76)	2,711	Ron Santo (1960–74)	2,254
Ernie Banks (1953–71)	2,583	Jose Cruz (1970–88)	2,251

LEADERS IN PITCHING CATEGORIES BY PITCHERS WHO NEVER PITCHED IN THE WORLD SERIES

Games Pitched	Lindy McDaniel	987
Games Started	Phil Niekro	716
Complete Games	Ted Lyons	356
Innings Pitched	Phil Niekro	5403.1
ERA (minimum 2000 Innings)	Addie Joss	1.88
Hits Allowed	Phil Niekro	5,044
Grand Slams Allowed	Ned Garver	9
	Milt Pappas	9
Victories	Phil Niekro	318
Losses	Phil Niekro	274
20-Win Seasons	Ferguson Jenkins	7
Saves	Gene Garber	218
Shutouts	Gaylord Perry	53
Walks	Phil Niekro	1809
Strikeouts	Gaylord Perry	3534

MOST WINS, NEVER APPEARED IN WORLD SERIES (Since 1903)

Phil Niekro (1964–87)	318	Mel Harder (1928–47)	223
Gaylord Perry (1962–83)	314	Hooks Dauss (1912–26)	221
Ferguson Jenkins (1965–83)	284	Wilbur Cooper (1912–26)	216
Ted Lyons (1923–42; 1946)	260	Milt Pappas (1957–73)	209
Jim Bunning (1955–71)	224		

PLAYERS WHOSE HOME RUN WON A WORLD SERIES GAME 1–0

1923   Casey Stengel, 3rd Game, NY NL versus NY, AL, pitcher Sam Jones

1949   Tommy Henrich, 1st Game, NY AL versus Bklyn., NL, pitcher Don Newcombe

1966   Paul Blair, 3rd game, Balt. AL versus L.A., NL, pitcher Claude Osteen

1966   Frank Robinson, 4th game, Balt. AL versus L.A., NL, pitcher Don Drysdale

BROTHERS IN SAME WORLD SERIES

Alou—Felipe (OF, San Francisco, NL) and Matty (OF, San Francisco, NL), 1968
Boyer—Clete (3B, New York, AL) and Ken (3B, St. Louis, NL), 1964
Cooper—Mort (P, St. Louis, NL) and Walker (C, St. Louis, NL), 1942, 1943 and 1944
Dean—Daffy (P, St. Louis, NL) and Dizzy (P, St. Louis, NL), 1934
Meusel—Bob (OF, New York, AL) and Irish (OF, New York, NL), 1921, 1922 and 1923
Waner—Lloyd (OF, Pittsburgh, NL) and Paul (OF, Pittsburgh, NL), 1927

BROTHERS WHO WERE WORLD SERIES TEAMMATES

1922   Jesse (Pitcher) and Virgil (Pitcher) Barnes NY Giants (NL)

1927   Paul (Outfielder) and Lloyd (Outfielder) Waner Pitt. Pirates (NL)

1934   Dizzy (Pitcher) and Paul (Pitcher) Dean St. L. Cardinals (NL)

1942–44   Mort (Pitcher) and Walker (Catcher) Cooper St. L. Cardinals (NL)

1962   Felipe (Outfielder) and Matty (Outfielder) Alou S.F. Giants (NL)

1980   George (3rd Base) and Ken (Pitcher) Brett K.C. Royals (AL)

BROTHERS FACING EACH OTHER IN WORLD SERIES

Clete (New York Yankees) versus Ken (St. Louis Cardinals) Boyer   1964
Jimmy (Brooklyn Dodgers) versus Wheeler (Cleveland Indians) Johnston   1920
Bob (New York Yankees) versus Irish (New York Giants) Meusel   1921, 1922, 1923

FATHERS AND SONS IN WORLD SERIES COMPETITION

Bagby—Jim, Sr. (Pitcher, Cleveland, AL, 1920)
        Jim, Jr. (Pitcher, Boston, AL, 1946)
Boone—Ray (Pinch hitter, Cleveland, AL, 1948)
        Bob (Catcher, Philadelphia, NL, 1980)
Hegan—Jim (Catcher, Cleveland, AL, 1948 and 1954)
        Mike (Pinch hitter and First Baseman, New York, AL 1964 and Oakland, AL 1972
Johnson—Ernie (Shortstop, New York, AL, 1923)
        Don (Second Baseman, Chicago, NL, 1945)
Kennedy—Bob (Outfielder, Cleveland, AL, 1948)
        Terry (Catcher, San Diego, NL, 1984)
Sullivan—Billy, Sr. (Catcher, Chicago, AL, 1906)
        Billy, Jr. (Catcher, Detroit, AL, 1940)

PLAYERS HITTING WORLD SERIES HOME RUNS IN EACH LEAGUE

Kirk Gibson	Det. (AL), 1984		Bill Skowron	NY (AL), 1955, 1956, 1958, 1960, 1961
	L.A. (NL), 1988			L.A. (NL), 1963
Roger Maris	NY (AL), 1960, 1961, 1962, 1964		Enos Slaughter	St. L. (NL), 1942, 1946
	St. L. (NL), 1967			NY (AL), 1956
Frank Robinson	Cinn. (NL), 1961		Reggie Smith	Bost. (AL), 1967
	Balt. (AL), 1966, 1969, 1970, 1971			St. L. (NL), 1977, 1978

WORLD SERIES TEAMS USING SIX DIFFERENT STARTING PITCHERS

1947　Bklyn. Dodgers (NL)
　　　Game One—Ralph Branca (Lost)
　　　Games Two and Six—Vic Lombardi (Lost and Won)
　　　Game Three—Joe Hatten (Won)
　　　Game Four—Harry Taylor (Won)
　　　Game Five—Rex Barney (Lost)
　　　Game Seven—Hal Gregg (Lost)
1955　Bklyn. Dodgers (NL)
　　　Game One—Don Newcombe (Lost)
　　　Game Two—Billy Loes (Lost)
　　　Games Three and Seven—Johnny Podres (Won and Won)

　　　Game Four—Carl Erskine (Won)
　　　Game Five—Roger Craig (Won)
　　　Game Six—Karl Spooner (Lost)
1971　Pitt. Pirates (NL)
　　　Game One—Dock Ellis (Lost)
　　　Game Two—Bob Johnson (Lost)
　　　Games Three and Seven—Steve Blass (Won and Won)
　　　Game Four—Luke Walker (Won)
　　　Game Five—Nelson Briles (Won)
　　　Game Six—Bob Moose (Lost)

ROOKIES STARTING SEVENTH GAME OF WORLD SERIES

1909　Babe Adams, Pittsburgh (NL) vs. Detroit (AL) winner, 8–0, complete game
1912　Hugh Bedient, Boston (AL) vs. New York (NL) went 7 innings, no decision, Boston wins 3–2
1947　Spec Shea, New York (AL), vs. Brooklyn (NL) went 1⅓ innings, no decision, New York wins 5–2
1952　Joe Black, Brooklyn (NL) vs. New York (AL) Went 5.1 innings, losing 4–2
1964　Mel Stottlemyre, New York (AL) vs. St. Louis (NL) went 4 innings, lost 7–5
1987　Joe Magrane, St. Louis (NL) vs. Minnesota (AL) went 4⅓ innings, no decision, Minnesota wins 4–2

MOST POSITIONS PLAYED IN WORLD SERIES COMPETITION (DURING CAREER)

Babe Ruth—pitcher, left field, right field, first base
Jackie Robinson—first base, second base, left field, third base
Elston Howard—left field, right field, first base, catcher
Tony Kubek—left field, third base, center field, shortstop
Pete Rose—right field, left field, third base, first base

PLAYERS STEALING HOME IN WORLD SERIES GAME

Bill Dahlen, NY Giants, 1905*   Game 3, 5th Inning
George Davis, Chic. White Sox, 1906*   Game 5, 3rd Inning
Jimmy Slagle, Chic. Cubs, 1907*   Game 4, 7th Inning
Ty Cobb, Det. Tigers, 1909   Game 2, 3rd Inning
Buck Herzog, NY Giants, 1912*   Game 6, 1st Inning
Butch Schmidt, Bost. Braves, 1914*   Game 1, 8th Inning
Mike McNally, NY Yankees, 1921   Game 1, 5th Inning
Bob Meusel, NY Yankees, 1921   Game 2, 8th Inning
Bob Meusel, NY Yankees, 1928*   Game 3, 6th Inning
Hank Greenberg, Det. Tigers, 1934*   Game 4, 8th Inning
Monte Irvin, NY Giants, 1951   Game 1, 1st Inning
Jackie Robinson, Bklyn. Dodgers, 1955   Game 1, 8th Inning
Tim McCarver, St. L. Cardinals, 1964*   Game 7, 4th Inning

*Front End of Double Steal

PITCHERS HITTING HOME RUNS IN WORLD SERIES PLAY

Jim Bagby, Sr., Cleveland Indians (AL), 5th game, 1920 Series vs. Brooklyn (NL)
Rosy Ryan, New York Giants (NL), 3rd game, 1924 Series vs. Washington (AL)
Jack Bentley, New York Giants (NL), 5th game, 1924 Series vs. Washington (AL)
Jesse Haines, St. Louis Cardinals (NL), 3rd game, 1926 Series vs. New York (AL)
Bucky Walters, Cincinnati Reds (NL), 6th game, 1940 Series vs. Detroit (AL)
Lew Burdette, Milwaukee Braves (NL), 2nd game, 1958 Series vs. New York (AL)
Jim "Mudcat" Grant, Minnesota Twins (AL), 6th game, 1965 Series vs. Los Angeles (NL)
Jose Santiago, Boston Red Sox (AL), 1st game, 1967 Series vs. St. Louis (NL)*
Bob Gibson, St. Louis Cardinals (NL), 4th game, 1967 Series vs. Boston (AL)
Mickey Lolich, Detroit Tigers (AL), 2nd game, 1968 Series vs. St. Louis (NL)
Dave McNally, Baltimore Orioles (AL), 5th game, 1969 Series vs. New York (NL)*
Dave McNally, Baltimore Orioles (AL), 3rd game, 1970 Series vs. Cincinnati (NL) (Grand Slam Homer)
Ken Holtzman, Oakland A's (AL), 4th game, 1974 Series vs. Los Angeles (NL)

*Losing effort

CY YOUNG WINNERS OPPOSING EACH OTHER IN WORLD SERIES GAMES

1968   Bob Gibson, St. L. vs. Denny McLain, Det.
        Games 1 and 4
1969   Tom Seaver, NY (NL) vs. Mike Cuellar, Balt.
        Games 1 and 4
1974   Catfish Hunter, Oak. vs. Mike Marshall, L.A.
        Games 1 and 3

WORLD SERIES IN WHICH NEITHER TEAM HAD A 20-GAME WINNER

1975   Cinn. (NL) vs. Bost. (AL)
1976   Cinn. (NL) vs. NY (AL)
1981   L.A. (NL) vs. NY (AL)*
1982   St. L. (NL) vs. Milw. (AL)

1983   Balt. (AL) vs. Phila. (NL)
1984   Det. (AL) vs. S.D. (NL)
1987   MN (AL) vs. St. L. (NL)

*Strike season

BLACK PITCHERS WINNING WORLD SERIES GAMES

Joe Black	1st game, 1952 Series, Bklyn. Dodgers
Bob Gibson	5th and 7th games, 1964 Series, St. L. Cardinals
	1st, 4th, and 7th games, 1967 Series, St. L. Cardinals
	1st and 4th games, 1968 Series, St. L. Cardinals
Mudcat Grant	1st and 6th games, 1965 Series, MN Twins
Grant Jackson	7th game, 1979 Series, Pitt. Pirates
Blue Moon Odom	5th game, 1974 Series, Oak. A's
Dave Stewart	1st and 3rd games, 1989 Series, Oak. A's
John Wyatt	6th game, 1967 Series, Bost. Red Sox

PITCHERS WITH LOWEST ERA IN TOTAL WORLD SERIES PLAY (Min. 25 Innings)

	INNINGS	RUNS	ERA
Jack Billingham, Cinn. (NL) (1972, '75, '76)	25.1	1	0.36
Harry Breechen, St. L. (NL) (1943, '44, '46)	32.2	3	0.83
Babe Ruth, Bost. (AL) (1916, '18)	31	3	0.87
Sherry Smith, Bklyn. (NL) (1916, '20)	30.1	3	0.89
Sandy Koufax, L.A. (NL) (1959, '63, '65, '66)	57	6	0.95
Hippo Vaughn, Chic. (NL) (1918)	27.0	3	1.00
Monte Pearson, NY (AL) (1936, '37, '38, '39)	35.2	4	1.01
Christy Mathewson, NY (NL) (1905, '11, '12, '13)	101.2	12	1.15
Babe Adams, Pitt. (NL) (1909, '25)	28.0	4	1.29

WORLD SERIES GRAND SLAM HOME RUNS

Elmer Smith, Cleveland (AL), October 10, 1920, 5th game, 1st inning, off Burleigh Grimes, Brooklyn
Tony Lazzeri, New York (AL), October 2, 1936, 2nd game, 3rd inning, off Dick Coffman, New York (NL)
Gil McDougald, New York (AL), October 9, 1951, 5th game, 3rd inning, off Larry Jansen, New York (NL)
Mickey Mantle, New York (AL), October 4, 1953, 5th game, 3rd inning, off Russ Meyer, Brooklyn
Yogi Berra, New York (AL), October 5, 1956, 2nd game, 2nd inning, off Don Newcombe, Brooklyn
Bill Skowron, New York (AL), October 10, 1956, 7th game, 7th inning, off Roger Craig, Brooklyn
Bobby Richardson, New York (AL), October 8, 1960, 3rd game, 1st inning, off Clem Labine, Pittsburgh
Chuck Hiller, San Francisco (NL), October 8, 1962, 4th game, 7th inning, off Marshall Bridges, New York
Ken Boyer, St. Louis (NL), October 11, 1964, 4th game, 6th inning, off Al Downing, New York
Joe Pepitone, New York (AL), October 14, 1964, 6th game, 8th inning, off Gordie Richardson, St. Louis
Jim Northrup, Detroit (AL), October 9, 1968, 6th game, 3rd inning, off Larry Jaster, St. Louis
Dave McNally, Baltimore (AL), October 13, 1970, 3rd game, 6th inning, off Wayne Granger, Cincinnati
Dan Gladden, Minnesota (AL), October 17, 1987, 1st game, 4th inning, off Bob Forsch, St. Louis
Kent Hrbek, Minnesota (AL), October 24, 1987, 6th game, 6th inning, off Ken Dayley, St. Louis
Jose Canseco, Oakland (AL), October 15, 1988, 1st game, 2nd inning, off Tim Belcher, Los Angeles

PLAYERS ON THREE DIFFERENT WORLD SERIES CLUBS

Don Baylor	Bost. Red Sox—1986
	MN Twins—1987
	Oak. A's—1988
Joe Bush	Phila. Athletics—1913, 1914
	Bost. Red Sox—1918
	NY Yankees—1922, 1923
Bobby Byrne	Pitt. Pirates—1909
	Phila. Phillies—1915
	Chic. White Sox—1917 (DNP)
Vic Davalillo	Pitt. Pirates—1971
	Oak. A's—1973
	L.A. Dodgers—1977, 1978
Paul Derringer	St. L. Cardinals—1931
	Cinn. Reds—1939, 1940
	Chic. Cubs—1945
Leo Durocher	NY Yankees—1928
	St. L. Cardinals—1934
	Bklyn. Dodgers—1941 (DNP)
Mike Gonzalez	NY Giants—1921 (DNP)
	Chic. Cubs—1929
	St. L. Cardinals—1931 (DNP)
Burleigh Grimes	Bklyn. Dodgers—1920
	St. L. Cardinals—1930, 1931
	Chic. Cubs—1932
Heinie Groh	NY Giants—1912 (DNP), 1922, 1923, 1924
	Cinn. Reds—1919
	Pitt. Pirates—1927
Pinky Higgins	Phila. Athletics—1930 (DNP)
	Det. Tigers—1940
	Bost. Red Sox—1946
Grant Jackson	Balt. Orioles—1971
	NY Yankees—1976
	Pitt. Pirates—1979
Mark Koenig	NY Yankees—1926, 1927, 1928
	Chic. Cubs—1932
	NY Giants—1936
Mike McCormick	Cinn. Reds—1940
	Bost. Braves—1948
	Bklyn. Dodgers—1949

Stuffy McInnis	Phila. Athletics—1910 (DNP), 1911, 1913, 1914
	Bost. Red Sox—1918
	Pitt. Pirates—1925
Fred Merkle	NY Giants—1911, 1912, 1913
	Bklyn. Dodgers—1916
	Chic. Cubs—1918
	NY Yankees—1926 (DNP)
Andy Pafko	Chic. Cubs—1945
	Bklyn. Dodgers—1952
	Milw. Braves—1957, 1958
Billy Pierce	Det. Tigers—1945 (DNP)
	Chic. White Sox—1959
	S.F. Giants—1962
Walter Ruether	Cinn. Reds—1919
	WA Senators—1925
	NY Yankees—1926, 1927 (DNP)
Wally Schang	Phila. Athletics—1913, 1914, 1930 (DNP)
	Bost. Red Sox—1918
	NY Yankees—1921, 1922
Everett Scott	Bost. Red Sox—1915, 1916, 1918
	NY Yankees—1922, 1923
	WA Senators—1925 (DNP)
Earl Smith	NY Giants—1921, 1922
	Pitt. Pirates—1925, 1927
	St. L. Cardinals—1928
Lonnie Smith	Phila. Phillies—1980
	St. L. Cardinals—1982
	K.C. Royals—1985
Tuck Stainback	Chic. Cubs—1935 (DNP)
	Det. Tigers—1940 (DNP)
	NY Yankees—1942, 1943
Eddie Stanky	Bklyn. Dodgers—1947
	Bost. Braves—1948
	NY Giants—1951

PLAYERS WITH SAME LIFETIME BATTING AVERAGE AS THEIR WORLD SERIES OVERALL AVERAGE

Duffy Lewis	11 years (1910–21), Lifetime BA	.284	Danny Murphy	16 years (1900–15), Lifetime BA	.288	
	3 World Series (1912, 1915, 1916)	.284		3 World Series (1905, 1910, 1911)	.288	
Phil Linz	7 years (1962–68), Lifetime BA	.235	Paul Waner	20 years (1926–45), Lifetime BA	.333	
	2 World Series (1963, 1964)	.235		One World Series (1927)	.333	

BATTING CHAMPIONS FACING EACH OTHER IN WORLD SERIES

1909	National League	Honus Wagner, Pitt. Pirates
	American League	Ty Cobb, Det. Tigers
1931	National League	Chick Hafey, St. L. Cardinals
	American League	Al Simmons, Phila. Athletics

| 1954 | National League | Willie Mays, NY Giants |
| | American League | Bobby Avila, Cleve. Indians |

HOME RUN CHAMPIONS FACING EACH OTHER IN WORLD SERIES

1921   Babe Ruth (NY Yankees) and George Kelly (NY Giants)
1928   Babe Ruth (NY Yankees) and Jim Bottomley (St. L. Cardinals)
1936   Lou Gehrig (NY Yankees) and Mel Ott (NY Giants)
1937   Joe DiMaggio (NY Yankees) and Mel Ott (NY Giants)
1956   Mickey Mantle (NY Yankees) and Duke Snider (Bklyn. Dodgers)

HIT HOME RUN IN FIRST TIME AT BAT IN WORLD SERIES

Joe Harris, Washington (AL), 1925
George Watkins, St. Louis (NL), 1930
Mel Ott, New York (NL), 1933
George Selkirk, New York (AL), 1936
Dusty Rhodes, New York (NL), 1954
Elston Howard, New York (AL), 1955
Roger Maris, New York (AL), 1960
Don Mincher, Minnesota (AL), 1965
Brooks Robinson, Baltimore (AL), 1966
Jose Santiago, Boston (AL), 1967

Mickey Lolich, Detroit (AL), 1968
Don Buford, Baltimore (AL), 1969
Gene Tenace*, Oakland (AL), 1972
Jim Mason, New York (AL), 1976
Doug DeCinces, Baltimore (AL), 1979
Amos Otis, Kansas City (AL), 1980
Bob Watson, New York (AL), 1981
Jim Dwyer, Baltimore (AL), 1983
Mickey Hatcher, Los Angeles (NL), 1988
Bill Bathe, S.F. (NL), 1989

*Hit home runs in first two times at bat in World Series

BEST WON-LOST PERCENTAGE IN WORLD SERIES PLAY (Teams Above .500)

	GAMES	WIN/LOSS	PERCENT
K.C.–Oakland A's (AL)	28	17–11	.607
New York Yankees (AL)	187	109–77–1	.586
Philadelphia A's (AL)	43	24–19	.558
New York Mets (NL)	19	11–8	.579
Baltimore Orioles (AL)	33	19–14	.576
Boston Red Sox (AL)	60	33–26–1	.559
Atlanta-Milw.-Boston Braves (NL)	24	13–11	.542
Cleveland Indians (AL)	17	9–8	.529

ROOKIES OF YEAR IN WORLD SERIES

NATIONAL LEAGUE

1947 Jackie Robinson, Bklyn. (1B)
1948 Alvin Dark, Bost. (SS)
1949 Don Newcombe, Bklyn. (P)
1952 Joe Black, Bklyn. (P)
1965 Jim Lefebvre, L.A. (2B)
1976 Pat Zachry, Cinn. (P)
1981 Fernando Valenzuela, L.A. (P)

AMERICAN LEAGUE

1951 Gil McDougald, NY (3B)
1957 Tony Kubek, NY (SS)
1962 Tom Tresh, NY (SS)
1975 Fred Lynn, Bost. (OF)
1988 Walt Weiss, Oak. (SS)

ALL-STAR GAME

PLAYERS WHO MADE THE ALL-STAR ROSTER AFTER STARTING SEASON IN THE MINORS

Don Newcombe, 1949 Brooklyn Dodgers (NL)—Started season with Montreal, International League
Don Schwall, 1961 Boston Red Sox (AL)—Started season with Seattle, PCL
Alvin Davis, 1984 Seattle Mariners (AL)—Started season with Salt Lake City, PCL

PITCHERS WINNING ALL-STAR GAME *AND* WORLD SERIES GAME, SAME SEASON

1937	Lefty Gomez, NY (AL)		1960	Vern Law, Pitt. (NL)
1940	Paul Derringer, Cinn. (NL)		1965	Sandy Koufax, L.A. (NL)
1947	Frank "Spec" Shea, NY (AL)		1977	Don Sutton, L.A. (NL)

PITCHERS WHO PITCHED MORE THAN 3 INNINGS IN ONE ALL-STAR GAME

6	Lefty Gomez, AL 1935	4	Lon Warneke, NL 1933	3.2	Bob Feller, AL 1939
5	Mel Harder, AL 1934	4	Hal Schumacher, NL 1935	3.1	Frank Sullivan, AL 1955
5	Al Benton, AL 1942	4	Spud Chandler, AL 1942	3.1	Joe Nuxhall, NL 1955
5	Larry Jansen, NL 1950	4	Johnny Antonelli, NL 1956	3.1	Ray Narleski, AL 1958
5	Catfish Hunter, AL 1967	4	Lew Burdette, NL 1957		

ALL-STAR MANAGERS WHO NEVER MANAGED IN WORLD SERIES

1961   Paul Richards, Baltimore (AL)—Replaced Casey Stengel, New York
1965   Gene Mauch, Philadelphia (NL)—Replaced Johnny Keane, St. Louis

BROTHERS APPEARING IN ALL-STAR GAME, SAME SEASON

Felipe (Atlanta) and Matty (Pittsburgh) Alou, 1968
Mort and Walker Cooper (both St. Louis, NL), 1942 & '43
Joe (New York, AL) and Dom (Boston, AL) DiMaggio, 1941, 1949 & '50
Carlos (Chicago, AL) and Lee (Cincinnati, NL) May, 1969
Gaylord (San Francisco, NL) and Jim (Minnesota, AL) Perry, 1970
Dixie (Pittsburgh, NL) and Harry (St. Louis and Philadelphia, NL) Walker 1943 & 1947

PLAYERS HITTING HOME RUNS IN ALL-STAR GAME *AND* WORLD SERIES, SAME SEASON

1934	Joe Medwick, St. L. Cardinals		1956	Mickey Mantle, NY Yankees
1936	Lou Gehrig, NY Yankees		1964	Ken Boyer, St. L. Cardinals
1937	Lou Gehrig, NY Yankees		1965	Harmon Killebrew, MN Twins
1939	Joe DiMaggio, NY Yankees		1971	Frank Robinson, Balt. Orioles
1952	Jackie Robinson, Bklyn. Dodgers		1971	Roberto Clemente, Pitt. Pirates
1955	Mickey Mantle, NY Yankees		1977	Steve Garvey, L.A. Dodgers

FATHERS AND SONS, BOTH OF WHOM PLAYED IN ALL-STAR GAME

Gus Bell, 1953, '54, '55, '56, Cincinnati (NL)
Buddy Bell, 1973, Cleveland (AL); 1980, '81, '82, '84, Texas (AL)

Ray Boone, 1954, '56, Detroit (AL)
Bob Boone, 1976, '78, '79, Philadelphia (NL); 1983, California (AL)

PITCHERS WITH NO VICTORIES NAMED TO ALL-STAR TEAM

1976   Dave Laroche, Cleve. (AL)   1987   Tom Henke, Tor. (AL)

MISCELLANY

OLYMPIANS WHO PLAYED MAJOR LEAGUE BASEBALL (In Official Medal Sports)

Ed "Cotton" Minahan	Pitcher, 1907 Cinn. Reds (NL)	1900 (Paris) Track and Field
Al Spalding	Pitcher, 1876–78 Chic. Cubs (NL)	1900 (Paris) Shooting
Jim Thorpe	Outfielder, 1913–15; 1917–19 NY Giants (NL)	1912 (Stockholm) Decathlon
	1917 Cinn. Reds (NL)	
	1919 Bost. Braves (NL)	

BABE RUTH'S YEARLY SALARIES

1914	Red Sox	$1,900	1922	Yankees	$52,000	1930	Yankees	$80,000
1915	Red Sox	$3,500	1923	Yankees	$52,000	1931	Yankees	$80,000
1916	Red Sox	$3,500	1924	Yankees	$52,000	1932	Yankees	$75,000
1917	Red Sox	$5,000	1925	Yankees	$52,000	1933	Yankees	$52,000
1918	Red Sox	$7,000	1926	Yankees	$52,000	1934	Yankees	$37,500
1919	Red Sox	$10,000	1927	Yankees	$70,000	1935	Braves	$25,000
1920	Yankees	$20,000	1928	Yankees	$70,000			
1921	Yankees	$30,000	1929	Yankees	$70,000	Totals	22 Seasons	$855,400

PLAYERS LEADING NEW YORK YANKEES IN HOME RUNS, TRADED BEFORE NEXT SEASON

1907 Danny Hoffman (4)—Traded to St. L. Browns with Jimmy Williams and Hobe Ferris for Fred Glade and Charlie Hemphill
1912 Guy Zinn (6)—Sold to Bost. Braves for cash
1969 Joe Pepitone (27)—Traded to Houst. for Curt Blefary
1975 Bobby Bonds (32)—Traded to CA for Mickey Rivers and Ed Figueroa
1988 Jack Clark (27)—Traded to S.D. for Jimmy Jones, Lance McCullers and Stan Jefferson

BILLY MARTIN'S FIGHTS

May, 1952—versus Jimmy Piersall, Boston Red Sox
July 14, 1952—versus Clint Courtney, St. Louis Browns
April 30, 1953—versus Clint Courtney, St. Louis Browns
July, 1953—versus Matt Batts, Detroit Tigers
May 16, 1957—at Copacabana, with Hank Bauer, Whitey Ford, Yogi Berra, Mickey Mantle, and Johnny Kucks versus patron of night club
August 4, 1960—versus Jim Brewer, Chicago Cubs
July 12, 1966—versus Howard Fox, Traveling Secretary, Minnesota Twins
August 6, 1969—versus Jim Boswell, Minnesota Twins
April 20, 1972—versus Tigers Fan
March 8, 1973—versus Lakeland, Florida, Policeman
May 30, 1974—versus Cleveland Indians Team
September 26, 1974—versus Burt Hawkins, Texas Ranger Traveling Secretary
June 18, 1977—versus Reggie Jackson, Yankees
November 10, 1978—versus Ray Hagar, Sportswriter, in Reno, Nevada
October 25, 1979—versus Joseph Cooper, marshmallow salesman, Minneapolis
May 25, 1983—versus Robin Wayne Olson, night club patron in Anaheim, California
September 20, 1985—versus patron at Cross Keys Inn, Baltimore
September 21, 1985—versus Ed Whitson, Yankees, Cross Keys Inn, Baltimore
May 6, 1988—versus unidentified assailant(s) in bathroom, Lace, Arlington, Texas

FOUR-DECADE PLAYERS

Nick Altrock	1898–1933*		"Minnie" Minoso	1949–1980*
Dan Brouthers	1879–1904		Bobo Newsom	1929–1953
Bill Buckner	1969–1990		Jack O'Connor	1887–1910
Eddie Collins	1906–1930		Jim O'Rourke	1876–1904
Darrell Evans	1969–1990		Jack Quinn	1909–1933
Kid Gleason	1888–1912		John Ryan	1889–1913
Jim Kaat	1959–1983		Nolan Ryan	1966–1990
Tim McCarver	1959–1980		Mickey Vernon	1939–1960
Willie McCovey	1959–1980		Ted Williams	1939–1960
Jim McGuire	1884–1912		Early Wynn	1939–1963

*5 decades

PLAYERS WITH PALINDRONIC SURNAMES (Last Name Same Spelled Forward and Backward)

Truck Hannah	1918–20 NY Yankees	Dave Otto	1987 Oak. A's
Toby Harrah	1969–71 WA Senators	Johnny Reder	1932 Bost. Red Sox
	1972–78 TX Rangers	Mark Salas	1984 St. L. Cardinals
	1979–83 Cleve. Indians		1985–87 MN Twins
	1984 NY Yankees		1987 NY Yankees
	1985–86 TX Rangers		
Eddie Kazak	1948–52 St. L. Cardinals		
	1952 Cinn. Reds		
Dick Nen	1963 L.A. Dodgers		
	1965–67 WA Senators		
	1968 Chic. Cubs		
	1970 WA Senators		

FIRST PLAYER TO BELONG TO ROSTER(S) OF EXPANSION CLUBS

LA Angels	Eli Grba	Seattle Pilots	Marv Staehle
WA Senators	John Gabler	K.C. Royals	Roger Nelson
NY Mets	Hobie Landrith	Mont. Expos	Manny Mota
Houst. Colt .45s	Ed Bressoud	Seattle Mariners	Dave Johnson
S.D. Padres	Ollie Brown	Tor. Blue Jays	Phil Roof

LAST ACTIVE PLAYER ONCE PLAYING FOR . . .

Casey Stengel	Tug McGraw (Played for Stengel in 1965, active until 1984.)
The Bklyn. Dodgers	Bob Aspromonte (Played for Bklyn. in 1956, active until 1971.)
The NY Giants	Willie Mays (Played for NY in 1957, active until 1973.)
The Bost. Braves	Eddie Mathews (Played for Bost. in 1952, active until 1968.)
The Phila. A's	Vic Power (Played for A's in 1954, active until 1965.)
The St. L. Browns	Don Larsen (Played for Browns in 1953, active until 1967.)
The Milw. Braves	Phil Niekro (Played for Milw. in 1965, active until 1987.)
The K.C. A's	Reggie Jackson (Played for K.C. A's in 1967, active until 1987.)
The Houst. Colt .45's	Rusty Staub (Played for Colt 45's in 1964, active until 1985.)
The L.A. Angels	Jim Fregosi (Played for L.A. in 1964, active until 1978.)
The Seattle Pilots	Fred Stanley (Played for Pilots in 1969, active until 1982.)
The WA Senators	Toby Harrah (Played for Senators in 1971, active until 1986.)

FIRST PLAYERS BORN IN TWENTIETH CENTURY TO PLAY IN MAJORS

Ed Corey, Chicago (AL)   Played in 1918; Born, July 13, 1900
John Cavanaugh, Philadelphia (NL)   Played in 1919; Born, June 5, 1900

LAST PLAYERS BORN IN NINETEENTH CENTURY TO PLAY IN MAJORS

Fred Johnson, St. L. (AL)   Played in 1939; Born, March 5, 1894
Jimmy Dykes, Chic. (AL)   Played in 1939; Born, November 10, 1896
Charlie Root, Chic. (NL)   Played in 1941; Born, March 17, 1899
Hod Lisenbee, Cinn. (NL)   Played in 1945; Born, September 23, 1898

NUMBERS RETIRED ON TWO DIFFERENT CLUBS

Henry Aaron   Atl. Braves and Milw. Brewers   44
Rod Carew   CA Angels and MN Twins   29
Casey Stengel   NY Mets and NY Yankees   37

PLAYERS WHO PITCHED AND CAUGHT IN THE SAME GAME

Roger Bresnahan   August 3, 1910   Jeff Newman   September 14, 1977
Bert Campaneris   September 8, 1965   Rick Cerone   July 19, 1987 and August 9, 1987
Cesar Tovar   September 22, 1968

MAJOR LEAGUERS WHO PLAYED FOOTBALL IN SAME SEASON

Red Badgro (OF), St. L. (AL)	1930	NY Giants
Charlie Berry (C), Phila. (AL)	1925	Pottsville Maroons
Joe Berry (2B), NY (NL)	1921	Rochester Jeffs
Garland Buckeye (P), Cleve. (AL)	1926	Chic. Bulls
Bruce Caldwell (OF), Cleve. (AL)	1928	NY Giants
Chuck Corgan (IF), Bklyn. (NL)	1925–27	K.C. Cowboys, NY Giants
Fred Crolius (OF), Pitt. (NL)	1902	Pitt. Pros
Steve Filipowicz (OF), NY (NL)	1945	NY Giants
Walter French (OF), Phila. (AL)	1925	Pottsville Maroons
George Halas (OF), NY (AL)	1919	Decateur Staleys
Bo Jackson (OF), K.C. (AL)	1987–89	L.A. Raiders
Vic Janowicz (3B), Pitt. (NL)	1954	WA Redskins
Bert Kuczynski (P), Phila. (AL)	1943	Det. Lions
Pete Layden (OF), St. L. (AL)	1948	NY Yankees
Christy Mathewson (P), NY (NL)	1902	Pitt. Pros
John Mohardt (2B), Det. (AL)	1922	Chic. Cardinals
Ernie Nevers (P), St. L. (AL)	1926–27	Duluth Eskimos
Ace Parker (SS), Phila. (AL)	1937–38	Bklyn. Dodgers
Al Pierotti (P), Bost. (NL)	1920	Cleve. Tigers
Pid Purdy (OF), Chic. (AL), Cinn. (NL)	1926–27	Green Bay Packers
Dick Reichle (OF), Bost. (AL)	1923	Milw. Badgers
Deion Sanders (OF), NY (AL)	1989	Atl. Falcons
John Scalzi (PH), Bost. (NL)	1931	Bklyn. Dodgers
Richard Smith (C), NY (NL)	1927	Green Bay Packers
Jim Thorpe (OF), NY, Cinn. & Bost. (NL)	1915–1919	Canton Bulldogs
Ernie Vick (C), St. L. (NL)	1925	Det. Panthers
Rube Waddell (P), Phila. (AL)	1902	Pitt. Pros
Tom Whelan (1B), Bost. (NL)	1920	Canton Bulldogs

PERFORMANCES BY OLDEST PLAYERS

	AGE (YEAR/MONTH)		AGE (YEAR/MONTH)
Pitched, Satchel Paige	59–2	Kansas City A's	9/25/65
Batted (0–1), Satchel Paige	59–2	Kansas City A's	9/25/65
Caught, Jim O'Rourke	52–1	New York Giants	9/20/04
Base hit, Minnie Minoso	53–9	Chicago White Sox	9/12/76
Double, Jack Quinn	47–11	Brooklyn Dodgers	6/7/32
Triple, Nick Altrock	48–0	Washington Senators	9/30/24
Homer, Jack Quinn	45–11	Philadelphia A's	6/7/30
Grand Slam Homer, Tony Perez	42–11	Cincinnati Reds	5/13/85
Run Scored, Charlie O'Leary	52–11	St. Louis Browns	9/30/34
RBI, Jack Quinn	47–11	Brooklyn Dodgers	6/7/32
Stolen base, Arlie Latham	50–5	New York Giants	8/18/09
Played 100 games, Cap Anson	45	Chicago Cubs	1897
Won Game (relief), Jack Quinn	48–1	Brooklyn Dodgers	8/14/32
Lost Game (relief), Hoyt Wilhelm	48–11	Los Angeles Dodgers	6/24/72
Pitched CG (won), Phil Niekro	46–5	New York Yankees	10/6/85
Shutout, Phil Niekro	46–6	New York Yankees	10/6/85
No-hitter, Cy Young	41–3	Boston Red Sox	6/30/08

OLDEST PLAYER, EACH POSITION

		AGE
1st Base	Dan Brouthers, 1904 NY Giants (NL)	46
	Cap Anson, 1897 Chic. Cubs (NL)	46
2nd Base	Arlie Latham, 1909 NY Giants (NL)	49
3rd Base	Jimmy Austin, 1929 St. L. Browns (AL)	49
Shortstop	Bobby Wallace, 1918 St. L. Cardinals (NL)	44
Outfield	Nick Altrock, 1929 WA Senators (AL)	53
	Sam Thompson, 1906 Det. Tigers (AL)	46
	Sam Rice, 1934 Cleve. Indians (AL)	44
	Carl Yastrzemski, 1983 Bost. Red Sox (AL)	44
Catcher	Jim O'Rourke, 1904 NY Giants (NL)	52
Pitcher	Satchel Paige, 1965 K.C. A's (AL)	59
Designated Hitter	Minnie Minoso, 1980 Chic. White Sox (AL)	57

YOUNGEST PLAYERS TO PLAY IN MAJORS

Fred Chapman	14 years, 8 months	Pitcher, Phila. (AA) 7/22/1887
Joe Nuxhall	15 years, 10 months	Pitcher, Cinn. (NL) 6/10/1944
Willie McGill	16 years, 6 months	Pitcher, Cleve. (P) 5/8/1890
Joe Stanley	16 years, 6 months	Outfielder, Balt. (U) 9/11/1897
Tommy Brown	16 years, 8 months	Shortstop, Bklyn. (NL) 8/3/1944
Carl Scheib	16 years, 8 months	Pitcher, Phila. (AL) 9/6/1943
Milton Scott	16 years, 9 months	First base, Chic. (NL) 9/30/1882
Jim Derrington	16 years, 10 months	Pitcher, Chic. (AL) 9/30/1956
Putsy Caballero	16 years, 10 months	Third Base, Phila. (NL) 9/14/1944
Rogers McKee	16 years, 11 months	Pitcher, Phila. (NL) 8/18/1943
Alex George	16 years, 11 months	Shortstop, K.C. (AL) 9/16/1955
Merito Acosta	17 years, 0 months	Outfielder, WA (AL) 6/5/1913

YOUNGEST PLAYER, EACH POSITION

POSITION		AGE	TEAM
First Base	Milton Scott	16	Chic. (NL) 1882
Second Base	Ted Sepkowski	18	Cleve. (AL) 1942
Third Base	Putsy Caballero	16	Phila. (NL) 1944
Shortstop	Tommy Brown	16	Bklyn. (NL) 1944
Outfielders	Merito Acosta	17	WA (AL) 1913
	Mel Ott	17	NY (NL) 1926
	Willie Crawford	17	L.A. (NL) 1964
Catcher	Jimmie Foxx	17	Phila. (AL) 1925
Pitchers:			
Right-Handed Pitcher	Fred Chapman	14	Phila. (AA) 1887
Left-Handed Pitcher	Joe Nuxhall	15	Cincinnati (NL) 1944

MOST PRESIDENTIAL ADMINISTRATIONS PLAYED IN

8 Cap Anson, 1876–1897
    Grant (1876)
    Hayes (1887–1881)
    Garfield (1881)
    Arthur (1881–1885)
    Cleveland (1885–1889)
    Harrison (1889–1893)
    Cleveland (1893–1897)
    McKinley (1897)

8 Jim O'Rourke, 1876–93, 1904
    Grant (1876)
    Hayes (1887–1881)
    Garfield (1881)
    Arthur (1881–1885)
    Cleveland (1885–1889)
    Harrison (1889–1893)
    Cleveland (1893)
    T. Roosevelt (1904)

7 Nick Altrock, 1898, 1902–19, 1924, 1929, 1931, 1933
    McKinley (1898)
    T. Roosevelt (1902–1909)
    Taft (1909–1913)
    Wilson (1913–1919)
    Coolidge (1924)
    Hoover (1929, 1931)
    F. Roosevelt (1933)

7 Jim Kaat, 1959–1983
    Eisenhower (1959–1961)
    Kennedy (1961–1963)
    Johnson (1963–1969)
    Nixon (1969–1975)
    Ford (1975–1977)
    Carter (1977–1981)
    Reagan (1959–1983)

TEN-YEAR MEN WHO NEVER PLAYED IN THE MINORS (Since 1900)

YEARS

22	Mel Ott, Outfielder	(1926–47, NY—NL)
22	Al Kaline, Outfielder	(1953–74, Det.—AL)
21	Eppa Rixey, Pitcher	(1912–33, Phila., Cinn.—NL)
21	Ted Lyons, Pitcher	(1923–46, Chic.—AL)
19	Tom Zachary, Pitcher	(1918–36, Phila., WA, St. L., NY—AL; Bost., Bklyn., Phila.—NL)
19	Frankie Frisch, 2nd-3rd Baseman	(1919–37, NY–St. L.—NL)
19	Ernie Banks, Shortstop, 1st Baseman	(1953–71, Chic.—NL)
18	Bob Feller, Pitcher	(1936–56, Cleve.—AL)
18	Eddie Yost, 3rd Baseman	(1944–62, WA, Det., CA—AL)
17	Eddie Plank, Pitcher	(1901–17, Phila., St. L.—AL; St. L.—FL)
17	Danny MacFayden, Pitcher	(1926–43, Bost., NY, WA—AL; Cinn., Bost., Pitt.—NL)
15	Jack Coombs, Pitcher	(1906–20, Phila.—AL; Bklyn.—NL)
15	Catfish Hunter, Pitcher	(1965–79, Oak., NY—AL)
14	Dick Groat, Shortstop	(1952–67, Pitt., St. L., Phila., S.F.—NL)
13	Ethan Allen, Outfielder	(1926–38, Cinn., NY, St. L., Phila., Chic.—NL, St. L.—AL)
13	Billy O'Dell, Pitcher	(1954–67, Balt.—AL; S.F., Milw.–Atl., Pitt.—NL)
12	Johnny Antonelli, Pitcher	(1948–61, Bost.–Milw., NY–S.F.—NL; Cleve.—AL)
12	Sandy Koufax, Pitcher	(1955–66, Bklyn.–L.A.—NL)
11	Jack Barry, Shortstop	(1908–19, Phila., Bost.—AL)
11	Milt Gaston, Pitcher	(1924–34, NY, St. L., WA, Bost., Chic.—AL)
11	Carl Schieb, Pitcher	(1943–54, Phila.—AL; St. L.—NL)

PLAYERS WITH ONE ADDRESS—ONE CLUB AND ONE CITY IN MAJORS, LONGEST

NATIONAL LEAGUE

Adrian "Cap" Anson, Chic. Cubs (Colts)	22 years (1876–97)
Stan Musial, St. L. Cardinals	22 years (1941–44; 1946–63)
Mel Ott, NY Giants	22 years (1926–47)
Willie Stargell, Pitt. Pirates	21 years (1962–82)
Ernie Banks, Chic. Cubs	19 years (1953–71)
Roberto Clemente, Pitt. Pirates	18 years (1955–72)
Ed Kranepool, NY Mets	18 years (1962–79)
Bob Gibson, St. L. Cardinals	17 years (1959–75)
Bill Mazeroski, Pitt. Pirates	17 years (1956–72)
Pie Traynor, Pitt. Pirates	17 years (1920–35; 1937)

AMERICAN LEAGUE

Brooks Robinson, Balt. Orioles	23 years (1955–77)
Carl Yastrzemski, Bost. Red Sox	23 years (1961–83)
Al Kaline, Det. Tigers	22 years (1953–74)
Walter Johnson, WA Senators	21 years (1907–27)
Ted Lyons, Chic. White Sox	21 years (1923–42; 1946)
Luke Appling, Chic. White Sox	20 years (1930–43; 1945–50)
Red Faber, Chic. White Sox	20 years (1914–33)
Mel Harder, Cleve. Indians	20 years (1928–47)
Charlie Gehringer, Det. Tigers	19 years (1924–42)
Ted Williams, Bost. Red Sox	19 years (1939–42; 1946–60)
Ossie Bluege, WA Senators	18 years (1922–39)
Bob Feller, Cleve. Indians	18 years (1936–41; 1945–56)
Mickey Mantle, NY Yankees	18 years (1951–68)
Frankie Crosetti, NY Yankees	17 years (1932–48)
Bill Dickey, NY Yankees	17 years (1928–43; 1946)
Lou Gehrig, NY Yankees	17 years (1923–39)

PLAYERS PLAYING MOST SEASONS IN CITY OF BIRTH

Phil Cavaretta	22	Chic. Cubs, 1935–53 Chic. White Sox, 1954–55
Pete Rose	19	Cinn. Reds, 1963–78, 1984–86
Ed Kranepool	18	NY Mets, 1962–79
Lou Gehrig	17	NY Yankees, 1923–39
Whitey Ford	16	NY Yankees, 1950, 1953–67
Harry Davis	16	Phila. Athletics, 1901–11, 1913–17

FIRST BLACKS ON EACH OF THE 16 ORIGINAL TEAMS

AMERICAN LEAGUE

Bost. Red Sox	Pumpsie Green, second baseman, 1959
Chic. White Sox	Sam Hairston, catcher, 1951
Cleve. Indians	Larry Doby, infielder, 1947
Det. Tigers	Ozzie Virgil, third baseman, 1958
NY Yankees	Elston Howard, outfielder, 1955
Phila. A's	Bob Trice, pitcher, 1953
St. L. Browns	Hank Thompson, second baseman, 1947
WA Senators	Carlos Paula, outfielder, 1954

NATIONAL LEAGUE

Bost. Braves	Sam Jethroe, outfielder, 1950
Bklyn. Dodgers	Jackie Robinson, first baseman, 1947
Chic. Cubs	Ernie Banks, shortstop, 1953
Cinn. Reds	Nino Escalera, outfielder, 1954
NY Giants	Hank Thompson, second baseman, 1949
Phila. Phillies	John Irvin Kennedy, third baseman, 1957
Pitt. Pirates	Curt Roberts, second baseman, 1954
St. L. Cardinals	Tom Alston, first baseman, 1954

PLAYERS WITH SAME SURNAME AS TOWN BORN IN

Estel Crabtree, OF	Crabtree, OH	(Cinn. (NL), 1929–32, 1943–44 St. L. (NL), 1933, 1941–42)
Charlie Gassaway, P	Gassaway, TN	(Chic. (NL), 1944; Phila. (AL), 1945; Cleve. (AL), 1946)
Elmer "Slim" Love, P	Love, MO	(WA (AL), 1913; NY (AL), 1916–18; Det. (AL), 1919–20)
Jack Ogden, P	Ogden, PA	(NY (NL), 1918; St. L. (AL), 1928–29; Cinn. (NL), 1931–32)
Warren "Curly" Ogden, P	Ogden, PA	(Phila. (AL), 1922–24; WA (AL), 1924–26)

THIRD BASEMEN ON TINKER-EVERS-TO-CHANCE CHICAGO CUBS TEAMS (1903–1910)

Doc Casey	1903, 1904, 1905	388 games
Solly Hoffman	1905, 1906, 1907, 1908	20 games
John Kane	1909, 1910	7 games
Bobby Lowe	1903	1 game
George Moriarity	1903, 1904	3 games
Tommy Raub	1903	4 games
Broadway Aleck Smith	1904	1 game
Harry Steinfeldt	1906, 1907, 1908, 1909, 1910	729 games
Otto Williams	1903, 1904	7 games
Heinie Zimmerman	1908, 1910	23 games

FIRST DESIGNATED HITTER FOR EACH AMERICAN LEAGUE TEAM

Balt. Orioles	Terry Crowley	Milw. Brewers	Ollie Brown
Bost. Red Sox	Orlando Cepeda	MN Twins	Tony Oliva
CA Angels	Tom McCraw	NY Yankees	Ron Blomberg
Chic. White Sox	Mike Andrews	Oak. A's	Billy North
Cleve. Indians	John Ellis	Seattle Mariners	Dave Collins
Det. Tigers	Gates Brown	TX Rangers	Rico Carty
K.C. Royals	Ed Kirkpatrick	Tor. Blue Jays	Otto Velez

PLAYERS KILLED AS DIRECT RESULT OF INJURIES SUSTAINED IN MAJOR LEAGUE GAMES

Maurice "Doc" Powers, Catcher, Philadelphia Athletics
  Died April 26, 1909 after three operations for "intestinal problems" after running into wall on April 12, 1909 at Shibe Park Inaugural Game
Ray Chapman, Shortstop, Cleveland Indians
  Died August 17, 1920 after being hit by pitch at the Polo Grounds on August 16, 1920, thrown by New York Yankees pitcher Carl Mays

PLAYERS WHO PLAYED FOR THREE NEW YORK TEAMS

Dan Brouthers	Troy, NY (NL), 1879–80
	Buffalo (NL), 1881–85
	NY (NL), 1904
Jack Doyle	NY (NL), 1893–95; 1898–1900; 1902
	Bklyn. (NL), 1903–04
	NY (AL), 1905
Dude Esterbrook	Buffalo (NL), 1880
	NY (AA), 1883–84; 1887
	NY (NL), 1885–86; 1890
	Bklyn. (NL), 1891
Burleigh Grimes	Bklyn. (NL), 1918–26
	NY (NL), 1927
	NY (AL), 1934
Benny Kauff	NY (AL), 1912
	Bklyn. (FL), 1915
	NY (NL), 1916–20
Willie Keeler	NY (NL), 1892–93; 1910
	Bklyn. (NL), 1893; 1899–1902
	NY (AL), 1903–09
Tony Lazzeri	NY (AL), 1926–37
	Bklyn. (NL), 1939
	NY (NL), 1939
Sal Maglie	NY (NL), 1945; 1950–55
	Bklyn. (NL), 1956–57
	NY (AL), 1957–58

Fred Merkle	NY (NL), 1907–16
	Bklyn. (NL), 1916–17
	NY (AL), 1925–26
Jack Nelson	Troy, NY (NL), 1879
	NY (AA), 1883–87
	NY (NL), 1887
	Bklyn. (AA), 1890
Lefty O'Doul	NY (AL), 1919–20; 1922
	NY (NL), 1928; 1933–34
	Bklyn. (NL), 1931–33
Dave Orr	NY (NL), 1883
	NY (AA), 1884–87
	Bklyn. (AA), 1888
	Bklyn. (PL), 1890
Zack Taylor	Bklyn. (NL), 1920–25; 1935
	NY (NL), 1927
	NY (AL), 1934
Monte Ward	NY (NL), 1883–89; 1893–94
	Bklyn. (PL), 1890
	Bklyn. (NL), 1891–92

PLAYERS WHO PLAYED FOR BOTH THE NEW YORK YANKEES AND THE METS

Neil Allen (Pitcher)	NY Yankees, 1985, 1987 NY Mets, 1979–83	Lee Mazzilli (Outfielder)	NY Yankees, 1982 NY Mets, 1976–81, 1986–88
Jack Aker (Pitcher)	NY Yankees, 1969–72 NY Mets, 1974	Doc Medich (Pitcher)	NY Yankees, 1972–75 NY Mets, 1977
Sandy Alomar (2nd baseman)	NY Yankees, 1974–76 NY Mets, 1967	Dale Murray (Pitcher)	NY Yankees, 1983–85 NY Mets, 1978–79
Tucker Ashford (3rd baseman)	NY Yankees, 1981 NY Mets, 1983	John Pacella (Pitcher)	NY Yankees, 1982 NY Mets, 1977, 1979–80
Yogi Berra (Catcher)	NY Yankees, 1946–63 NY Mets, 1965	Lenny Randle (3rd, 2nd Baseman)	NY Yankees, 1979 NY Mets, 1977–78
Ray Burris (Pitcher)	NY Yankees, 1979 NY Mets, 1979–80	Hal Reniff (Pitcher)	NY Yankees, 1961–67 NY Mets, 1967
John Candelaria (Pitcher)	NY Yankees, 1988 NY Mets, 1987	Rafael Santana (Shortstop)	NY Yankees, 1988 NY Mets, 1984–87
Duke Carmel (Outfielder)	NY Yankees, 1965 NY Mets, 1963	Bill Short (Pitcher)	NY Yankees, 1960 NY Mets, 1968
Billy Cowan (Outfielder)	NY Yankees, 1969 NY Mets, 1965	Charley Smith (3rd Baseman)	NY Yankees, 1967–68 NY Mets, 1964–65
Dock Ellis (Pitcher)	NY Yankees, 1977 NY Mets, 1979	Roy Staiger (3rd Baseman)	NY Yankees, 1979 NY Mets, 1975–77
Tim Foli (Shortstop)	NY Yankees, 1984 NY Mets, 1970–71, 1979	Tom Sturdivant (Pitcher)	NY Yankees, 1955–59 NY Mets, 1964
Bob Friend (Pitcher)	NY Yankees, 1966 NY Mets, 1966	Bill Sudakis (3rd Baseman, DH, 1st Baseman)	NY Yankees, 1974 NY Mets, 1972
Billy Gardner (2nd Baseman)	NY Yankees, 1961–62 NY Mets, 1954–55	Ron Swoboda (Outfielder)	NY Yankees, 1971–73 NY Mets, 1965–70
Jesse Gonder (Catcher)	NY Yankees, 1960–61 NY Mets, 1963–65	Ralph Terry (Pitcher)	NY Yankees, 1956–57, 1959–64 NY Mets, 1966–67
Dave Kingman (Outfielder)	NY Yankees, 1977 NY Mets, 1975–77, 1981–83	Marv Throneberry (1st Baseman)	NY Yankees, 1955, 1958–59 NY Mets, 1962–63
Phil Linz (Shortstop)	NY Yankees, 1962–65 NY Mets, 1967–68	Dick Tidrow (Pitcher)	NY Yankees, 1974–79 NY Mets, 1984
Phil Lombardi (Catcher)	NY Yankees, 1986–87 NY Mets, 1989	Mike Torrez (Pitcher)	NY Yankees, 1977 NY Mets, 1983–84
Elliott Maddox (Outfielder, 3rd Baseman)	NY Yankees, 1974–76 NY Mets, 1978–80	Gene Woodling (Outfielder)	NY Yankees, 1949–54 NY Mets, 1962

PLAYERS WITH BOTH ORIGINAL AND EXPANSION WASHINGTON SENATORS

Rudy Hernandez (Pitcher)   Original Senators, 1960; Expansion Senators, 1961
Hector Maestri (Pitcher)   Original Senators, 1960; Expansion Senators, 1961
Camilo Pascual (Pitcher)   Original Senators, 1954–60; Expansion Senators, 1967–69
Pedro Pamos (Pitcher)   Original Senators, 1955–60; Expansion Senators, 1970
Zoilo Versalles (Shortstop)   Original Senators, 1959–60; Expansion Senators, 1969

PLAYERS WITH BOTH KANSAS CITY As AND KANSAS CITY ROYALS

Moe Drabowsky (Pitcher)   K.C. A's, 1963–65
    K.C. Royals, 1969–70
Aurelio Monteagudo (Pitcher)   K.C. A's, 1963–66
    K.C. Royals, 1970

Ken Sanders (Pitcher)   K.C. A's, 1964; 1966
    K.C. Royals, 1976
Dave Wickersham (Pitcher)   K.C. A's, 1960–63
    K.C. Royals, 1969

PLAYERS PLAYING FOR BOTH MILWAUKEE BRAVES AND MILWAUKEE BREWERS

Hank Aaron (Outfielder, Designated Hitter)   Milw. Braves, 1954–65
    Milw. Brewers, 1975–76
Phil Roof (Catcher)   Milw. Braves, 1961; 1964
    Milw. Brewers, 1970–71

PITCHERS WHO GAVE UP MOST HITS TO PETE ROSE

64 Phil Niekro
60 Don Sutton
42 Juan Marichal
     Gaylord Perry
39 Joe Niekro

38 Claude Osteen
     Ron Reed
36 Bob Gibson
     Ferguson Jenkins

2,500 GAMES IN ONE UNIFORM (Since 1900)

Ernie Banks (Chic. Cubs, 1953–71)   2528
Al Kaline (Det. Tigers, 1953–74)   2834
Stan Musial (St. L. Cardinals, 1941–44; 1946–63)   3026

Mel Ott (NY Giants, 1926–47)   2732
Brooks Robinson (Balt. Orioles, 1955–77)   2896
Carl Yastrzemski (Bost. Red Sox, 1961–83)   3308

TEAM-BY-TEAM LEADERS NATIONAL LEAGUE

ATLANTA BRAVES (BOSTON AND MILWAUKEE)

BATTING

ALL-TIME GAME LEADERS

Hank Aaron (1954–74)	3,076	Herman Long (1890–1902)	1,642
Eddie Mathews (1952–66)	2,223	Bobby Lowe (1890–1901)	1,403
Dale Murphy (1976–1989)	1,829	Del Crandall (1949–50; 1953–63)	1,394
Rabbit Maranville (1912–20; 1929–32; 1935)	1,795	Johnny Logan (1951–61)	1,351
Fred Tenney (1894–1907; 1911)	1,737	Tommy Holmes (1942–51)	1,289

ALL-TIME AT BAT LEADERS

Hank Aaron (1954–74)	11,628	Fred Tenney (1894–1907; 1911)	6,629
Eddie Mathews (1952–66)	8,049	Bobby Lowe (1890–1901)	5,580
Herman Long (1890–1902)	6,767	Tommy Holmes (1942–51)	4,956
Dale Murphy (1976–1989)	6,749	Johnny Logan (1951–61)	4,931
Rabbit Maranville (1912–20; 1929–32; 1935)	6,724	John Morrill (1876–88)	4,759

ALL-TIME RUN LEADERS

Hank Aaron (1954–74)	2,107	Hugh Duffy (1892–1900)	998
Eddie Mathews (1952–66)	1,452	Bobby Lowe (1890–1901)	997
Herman Long (1890–1902)	1,294	Billy Nash (1885–1889; 1891–1895)	857
Fred Tenney (1894–1907; 1911)	1,127	Rabbit Maranville (1912–20; 1929–32; 1935)	801
Dale Murphy (1976–1989)	1,065	John Morrill (1876–88)	800

ALL-TIME HIT LEADERS

Hank Aaron (1954–74)	3,600	Rabbit Maranville (1912–20; 1929–32; 1935)	1,696
Eddie Mathews (1952–66)	2,201	Bobby Lowe (1890–1901)	1,606
Fred Tenney (1894–1907; 1911)	2,002	Hugh Duffy (1892–1900)	1,560
Herman Long (1890–1902)	1,911	Tommy Holmes (1942–51)	1,503
Dale Murphy (1976–89)	1,820	Billy Nash (1885–89; 1891–95)	1,345

ALL-TIME DOUBLE LEADERS

Hank Aaron (1954–74)	600	Wally Berger (1930–37)	248
Eddie Mathews (1952–66)	338	Rabbit Maranville (1912–20; 1929–32; 1935)	244
Dale Murphy (1976–89)	292	Fred Tenney (1894–1907; 1911)	236
Tommy Holmes (1942–51)	291	John Morrill (1876–88)	234
Herman Long (1890–1902)	277	Johnny Logan (1951–61)	207

ALL-TIME TRIPLE LEADERS

Rabbit Maranville (1912–20; 1929–32; 1935)	103	Fred Tenney (1894–1907; 1911)	77
Hank Aaron (1954–66)	96	Billy Nash (1885–89; 1891–95)	76
Herman Long (1890–1902)	89	Hugh Duffy (1892–1900)	72
John Morrill (1876–88)	80	Bobby Lowe (1890–1901)	70
Bill Bruton (1953–60)	79	Eddie Mathews (1952–66)	70

ALL-TIME HOME RUN LEADERS

Hank Aaron (1954–76)	733	Wally Berger (1930–37)	199
Eddie Mathews (1952–66)	493	Del Crandall (1949–50; 1953–63)	170
Dale Murphy (1976–89)	354	Joe Torre (1960–68)	142
Joe Adcock (1953–62)	239	Darrell Evans (1969–76)	120
Bob Horner (1978–86)	215	Rico Carty (1963–72)	109

ALL-TIME TOTAL BASE LEADERS

Hank Aaron (1954–76)	6,591	Rabbit Maranville (1912–20; 1929–32; 1935)	2,215
Eddie Mathews (1952–66)	4,158	Wally Berger (1930–37)	2,212
Dale Murphy (1976–89)	3,248	Joe Adcock (1953–62)	2,162
Herman Long (1890–1902)	2,630	Tommy Holmes (1942–51)	2,152
Fred Tenney (1894–1907; 1911)	2,440	Bobby Lowe (1890–1901)	2,113

ALL-TIME RBI LEADERS

Hank Aaron (1954–76)	2,202	Billy Nash (1885–89; 1891–95)	809
Eddie Mathews (1952–66)	1,388	Joe Adcock (1953–62)	760
Dale Murphy (1976–89)	1,088	Wally Berger (1930–37)	746
Herman Long (1890–1902)	961	Bob Horner (1978–86)	652
Bobby Lowe (1890–1901)	872		

ALL-TIME EXTRA BASE HIT LEADERS

Hank Aaron (1954–76)	1,429	Herman Long (1890–1902)	454
Eddie Mathews (1952–66)	901	Tommy Holmes (1942–51)	426
Dale Murphy (1976–89)	683	Bob Horner (1978–86)	382
Wally Berger (1930–37)	499	Rabbit Maranville (1912–20; 1929–32; 1935)	370
Joe Adcock (1953–62)	458	Del Crandall (1949–50; 1953–63)	354

ALL-TIME BATTING AVERAGE LEADERS
(500 or more games)

Billy Hamilton (1896–1901)	.338	Lance Richbourg (1927–31)	.311
Hugh Duffy (1892–1900)	.336	Hank Aaron (1954–74)	.310
Chick Stahl (1897–1900)	.328	Jimmy Collins (1895–1900)	.310
Ralph Garr (1968–75)	.317	Wally Berger (1930–37)	.304
Rico Carty (1963–72)	.317	Tommy Holmes (1942–51)	.303

ALL-TIME STOLEN BASE LEADERS

Hank Aaron (1954–74)	240	Fred Tenney (1894–1907; 1911)	145
Rabbit Maranville (1912–20; 1929–32; 1935)	194	Bill Bruton (1953–60)	143
Jerry Royster (1976–84)	174	Ralph Garr (1968–75)	137
Bill Sweeney (1907–13)	153	Claudell Washington (1981–86)	115
Dale Murphy (1976–89)	151	Sam Jethroe (1950–52)	98

PITCHING

ALL-TIME GAME LEADERS

Warren Spahn (1942; 1946–64)	714	Rick Camp (1976–85)	414
Phil Niekro (1964–83)	689	Bob Smith (1925–30; 1933–37)	349
Gene Garber (1978–87)	557	Ed Brandt (1928–36)	321
Kid Nichols (1890–1901)	543	Vic Willis (1898–1905)	320
Lew Burdette (1951–63)	468	Ben Cantwell (1928–36)	290

ALL-TIME WIN LEADERS

Warren Spahn (1942; 1946–64)	356	Vic Willis (1898–1905)	149
Kid Nichols (1890–1901)	330	John Clarkson (1888–1892)	148
Phil Niekro (1964–83)	268	Jim Whitney (1881–85)	133
Lew Burdette (1951–63)	179	Jack Stivetts (1892–98)	130
Tommy Bond (1877–81)	149	Dick Rudolph (1913–23; 1927)	122

ALL-TIME INNINGS PITCHED LEADERS

Warren Spahn (1942; 1946–64)	5,046	Jim Whitney (1881–85)	2,263
Kid Nichols (1890–1901)	4,570	Tommy Bond (1877–81)	2,127
Phil Niekro (1964–83)	4,532	John Clarkson (1888–92)	2,093
Lew Burdette (1951–63)	2,639	Dick Rudolph (1913–23; 1927)	2,034
Vic Willis (1898–1905)	2,575	Ed Brandt (1928–36)	1,996

ALL-TIME LOSS LEADERS

Phil Niekro (1964–83)	230	Lew Burdette (1951–63)	120
Warren Spahn (1942; 1946–64)	229	Bob Smith (1925–30; 1933–37)	120
Kid Nichols (1890–1901)	182	Ed Brandt (1928–36)	119
Vic Willis (1898–1905)	146	Dick Rudolph (1913–23; 1927)	107
Jim Whitney (1881–85)	121	Ben Cantwell (1928–36)	106

ALL-TIME SHUTOUT LEADERS

Warren Spahn (1942; 1946–64)	63	Vic Willis (1898–1905)	26
Kid Nichols (1890–1901)	44	Dick Rudolph (1913–23; 1927)	25
Phil Niekro (1964–83)	43	Lefty Tyler (1910–17)	21
Tommy Bond (1877–81)	30	John Clarkson (1888–92)	20
Lew Burdette (1951–63)	30	Charlie Buffinton (1882–86)	19

ALL-TIME STRIKEOUT LEADERS

Phil Niekro (1964–83)	2,855	Lew Burdette (1951–63)	923
Warren Spahn (1942; 1946–64)	2,493	Charlie Buffinton (1882–86)	911
Kid Nichols (1890–1901)	1,684	Denny Lemaster (1962–67)	842
Vic Willis (1898–1905)	1,161	John Clarkson (1888–92)	834
Jim Whitney (1881–85)	1,157	Tony Cloninger (1961–68)	834

ALL-TIME WALK LEADERS

Phil Niekro (1964–83)	1,452	Lefty Tyler (1910–17)	678
Warren Spahn (1942; 1946–64)	1,378	Ed Brandt (1928–36)	676
Kid Nichols (1890–1901)	1,159	John Clarkson (1888–92)	676
Vic Willis (1898–1905)	854	Jack Stivetts (1892–98)	651
Bob Buhl (1953–62)	782	Bob Smith (1925–30; 1933–37)	561

ALL-TIME WON-LOST PERCENTAGE LEADERS

Fred Klobedanz (1896–99; 1902)	.679	Jack Stivetts (1892–98)	.625
Harry Staley (1891–94)	.655	Ted Lewis (1896–1901)	.624
Kid Nichols (1890–1901)	.645	Warren Spahn (1942; 1946–64)	.609
John Clarkson (1888–92)	.643	Bob Buhl (1953–62)	.602
Tommy Bond (1877–81)	.631	Lew Burdette (1951–63)	.599

ALL-TIME SAVES LEADERS

Gene Garber (1978–87)	141	Bruce Stutter (1985–88)	40
Cecil Upshaw (1966–73)	78	Bob Smith (1925–30; 1933–37)	36
Rick Camp (1976–85)	57	Claude Raymond (1961–63; 1967–69)	33
Don McMahon (1957–62)	50	Phil Niekro (1964–83)	29
Steve Bedrosian (1981–85)	41	Warren Spahn (1942; 1946–64)	29

BRAVES LEAGUE LEADERS

BATTING

BATTING AVERAGE
R. Hornsby, 1928
E. Lombardi, 1942
H. Aaron, 1954, '59
R. Carty, 1970
R. Garr, 1974

HOME RUNS
H. Long, 1900
D. Brain, 1907
F. Beck, 1910 (Tie)
W. Berger, 1935
T. Holmes, 1945
E. Mathews, 1953, '59
H. Aaron, 1957, '63 (Tie), '66, '67
D. Murphy, 1984 (Tie), '85

HITS
G. Beaumont, 1907
D. Miller, 1911
E. Brown, 1926
T. Holmes, 1945, '47
H. Aaron, 1956, '59
R. Schoendienst, 1957 (Also with NY)
F. Alou, 1966, '68 (Tie)
R. Garr, 1974

RBI
W. Berger, 1935
H. Aaron, 1957, '60, '63, '66
D. Murphy, 1982 (Tie), '83

RUNS SCORED
E. Torgeson, 1950
H. Aaron, 1957, '63, '67 (Tie)
B. Bruton, 1960
F. Alou, 1966
D. Murphy, 1985

DOUBLES
T. Holmes, 1945
H. Aaron, 1955 (Tie), '56, '61, '65
J. Logan, 1955 (Tie)
L. Maye, 1964

TRIPLES
R. Powell, 1921 (Tie)
B. Bruton, 1956, '60
R. Garr, 1974, '75
B. Butler, 1983

STOLEN BASES
S. Jethroe, 1950, '51
B. Bruton, 1953, '54, '55

PITCHING
(Post–1900)

WON-LOST PERCENTAGE
W. James, 1914
T. Hughes, 1916
L. Benton, 1927 (Also NY)
B. Cantwell, 1933
R. Buhl, 1957
W. Spahn, 1958
P. Niekro, 1982

WINS
R. Rudolph, 1914
C. Barrett, 1945 (Also St. L.)
J. Sain, 1948
W. Spahn, 1949, 1950, 1953, 1957, 1958, 1959, 1960, 1961
L. Burdette, 1959 (Tie)
P. Niekro, 1974, 1979 (Tie)

STRIKEOUTS
W. Spahn, 1949, 1950, 1951, 1952
P. Niekro, 1977

ERA
J. Turner, 1937
W. Spahn, 1947, 1953, 1961
C. Nichols, 1951
L. Burdette, 1956
P. Niekro, 1967
L. Capra, 1974

SAVES
V. Willis, 1902
D. McMahon, 1959 (Tie)

MOST VALUABLE PLAYERS
J. Evers, 1914
B. Elliott, 1947
H. Aaron, 1957
D. Murphy, 1982, '83

ROOKIES OF THE YEAR
A. Dark, 1948
S. Jethroe, 1950
E. Williams, 1971
B. Horner, 1978

CY YOUNG WINNER
W. Spahn, 1957

CHICAGO CUBS

BATTING

ALL-TIME GAME LEADERS

Ernie Banks (1953–71)	2,528	Stan Hack (1932–47)	1,938
Cap Anson (1876–97)	2,253	Gabby Hartnett (1922–40)	1,926
Billy Williams (1959–74)	2,213	Jimmy Ryan (1885–89; 1891–1900)	1,656
Ron Santo (1960–73)	2,126	Don Kessinger (1964–75)	1,648
Phil Cavaretta (1934–53)	1,953	Wildfire Schulte (1904–16)	1,558

ALL-TIME AT BAT LEADERS

Ernie Banks (1953–71)	9,421	Jimmy Ryan (1885–89; 1891–1900)	6,803
Cap Anson (1876–97)	9,084	Phil Cavaretta (1934–53)	6,592
Billy Williams (1959–74)	8,479	Don Kessinger (1964–75)	6,355
Ron Santo (1960–73)	7,768	Gabby Hartnett (1922–40)	6,282
Stan Hack (1932–47)	7,278	Wildfire Schulte (1904–16)	5,837

ALL-TIME RUN LEADERS

Cap Anson (1876–97)	1,712	Ron Santo (1960–73)	1,109
Jimmy Ryan (1885–89; 1891–1900)	1,406	Phil Cavaretta (1934–53)	968
Billy Williams (1959–74)	1,306	Bill Dahlen (1891–98)	899
Ernie Banks (1953–71)	1,305	Billy Herman (1931–41)	875
Stan Hack (1932–47)	1,239	Gabby Hartnett (1922–40)	847

ALL-TIME HIT LEADERS

Cap Anson (1876–97)	3,081	Jimmy Ryan (1885–89; 1891–1900)	2,153
Ernie Banks (1953–71)	2,583	Phil Cavaretta (1934–53)	1,927
Billy Williams (1959–74)	2,510	Gabby Hartnett (1922–40)	1,867
Stan Hack (1932–47)	2,193	Billy Herman (1931–41)	1,710
Ron Santo (1960–73)	2,171	Don Kessinger (1964–75)	1,619

ALL-TIME DOUBLE LEADERS

Cap Anson (1876–97)	530	Ron Santo (1960–73)	353
Ernie Banks (1953–71)	407	Jimmy Ryan (1885–89; 1891–1900)	350
Billy Williams (1959–74)	402	Billy Herman (1931–41)	346
Gabby Hartnett (1922–40)	391	Phil Cavaretta (1934–53)	341
Stan Hack (1932–47)	363	Charlie Grimm (1925–36)	270

ALL-TIME TRIPLE LEADERS

Jimmy Ryan (1885–89; 1891–1900)	136	Joe Tinker (1902–12; 1916)	93
Cap Anson (1876–97)	129	Ernie Banks (1953–71)	90
Wildfire Schulte (1904–16)	117	Billy Williams (1959–74)	87
Bill Dahlen (1891–98)	106	Bill Lange (1893–99)	83
Phil Cavaretta (1934–53)	99	Stan Hack (1932–47)	81

ALL-TIME HOME RUN LEADERS

Ernie Banks (1953–71)	512	Hank Sauer (1949–55)	198
Billy Williams (1959–74)	392	Hack Wilson (1926–31)	190
Ron Santo (1960–73)	337	Leon Durham (1981–87)	135
Gabby Hartnett (1922–40)	231	Andy Pafko (1943–51)	126
Bill Nicholson (1939–48)	205	Jody Davis (1981–87)	116

ALL-TIME TOTAL BASE LEADERS

Ernie Banks (1953–71)	4,706	Jimmy Ryan (1885–89; 1891–1900)	3,054
Billy Williams (1959–74)	4,262	Stan Hack (1932–47)	2,889
Cap Anson (1876–97)	4,145	Phil Cavaretta (1934–53)	2,742
Ron Santo (1960–73)	3,667	Wildfire Schulte (1904–16)	2,351
Gabby Hartnett (1922–40)	3,079	Billy Herman (1931–41)	2,305

ALL-TIME RBI LEADERS

Cap Anson (1876–97)	1,715	Jimmy Ryan (1885–89; 1891–1900)	914
Ernie Banks (1953–71)	1,636	Phil Cavaretta (1934–53)	896
Billy Williams (1959–74)	1,354	Bill Nicholson (1939–48)	833
Ron Santo (1960–73)	1,290	Hack Wilson (1926–31)	768
Gabby Hartnett (1922–40)	1,153	Wildfire Schulte (1904–16)	712

ALL-TIME EXTRA BASE HIT LEADERS

Ernie Banks (1953–71)	1,009	Jimmy Ryan (1885–89; 1981–1900)	579
Billy Williams (1959–74)	881	Phil Cavaretta (1934–53)	532
Ron Santo (1960–73)	756	Bill Nicholson (1939–48)	503
Cap Anson (1876–97)	751	Stan Hack (1932–47)	501
Gabby Hartnett (1922–40)	686	Wildfire Schulte (1904–16)	462

ALL-TIME BATTING AVERAGE LEADERS (500 or more games)

Cap Anson (1876–97)	.339	Hack Wilson (1926–31)	.322
Riggs Stephenson (1926–34)	.336	George Gore (1879–86)	.316
Bill Lange (1893–99)	.336	Jimmy Ryan (1885–89; 1891–1900)	.316
Bill Everett (1895–1900)	.326	King Kelly (1880–86)	.314
Kiki Cuyler (1928–35)	.325	Frank Demaree (1932–38)	.309

ALL-TIME STOLEN BASE LEADERS

Frank Chance (1898–1912)	387	Stan Hack (1932–47)	165
Joe Tinker (1902–12; 1916)	304	Jimmy Sheckard (1906–12)	163
Johnny Evers (1902–13)	281	Ivan DeJesus (1977–81)	154
Ryne Sandberg (1982–89)	250	Kiki Cuyler (1928–35)	153
Wildfire Schulte (1904–16)	200	Solly Hofman (1904–12; 1916)	153
Jimmy Slagle (1902–08)	198		

PITCHING

ALL-TIME GAME LEADERS

Charlie Root (1926–41)	605	Bill Hutchinson (1889–95)	367
Lee Smith (1980–87)	458	Bill Lee (1934–43; 1947)	364
Don Elston (1953–64)	449	Rick Reuschel (1972–84)	358
Guy Bush (1923–34)	428	Mordecai "Three Finger" Brown (1904–12; 1916)	346
Ferguson Jenkins (1966–73; 1982–83)	401	Bob Rush (1948–57)	339

ALL-TIME WIN LEADERS

Charlie Root (1926–41)	201	Clark Griffith (1893–1900)	152
Mordecai "Three Finger" Brown (1904–12; 1916)	188	James "Hippo" Vaughn (1913–21)	151
Bill Hutchinson (1889–95)	181	Bill Lee (1934–43; 1947)	139
Ferguson Jenkins (1966–73; 1982–83)	167	John Clarkson (1884–87)	136
Guy Bush (1923–34)	152	Ed Reulbach (1905–13)	136

ALL-TIME INNINGS PITCHED LEADERS

Charlie Root (1926–41)	3,138	Rick Reuschel (1972–84)	2,291
Bill Hutchinson (1889–95)	3,026	Bill Lee (1934–43; 1947)	2,271
Ferguson Jenkins (1966–73; 1982–83)	2,673	James "Hippo" Vaughn (1913–21)	2,216
Larry Corcoran (1880–85)	2,338	Guy Bush (1923–35)	2,201
Three Finger Brown (1904–12; 1916)	2,329	Clark Griffith (1893–1900)	2,189

ALL-TIME LOSS LEADERS

Charlie Root (1926–41)	156	Bill Lee (1934–43; 1947)	123
Bill Hutchinson (1889–95)	154	Dick Ellsworth (1958; 1960–66)	110
Bob Rush (1948–57)	140	James "Hippo" Vaughn (1913–21)	104
Ferguson Jenkins (1966–73; 1982–83)	132	Guy Bush (1923–35)	101
Rick Reuschel (1972–84)	127	Claude Passeau (1939–47)	94

ALL-TIME SHUTOUT LEADERS

Mordecai "Three Finger" Brown (1904–12; 1916) 50
James "Hippo" Vaughn (1913–21) 35
Ed Reulbach (1905–13) 31
Ferguson Jenkins (1966–73; 1982–83) 29
Orval Overall (1906–10; 1913) 28

Bill Lee (1934–43; 1947) 25
Bill Hutchinson (1890–95) 21
Larry French (1935–41) 21
Charlie Root (1926–41) 21
Carl Lundgren (1902–09) 19

ALL-TIME STRIKEOUT LEADERS

Ferguson Jenkins (1966–73; 1982–83) 2,038
Charlie Root (1926–41) 1,432
Rick Reuschel (1972–84) 1,367
Bill Hutchinson (1889–95) 1,226
James "Hippo" Vaughn (1913–21) 1,138

Larry Corcoran (1880–85) 1,086
Bob Rush (1948–57) 1,076
Three Finger Brown (1904–12; 1916) 1,043
John Clarkson (1884–87) 997
Ken Holtzman (1965–71; 1978–79) 988

ALL-TIME WALK LEADERS

Bill Hutchinson (1889–95) 1,106
Charlie Root (1926–41) 871
Guy Bush (1923–35) 734
Bob Rush (1948–57) 725
Bill Lee (1934–43; 1947) 704

Sheriff Blake (1924–31) 661
Ed Reulbach (1905–13) 650
Rick Reuschel (1972–84) 640
James "Hippo" Vaughn (1913–21) 621
Ferguson Jenkins (1966–73; 1982–83) 600

ALL-TIME ERA LEADERS

Three Finger Brown (1904–12; 1916) 1.80
Jack Pfiester (1906–11) 1.86
Orval Overall (1906–10; 1913) 1.92
Jake Weimer (1903–05) 2.15
Ed Reulbach (1905–13) 2.24

Larry Corcoran (1880–85) 2.26
James "Hippo" Vaughn (1913–21) 2.33
Terry Larkin (1878–79) 2.34
John Clarkson (1884–87) 2.39
Carl Lundgren (1902–09) 2.42

ALL-TIME WON-LOST PERCENTAGE LEADERS

John Clarkson (1884–87) .705
Three Finger Brown (1904–12; 1916) .689
Ed Reulbach (1905–13) .680
Larry Corcoran (1880–85) .670
Orval Overall (1906–10; 1913) .662

Jack Pfiester (1906–11) .636
Fred Goldsmith (1880–84) .633
Jake Weimer (1903–05) .628
Carl Lundgren (1902–09) .621
Clark Griffith (1893–1900) .620

ALL-TIME SAVE LEADERS

Lee Smith (1980–87)	180	Three Finger Brown (1904–12; 1916)	39
Bruce Sutter (1976–80)	133	Lindy McDaniel (1963–65)	39
Don Elston (1953; 1957–64)	63	Jack Aker (1972–73)	29
Phil Regan (1969–72)	60	Dutch Leonard (1949–53)	28
Charlie Root (1926–41)	40	Turk Lown (1951–58)	28
Ted Abernathy (1965–66; 1969–70)	39		

CUBS LEAGUE LEADERS

BATTING

BATTING AVERAGE
 H. Zimmerman, 1912
 P. Cavaretta, 1945
 B. Williams, 1972
 B. Madlock, 1975, '76
 B. Buckner, 1980

HOME RUNS
 W. Schulte, 1910 (Tie), '11
 H. Zimmerman, 1912
 H. Wilson, 1926, '27 (Tie), '28 (Tie), '30
 B. Nicholson, 1943, '44
 H. Sauer, 1952 (Tie)
 E. Banks, 1958, '60
 D. Kingman, 1979
 A. Dawson, 1987

HITS
 H. Steinfeldt, 1906
 H. Zimmerman, 1912
 C. Hollocher, 1918
 B. Herman, 1935
 S. Hack, 1940 (Tie), '41
 P. Cavaretta, 1944 (Tie)
 B. Williams, 1970 (Tie)

RBI
 H. Steinfeldt, 1906 (Tie)
 W. Schulte, 1911
 H. Zimmerman, 1912, '16 (Also with NY)
 H. Wilson, 1929, '30
 B. Nicholson, 1943, '44
 H. Sauer, 1952
 E. Banks, 1958, '59
 A. Dawson, 1987

RUNS SCORED
 F. Chance, 1906 (Tie)
 J. Sheckard, 1911
 T. Leach, 1913 (Tie)
 R. Hornsby, 1929
 A. Galan, 1935
 B. Nicholson, 1944
 G. Beckert, 1968
 B. Williams, 1970
 I. DeJesus, 1978
 R. Sandberg, 1984

DOUBLES
 H. Zimmerman, 1912
 R. Stephenson, 1927
 K. Cuyler, 1934
 B. Herman, 1935
 B. Buckner, 1981

TRIPLES
 W. Schulte, 1906 (Tie)
 V. Saier, 1913
 B. Herman, 1939

 G. Altman, 1960
 R. Sandberg, 1984 (Tie)

STOLEN BASES
 F. Chance, 1903 (Tie), '06
 B. Maloney, 1905 (Tie)
 K. Cuyler, 1928, '29, '30
 A. Galan, 1935, '37
 S. Hack, 1938, '39 (Tie)

PITCHING
(Post–1900)

WON-LOST PERCENTAGE
 E. Reulbach, 1906, 1907, 1908
 K. Cole, 1910
 B. Humphries, 1913
 C. Hendrix, 1918
 C. Root, 1929
 L. Warneke, 1932
 W. Lee, 1935, 1938

WINS
 M. Brown, 1909
 L. Cheney, 1912
 J. Vaughn, 1918
 G. Alexander, 1920
 C. Root, 1927
 P. Malone, 1929, 1930
 L. Warneke, 1932
 W. Lee, 1938
 L. Jackson, 1964
 F. Jenkins, 1971
 R. Sutcliffe, 1987

STRIKEOUTS
 F. Beebe, 1906 (Also St. L.)
 O. Overall, 1909
 J. Vaughn, 1918, 1919
 P. Malone 1929
 C. Bryant, 1938
 C. Passeau, 1939 (Also Phila.)
 J. Schmitz, 1946
 S. Jones, 1955, 1956
 F. Jenkins, 1969

ERA
 J. Taylor, 1902
 M. Brown, 1906
 J. Pfiester, 1907
 J. Vaughn, 1918
 G. Alexander, 1919, 1920
 L. Warneke, 1932
 W. Lee, 1938
 H. Borowy, 1945 (Also NY)

SAVES
 C. Lundgren, 1903 (Tie)
 M. Brown, 1908 (Tie), '09, '10, '11
 L. Cheney, 1913

G. Bush, 1925 (Tie), '29 (Tie)
L. McDaniel, 1963
T. Abernathy, 1965
P. Regan, 1968 (Also with L.A.)
B. Sutter, 1979, '80
L. Smith, 1983

MOST VALUABLE PLAYERS
W. Schulte, 1911
R. Hornsby, 1929
G. Hartnett, 1935
P. Cavaretta, 1945
H. Sauer, 1952
E. Banks, 1958, 1959

R. Sandberg, 1984
A. Dawson, 1987

ROOKIES OF YEAR
B. Williams, 1961
K. Hubbs, 1962
T. Walton, 1989

CY YOUNG WINNERS
F. Jenkins, 1971
B. Sutter, 1979
R. Sutcliffe, 1984

CINCINNATI REDS

BATTING

ALL-TIME GAME LEADERS

Pete Rose (1963–78; 1984–86)	2,722	Frank Robinson (1956–65)	1,502
Dave Concepcion (1970–88)	2,488	Dan Driessen (1973–84)	1,480
Johnny Bench (1967–83)	2,158	Edd Roush (1916–26; 1931)	1,399
Tony Perez (1964–76; 1984–86)	1,948	Roy McMillan (1951–60)	1,348
Vada Pinson (1958–68)	1,565	Ted Kluszewski (1947–57)	1,339

ALL-TIME AT BAT LEADERS

Pete Rose (1963–78; 1984–86)	10,934	Frank Robinson (1956–65)	5,527
Dave Concepcion (1970–88)	8,723	Edd Roush (1916–26; 1931)	5,384
Johnny Bench (1967–83)	7,658	Ted Kluszewski (1947–57)	4,961
Tony Perez (1964–76; 1984–86)	6,846	Frank McCormick (1934–45)	4,787
Vada Pinson (1958–68)	6,335	Dan Driessen (1973–84)	4,717

ALL-TIME RUN LEADERS

Pete Rose (1963–78; 1984–86)	1,741	Tony Perez (1964–76; 1984–86)	936
Johnny Bench (1967–83)	1,091	Bid McPhee (1890–99)	919
Frank Robinson (1956–65)	1,043	Joe Morgan (1972–79)	816
Dave Concepcion (1970–88)	993	Edd Roush (1916–26; 1931)	815
Vada Pinson (1958–68)	978	Ted Kluszewski (1947–57)	745

ALL-TIME HIT LEADERS

Pete Rose (1963–78; 1984–86)	3,358	Edd Roush (1916–26; 1931)	1,784
Dave Concepcion (1970–88)	2,326	Frank Robinson (1956–65)	1,673
Johnny Bench (1967–83)	2,048	Ted Kluszewski (1947–57)	1,499
Tony Perez (1964–76; 1984–86)	1,934	Frank McCormick (1934–45)	1,439
Vada Pinson (1958–68)	1,881	Gus Bell (1953–61)	1,343

ALL-TIME DOUBLE LEADERS

Pete Rose (1963–78; 1984–86)	601	Frank Robinson (1956–65)	318
Dave Concepcion (1970–88)	389	Frank McCormick (1934–45)	285
Johnny Bench (1967–83)	381	Edd Roush (1916–26; 1931)	260
Vada Pinson (1958–68)	342	Ted Kluszewski (1947–57)	244
Tony Perez (1964–76; 1984–86)	339	Dan Driessen (1973–84)	240

ALL-TIME TRIPLE LEADERS

Edd Roush (1916–26; 1931)	153	Mike Mitchell (1907–12)	88
Pete Rose (1963–78; 1984–86)	115	Jake Beckley (1897–1903)	80
Bid McPhee (1890–99)	111	Ival Goodman (1935–42)	79
Vada Pinson (1958–68)	96	Jake Daubert (1919–24)	78
Curt Walker (1924–30)	94	Heinie Groh (1913–21)	75

REDS ALL-TIME HOME RUN LEADERS

Johnny Bench (1967–83)	389	Vada Pinson (1958–68)	186
Frank Robinson (1956–65)	324	Wally Post (1949–57; 1960–63)	172
Tony Perez (1964–76; 1984–86)	287	Gus Bell (1953–61)	160
Ted Kluszewski (1947–57)	251	Joe Morgan (1972–79)	152
George Foster (1971–81)	244	Pete Rose (1963–78; 1984–86)	152

ALL-TIME TOTAL BASE LEADERS

Pete Rose (1963–78; 1984–86)	4,645	Vada Pinson (1958–68)	2,973
Johnny Bench (1967–83)	3,644	Ted Kluszewski (1947–57)	2,542
Tony Perez (1964–76; 1984–86)	3,246	Edd Roush (1916–26; 1931)	2,488
Dave Concepcion (1970–88)	3,114	George Foster (1971–81)	2,289
Frank Robinson (1956–65)	3,063	Gus Bell (1953–61)	2,121

ALL-TIME RBI LEADERS

Johnny Bench (1967–83)	1,376	Ted Kluszewski (1947–57)	886
Tony Perez (1964–76; 1984–86)	1,192	George Foster (1971–81)	861
Pete Rose (1963–78; 1984–86)	1,036	Vada Pinson (1958–68)	814
Frank Robinson (1956–65)	1,009	Frank McCormick (1934–45)	803
Dave Concepcion (1970–88)	950	Edd Roush (1916–26; 1931)	459

ALL-TIME EXTRA BASE HIT LEADERS

Pete Rose (1963–78; 1984–86)	868	Dave Concepcion (1970–88)	538
Johnny Bench (1967–83)	794	Ted Kluszewski (1947–57)	518
Frank Robinson (1956–65)	692	George Foster (1971–81)	488
Tony Perez (1964–76; 1985–86)	682	Edd Roush (1916–26; 1931)	459
Vada Pinson (1958–68)	624	Gus Bell (1953–61)	423

ALL-TIME BATTING AVERAGE LEADERS
(500 or more games)

Cy Seymour (1902–06)	.333	Rube Bressler (1917–27)	.311
Edd Roush (1916–26; 1931)	.331	Ernie Lombardi (1932–41)	.311
Jake Beckley (1897–1903)	.324	Ken Griffey (1973–81)	.310
Bug Holliday (1890–98)	.315	Dusty Miller (1895–99)	.308
Bubbles Hargrave (1921–28)	.314	Pete Rose (1963–78; 1984–86)	.307

ALL-TIME STOLEN BASE LEADERS

Joe Morgan (1972–79)	406	Edd Roush (1916–26; 1931)	199
Dave Concepcion (1970–88)	321	Hans Lobert (1906–10)	168
Bob Bescher (1908–13)	320	Mike Mitchell (1907–12)	165
Vada Pinson (1958–68)	221	Frank Robinson (1956–65)	161
Eric Davis (1984–89)	212	Dick Egan (1908–13)	154

PITCHING

ALL-TIME GAMES LEADERS

Pedro Borbon (1970–79)	531	Dolf Luque (1918–29)	395
Clay Carroll (1968–75)	486	Paul Derringer (1933–42)	393
Joe Nuxhall (1944; 1952–60; 1962–66)	484	Johnny Franco (1984–88)	333
Tom Hume (1977–85)	457	Pete Donohue (1921–30)	316
Eppa Rixey (1921–33)	440	Johnny Vander Meer (1937–43; 1946–49)	313

ALL-TIME WIN LEADERS

Eppa Rixey (1921–33)	179	Frank Dwyer (1892–99)	132
Paul Derringer (1933–42)	161	Joe Nuxhall (1944; 1952–60; 1962–66)	130
Bucky Walters (1938–48)	160	Pete Donohue (1921–30)	127
Dolf Luque (1918–29)	154	Noodles Hahn (1899–1905)	127
Jim Maloney (1960–70)	134	Johnny Vander Meer (1937–43; 1946–49)	116

ALL-TIME SHUTOUT LEADERS

Bucky Walters (1938–48)	32	Dolf Luque (1918–29)	24
Jim Maloney (1960–70)	30	Eppa Rixey (1921–33)	23
Johnny Vander Meer (1937–43; 1946–49)	30	Joe Nuxhall (1944; 1952–60; 1962–66)	20
Ken Raffensberger (1947–54)	25	Jack Billingham (1972–77)	18
Paul Derringer (1933–42)	24	Red Lucas (1926–33)	18
Noodles Hahn (1899–1905)	24		

ALL-TIME INNINGS PITCHED LEADERS

Eppa Rixey (1921–33)	2,890	Johnny Vander Meer (1937–43; 1946–49)	2,027
Dolf Luque (1918–29)	2,669	Bob Ewing (1902–09)	2,022
Paul Derringer (1930–42)	2,616	Pete Donohue (1921–30)	1,996
Bucky Walters (1938–48)	2,355	Frank Dwyer (1892–99)	1,983
Joe Nuxhall (1944; 1952–60; 1962–66)	2,171	Noodles Hahn (1899–1905)	1,979

ALL-TIME LOSS LEADERS

Dolf Luque (1918–29)   152
Paul Derringer (1933–42)   150
Eppa Rixey (1921–33)   148
Johnny Vander Meer (1937–43; 1946–49)   116
Pete Donohue (1921–30)   110
Joe Nuxhall (1944; 1952–60; 1962–66)   109

Bucky Walters (1938–48)   107
Bob Ewing (1902–09)   103
Frank Dwyer (1892–99)   101
Red Lucas (1926–33)   99
Ken Raffensberger (1947–54)   99

ALL-TIME STRIKEOUT LEADERS

Jim Maloney (1960–70)   1,592
Mario Soto (1977–87)   1,415
Joe Nuxhall (1944; 1952–60; 1962–66)   1,289
Johnny Vander Meer (1937–43; 1946–49)   1,251
Paul Derringer (1933–42)   1,062

Gary Nolan (1967–77)   1,035
Jim O'Toole (1958–66)   1,002
Dolf Luque (1918–29)   970
Noodles Hahn (1899–1905)   895
Bob Ewing (1902–09)   884

ALL-TIME WALK LEADERS

Johnny Vander Meer (1937–43; 1946–49)   1,072
Bucky Walters (1938–48)   806
Jim Maloney (1960–70)   786
Dolf Luque (1981–29)   756
Joe Nuxhall (1944; 1952–60; 1962–66)   706

Mario Soto (1977–88)   657
Eppa Rixey (1921–33)   603
Fred Norman (1974–79)   531
Jim O'Toole (1958–66)   528
Bob Ewing (1902–09)   513

ALL-TIME WON-LOST PERCENTAGE LEADERS

Don Gullett (1970–76)   .674
Pedro Borbon (1970–79)   .653
Clay Carroll (1968–75)   .623
Jim Maloney (1960–70)   .623
Gary Nolan (1967–1977)   .621

Tom Seaver (1977–82)   .620
Elmer Riddle (1939–45; 1947)   .605
Tom Browning (1984–89)   .600
Hod Eller (1917–21)   .600
Bucky Walters (1938–48)   .599

ALL-TIME SAVE LEADERS

John Franco (1984–89)   148
Clay Carroll (1968–75)   104
Tom Hume (1977–85)   88
Pedro Borbon (1970–79)   76
Wayne Granger (1969–71)   73

Bill Henry (1958–65)   64
Rawley Eastwick (1974–77)   57
Doug Blair (1978–81)   50
Billy McCool (1964–68)   50
Jim Brosnan (1959–63)   43

REDS LEAGUE LEADERS

BATTING

BATTING AVERAGE
C. Seymour, 1905
H. Chase, 1916
E. Roush, 1917, '19
B. Hargrave, 1926
E. Lombardi, 1938
P. Rose, 1968, '69, '73

HOME RUNS
S. Crawford, 1901
F. Odwell, 1905
T. Kluszewski, 1954
J. Bench, 1970, '72
G. Foster, 1977, '78

HITS
C. Seymour, 1905
H. Chase, 1916
H. Groh, 1917
F. McCormick, 1938, '39, '40 (Tie)
T. Kluszewski, 1955
V. Pinson, 1961, '63
P. Rose, 1965, '68 (Tie), '70 (Tie), '72, '73, '76

RBI
C. Seymour, 1905
S. Magee, 1918
F. McCormick, 1939
T. Kluszewski, 1954
D. Johnson, 1965
J. Bench, 1970, '72, '74
G. Foster, 1976, '77, '78
D. Parker, 1985

RUNS SCORED
B. Bescher, 1912
H. Groh, 1918
B. Weber, 1939
V. Pinson, 1959
F. Robinson, 1956, '62
T. Harper, 1965
P. Rose, 1969 (Tie), '74, '75, '76
J. Morgan, 1972
G. Foster, 1977

DOUBLES
J. Beckley, 1901 (Tie)
H. Steinfeldt, 1903 (Tie)
C. Seymour, 1905
H. Groh, 1917, '18
E. Roush, 1923
F. McCormick, 1940
E. Miller, 1947
D. Hoak, 1957
V. Pinson, 1959, '60
F. Robinson, 1962
P. Rose, 1974, '75, '76, '78
D. Parker, 1985

TRIPLES
S. Crawford, 1902
C. Seymour, 1905
J. Ganzel, 1907 (Tie)
M. Mitchell, 1909, '10
J. Daubert, 1922
E. Roush, 1924
B. Herman, 1932
I. Goodman, 1935, '36
V. Pinson, 1963, '67

STOLEN BASES
B. Bescher, 1909, '10, '11, '12
L. Frey, 1940
B. Tolan, 1970

PITCHING
(Post–1900)

WON-LOST PERCENTAGE
D. Reuther, 1919
P. Donohue, 1922
D. Luque, 1923
P. Derringer, 1939
E. Riddle, 1941
R. Purkey, 1962
D. Gullett, 1971
G. Nolan, 1972
T. Seaver, 1981
M. Soto, 1984

WINS
E. Rixey, 1922
D. Luque, 1923
P. Donohue, 1926
P. Derringer, 1939
W. Walters, 1940, 1944
E. Riddle, 1943
E. Blackwell, 1947
J. Jay, 1961
T. Seaver, 1981
D. Jackson, 1988 (Tie)

STRIKEOUTS
F. Hahn, 1901
W. Walters, 1939
J. Vander Meer, 1941, 1942, 1943
E. Blackwell, 1947

ERA
D. Luque, 1923, 1925
W. Walters, 1939, 1940
E. Riddle, 1941
E. Heusser, 1944

SAVES
L. Ames, 1914 (Tie)
R. Benton, 1915 (Tie—also with NY)
F. Toney, 1918 (Tie—also with NY)
J. May, 1924

J. Beggs, 1940 (Tie)
H. Bumbert, 1948
T. Abernathy, 1967
W. Granger, 1970
C. Carroll, 1972
R. Eastwick, 1975 (Tie), '76
J. Franco, 1988

MOST VALUABLE PLAYERS
E. Lombardi, 1938
B. Walters, 1939
F. McCormick, 1940
F. Robinson, 1961
J. Bench, 1970, '72

P. Rose, 1973
J. Morgan, 1975, '76
G. Foster, 1977

ROOKIES OF YEAR
F. Robinson, 1956
P. Rose, 1963
T. Helms, 1966
J. Bench, 1968
P. Zachry, 1976 (Tie)

CY YOUNG WINNERS

HOUSTON ASTROS

BATTING

ALL-TIME GAME LEADERS

Jose Cruz (1975–87)	1,870	Doug Rader (1967–75)	1,178
Cesar Cedeno (1970–81)	1,512	Joe Morgan (1963–71)	1,032
Terry Puhl (1977–89)	1,479	Bob Aspromonte (1962–68)	1,007
Jimmy Wynn (1963–73)	1,426	Enos Cabell (1975–80; 1984–85)	1,007
Bob Watson (1966–79)	1,381	Denny Walling (1977–87)	1,004

ALL-TIME AT BAT LEADERS

Jose Cruz (1975–87)	6,629	Doug Rader (1967–75)	4,232
Cesar Cedeno (1970–81)	5,732	Enos Cabell (1975–80; 1984–85)	3,862
Jimmy Wynn (1963–73)	5,063	Joe Morgan (1963–71)	3,729
Bob Watson (1966–79)	4,883	Bob Aspromonte (1962–68)	3,588
Terry Puhl (1977–89)	4,796	Roger Metzger (1971–78)	3,555

ALL-TIME RUN LEADERS

Cesar Cedeno (1970–81)	890	Joe Morgan (1963–71)	597
Jose Cruz (1975–87)	871	Bill Doran (1982–89)	562
Jimmy Wynn (1963–73)	829	Doug Rader (1967–75)	520
Terry Puhl (1977–89)	671	Enos Cabell (1975–80; 1984–85)	502
Bob Watson (1966–79)	640	Roger Metzger (1971–78)	396

ALL-TIME HIT LEADERS

Jose Cruz (1975–87)	1,937	Enos Cabell (1975–80; 1984–85)	1,089
Cesar Cedeno (1970–81)	1,659	Doug Rader (1967–75)	1,060
Bob Watson (1966–79)	1,448	Joe Morgan (1963–71)	972
Terry Puhl (1977–89)	1,345	Bob Aspromonte (1962–68)	925
Jimmy Wynn (1963–73)	1,291	Roger Metzger (1971–78)	817

ALL-TIME DOUBLE LEADERS

Cesar Cedeno (1970–81)	343	Doug Rader (1967–75)	197
Jose Cruz (1975–87)	335	Enos Cabell (1975–80; 1984–85)	167
Bob Watson (1966–79)	241	Rusty Staub (1963–68)	156
Jimmy Wynn (1963–73)	228	Joe Morgan (1963–71)	153
Terry Puhl (1977–89)	225	Alan Ashby (1979–89)	136

ALL-TIME TRIPLE LEADERS

Jose Cruz (1975–87)	80	Enos Cabell (1975–80; 1984–85)	44
Joe Morgan (1963–71)	63	Bill Doran (1982–89)	33
Roger Metzger (1971–78)	61	Jimmy Wynn (1963–73)	32
Terry Puhl (1977–89)	56	Phil Garner (1981–87)	30
Cesar Cedeno (1970–81)	55	Doug Rader (1967–75)	30
Craig Reynolds (1979–88)	55	Bob Watson (1966–79)	30

ALL-TIME HOME RUN LEADERS

Jimmy Wynn (1963–73)	223	Lee May (1972–74)	81
Cesar Cedeno (1970–81)	163	Kevin Bass (1983–88)	73
Glenn Davis (1984–89)	144	Joe Morgan (1963–71)	72
Bob Watson (1966–79)	139	Alan Ashby (1979–89)	69
Jose Cruz (1975–87)	138	Terry Puhl (1977–89)	62

ALL-TIME TOTAL BASE LEADERS

Jose Cruz (1975–87)	2,846	Doug Rader (1967–75)	1,701
Cesar Cedeno (1970–81)	2,601	Enos Cabell (1975–80; 1984–85)	1,473
Jimmy Wynn (1963–73)	2,252	Joe Morgan (1963–71)	1,467
Bob Watson (1966–79)	2,166	Bob Aspromonte (1962–68)	1,237
Terry Puhl (1977–89)	1,868	Rusty Staub (1963–68)	1,143

ALL-TIME RBI LEADERS

Jose Cruz (1975–87)	942	Terry Puhl (1977–89)	424
Bob Watson (1966–79)	782	Enos Cabell (1975–80; 1984–85)	391
Cesar Cedeno (1970–81)	778	Alan Ashby (1979–89)	388
Jimmy Wynn (1963–73)	719	Bob Aspromonte (1962–68)	385
Doug Rader (1967–75)	600	Rusty Staub (1963–68)	370

ALL-TIME EXTRA BASE HIT LEADERS

Cesar Cedeno (1970–81)	561	Terry Puhl (1977–89)	343
Jose Cruz (1975–87)	553	Joe Morgan (1963–71)	288
Jimmy Wynn (1963–73)	483	Enos Cabell (1975–80; 1984–85)	254
Bob Watson (1966–79)	410	Rusty Staub (1963–68)	225
Doug Rader (1967–75)	355	Phil Garner (1981–87)	198

ALL-TIME BATTING AVERAGE LEADERS (500 game minimum)

Bob Watson (1966–79)	.297	Terry Puhl (1977–89)	.280
Jose Cruz (1975–88)	.292	Denny Walling (1977–88)	.280
Cesar Cedeno (1970–81)	.289	Kevin Bass (1983–89)	.276
Jesus Alou (1969–73)	.282	Rusty Staub (1963–68)	.273
Enos Cabell (1975–80; 1984–85)	.282	Bill Doran (1982–89)	.265

ALL-TIME STOLEN BASE LEADERS

Cesar Cedeno (1970–81)	487	Bill Doran (1982–89)	173
Jose Cruz (1975–87)	288	Billy Hatcher (1986–89)	145
Joe Morgan (1963–71)	219	Kevin Bass (1983–88)	100
Terry Puhl (1977–89)	216	Dickie Thon (1981–87)	94
Enos Cabell (1975–80; 1984–85)	188	Sonny Jackson (1963–67)	73
Jimmy Wynn (1963–73)	180		

PITCHING

ALL-TIME GAME LEADERS

Dave Smith (1980–89)	514	Bob Knepper (1981–89)	284
Joe Niekro (1975–85)	431	Nolan Ryan (1980–88)	282
Ken Forsch (1970–80)	421	Jim Ray (1965–73)	280
Joe Sambito (1976–82; 1984)	353	Don Wilson (1966–74)	266
Larry Dierker (1964–76)	345	J. R. Richard (1971–81)	238

ALL-TIME WIN LEADERS

Joe Niekro (1975–85)	144	Bob Knepper (1981–89)	93
Larry Dierker (1964–76)	137	Ken Forsch (1970–80)	78
J. R. Richard (1971–81)	107	Dick Farrell (1962–67)	53
Nolan Ryan (1980–88)	106	Dave Giusti (1962; 1964–68)	47
Don Wilson (1966–74)	104	Dave A. Roberts (1972–75)	47
Mike Scott (1983–89)	101		

ALL-TIME INNINGS PITCHED LEADERS

Larry Dierker (1964–76)	2,295	J. R. Richard (1971–81)	1,606
Joe Niekro (1975–85)	2,270	Ken Forsch (1970–80)	1,492
Nolan Ryan (1980–88)	1,855	Mike Scott (1983–89)	1,491
Don Wilson (1966–74)	1,749	Dick Farrell (1962–67)	1,015
Bob Knepper (1981–89)	1,738	Dave Giusti (1962; 1964–68)	913

ALL-TIME LOSS LEADERS

Larry Dierker (1964–76)	117	Ken Forsch (1970–80)	81
Joe Niekro (1975–85)	116	J. R. Richard (1971–81)	71
Bob Knepper (1981–89)	100	Mike Scott (1983–89)	66
Nolan Ryan (1980–88)	94	Dick Farrell (1962–67)	64
Don Wilson (1966–74)	92	Tom Griffin (1969–76)	60

ALL-TIME SHUTOUT LEADERS

Larry Dierker (1964–76)	25		Bob Knepper (1981–89)	18
Joe Niekro (1975–85)	21		Nolan Ryan (1980–88)	13
Don Wilson (1966–74)	20		Dave A. Roberts (1972–75)	11
J. R. Richard (1971–81)	19		Ken Forsch (1970–80)	9
Mike Scott (1983–89)	19		Tom Griffin (1969–76)	9

ALL-TIME STRIKEOUT LEADERS

Nolan Ryan (1980–88)	1,866		Joe Niekro (1975–85)	1,178
J. R. Richard (1971–81)	1,493		Bob Knepper (1981–89)	946
Larry Dierker (1964–76)	1,487		Ken Forsch (1970–80)	815
Don Wilson (1966–74)	1,283		Dick Farrell (1962–67)	694
Mike Scott (1983–89)	1,194		Tom Griffin (1969–76)	652

ALL-TIME WALK LEADERS

Joe Niekro (1975–85)	818		Bob Knepper (1981–89)	521
Nolan Ryan (1980–88)	796		Tom Griffin (1969–76)	441
J. R. Richard (1971–81)	770		Mike Scott (1983–89)	435
Larry Dierker (1964–76)	695		Ken Forsch (1970–80)	428
Don Wilson (1966–74)	640		Joaquin Andujar (1976–81)	340

ALL-TIME ERA LEADERS

Joe Sambito (1976–82; 1984)	2.42		J. R. Richard (1971–81)	3.15
Dave Smith (1980–89)	2.54		Ken Forsch (1970–80)	3.18
Mike Cuellar (1965–68)	2.74		Mike Scott (1983–89)	3.18
Nolan Ryan (1980–88)	3.08		Joe Niekro (1975–85)	3.22
Don Wilson (1966–74)	3.14		Larry Dierker (1964–76)	3.28

ALL-TIME WON-LOST PERCENTAGE LEADERS

Mike Scott (1983–89)	.605		Don Wilson (1966–74)	.531
J. R. Richard (1971–80)	.601		Nolan Ryan (1980–88)	.530
Joe Niekro (1975–85)	.554		Dave Roberts (1972–75)	.516
Larry Dierker (1964–76)	.539		Ken Forsch (1970–80)	.491
Dave Smith (1980–89)	.534		Bob Knepper (1981–89)	.482

ALL-TIME SAVE LEADERS

Dave Smith (1980–89)	176	Hal Woodeshick (1962–65)	31
Fred Gladding (1968–73)	76	Frank LaCorte (1979–83)	26
Joe Sambito (1976–82; 1984)	72	Jim Ray (1965–73)	23
Ken Forsch (1970–80)	50	Claude Raymond (1964–67)	22
Frank DiPino (1980–86)	43	Bill Dawley (1983–85)	21

ASTROS LEAGUE LEADERS

BATTING

HITS
J. Cruz, 1983 (Tie)

DOUBLES
R. Staub, 1967
C. Cedeno, 1971, '72 (Tie)

TRIPLES
J. Morgan, 1971 (Tie)
R. Metzger, 1971 (Tie), '73
C. Reynolds, 1981 (Tie)
D. Thon, 1982

PITCHING
WON-LOST PERCENTAGE

WINS
J. Niekro, 1979 (Tie)
M. Scott, 1989

STRIKEOUTS
J. R. Richard, 1978, 1979
M. Scott, 1986
N. Ryan, 1987, 1988

ERA
J. R. Richard, 1979
N. Ryan, 1981, 1987
M. Scott, 1986

SAVES
H. Woodeshick, 1964
F. Gladding, 1969

MOST VALUABLE PLAYERS
none

ROOKIES OF YEAR
none

CY YOUNG WINNERS
M. Scott, 1986

LOS ANGELES DODGERS (BROOKLYN)

BATTING

ALL-TIME GAME LEADERS

Zack Wheat (1909–26)	2,318	Willie Davis (1960–73)	1,952
Bill Russell (1969–86)	2,181	Duke Snider (1947–63)	1,923
Pee Wee Reese (1940–58)	2,166	Carl Furillo (1946–60)	1,806
Gil Hodges (1943; 1947–61)	2,006	Steve Garvey (1969–82)	1,727
Junior Gilliam (1953–66)	1,956	Maury Wills (1959–66; 1969–72)	1,593

ALL-TIME AT BAT LEADERS

Zack Wheat (1909–26)	8,859	Gil Hodges (1943; 1947–61)	6,881
Pee Wee Reese (1940–58)	8,058	Duke Snider (1947–63)	6,640
Willie Davis (1960–73)	7,495	Steve Garvey (1969–82)	6,543
Bill Russell (1969–86)	7,318	Carl Furillo (1946–60)	6,378
Junior Gilliam (1953–66)	7,119	Maury Wills (1959–66; 1969–72)	6,156

ALL-TIME RUN LEADERS

Pee Wee Reese (1940–58)	1,338	Willie Davis (1960–73)	1,004
Zack Wheat (1909–26)	1,255	Jackie Robinson (1947–56)	947
Duke Snider (1947–63)	1,199	Carl Furillo (1946–60)	895
Junior Gilliam (1953–66)	1,163	Mike Griffin (1891–98)	886
Gil Hodges (1943; 1946–61)	1,088	Maury Wills (1959–66; 1969–72)	876

ALL-TIME HIT LEADERS

Zack Wheat (1909–26)	2,804	Bill Russell (1969–88)	1,926
Pee Wee Reese (1940–58)	2,170	Carl Furillo (1946–60)	1,910
Willie Davis (1960–73)	2,091	Junior Gilliam (1953–66)	1,889
Duke Snider (1947–63)	1,995	Gil Hodges (1943; 1946–61)	1,884
Steve Garvey (1969–82)	1,968	Maury Wills (1959–66; 1969–72)	1,732

ALL-TIME DOUBLE LEADERS

Zack Wheat (1909–26)	464	Willie Davis (1960–73)	321
Duke Snider (1947–63)	343	Junior Gilliam (1953–66)	304
Steve Garvey (1969–82)	333	Gil Hodges (1943; 1946–61)	294
Pee Wee Reese (1940–58)	330	Bill Russell (1969–88)	293
Carl Furillo (1946–60)	324	Dixie Walker (1939–47)	274

ALL-TIME TRIPLE LEADERS

Zack Wheat (1909–26)	171	Duke Snider (1947–63)	82
Willie Davis (1960–73)	110	Pee Wee Reese (1940–58)	80
Hy Myers (1909; 1911; 1914–22)	97	Jimmy Sheckard (1897–98; 1902–05)	80
Jake Daubert (1910–18)	87	Tom Daly (1890–1901)	74
John Hummel (1905–15)	82	Jimmy Johnston (1916–25)	73

ALL-TIME HOME RUN LEADERS

Duke Snider (1947–63)	389	Carl Furillo (1946–60)	192
Gil Hodges (1943; 1947–61)	361	Pedro Guerrero (1978–88)	166
Roy Campanella (1948–57)	242	Willie Davis (1960–73)	154
Ron Cey (1971–82)	228	Dusty Baker (1976–83)	144
Steve Garvey (1969–82)	211	Dolf Camilli (1938–43)	139

ALL-TIME TOTAL BASE LEADERS

Zack Wheat (1909–26)	4,003	Steve Garvey (1969–82)	3,004
Duke Snider (1947–63)	3,669	Carl Furillo (1946–60)	2,922
Gil Hodges (1943; 1947–61)	3,357	Junior Gilliam (1953–66)	2,530
Willie Davis (1960–73)	3,094	Bill Russell (1969–86)	2,471
Pee Wee Reese (1940–58)	3,038	Ron Cey (1971–82)	2,321

ALL-TIME RBI LEADERS

Duke Snider (1947–63)	1,271	Pee Wee Reese (1940–58)	885
Gil Hodges (1943; 1947–61)	1,254	Roy Campanella (1948–57)	856
Zack Wheat (1909–26)	1,227	Willie Davis (1960–73)	849
Carl Furillo (1946–60)	1,058	Ron Cey (1971–82)	842
Steve Garvey (1969–82)	992	Jackie Robinson (1947–56)	734

ALL-TIME EXTRA BASE HIT LEADERS

Duke Snider (1947–63)	814	Carl Furillo (1946–60)	572
Zack Wheat (1909–26)	766	Pee Wee Reese (1940–58)	536
Gil Hodges (1943; 1947–61)	703	Ron Cey (1971–82)	469
Willie Davis (1960–73)	585	Jackie Robinson (1947–56)	464
Steve Garvey (1969–82)	579	Junior Gilliam (1953–66)	440

ALL-TIME BATTING AVERAGE LEADERS (500 games min.)

Willie Keeler (1893; 1899–1902)	.360	Fielder Jones (1896–1900)	.315
Babe Herman (1926–31; 1945)	.339	Manny Mota (1969–82)	.315
Jack Fournier (1923–26)	.337	Jackie Robinson (1947–56)	.311
Zack Wheat (1909–26)	.317	Dixie Walker (1939–47)	.311
Babe Phelps (1935–41)	.315	Pedro Guerrero (1978–88)	.310

ALL-TIME STOLEN BASE LEADERS

Maury Wills (1959–66; 1969–72)	450	Junior Gilliam (1953–66)	203
Davey Lopes (1972–81)	413	Zack Wheat (1909–26)	203
Willie Davis (1960–73)	335	Jimmy Sheckard (1897–98; 1902–05)	199
Steve Sax (1981–88)	290	Jackie Robinson (1947–56)	197
Pee Wee Reese (1940–58)	232	Bill Russell (1969–86)	167

PITCHING

ALL-TIME GAME LEADERS

Don Sutton (1966–80; 1988)	550	Charlie Hough (1970–80)	401
Don Drysdale (1956–69)	518	Sandy Koufax (1955–66)	397
Jim Brewer (1964–75)	474	Brickyard Kennedy (1892–1901)	381
Ron Perranoski (1961–67; 1972)	457	Dazzy Vance (1922–32)	378
Clem Labine (1950–60)	425	Johnny Podres (1953–55; 1957–66)	366

ALL-TIME WIN LEADERS

Don Sutton (1966–80; 1988)	233	Burleigh Grimes (1918–26)	158
Don Drysdale (1956–69)	209	Claude Osteen (1965–73)	147
Dazzy Vance (1922–32)	190	Johnny Podres (1953–55; 1957–66)	136
Brickyard Kennedy (1892–1901)	174	Nap Rucker (1907–16)	134
Sandy Koufax (1955–66)	165	Don Newcombe (1949–58)	123

ALL-TIME INNINGS PITCHED LEADERS

Don Sutton (1966–80; 1988)	3,815	Claude Osteen (1965–73)	2,397
Don Drysdale (1956–69)	3,432	Nap Rucker (1907–16)	2,375
Brickyard Kennedy (1892–1901)	2,857	Sandy Koufax (1955–66)	2,324
Dazzy Vance (1922–32)	2,758	Johnny Podres (1953–55; 1957–66)	2,030
Burleigh Grimes (1918–26)	2,426	Burt Hooton (1975–84)	1,863

ALL-TIME LOSS LEADERS

Don Sutton (1966–80; 1988)	181	Claude Osteen (1965–73)	126
Don Drysdale (1956–69)	166	Burleigh Grimes (1918–26)	121
Brickyard Kennedy (1892–1901)	149	Johnny Podres (1953–55; 1957–66)	104
Nap Rucker (1907–16)	136	Van Lingle Mungo (1931–41)	99
Dazzy Vance (1922–32)	131	Watty Clark (1927–33; 1934–37)	88

ALL-TIME SHUTOUT LEADERS

Don Sutton (1966–80; 1988)	52		Dazzy Vance (1922–32)	30
Don Drysdale (1956–69)	49		Fernando Valenzuela (1980–89)	27
Sandy Koufax (1955–66)	40		Jeff Pfeffer (1913–21)	25
Nap Rucker (1907–16)	38		Johnny Podres (1953–55; 1957–66)	23
Claude Osteen (1965–73)	34		Bob Welch (1978–87)	23

ALL-TIME STRIKEOUT LEADERS

Don Sutton (1966–80; 1988)	2,696		Johnny Podres (1953–55; 1957–66)	1,331
Don Drysdale (1956–69)	2,486		Bob Welch (1978–87)	1,292
Sandy Koufax (1955–66)	2,396		Nap Rucker (1907–16)	1,217
Dazzy Vance (1922–32)	1,918		Claude Osteen (1965–73)	1,162
Fernando Valenzuela (1980–89)	1,644		Burt Hooton (1975–84)	1,042

ALL-TIME WALK LEADERS

Brickyard Kennedy (1892–1901)	1,128		Dazzy Vance (1922–32)	764
Don Sutton (1966–80; 1988)	966		Burleigh Grimes (1918–26)	744
Don Drysdale (1956–69)	855		Nap Rucker (1907–16)	701
Fernando Valenzuela (1980–89)	838		Van Lingle Mungo (1931–41)	697
Sandy Koufax (1955–66)	817		Johnny Podres (1953–55; 1957–66)	670

ALL-TIME ERA LEADERS (1100 Inns. Min.)

Jeff Pfeffer (1913–21)	2.31		Tommy John (1972–74; 1976–78)	2.98
Nap Rucker (1907–16)	2.43		Bill Singer (1964–72)	3.03
Sandy Koufax (1955–66)	2.76		Don Sutton (1966–80; 1988)	3.08
Sherry Smith (1915–22)	2.91		Claude Osteen (1965–73)	3.09
Don Drysdale (1956–69)	2.95		Fernando Valenzuela (1980–89)	3.19
Doc Scanlan (1904–07; 1909–11)	2.96			

ALL-TIME WON-LOST PERCENTAGE LEADERS

Preacher Roe (1948–54)	.715		Don Newcombe (1949–58)	.651
Jim Hughes (1899–1902)	.674		Kirby Higbe (1941–43; 1946–47)	.648
Tommy John (1972–74; 1976–78)	.674		Whit Wyatt (1939–44)	.640
Billy Loes (1950–56)	.658		Hugh Casey (1939–42; 1946–48)	.631
Sandy Koufax (1955–66)	.655		Orel Hershiser (1983–1989)	.605

ALL-TIME SAVE LEADERS

Jim Brewer (1964–75)	125	Hugh Casey (1939–42; 1946–48)	50
Ron Perranoski (1961–67; 1972)	101	Ed Roebuck (1955–63)	43
Clem Labine (1950–60)	83	Mike Marshall (1974–76)	42
Tom Niedenfuer (1981–87)	64	Jim Hughes (1952–56)	39
Charlie Hough (1970–80)	60	Larry Sherry (1958–63)	39
Steve Howe (1980–85)	59		

DODGERS LEAGUE LEADERS

BATTING

BATTING AVERAGE
J. Daubert, 1913, '14
Z. Wheat, 1918
L. O'Doul, 1932
P. Reiser, 1941
D. Walker, 1944
J. Robinson, 1949
C. Furillo, 1953
T. Davis, 1962, '63

HOME RUNS
J. Sheckard, 1903
H. Lumley, 1904
T. Jordan, 1906, '08
J. Fournier, 1924
D. Camili, 1941
D. Snider, 1956

HITS
W. Keeler, 1900
I. Olson, 1919
D. Snider, 1950
T. Davis, 1962
S. Garvey, 1978, '80

RBI
H. Myers, 1919
D. Camili, 1941
D. Walker, 1945
R. Campanella, 1953
D. Snider, 1955
T. Davis, 1962

RUNS SCORED
P. Reiser, 1941
A. Vaughan, 1943
E. Stanky, 1945
P. Reese, 1949
D. Snider, 1953, '54 (Tie), '55

DOUBLES
R. Smith, 1913
J. Frederick, 1929
P. Reiser, 1914 (Tie)
W. Parker, 1970

TRIPLES
J. Sheckard, 1901
H. Lumley, 1904
W. Alperman, 1907 (Tie)
J. Daubert, 1918
H. Myers, 1919 (Tie), '20
P. Reiser, 1941
L. Olmo, 1945
J. Gilliam, 1953
C. Neal, 1959 (Tie)
W. Moon, 1959 (Tie)
W. Davis, 1962 (Tie), '70
M. Wills, 1962 (Tie)

STOLEN BASES
J. Sheckard, 1903 (Tie)
P. Reiser, 1942, '46
A. Vaughan, 1943
J. Robinson, 1947, '49
P. Reese, 1952
M. Wills, 1960, '61, '62, '63, '64, '65
D. Lopes, 1975, '76

PITCHING
(Post-1900)

WON-LOST PERCENTAGE
B. Grimes, 1920
F. Fitzsimmons, 1940
L. French, 1942
P. Roe, 1949, 1950
C. Erskine, 1953
D. Newcombe, 1955, 1956
J. Podres, 1961
R. Perranoski, 1963
S. Koufax, 1964, 1965
T. John, 1973
A. Messersmith, 1974
O. Hershiser, 1985

WINS
J. McGinnity, 1900
W. Donovan, 1901
B. Grimes, 1921
C. Vance, 1924, 1925
K. Higbe, 1941 (Tie)
W. Wyatt, 1941 (Tie)
D. Newcombe, 1956
D. Drysdale, 1962
S. Koufax, 1963, 1965, 1966
A. Messersmith, 1974
F. Valenzuela, 1986
O. Hershiser, 1988 (Tie)

STRIKEOUTS
B. Grimes, 1921
C. Vance, 1922, 1923, 1924, 1925, 1926, 1927, 1928
V. L. Mungo, 1936
K. Higbe, 1940
D. Newcombe, 1951
D. Drysdale, 1959, 1960, 1962
S. Koufax, 1961, 1963, 1965, 1966
F. Valenzuela, 1981

ERA
C. Vance, 1924, 1928, 1930
J. Podres, 1957
S. Koufax, 1962, 1963, 1964, 1965, 1966
D. Sutton, 1980
A. Pena, 1984

SAVES
F. Kitson, 1900
J. Morrison, 1929 (Tie)

J. Quinn, 1931, '32
D. Leonard, 1935
H. Casey, 1942, '47
L. Webber, 1943
J. Hughes, 1954
C. Labine, 1956, '57
P. Regan, 1966, '68 (Also with Chic.)
M. Marshall, 1974

MOST VALUABLE PLAYERS
J. Daubert, 1913
D. Vance, 1924
D. Camili, 1941
J. Robinson, 1949
R. Campanella, 1951, '53, '55
D. Newcombe, 1956
M. Wills, 1962
S. Koufax, 1963
S. Garvey, 1974
K. Gibson, 1988

ROOKIES OF YEAR
J. Robinson, 1947
D. Newcombe, 1949
J. Black, 1952
J. Gilliam, 1953
F. Howard, 1960
J. Lefebvre, 1965
T. Sizemore, 1969
R. Sutcliffe, 1979
S. Howe, 1980
F. Valenzuela, 1981
S. Sax, 1982

CY YOUNG WINNERS
D. Newcombe, 1956
D. Drysdale, 1962
S. Koufax, 1963, '65, '66
M. Marshall, 1974
F. Valenzuela, 1981
O. Hershiser, 1988

MONTREAL EXPOS

BATTING

ALL-TIME GAME LEADERS

Andre Dawson (1976–86)	1,443	Larry Parrish (1974–81)	967
Gary Carter (1974–84)	1,408	Bob Bailey (1969–75)	951
Tim Wallach (1980–89)	1,305	Chris Speier (1977–84)	895
Tim Raines (1979–89)	1,275	Ron Fairly (1969–74)	718
Warren Cromartie (1974–83)	1,038	Tim Foli (1972–77)	710

ALL-TIME AT BAT LEADERS

Andre Dawson (1976–86)	5,628	Larry Parrish (1974–81)	3,411
Gary Carter (1974–84)	5,018	Bob Bailey (1969–75)	2,991
Tim Raines (1979–89)	4,848	Chris Speier (1977–84)	2,902
Tim Wallach (1980–89)	4,789	Tim Foli (1972–77)	2,614
Warren Cromartie (1974–83)	3,796	Ellis Valentine (1975–81)	2,351

ALL-TIME RUN LEADERS

Tim Raines (1979–89)	869	Larry Parrish (1974–81)	421
Andre Dawson (1976–86)	828	Bob Bailey (1969–75)	412
Gary Carter (1974–84)	683	Ron Fairly (1969–74)	303
Tim Wallach (1980–89)	555	Ellis Valentine (1975–81)	297
Warren Cromartie (1974–83)	446	Rusty Staub (1969–71; 1979)	290

ALL-TIME HIT LEADERS

Andre Dawson (1976–86)	1,575	Larry Parrish (1974–81)	896
Tim Raines (1979–89)	1,467	Bob Bailey (1969–75)	791
Gary Carter (1974–84)	1,365	Chris Speier (1977–84)	710
Tim Wallach (1980–89)	1,259	Ellis Valentine (1975–81)	676
Warren Cromartie (1974–83)	1,063	Tim Foli (1972–77)	642

ALL-TIME DOUBLE LEADERS

Andre Dawson (1976–86)	295	Ellis Valentine (1975–81)	136
Tim Wallach (1980–89)	272	Chris Speier (1977–84)	123
Tim Raines (1979–89)	262	Bob Bailey (1969–75)	116
Gary Carter (1974–84)	256	Tim Foli (1972–77)	99
Warren Cromartie (1974–83)	222	Tony Perez (1977–79)	99
Larry Parrish (1974–81)	208		

ALL-TIME TRIPLE LEADERS

Tim Raines (1979–89)	76	Gary Carter (1974–84)	23
Andre Dawson (1976–86)	67	Mitch Webster (1985–87)	23
Warren Cromartie (1974–83)	30	Chris Speier (1977–84)	22
Larry Parrish (1974–81)	24	Rodney Scott (1976; 1979–82)	21
Bob Bailey (1969–75)	23	Rusty Staub (1969–71; 1979)	18

ALL-TIME HOME RUN LEADERS

Andre Dawson (1976–86)	225	Ellis Valentine (1975–81)	95
Gary Carter (1974–84)	215	Tim Raines (1979–89)	87
Tim Wallach (1980–89)	161	Ron Fairly (1969–74)	86
Bob Bailey (1969–75)	118	Rusty Staub (1969–71; 1979)	81
Larry Parrish (1974–81)	100	Warren Cromartie (1974–83)	60

ALL-TIME TOTAL BASE LEADERS

Andre Dawson (1976–86)	2,679	Larry Parrish (1974–81)	1,452
Gary Carter (1974–84)	2,312	Bob Bailey (1969–75)	1,307
Tim Raines (1979–89)	2,142	Ellis Valentine (1975–81)	1,119
Tim Wallach (1980–89)	1,832	Ron Fairly (1969–74)	979
Warren Cromartie (1974–83)	1,525	Chris Speier (1977–84)	964

ALL-TIME RBI LEADERS

Andre Dawson (1976–86)	838	Larry Parrish (1974–81)	444
Gary Carter (1974–84)	724	Warren Cromartie (1974–83)	371
Tim Wallach (1980–89)	675	Ellis Valentine (1975–81)	358
Tim Raines (1979–89)	490	Ron Fairly (1969–74)	331
Bob Bailey (1969–75)	466	Rusty Staub (1969–71; 1979)	284

ALL-TIME EXTRA BASE HIT LEADERS

Andre Dawson (1976–86)	587	Warren Cromartie (1974–83)	312
Gary Carter (1974–84)	494	Bob Bailey (1969–75)	257
Tim Wallach (1980–89)	457	Ellis Valentine (1975–81)	242
Tim Raines (1979–89)	425	Ron Fairly (1969–74)	185
Larry Parrish (1974–81)	332	Rusty Staub (1969–71; 1979)	185

ALL-TIME BATTING AVERAGE LEADERS (300 game min.)

Tim Raines (1979–89)	.303	Mitch Webster (1985–88)	.283
Rusty Staub (1969–71; 1979)	.295	Tony Perez (1977–79)	.281
Terry Francona (1981–85)	.290	Warren Cromartie (1974–83)	.280
Ellis Valentine (1975–81)	.288	Andre Dawson (1976–86)	.280
Ken Singleton (1972–74)	.285	Hubie Brooks (1985–89)	.279

ALL-TIME STOLEN BASE LEADERS

Tim Raines (1979–89)	585	Larry Lintz (1973–75)	79
Andre Dawson (1976–86)	253	Herm Winningham (1985–88)	61
Rodney Scott (1976; 1979–82)	139	Pepe Mangual (1972–76)	57
Ron LeFlore (1980)	97	Ellis Valentine (1975–81)	56
Mitch Webster (1985–88)	84	Jerry White (1974–78; 1979–83)	53

PITCHING

ALL-TIME GAME LEADERS

Steve Rogers (1973–85)	399	Dan Schatzeder (1977–79; 1982–86)	241
Jeff Reardon (1981–86)	359	Steve Renko (1969–79)	238
Woodie Fryman (1978–83)	297	Stan Bahnsen (1977–81)	204
Bryn Smith (1981–89)	284	Andy McGaffigan (1984; 1986–88)	201
Tim Burke (1985–89)	262	Dale Murray (1974–76; 1979)	201
Mike Marshall (1970–73)	247		

ALL-TIME WIN LEADERS

Steve Rogers (1973–85)	158	Charlie Lea (1980–87)	55
Bryn Smith (1981–89)	81	Bill Stoneman (1969–73)	51
Bill Gullickson (1979–85)	72	Mike Torrez (1971–74)	40
Steve Renko (1969–76)	68	David Palmer (1978–80; 1982; 1984–85)	38
Scott Sanderson (1978–83)	56	Dan Schatzeder (1977–79; 1982–86)	37

ALL-TIME INNINGS PITCHED LEADERS

Steve Rogers (1973–85)	2,839	Scott Sanderson (1978–83)	882
Bryn Smith (1981–89)	1,401	Charlie Lea (1980–87)	793
Steve Renko (1969–76)	1,359	Dan Schatzeder (1977–79; 1982–86)	750
Bill Gullickson (1979–85)	1,186	Woodie Fryman (1978–83)	722
Bill Stoneman (1969–73)	1,085	Carl Morton (1969–72)	700

ALL-TIME LOSS LEADERS

Steve Rogers (1973–85)	152	Woodie Fryman (1978–83)	52
Steve Renko (1969–76)	82	Ernie McAnally (1971–74)	49
Bill Stoneman (1969–73)	72	Scott Sanderson (1978–83)	47
Bryn Smith (1981–89)	71	Carl Morton (1969–72)	45
Bill Gullickson (1979–85)	61	Charlie Lea (1980–87)	41

ALL-TIME SHUTOUT LEADERS

Steve Rogers (1973–85)	37	Bryn Smith (1981–89)	8
Bill Stoneman (1969–73)	15	Bill Gullickson (1979–85)	7
Woodie Fryman (1978–83)	8	Ernie McAnally (1971–74)	7
Charlie Lea (1980–87)	8	Steve Renko (1969–76)	7
Scott Sanderson (1978–83)	8	Floyd Youmans (1985–88)	7

ALL-TIME STRIKEOUT LEADERS

Steve Rogers (1973–85)	1,621	Scott Sanderson (1978–83)	603
Bryn Smith (1981–89)	838	Woodie Fryman (1978–83)	469
Bill Stoneman (1969–73)	831	Charlie Lea (1980–87)	463
Steve Renko (1969–76)	810	Dan Schatzeder (1977–79; 1982–86)	438
Bill Gullickson (1979–85)	678	Floyd Youmans (1985–88)	404

ALL-TIME WALK LEADERS

Steve Rogers (1973–85)	876	Charlie Lea (1980–87)	291
Steve Renko (1969–76)	624	Bill Gullickson (1979–85)	288
Bill Stoneman (1969–73)	535	Carl Morton (1969–72)	279
Bryn Smith (1981–89)	341	Woodie Fryman (1978–83)	273
Mike Torrez (1971–74)	303	Ernie McAnally (1971–74)	268

ALL-TIME WON-LOST PERCENTAGE LEADERS

Andy McGaffigan (1984; 1986–88)	.686	Ross Grimsley (1978–80)	.571
Tim Burke (1985–88)	.636	Dennis Martinez (1987–88)	.558
Joe Hesketh (1984–88)	.595	Mike Torrez (1971–74)	.556
David Palmer (1978–80; 1982; 1984–85)	.594	Scott Sanderson (1978–83)	.544
Charlie Lea (1980–87)	.573	Dan Schatzeder (1977–79; 1982–86)	.544

ALL-TIME SAVE LEADERS

Jeff Reardon (1981–86)	152	Elias Sosa (1979–81)	30
Mike Marshall (1970–73)	75	Claude Raymond (1969–71)	24
Woodie Fryman (1978–83)	52	Andy McGaffigan (1984; 1986–88)	19
Tim Burke (1985–88)	48	Stan Bahnsen (1977–81)	17
Dale Murray (1974–76; 1979)	33	Chuck Taylor (1973–76)	17

EXPOS LEAGUE LEADERS

BATTING

BATTING AVERAGE
A. Oliver, 1982
T. Raines, 1986

HITS
A. Oliver, 1982
A. Dawson, 1983 (Tie)

RBI
A. Oliver, 1982 (Tie)
G. Carter, 1984 (Tie)

RUNS
T. Raines, 1983, '87

DOUBLES
A. Oliver, 1982, '83 (Tie)
T. Raines, 1984 (Tie)
T. Wallach, 1987

TRIPLES
R. Scott, 1980 (Tie)
M. Webster, 1986

STOLEN BASES
R. LeFlore, 1980
T. Raines, 1981, '82, '83, '84

PITCHING

ERA
S. Rogers, 1982

SAVES
M. Marshall, 1973
J. Reardon, 1985

MOST VALUABLE PLAYERS
none

ROOKIES OF YEAR
C. Morton, 1970
A. Dawson, 1977

CY YOUNG WINNERS

NEW YORK METS

BATTING

ALL-TIME GAME LEADERS

Ed Kranepool (1962–79)	1,853	Lee Mazzilli (1976–82; 1986–89)	979
Bud Harrelson (1965–77)	1,322	Darryl Strawberry (1983–89)	957
Jerry Grote (1966–77)	1,235	Rusty Staub (1972–75; 1981–85)	942
Cleon Jones (1963–75)	1,201	Wayne Garrett (1969–76)	883
Mookie Wilson (1980–89)	1,116	John Stearns (1975–84)	809

ALL-TIME AT BAT LEADERS

Ed Kranepool (1962–79)	5,436	Darryl Strawberry (1983–89)	3,361
Bud Harrelson (1965–77)	4,390	Keith Hernandez (1983–89)	3,164
Cleon Jones (1963–75)	4,223	Lee Mazzilli (1976–82; 1986–89)	3,013
Jerry Grote (1966–77)	3,881	Wayne Garrett (1969–79)	2,817
Mookie Wilson (1980–88)	3,778	John Stearns (1975–84)	2,679

ALL-TIME HIT LEADERS

Ed Kranepool (1962–79)	1,418	Keith Hernandez (1983–89)	939
Cleon Jones (1963–75)	1,188	Darryl Strawberry (1983–89)	875
Mookie Wilson (1980–89)	1,112	Lee Mazzilli (1976–82; 1986–89)	796
Bud Harrelson (1965–77)	1,029	Felix Millan (1973–77)	743
Jerry Grote (1966–77)	994	Rusty Staub (1972–75; 1981–85)	709

ALL-TIME RUN LEADERS

Mookie Wilson (1980–89)	592		Keith Hernandez (1983–89)	455
Cleon Jones (1963–75)	563		Lee Mazzilli (1976–82; 1986–89)	404
Ed Kranepool (1962–79)	536		Wayne Garrett (1969–76)	389
Darryl Strawberry (1983–89)	570		Tommie Agee (1968–72)	344
Bud Harrelson (1965–77)	490		John Stearns (1975–84)	334

ALL-TIME DOUBLE LEADERS

Ed Kranepool (1962–79)	225		John Stearns (1975–84)	152
Cleon Jones (1963–75)	182		Lee Mazzilli (1976–82; 1986–89)	148
Mookie Wilson (1980–89)	170		Jerry Grote (1966–77)	143
Darryl Strawberry (1983–89)	169		Rusty Staub (1972–75; 1981–85)	130
Keith Hernandez (1983–89)	159		Bud Harrelson (1965–77)	123

ALL-TIME TRIPLE LEADERS

Mookie Wilson (1980–89)	62		Doug Flynn (1977–81)	26
Bud Harrelson (1965–77)	45		Ed Kranepool (1962–79)	25
Cleon Jones (1963–75)	33		Lee Mazzilli (1976–82; 1986–89)	22
Steve Henderson (1977–80)	31		Wayne Garrett (1969–76)	20
Darryl Strawberry (1983–89)	29		Ron Swoboda (1965–70)	20

ALL-TIME HOME RUN LEADERS

Darryl Strawberry (1983–89)	215		Cleon Jones (1963–75)	93
Dave Kingman (1975–77; 1981–83)	154		Gary Carter (1985–89)	89
Ed Kranepool (1962–79)	118		Tommie Agee (1968–72)	82
George Foster (1982–86)	99		Keith Hernandez (1983–89)	80
John Milner (1971–77)	94		Rusty Staub (1972–75; 1981–85)	75

ALL-TIME TOTAL BASE LEADERS

Ed Kranepool (1962–79)	2,047		Jerry Grote (1966–77)	1,278
Darryl Strawberry (1983–89)	1,747		Bud Harrelson (1965–77)	1,260
Cleon Jones (1963–75)	1,715		Lee Mazzilli (1976–82; 1986–89)	1,192
Mookie Wilson (1980–89)	1,586		Rusty Staub (1972–75; 1981–85)	1,078
Keith Hernandez (1983–89)	1,358		Dave Kingman (1975–77; 1981–83)	1,053

ALL-TIME RBI LEADERS

Darryl Strawberry (1983–89)	625	Dave Kingman (1975–77; 1981–83)	389
Ed Kranepool (1962–79)	614	George Foster (1982–86)	361
Cleon Jones (1963–75)	521	Jerry Grote (1966–77)	357
Keith Hernandez (1983–89)	468	Lee Mazzilli (1976–82; 1986–89)	353
Rusty Staub (1972–75; 1981–85)	399	John Milner (1971–77)	338

ALL-TIME EXTRA BASE HIT LEADERS

Darryl Strawberry (1983–89)	413	Lee Mazzilli (1976–82; 1986–89)	234
Ed Kranepool (1962–79)	368	Dave Kingman (1976–82; 1986–88)	230
Cleon Jones (1963–75)	308	Rusty Staub (1972–75; 1981–85)	212
Mookie Wilson (1980–89)	292	John Stearns (1975–84)	208
Keith Hernandez (1983–89)	249	John Milner (1971–77)	206

ALL-TIME BATTING LEADERS
(500 game min.)

Keith Hernandez (1983–89)	.297	Rusty Staub (1972–75; 1981–85)	.276
Wally Backman (1980–88)	.283	Joel Youngblood (1978–82)	.274
Cleon Jones (1963–75)	.281	Hubie Brooks (1980–84)	.272
Felix Millan (1973–77)	.278	Darryl Strawberry (1983–88)	.266
Mookie Wilson (1980–89)	.276	Lee Mazzilli (1976–82; 1986–89)	.257

ALL-TIME STOLEN BASE LEADERS

Mookie Wilson (1980–89)	281	Wally Backman (1980–89)	106
Darryl Strawberry (1983–89)	176	Tommie Agee (1968–72)	92
Lee Mazzilli (1976–82; 1986–89)	152	Cleon Jones (1963–75)	91
Len Dykstra (1985–89)	116	John Stearns (1975–84)	91
Bud Harrelson (1965–77)	115	Frank Taveras (1979–81)	74

PITCHING

ALL-TIME GAME LEADERS

Tom Seaver (1967–77; 1983) 401
Jerry Koosman (1967–78) 376
Jesse Orosco (1979–87) 372
Tug McGraw (1965–74) 364
Ron Taylor (1967–71) 269

Doug Sisk (1983–87) 263
Craig Swan (1973–84) 229
Skip Lockwood (1975–79) 227
Neil Allen (1979–83) 223
Jon Matlack (1971–77) 203

ALL-TIME WIN LEADERS

Tom Seaver (1967–77; 1983) 198
Jerry Koosman (1967–78) 140
Dwight Gooden (1984–89) 100
Ron Darling (1983–89) 87
Jon Matlack (1971–77) 82

Sid Fernandez (1984–89) 69
Craig Swan (1973–84) 59
Tug McGraw (1965–74) 47
Jesse Orosco (1979–87) 47
Al Jackson (1962–65; 1968–69) 43

ALL-TIME INNINGS PITCHED LEADERS

Tom Seaver (1967–77; 1983) 3,045
Jerry Koosman (1967–78) 2,545
Jon Matlack (1971–77) 1,448
Ron Darling (1983–89) 1,391
Dwight Gooden (1984–89) 1,291

Craig Swan (1973–84) 1,229
Sid Fernandez (1984–89) 1,027
Al Jackson (1962–65; 1968–69) 980
Jack Fisher (1964–67) 932
Tug McGraw (1965–74) 793

ALL-TIME LOSS LEADERS

Jerry Koosman (1967–78) 137
Tom Seaver (1967–77; 1983) 124
Jon Matlack (1971–77) 81
Al Jackson (1962–65; 1968–69) 80
Jack Fisher (1964–67) 73
Craig Swan (1973–84) 71

Tug McGraw (1965–74) 55
Ron Darling (1983–89) 55
Jim McAndrew (1968–73) 49
Roger Craig (1962–63) 46
Pat Zachry (1977–82) 46

ALL-TIME SHUTOUT LEADERS

Tom Seaver (1967–77; 1983)	44	Bob Ojeda (1986–89)	9
Jerry Koosman (1967–78)	26	Gary Gentry (1969–72)	8
Jon Matlack (1971–77)	26	Craig Swan (1973–84)	7
Dwight Gooden (1984–89)	19	David Cone (1987–89)	6
Ron Darling (1983–89)	10	Jim McAndrew (1968–73)	6
Al Jackson (1962–65; 1968–69)	10	Pat Zachry (1977–82)	6

ALL-TIME STRIKEOUT LEADERS

Tom Seaver (1967–77; 1983)	2,541	Sid Fernandez (1984–89)	972
Jerry Koosman (1967–78)	1,799	Craig Swan (1973–84)	671
Dwight Gooden (1984–89)	1,168	Tug McGraw (1965–74)	618
Jon Matlack (1971–77)	1,023	Gary Gentry (1969–72)	563
Ron Darling (1983–89)	991	Al Jackson (1962–65; 1968–69)	561

ALL-TIME WALK LEADERS

Tom Seaver (1967–77; 1983)	847	Dwight Gooden (1984–89)	379
Jerry Koosman (1967–78)	820	Craig Swan (1973–84)	368
Ron Darling (1983–89)	542	Tug McGraw (1965–74)	350
Jon Matlack (1971–77)	419	Nolan Ryan (1966–71)	344
Sid Fernandez (1984–89)	417	Gary Gentry (1969–72)	324

ALL-TIME ERA LEADERS (Min. 500 IP)

Tom Seaver (1967–77; 1983)	2.57	Jerry Koosman (1967–78)	3.09
Dwight Gooden (1984–89)	2.64	Tug McGraw (1965–74)	3.17
Jesse Orosco (1979–87)	2.74	Sid Fernandez (1984–89)	3.21
David Cone (1987–89)	3.01	Ray Sadecki (1970–74; 1977)	3.35
Jon Matlack (1971–77)	3.03	Ron Darling (1983–89)	3.38

ALL-TIME WON-LOST PERCENTAGE LEADERS

Dwight Gooden (1984–89)	.719	Rick Aguilera (1985–89)	.578
David Cone (1987–89)	.696	Roger McDowell (1985–88)	.571
Tom Seaver (1967–77; 1983)	.615	Bob Ojeda (1986–89)	.564
Ron Darling (1983–89)	.613	Ray Sadecki (1970–74; 1977)	.545
Sid Fernandez (1984–1989)	.611	Jerry Koosman (1967–78)	.505

ALL-TIME SAVE LEADERS (Since 1969)

Jesse Orosco (1979–87)	107		Randy Myers (1985–89)	56
Tug McGraw (1965–74)	85		Doug Sisk (1983–87)	33
Roger McDowell (1985–89)	84		Ron Taylor (1967–71)	28
Neil Allen (1979–83)	69		Bob Apodaca (1973–77)	26
Skip Lockwood (1975–79)	65		Danny Frisella (1967–72)	24

METS LEAGUE LEADERS

BATTING

HOME RUNS
D. Kingman, 1982
H. Johnson, 1989 (Tie)

PITCHING

WON-LOST PERCENTAGE
T. Seaver, 1969, 1975, 1979
R. Ojeda, 1986
D. Cone, 1988
S. Fernandez, 1989 (Tie)

WINS
T. Seaver, 1969, 1975
D. Gooden, 1985

STRIKEOUTS
T. Seaver, 1970, 1971, 1973, 1975, 1976
D. Gooden, 1984, 1985

ERA
T. Seaver, 1970, 1971, 1973
C. Swan, 1978
D. Gooden, 1985

MOST VALUABLE PLAYERS
none

ROOKIES OF YEAR
T. Seaver, 1967
J. Matlack, 1972
D. Strawberry, 1983
D. Gooden, 1984

CY YOUNG WINNERS
T. Seaver, 1969, '73, '75
D. Gooden, 1985

PHILADELPHIA PHILLIES

BATTING

ALL-TIME GAME LEADERS

Mike Schmidt (1972–89)	2,404	Ed Delahanty (1888–89; 1891–1901)	1,544
Richie Ashburn (1948–59)	1,794	Puddin' Head Jones (1947–59)	1,520
Larry Bowa (1970–81)	1,739	Sherry Magee (1904–14)	1,518
Tony Taylor (1960–71; 1974–76)	1,669	Granny Hamner (1944–59)	1,501
Del Ennis (1946–56)	1,630	Cy Williams (1918–30)	1,463

ALL-TIME AT BAT LEADERS

Mike Schmidt (1972–89)	8,352	Tony Taylor (1960–71; 1974–76)	5,799
Richie Ashburn (1948–59)	7,122	Granny Hamner (1944–59)	5,772
Larry Bowa (1970–81)	6,815	Sherry Matee (1904–14)	5,505
Ed Delahanty (1888–89; 1891–1901)	6,352	Puddin' Head Jones (1947–59)	5,419
Del Ennis (1946–56)	6,327	Johnny Callison (1960–69)	5,306

ALL-TIME RUN LEADERS

Mike Schmidt (1972–89)	1,506	Roy Thomas (1899–1908)	916
Ed Delahanty (1888–89; 1891–1901)	1,365	Sherry Magee (1904–14)	898
Richie Ashburn (1948–59)	1,114	Del Ennis (1946–56)	891
Chuck Klein (1928–33; 1936–39; 1940–44)	963	Billy Hamilton (1890–95)	877
Sam Thompson (1889–98)	928	Cy Williams (1918–30)	825

ALL-TIME HIT LEADERS

Mike Schmidt (1972–89)	2,234	Chuck Klein (1928–33; 1936–39; 1940–44)	1,705
Richie Ashburn (1948–59)	2,217	Sherry Magee (1904–14)	1,647
Ed Delahanty (1888–89; 1891–1901)	2,211	Cy Williams (1918–30)	1,553
Del Ennis (1946–56)	1,812	Granny Hamner (1944–59)	1,518
Larry Bowa (1970–81)	1,798	Tony Taylor (1960–71; 1974–76)	1,511

ALL-TIME DOUBLE LEADERS

Ed Delahanty (1888–89; 1891–1901)	432	Richie Ashburn (1948–59)	287
Mike Schmidt (1972–88)	401	Granny Hamner (1944–59)	271
Sherry Magee (1904–14)	337	Johnny Callison (1960–69)	265
Chuck Klein (1928–33; 1936–39; 1940–44)	336	Sam Thompson (1889–98)	258
Del Ennis (1946–56)	310	Greg Luzinski (1970–80)	253

ALL-TIME TRIPLE LEADERS

Ed Delahanty (1888–89; 1891–1901)	151	Gavvy Cravath (1912–20)	72
Sherry Magee (1904–14)	127	Del Ennis (1946–56)	65
Sam Thompson (1889–98)	103	Richie Allen (1963–69)	64
Richie Ashburn (1948–59)	97	Chuck Klein (1928–33; 1936–39; 1940–44)	64
Johnny Callison (1960–69)	84	Nap Lajoie (1896–1900)	64
Larry Bowa (1970–81)	81	John Titus (1903–12)	64

ALL-TIME HOME RUN LEADERS

Mike Schmidt (1972–89)	548	Richie Allen (1963–69)	204
Del Ennis (1946–56)	259	Johnny Callison (1960–69)	185
Chuck Klein (1928–33; 1936–39; 1940–44)	243	Puddin' Head Jones (1947–59)	180
Greg Luzinski (1970–80)	223	Andy Seminick (1943–51; 1956–57)	123
Cy Williams (1918–30)	217	Gavvy Cravath (1912–20)	117

ALL-TIME TOTAL BASE LEADERS

Mike Schmidt (1972–89)	4,404	Cy Williams (1918–30)	2,539
Ed Delahanty (1888–89; 1891–1901)	3,197	Sherry Magee (1904–14)	2,463
Del Ennis (1946–56)	3,029	Johnny Callison (1960–69)	2,426
Chuck Klein (1928–33; 1936–39; 1940–44)	2,898	Greg Luzinski (1970–80)	2,263
Richie Ashburn (1948–59)	2,764	Puddin' Head Jones (1947–59)	2,236

ALL-TIME RBI LEADERS

Mike Schmidt (1972–89)	1,595	Sherry Magee (1904–14)	889
Ed Delahanty (1888–89; 1891–1901)	1,286	Greg Luzinski (1970–80)	811
Del Ennis (1946–56)	1,124	Cy Williams (1918–30)	796
Chuck Klein (1928–33; 1936–39; 1940–44)	983	Puddin' Head Jones (1947–59)	753
Sam Thompson (1889–98)	958	Pinky Whitney (1928–33; 1936–39)	734

ALL-TIME EXTRA BASE HIT LEADERS

Mike Schmidt (1972–89)	1,115	Johnny Callison (1960–69)	534
Ed Delahanty (1888–89; 1891–1901)	667	Cy Williams (1918–30)	503
Chuck Klein (1928–33; 1936–39; 1940–44)	643	Greg Luzinski (1970–80)	497
Del Ennis (1946–56)	634	Richie Allen (1963–69)	472
Sherry Magee (1904–14)	539	Sam Thompson (1889–98)	456

ALL-TIME BATTING AVERAGE LEADERS (500 game min.)

Billy Hamilton (1890–95)	.362	Spud Davis (1928–33; 1938–39)	.321
Ed Delahanty (1888–89; 1891–1901)	.348	Freddy Leach (1923–28)	.312
Elmer Flick (1898–1901)	.345	Richie Ashburn (1948–59)	.311
Sam Thompson (1889–98)	.335	Pinky Whitney (1928–33; 1936–39)	.307
Chuck Klein (1928–33; 1936–39; 1940–44)	.326	Cy Williams (1918–30)	.306

ALL-TIME STOLEN BASE LEADERS

Sherry Magee (1904–14)	387	Garry Maddox (1975–86)	189
Larry Bowa (1970–81)	288	Mike Schmidt (1972–88)	174
Juan Samuel (1983–89)	249	Dode Paskert (1911–17)	149
Roy Thomas (1899–1908)	224	Tony Taylor (1960–71; 1974–76)	136
Richie Ashburn (1948–59)	199	Red Dooin (1902–14)	132

PITCHING

ALL-TIME GAME LEADERS

Robin Roberts (1948–61)	529	Dick Farrell (1956–61; 1967–69)	359
Steve Carlton (1972–86)	499	Grover C. Alexander (1911–17)	338
Tug McGraw (1975–84)	463	Jack Baldschun (1961–65)	333
Chris Short (1959–72)	459	Curt Simmons (1947–50; 1952–60)	325
Ron Reed (1976–83)	458	Jim Konstanty (1948–54)	314

ALL-TIME WIN LEADERS

Steve Carlton (1972–86)	241	Al Orth (1895–1901)	101
Robin Roberts (1948–61)	234	Tully Sparks (1903–10)	94
Grover C. Alexander (1911–17)	190	Bill Duggleby (1898; 1901; 1902–07)	91
Chris Short (1959–72)	132	Jim Bunning (1964–67; 1970–71)	89
Curt Simmons (1947–50; 1952–60)	115	Eppa Rixey (1912–17; 1919–20)	87

ALL-TIME INNINGS PITCHED LEADERS

Robin Roberts (1948–61)	3,740	Tully Sparks (1903–10)	1,691
Steve Carlton (1972–86)	3,696	Bill Duggleby (1898; 1901; 1902–07)	1,642
Grover C. Alexander (1911–17)	2,513	Eppa Rixey (1912–17; 1919–20)	1,604
Chris Short (1959–72)	2,252	Jim Bunning (1964–67; 1970–71)	1,520
Curt Simmons (1947–50; 1952–60)	1,939	Al Orth (1895–1901)	1,505

ALL-TIME LOSS LEADERS

Robin Roberts (1948–61)	199	Bill Duggleby (1898; 1901; 1902–07)	101
Steve Carlton (1972–86)	161	Jimmy Ring (1921–25; 1928)	98
Chris Short (1959–72)	127	Tully Sparks (1903–10)	95
Curt Simmons (1947–50; 1952–60)	110	Grover C. Alexander (1911–17)	91
Eppa Rixey (1912–17; 1919–20)	103	Ray Benge (1928–32; 1936)	82

ALL-TIME SHUTOUT LEADERS

Grover C. Alexander (1911–17)	61	Curt Simmons (1947–50; 1952–60)	18
Steve Carlton (1972–86)	39	Tully Sparks (1903–10)	18
Robin Roberts (1948–61)	35	George McQuillan (1907–10; 1915–16)	17
Chris Short (1959–72)	24	Bill Duggleby (1898; 1901; 1902–07)	16
Jim Bunning (1964–67; 1970–71)	23	Eppa Rixey (1912–17; 1919–20)	16
Earl Moore (1908–13)	18		

ALL-TIME STRIKEOUT LEADERS

Steve Carlton (1972–86)	3,030	Curt Simmons (1947–50; 1952–60)	1,052
Robin Roberts (1948–61)	1,871	Larry Christenson (1973–83)	781
Chris Short (1959–72)	1,585	Dick Ruthven (1973–75; 1978–83)	717
Grover C. Alexander (1911–17)	1,409	Rick Wise (1964; 1966–71)	717
Jim Bunning (1964–67; 1970–71)	1,197	Eppa Rixey (1912–17; 1919–20)	690

ALL-TIME WALK LEADERS

Steve Carlton (1972–86)	1,252	Grover C. Alexander (1911–17)	561
Chris Short (1959–72)	762	Earl Moore (1908–13)	537
Robin Roberts (1948–61)	718	Phil Collins (1929–35)	496
Curt Simmons (1947–50; 1952–60)	718	Eppa Rixey (1912–17; 1919–20)	479
Jimmy Ring (1921–25; 1928)	630	Dick Ruthven (1973–75; 1978–83)	475

ALL-TIME WON-LOST PERCENTAGE LEADERS

Grover C. Alexander (1911–17)	.683	Ron Reed (1976–83)	.600
Charlie Ferguson (1884–87)	.607	Wiley Piatt (1898–1900)	.589
Charlie Buffinton (1887–89)	.606	Al Orth (1895–1901)	.581
Red Donahue (1898–1901)	.603	Gus Weyhing (1892–95)	.573
Steve Carlton (1972–86)	.600	Schoolboy Rowe (1943; 1946–49)	.571

ALL-TIME SAVE LEADERS

Steve Bedrosian (1986–89)	103	Al Holland (1983–85)	55
Tug McGraw (1975–84)	94	Jim Konstanty (1948–54)	54
Ron Reed (1976–83)	90	Gene Garber (1974–78)	51
Dick Farrell (1956–61; 1967–69)	65	Dick Selma (1970–73)	26
Jack Baldschun (1961–65)	59	Robin Roberts (1948–61)	24

PHILLIES LEAGUE LEADERS

BATTING

BATTING AVERAGE
S. Magee, 1910
L. O'Doul, 1929
C. Klein, 1933
H. Walker, 1947 (Also with St. Louis)
R. Ashburn, 1955, '58

HOME RUNS
G. Cravath, 1913, '14, '15, '17 (Tie), '18, '19
C. Williams, 1920, '23, '27 (Tie)
C. Klein, 1929, '31, '32 (Tie), '33
M. Schmidt, 1974, '75, '76, '80, '81, '83, '84 (Tie), '86

HITS
G. Cravath, 1913
S. Magee, 1914
L. O'Doul, 1929
C. Klein, 1932, '33
R. Ashburn, 1951, '53, '58
D. Cash, 1975
P. Rose, 1981

RBI
E. Flick, 1900
S. Magee, 1907, '10, '14
G. Cravath, 1913, '15
C. Klein, 1931, '33
D. Hurst, 1932
D. Ennis, 1950
G. Luzinski, 1975
M. Schmidt, 1981, '84 (Tie), '86

RUNS SCORED
R. Thomas, 1900
S. Magee, 1910
G. Cravath, 1915
C. Klein, 1930, '31 (Tie), '32
R. Allen, 1964
M. Schmidt, 1981
V. Hayes, 1986 (Tie)

DOUBLES
E. Delehanty, 1901 (Tie)
S. Magee, 1914
B. Niehoff, 1916
C. Klein, 1930, '33
E. Allen, 1934 (Tie)
J. Callison, 1966
W. Montanez, 1972 (Tie)
P. Rose, 1980
V. Hayes, 1986

TRIPLES
H. Walker, 1947 (Also with St. Louis)
R. Ashburn, 1950, '58
R. Allen, 1964 (Tie)
J. Callison, 1962 (Tie), '65
L. Bowa, 1972

D. Cash, 1976
J. Samuel, 1984 (Tie), '87

STOLEN BASES
C. Klein, 1932
D. Murtaugh, 1941
R. Ashburn, 1948

PITCHING
(Post-1900)

WON-LOST PERCENTAGE
G. Alexander, 1915
S. Carlton, 1976
J. Denny, 1983

WINS
G. Alexander, 1911, 1914, 1915, 1916, 1917
T. Seaton, 1913
J. Elliott, 1931
R. Roberts, 1952, 1953, 1954, 1955
S. Carlton, 1972, 1977, 1980, 1982
J. Denny, 1983

STRIKEOUTS
E. Moore, 1910
G. Alexander, 1911, 1912, 1914, 1915, 1916, 1917
T. Seaton, 1913
C. Passeau, 1939 (Also Chicago)
R. Roberts, 1954
J. Sanford, 1957
J. Bunning, 1967
S. Carlton, 1972, 1980, 1982, 1983

ERA
G. McQuillan, 1910
G. Alexander, 1915, 1916, 1917
S. Carlton, 1972

SAVES
J. O'Farrell, 1918 (Tie)
P. Collins, 1933
A. Karl, 1945 (Tie)
K. Raffensberger, 1946
J. Konstanty, 1950
J. Meyer, 1955
S. Bedrosian, 1987

MOST VALUABLE PLAYERS
C. Klein, 1932
J. Konstanty, 1950
M. Schmidt, 1980, '81, '86

ROOKIES OF YEAR
J. Sanford, 1957
R. Allen, 1964

CY YOUNG WINNERS
S. Carlton, 1972, '77, '80, '82
J. Denny, 1983
S. Bedrosian, 1987

PITTSBURGH PIRATES

BATTING

ALL-TIME GAME LEADERS

Roberto Clemente (1955–72)	2,433	Paul Waner (1926–40)	2,154
Honus Wagner (1900–17)	2,432	Pie Traynor (1920–37)	1,941
Willie Stargell (1962–82)	2,360	Lloyd Waner (1927–41; 1944–45)	1,803
Max Carey (1910–26)	2,171	Tommy Leach (1900–12; 1918)	1,548
Bill Mazeroski (1956–72)	2,163	Fred Clarke (1900–11; 1913–15)	1,442

ALL-TIME AT BAT LEADERS

Roberto Clemente (1955–72)	9,454	Bill Mazeroski (1956–72)	7,755
Honus Wagner (1900–17)	9,046	Pie Traynor (1920–37)	7,559
Paul Waner (1926–40)	8,429	Lloyd Waner (1972–41; 1944–45)	7,256
Max Carey (1910–26)	8,406	Tommy Leach (1900–12; 1918)	5,909
Willie Stargell (1962–82)	7,927	Fred Clarke (1900–11; 1913–15)	5,471

ALL-TIME RUN LEADERS

Honus Wagner (1900–17)	1,520	Pie Traynor (1920–37)	1,183
Paul Waner (1926–40)	1,492	Lloyd Waner (1927–41; 1944–45)	1,151
Roberto Clemente (1955–72)	1,416	Fred Clarke (1900–11; 1913–15)	1,017
Max Carey (1910–26)	1,414	Tommy Leach (1900–12; 1918)	1,007
Willie Stargell (1962–82)	1,195	Arky Vaughan (1932–41)	936

ALL-TIME HIT LEADERS

Roberto Clemente (1955–72)	3,000	Lloyd Waner (1927–41; 1944–45)	2,317
Honus Wagner (1900–17)	2,970	Willie Stargell (1962–82)	2,232
Paul Waner (1926–40)	2,868	Bill Mazeroski (1956–72)	2,016
Max Carey (1910–26)	2,416	Arky Vaughan (1932–41)	1,709
Pie Traynor (1920–37)	2,416	Fred Clarke (1900–11; 1913–15)	1,638

ALL-TIME DOUBLE LEADERS

Honus Wagner (1900–17)	556	Dave Parker (1973–83)	296
Paul Waner (1926–40)	556	Bill Mazeroski (1956–72)	294
Roberto Clemente (1955–72)	440	Arky Vaughan (1932–41)	291
Willie Stargell (1962–82)	423	Al Oliver (1968–77)	276
Max Carey (1910–26)	375	Gus Suhr (1930–39)	276
Pie Traynor (1920–37)	371		

ALL-TIME TRIPLE LEADERS

Honus Wagner (1900–17)	231	Max Carey (1910–26)	148
Paul Waner (1926–40)	186	Tommy Leach (1900–12; 1918)	137
Roberto Clemente (1955–72)	166	Arky Vaughan (1932–41)	116
Pie Traynor (1920–37)	164	Jake Beckley (1888–89; 1891–96)	114
Fred Clarke (1900–11; 1913–15)	155	Lloyd Waner (1927–41; 1944–45)	114

ALL-TIME HOME RUN LEADERS

Willie Stargell (1962–82)	475	Bill Mazeroski (1956–72)	138
Ralph Kiner (1946–53)	301	Al Oliver (1968–77)	135
Roberto Clemente (1955–72)	240	Richie Hebner (1968–76; 1982–83)	128
Dave Parker (1973–83)	166	Dick Stuart (1958–62)	117
Frank Thomas (1951–58)	163	Bill Robinson (1975–82)	109

ALL-TIME TOTAL BASE LEADERS

Roberto Clemente (1955–72)	4,492	Max Carey (1910–26)	3,285
Honus Wagner (1900–17)	4,234	Lloyd Waner (1927–41; 1944–45)	2,898
Willie Stargell (1962–82)	4,190	Bill Mazeroski (1956–72)	2,848
Paul Waner (1926–40)	4,120	Arky Vaughan (1932–41)	2,484
Pie Traynor (1920–37)	3,289	Dave Parker (1973–83)	2,397

ALL-TIME RBI LEADERS

Willie Stargell (1962–82)	1,540	Bill Mazeroski (1956–72)	853
Honus Wagner (1900–17)	1,475	Ralph Kiner (1946–53)	801
Roberto Clemente (1955–72)	1,305	Gus Suhr (1930–39)	789
Pie Traynor (1920–37)	1,273	Arky Vaughan (1932–41)	764
Paul Waner (1926–40)	1,177	Dave Parker (1973–83)	758

ALL-TIME EXTRA BASE HIT LEADERS

Willie Stargell (1962–82)	953	Max Carey (1910–26)	589
Honus Wagner (1900–17)	869	Dave Parker (1973–83)	524
Paul Waner (1926–40)	850	Bill Mazeroski (1956–72)	494
Roberto Clemente (1955–72)	846	Arky Vaughan (1932–41)	491
Pie Traynor (1920–37)	593	Ralph Kiner (1946–53)	486

ALL-TIME BATTING AVERAGE LEADERS (500 game min.)

Paul Waner (1926–40)	.340	Arky Vaughan (1932–41)	.324
Kiki Cuyler (1921–27)	.336	Ginger Beaumont (1899–1906)	.321
Elmer Smith (1892–97; 1901)	.328	Pie Traynor (1920–37)	.320
Honus Wagner (1900–17)	.328	Lloyd Waner (1927–41; 1944–45)	.319
Matty Alou (1966–70)	.327	Roberto Clemente (1955–72)	.317

ALL-TIME STOLEN BASE LEADERS

Max Carey (1910–26)	678	Frank Taveras (1971–79)	206
Honus Wagner (1900–17)	639	Carson Bigbee (1916–26)	182
Omar Moreno (1975–82)	412	Ginger Beaumont (1899–1906)	169
Fred Clarke (1900–11; 1913–15)	261	Pie Traynor (1920–37)	158
Tommy Leach (1900–12; 1918)	249	Lee Lacy (1979–84)	140

PITCHING

ALL-TIME WIN LEADERS

Wilbur Cooper (1912–24)	202	Ray Kremer (1924–33)	143
Babe Adams (1907; 1909–26)	194	Rip Sewell (1938–49)	143
Sam Leever (1898–1910)	194	John Candelaria (1975–85)	124
Bob Friend (1951–65)	191	Jesse Tannehill (1897–1902)	116
Deacon Phillippe (1900–11)	165	Bob Veale (1962–72)	116
Vern Law (1950–51; 1954–67)	162		

ALL-TIME GAME LEADERS

Roy Face (1953–68)	802	Wilbur Cooper (1912–24)	469
Kent Tekulve (1974–85)	722	Dave Giusti (1970–76)	410
Bob Friend (1951–65)	568	Sam Leever (1898–1910)	388
Babe Adams (1907; 1909–26)	483	Rip Sewell (1938–49)	385
Vern Law (1950–51; 1954–67)	483	Don Robinson (1978–87)	343

ALL-TIME INNINGS PITCHED LEADERS

Bob Friend (1951–65)	3,481	Deacon Phillippe (1900–11)	2,283
Wilbur Cooper (1912–24)	3,201	Rip Sewell (1938–49)	2,108
Babe Adams (1907; 1909–26)	2,991	Ray Kremer (1924–33)	1,955
Vern Law (1950–51; 1954–67)	2,673	Bob Veale (1962–72)	1,869
Sam Leever (1898–1910)	2,645	John Candelaria (1975–85)	1,854

ALL-TIME LOSS LEADERS

Bob Friend (1953–68)	218	Rip Sewell (1938–49)	97
Wilbur Cooper (1912–24)	159	Roy Face (1953–68)	93
Vern Law (1950–51; 1954–67)	147	Deacon Phillippe (1900–11)	93
Babe Adams (1907; 1909–26)	139	Ron Kline (1952; 1955–59; 1968–69)	91
Sam Leever (1898–1910)	100	Bob Veale (1962–72)	91

ALL-TIME SHUTOUT LEADERS

Babe Adams (1907; 1909–26)	47		Vern Law (1950–51; 1954–67)	28
Sam Leever (1898–1910)	39		Deacon Phillippe (1900–11)	25
Bob Friend (1951–65)	35		Vic Willis (1906–09)	23
Wilbur Cooper (1912–24)	34		Rip Sewell (1938–49)	20
Lefty Leifield (1905–12)	29		Bob Veale (1962–72)	20

ALL-TIME STRIKEOUT LEADERS

Bob Friend (1951–65)	1,682		Babe Adams (1907; 1909–26)	1,036
Bob Veale (1962–72)	1,652		Steve Blass (1964; 1966–74)	896
Wilbur Cooper (1912–24)	1,191		Dock Ellis (1968–75)	869
John Candelaria (1975–85)	1,142		Deacon Phillippe (1900–11)	853
Vern Law (1950–51; 1954–67)	1,092		Rick Rhoden (1979–86)	852

ALL-TIME WALK LEADERS

Bob Friend (1951–65)	869		Vern Law (1950–51; 1954–67)	597
Bob Veale (1962–72)	839		Sam Leever (1898–1910)	587
Wilbur Cooper (1912–24)	762		Howie Camnitz (1904; 1906–13)	532
Rip Sewell (1938–49)	740		Frank Killen (1893–98)	519
Steve Blass (1964; 1966–74)	597		Ray Kremer (1924–33)	483

ALL-TIME WON-LOST PERCENTAGE LEADERS

Jesse Tannehill (1897–1902)	.667		Ray Kremer (1924–33)	.627
Sam Leever (1898–1910)	.661		Jim Bibby (1978–83)	.610
Vic Willis (1906–09)	.659		Al McBean (1961–68; 1970)	.602
Jack Chesbro (1899–1902)	.648		John Candelaria (1975–85)	.596
Deacon Phillippe (1900–11)	.645		Rip Sewell (1938–49)	.596
Lee Meadows (1923–29)	.629			

ALL-TIME SAVE LEADERS

Roy Face (1953–68)	186		Ramon Hernandez (1971–76)	39
Kent Tekulve (1974–85)	158		Grant Jackson (1977–81)	36
Dave Giusti (1970–76)	133		Rod Scurry (1980–85)	34
Don Robinson (1978–87)	43		Goose Gossage (1977)	26
Jim Gott (1987–88)	42		Enrique Romero (1979–82)	26

PIRATES LEAGUE LEADERS

BATTING

BATTING AVERAGE
H. Wagner, 1900, '03, '04, '06, '07, '08, '09, '11
G. Beaumont, 1902
P. Waner, 1927, '34, '36
A. Vaughan, 1935
D. Garms, 1940
D. Groat, 1960
R. Clemente, 1961, '64, '65, '67
M. Alou, 1966
D. Parker, 1977, '78
B. Madlock, 1981, '83

HOME RUNS
T. Leach, 1902
R. Kiner, 1946, '47 (Tie), '48 (Tie), '49, '50, '51, '52 (Tie)
W. Stargell, 1971, '73

HITS
G. Beaumont, 1903, '04
H. Wagner, 1908
B. Byrne, 1910
P. Waner, 1927, '34
L. Waner, 1931
R. Clemente, 1964 (Tie), '67
M. Alou, 1969
D. Parker, 1977

RBI
H. Wagner, 1901, '02, '08, '09
J. Nealon, 1906 (Tie)
P. Waner, 1927
R. Kiner, 1949
W. Stargell, 1973

RUNS
H. Wagner, 1902, '06 (Tie)
G. Beaumont, 1903
T. Leach, 1909
M. Carey, 1913
K. Cuyler, 1925, '26
L. Waner, 1927
P. Waner, 1928, '34
A. Vaughan, 1936, '40
R. Kiner, 1951 (Tie)

DOUBLES
H. Wagner, 1900, '01 (Tie), '02, '04, '06, '07, '08, '09
F. Clarke, 1903 (Tie)
B. Byrne, 1910
P. Waner, 1928, '32
M. Alou, 1969
W. Stargell, 1973
D. Parker, 1977
J. Ray, 1983 (Tie), '84 (Tie)

TRIPLES
H. Wagner, 1900, '01 (Tie), '03, '08
F. Clarke, 1906 (Tie)
O. Wilson, 1912

M. Carey, 1914, '23 (Tie)
B. Hinchman, 1916
B. Southworth, 1919 (Tie)
P. Traynor, 1923 (Tie)
K. Cuyler, 1925
P. Waner, 1926, '27
L. Waner, 1929
A. Comorosky, 1930
A. Vaughan, 1933, '37, '40
J. Barrett, 1944
G. Bell, 1951 (Tie)
D. Long, 1955
B. Virdon, 1962 (Tie)
R. Clemente, 1969
O. Moreno, 1980

STOLEN BASES
K. Cuyler, 1926
L. Handley, 1939
J. Barrett, 1944
F. Taveras, 1977
O. Moreno, 1978, '79

PITCHING
(Post–1900)

WON-LOST PERCENTAGE
J. Tannehill, 1900
J. Chesbro, 1901, 1902
S. Leever, 1903
C. Hendrix, 1912
E. Yde, 1924
R. Kremer, 1926
R. Face, 1959
S. Blass, 1968
J. Candelaria, 1977
J. Bibby, 1980
M. Dunne, 1987

WINS
J. Chesbro, 1902
W. Cooper, 1921
L. Meadows, 1926 (Tie)
R. Kremer, 1926 (Tie), 1930
B. Grimes, 1928
H. Meine, 1931
R. Sewell, 1943 (Tie)
R. Friend, 1958

STRIKEOUTS
R. Waddell, 1900
P. Roe, 1945
R. Veale, 1964

ERA
R. Waddell, 1900
J. Tannehill, 1901
S. Leever, 1903
R. Kremer, 1926, 1927
C. Blanton, 1935

R. Friend, 1955
J. Candelaria, 1977

SAVES
W. Cooper, 1918 (Tie)
J. Morrison, 1924 (Tie)
M. Brown, 1937 (Tie), '40 (Tie)
T. Wilks, 1951 (Also with St. Louis)
R. Face 1958, '61 (Tie), '62
D. Giusti, 1971

MOST VALUABLE PLAYERS
P. Waner, 1927
D. Groat, 1960

R. Clemente, 1966
D. Parker, 1978
W. Stargell, 1979 (Tie)

ROOKIES OF YEAR
none

CY YOUNG WINNERS
V. Law, 1960

ST. LOUIS CARDINALS

BATTING

ALL-TIME GAME LEADERS

Stan Musial (1941–44; 1946–63)	3,026	Ken Boyer (1955–65)	1,667
Lou Brock (1964–79)	2,289	Rogers Hornsby (1915–26; 1933)	1,580
Enos Slaughter (1938–53)	1,820	Julian Javier (1960–71)	1,578
Red Schoendienst (1945–56; 1961–63)	1,795	Ted Simmons (1968–80)	1,564
Curt Flood (1958–69)	1,738	Marty Marion (1940–50)	1,502

ALL-TIME AT BAT LEADERS

Stan Musial (1941–44; 1946–63)	10,972	Curt Flood (1958–69)	6,318
Lou Brock (1964–79)	9,125	Rogers Hornsby (1915–26; 1933)	5,881
Red Schoendienst (1945–56; 1961–63)	6,841	Ted Simmons (1968–80)	5,725
Enos Slaughter (1938–53)	6,775	Julian Javier (1960–71)	5,631
Ken Boyer (1955–65)	6,334	Jim Bottomley (1922–32)	5,314

ALL-TIME RUN LEADERS

Stan Musial (1941–44; 1946–63)	1,949	Ken Boyer (1955–65)	988
Lou Brock (1964–79)	1,427	Jim Bottomley (1922–32)	921
Rogers Hornsby (1915–26; 1933)	1,089	Curt Flood (1958–69)	845
Enos Slaughter (1938–53)	1,071	Frankie Frisch (1927–37)	831
Red Schoendienst (1945–56; 1961–63)	1,025	Joe Medwick (1932–40; 1947–48)	811

ALL-TIME HIT LEADERS

Stan Musial (1941–44; 1946–63)	3,630	Ken Boyer (1955–65)	1,855
Lou Brock (1964–79)	2,713	Curt Flood (1958–69)	1,853
Rogers Hornsby (1915–26; 1933)	2,110	Jim Bottomley (1922–32)	1,727
Enos Slaughter (1938–53)	2,064	Ted Simmons (1968–80)	1,704
Red Schoendienst (1945–56; 1961–63)	1,980	Joe Medwick (1932–40; 1947–48)	1,590

ALL-TIME DOUBLE LEADERS

Stan Musial (1941–44; 1946–63)	725	Red Schoendienst (1945–56; 1961–63)	352
Lou Brock (1964–79)	434	Jim Bottomley (1922–32)	344
Joe Medwick (1932–40; 1947–48)	377	Ted Simmons (1968–80)	332
Rogers Hornsby (1915–26; 1933)	367	Frankie Frisch (1927–37)	286
Enos Slaughter (1938–53)	366	Curt Flood (1958–69)	271

ALL-TIME TRIPLE LEADERS

Stan Musial (1941–44; 1946–63)	177	Ed Konetchy (1907–13)	93
Rogers Hornsby (1915–26; 1933)	143	Joe Medwick (1932–40; 1947–48)	81
Enos Slaughter (1938–53)	135	Pepper Martin (1928; 1930–40; 1944)	75
Lou Brock (1964–79)	121	Garry Templeton (1976–81)	69
Jim Bottomley (1922–32)	119	Johnny Mize (1936–41)	66

ALL-TIME HOME RUN LEADERS

Stan Musial (1941–44; 1946–63)	475	Johnny Mize (1936–41)	158
Ken Boyer (1955–65)	255	Joe Medwick (1932–40; 1947–48)	152
Rogers Hornsby (1915–26; 1933)	193	Enos Slaughter (1938–53)	146
Jim Bottomley (1922–32)	181	Bill White (1959–65)	140
Ted Simmons (1968–80)	172	Lou Brock (1964–79)	129

ALL-TIME TOTAL BASE LEADERS

Stan Musial (1941–44; 1946–63)	6,134	Jim Bottomley (1922–32)	2,852
Lou Brock (1964–79)	3,776	Red Schoendienst (1945–56; 1961–63)	2,657
Rogers Hornsby (1916–26; 1933)	3,342	Ted Simmons (1968–80)	2,626
Enos Slaughter (1938–53)	3,138	Joe Medwick (1932–40; 1947–48)	2,585
Ken Boyer (1955–65)	3,011	Curt Flood (1958–69)	2,464

ALL-TIME RBI LEADERS

Stan Musial (1941–44; 1946–63)	1,951	Ted Simmons (1968–80)	929
Enos Slaughter (1938–53)	1,148	Joe Medwick (1932–40; 1947–48)	923
Jim Bottomley (1922–32)	1,105	Lou Brock (1964–79)	814
Rogers Hornsby (1915–26; 1933)	1,067	Frankie Frisch (1927–37)	720
Ken Boyer (1955–65)	1,001	Johnny Mize (1936–41)	653

ALL-TIME EXTRA BASE HIT LEADERS

Stan Musial (1941–44; 1946–63)	1,377	Joe Medwick (1932–40; 1947–48)	610
Rogers Hornsby (1915–26; 1933)	703	Ken Boyer (1955–65)	585
Lou Brock (1964–79)	684	Ted Simmons (1968–80)	541
Enos Slaughter (1938–53)	647	Red Schoendienst (1945–56; 1961–63)	482
Jim Bottomley (1922–32)	644	Johnny Mize (1936–41)	442

ALL-TIME BATTING AVERAGE LEADERS (500 game min.)

Rogers Hornsby (1915–26; 1933)	.359	Jim Bottomley (1922–32)	.325
Johnny Mize (1936–41)	.336	Frankie Frisch (1927–37)	.312
Joe Medwick (1932–40; 1947–48)	.335	George Watkins (1930–33)	.309
Stan Musial (1941–44; 1946–63)	.331	Joe Torre (1969–74)	.308
Chick Hafey (1924–31)	.326	Ripper Collins (1931–36)	.307

ALL-TIME STOLEN BASE LEADERS

Lou Brock (1964–79)	833	Jack Smith (1915–26)	203
Vince Coleman (1985–89)	472	Miller Huggins (1910–16)	174
Ozzie Smith (1982–89)	285	Lonnie Smith (1982–85)	173
Willie McGee (1982–89)	246	Tommy Herr (1979–88)	152
Frankie Frisch (1927–37)	195	Ed Konetchy (1907–13)	151

PITCHING

ALL-TIME GAME LEADERS

Jesse Haines (1920–37)	554	Bill Doak (1913–24; 1929)	376
Bob Gibson (1959–75)	528	Lindy McDaniel (1955–62)	336
Bill Sherdel (1918–30; 1932)	465	Larry Jackson (1955–62)	330
Al Brazle (1943; 1946–54)	441	Al Hrabosky (1970–77)	329
Bob Forsch (1974–88)	425	Slim Sallee (1908–16)	316

ALL-TIME WIN LEADERS

Bob Gibson (1959–75)	251	Harry Brecheen (1940; 1943–52)	127
Jesse Haines (1920–37)	210	Mort Cooper (1938–45)	105
Bob Forsch (1974–88)	154	Slim Sallee (1908–16)	105
Bill Sherdel (1918–30; 1932)	153	Larry Jackson (1955–62)	101
Bill Doak (1913–24; 1929)	145	Max Lanier (1938–46; 1949–51)	101
Dizzy Dean (1930; 1932–37)	134		

ALL-TIME INNINGS PITCHED LEADERS

Bob Gibson (1959–75)	3,885	Slim Sallee (1908–16)	1,902
Jesse Haines (1920–37)	3,204	Ted Breitenstein (1892–96; 1901)	1,897
Bob Forsch (1974–88)	2,550	Harry Brecheen (1940; 1943–52)	1,790
Bill Sherdel (1918–30; 1932)	2,450	Dizzy Dean (1930; 1932–37)	1,736
Bill Doak (1913–24; 1929)	2,387	Larry Jackson (1955–62)	1,672

ALL-TIME LOSS LEADERS

Bob Gibson (1959–75)	174	Ted Breitenstein (1892–96; 1901)	124
Jesse Haines (1920–37)	158	Slim Sallee (1908–16)	107
Bill Doak (1913–24; 1929)	136	Larry Jackson (1955–62)	86
Bill Sherdel (1918–30; 1932)	131	Bob Harmon (1909–13)	81
Bob Forsch (1974–89)	127	Harry Brecheen (1940; 1943–52)	79

ALL-TIME SHUTOUT LEADERS

Bob Gibson (1959–75)	56	Dizzy Dean (1930; 1932–37)	23
Bill Doak (1913–24; 1929)	32	Max Lanier (1938–46; 1949–51)	20
Mort Cooper (1938–45)	28	Howie Pollet (1941–43; 1946–51)	20
Harry Brecheen (1940; 1943–52)	25	Ernie Broglio (1959–64)	18
Jesse Haines (1920–37)	24	Bob Forsch (1974–88)	18

ALL-TIME STRIKEOUT LEADERS

Bob Gibson (1959–75)	3,117	Bill Doak (1913–24; 1929)	938
Dizzy Dean (1930; 1932–37)	1,087	Larry Jackson (1955–62)	899
Bob Forsch (1974–88)	1,039	Harry Brecheen (1940; 1943–52)	857
Jesse Haines (1920–37)	979	Vinegar Bend Mizell (1952–60)	789
Steve Carlton (1965–71)	951	Bill Hallahan (1925–36)	784

ALL-TIME WALK LEADERS

Bob Gibson (1959–75)	1,336	Bill Hallahan (1925–36)	651
Jesse Haines (1920–37)	870	Bill Sherdel (1918–30; 1932)	595
Ted Breitenstein (1892–96; 1901)	825	Bob Harmon (1909–13)	594
Bob Forsch (1974–88)	742	Vinegar Bend Mizell (1952–60)	568
Bill Doak (1913–24; 1929)	740	Max Lanier (1938–46; 1949–51)	524

ALL-TIME ERA LEADERS

Slim Sallee (1908–16)	2.67	Fred Beebe (1906–09)	2.79
Jack Taylor (1904–06)	2.67	Max Lanier (1938–46; 1949–51)	2.84
Red Ames (1915–19)	2.74	Harry Brecheen (1940; 1943–52)	2.91
Johnny Lush (1907–10)	2.74	Bob Gibson (1959–75)	2.91
Mort Cooper (1938–45)	2.77	Bill Doak (1913–24; 1929)	2.93

ALL-TIME WON-LOST PERCENTAGE LEADERS

Mort Cooper (1938–45)	.677	Al Brazle (1943; 1946–54)	.602
Dizzy Dean (1930; 1932–37)	.641	George Munger (1943–44; 1946–52)	.602
Lon Warneke (1937–42)	.629	Howie Pollet (1941–43; 1946–51)	.599
Grover C. Alexander (1926–29)	.618	Max Lanier (1938–46; 1949–51)	.594
Harry Brecheen (1940; 1943–52)	.617	Bob Gibson (1959–75)	.591

ALL-TIME SAVE LEADERS

Bruce Sutter (1981–84)	127	Al Hrabosky (1970–77)	59
Todd Worrell (1985–89)	94	Dizzy Dean (1930; 1932–37)	30
Lindy McDaniel (1955–62)	64	Ted Wilks (1944–51)	29
Al Brazle (1943; 1946–54)	60	Mark Littell (1978–82)	28
Joe Hoerner (1966–69)	60	Diego Segui (1972–73)	26

CARDINALS LEAGUE LEADERS

BATTING

BATTING AVERAGE
J. Burkett, 1901
R. Hornsby, 1920, '21, '22, '23, '24, '25
C. Hafey, 1931
J. Medwick, 1937
J. Mize, 1939
S. Musial, 1943, '46, '48, '50, '51, '52, '57
H. Walker, 1947 (Also with Philadelphia)
J. Torre, 1971
K. Hernandez, 1979
W. McGee, 1985

HOME RUNS
R. Hornsby, 1922, '25
J. Bottomley, 1928 (Tie)
R. Collins, 1934 (Tie)
J. Mize, 1939, '40

HITS
J. Burkett, 1901
R. Hornsby, 1920, '21, '22, '24, '25
J. Bottomley, 1925
J. Medwick, 1936, '37
E. Slaughter, 1942
S. Musial, 1943, '44 (Tie) '46, '48, '49, '52
J. Torre, 1971
C. Flood, 1964 (Tie)
G. Templeton, 1979
W. McGee, 1985

RBI
R. Hornsby, 1920 (Tie), '21, '22, '25
J. Bottomley, 1926, '28
J. Medwick, 1936, '37, '38
J. Mize, 1940
E. Slaughter, 1946
S. Musial, 1948, '56
K. Boyer, 1964
O. Cepeda, 1967
J. Torre, 1971

RUNS
J. Burkett, 1901
R. Hornsby, 1921, '22, '24 (Tie)
P. Martin, 1933
J. Medwick, 1937
S. Musial, 1946, '48, '51 (Tie), '52 (Tie), '54 (Tie)
S. Hemus, 1952 (Tie)
L. Brock, 1967 (Tie), 1971
K. Hernandez, 1979, '80
L. Smith, 1982

DOUBLES
E. Konetchy, 1911
R. Hornsby, 1920, '21, '22, '24
J. Bottomley, 1925
S. Adams, 1931
J. Medwick, 1936, '37, '38
E. Slaughter, 1939

J. Mize, 1941 (Tie)
M. Marion, 1942
S. Musial, 1943, '44, '46, '48, '49, '52, '53, '54
R. Schoendienst, 1950
D. Groat, 1963
L. Brock, 1968
K. Hernandez, 1979

TRIPLES
T. Long, 1915
R. Hornsby, 1917, '21 (Tie)
J. Bottomley, 1928
J. Medwick, 1934
J. Mize, 1938
E. Slaughter, 1942, '49 (Tie)
S. Musial, 1943, '46, '48, '49 (Tie), '51 (Tie)
H. Walker, 1947 (Also with Philadelphia)
T. McCarver, 1966
L. Brock, 1968
G. Templeton, 1977, '78, '79
W. McGee, 1985

STOLEN BASES
P. Donovan, 1900 (Tie)
F. Frisch, 1927, '31
P. Martin, 1933, '34, '36
R. Schoendienst, 1945
L. Brock, 1966, '67, '68, '69, '71, '72, '73, '74
V. Coleman, 1985, '86, '87

PITCHING
(Post–1900)

WON-LOST PERCENTAGE
W. Doak, 1921
W. Sherdel, 1925
P. Derringer, 1931
J. Dean, 1934
M. Cooper, 1943
T. Wilks, 1944
K. Burkhart, 1945
M. Dickson, 1946
H. Brecheen, 1948
E. Broglio, 1960
D. Hughes, 1967
R. Gibson, 1970

WINS
F. Rhem, 1926
W. Hallahan, 1931
J. Dean, 1934, 1935
M. Cooper, 1942, 1943
C. Barrett, 1945 (Also Boston)
H. Pollett, 1946
E. Broglio, 1960
R. Gibson, 1970
J. Andujar, 1984

STRIKEOUTS
F. Beebe, 1906 (Also Chicago)

W. Hallahan, 1930, 1931
J. Dean, 1932, 1933, 1934, 1935
H. Brecheen, 1948
S. Jones, 1958
R. Gibson, 1968
J. Deleon, 1989

ERA
W. Doak, 1914, 1921
M. Cooper, 1942
H. Pollett, 1943, 1946
H. Brecheen, 1948
J. Hearn, 1950 (Also New York)
R. Gibson, 1968
J. Denny, 1976
J. Magrane, 1988

SAVES
H. Sallee, 1912, '14 (Tie)
L. Ames, 1916
O. Tuero, 1919
W. Sherdel, 1920, '27, '28 (Tie)
L. North, 1921
H. Haid, 1928
H. Bell, 1930
J. Dean, 1936
R. Bowman, 1939 (Tie)
C. Shoun, 1939 (Tie)
T. Wilks, 1949, '51 (Also with Pittsburgh)
A. Brazle, 1952, '53
L. McDaniel, 1959 (Tie), '60
A. Hrabosky, 1975 (Tie)

B. Sutter, 1981, '82, '84
T. Worrell, 1986

MOST VALUABLE PLAYERS
R. Hornsby, 1925
B. O'Farrell, 1926
J. Bottomley, 1928
F. Frisch, 1931
D. Dean, 1934
J. Medwick, 1937
M. Cooper, 1942
S. Musial, 1943, '46, '48
M. Marion, 1944
K. Boyer, 1964
O. Cepeda, 1967
B. Gibson, 1968
J. Torre, 1971
K. Hernandez, 1979 (Tie)
W. McGee, 1985

ROOKIES OF YEAR
W. Moon, 1954
B. Virdon, 1955
B. McBride, 1974
V. Coleman, 1985
T. Worrell, 1986

CY YOUNG WINNERS
B. Gibson, 1968, '70

SAN DIEGO PADRES

BATTING

ALL-TIME GAME LEADERS

Dave Winfield (1973–80)	1,117	Nate Colbert (1969–74)	866
Garry Templeton (1982–89)	1,110	Terry Kennedy (1981–86)	835
Tony Gwynn (1982–89)	1,060	Clarence Gaston (1969–74)	766
Tim Flannery (1979–89)	972	Fred Kendall (1969–76)	754
Gene Richards (1977–83)	939	Enzo Hernandez (1971–77)	710

ALL-TIME AT BAT LEADERS

Tony Gwynn (1982–89)	4,078	Terry Kennedy (1981–86)	2,987
Dave Winfield (1973–80)	3,997	Clarence Gaston (1969–74)	2,615
Garry Templeton (1982–89)	3,950	Enzo Hernandez (1971–77)	2,324
Gene Richards (1977–83)	3,414	Steve Garvey (1983–87)	2,292
Nate Colbert (1969–74)	3,080	Ozzie Smith (1978–81)	2,236

ALL-TIME RUN LEADERS

Tony Gwynn (1982–89)	617	Terry Kennedy (1981–86)	308
Dave Winfield (1973–80)	599	Steve Garvey (1983–87)	291
Gene Richards (1977–83)	484	Clarence Gaston (1969–74)	269
Nate Colbert (1969–74)	422	Ozzie Smith (1978–81)	266
Garry Templeton (1982–89)	380	Enzo Hernandez (1971–77)	241

ALL-TIME HIT LEADERS

Tony Gwynn (1982–89)	1,354	Nate Colbert (1969–74)	780
Dave Winfield (1973–80)	1,134	Clarence Gaston (1969–74)	672
Garry Templeton (1982–89)	999	Steve Garvey (1983–87)	631
Gene Richards (1977–83)	994	Tim Flannery (1979–89)	631
Terry Kennedy (1981–86)	817	Luis Salazar (1980–84; 1987)	532

ALL-TIME DOUBLE LEADERS

Tony Gwynn (1982–89)	192	Gene Richards (1977–83)	123
Dave Winfield (1973–80)	179	Carmelo Martinez (1984–89)	111
Garry Templeton (1982–89)	169	Steve Garvey (1983–87)	107
Terry Kennedy (1981–86)	158	Johnny Grubb (1972–76)	101
Nate Colbert (1969–74)	130	Clarence Gaston (1969–74)	93

ALL-TIME TRIPLE LEADERS

Gene Richards (1977–83)	63	Nate Colbert (1969–74)	22
Tony Gwynn (1982–89)	51	Luis Salazar (1980–84; 1987)	22
Dave Winfield (1973–80)	39	Tim Flannery (1979–89)	21
Garry Templeton (1982–89)	32	Ozzie Smith (1978–81)	19
Clarence Gaston (1969–74)	29	Kevin McReynolds (1983–86)	17

ALL-TIME HOME RUN LEADERS

Nate Colbert (1969–74)	163	Gene Tenace (1977–80)	68
Dave Winfield (1973–80)	154	Kevin McReynolds (1983–86)	65
Carmelo Martinez (1984–89)	82	Steve Garvey (1983–87)	61
Clarence Gaston (1969–74)	77	Ollie Brown (1969–72)	52
Terry Kennedy (1981–86)	76	Willie McCovey (1974–76)	52

ALL-TIME TOTAL BASE LEADERS

Dave Winfield (1973–80)	1,853	Terry Kennedy (1981–86)	1,217
Tony Gwynn (1982–89)	1,783	Clarence Gaston (1969–74)	1,054
Nate Colbert (1977–83)	1,443	Steve Garvey (1983–87)	937
Garry Templeton (1982–89)	1,331	Kevin McReynolds (1983–86)	783
Gene Richards (1977–83)	1,321	Luis Salazar (1980–84; 1987)	738

ALL-TIME RBI LEADERS

Dave Winfield (1973–80)	626		Steve Garvey (1983–87)	316
Nate Colbert (1969–74)	481		Clarence Gaston (1969–74)	316
Terry Kennedy (1981–86)	424		Kevin McReynolds (1983–86)	260
Tony Gwynn (1982–89)	416		Gene Richards (1977–83)	251
Garry Templeton (1982–88)	322		Gene Tenace (1977–80)	239

ALL-TIME EXTRA BASE HIT LEADERS

Dave Winfield (1973–80)	372		Clarence Gaston (1969–74)	199
Nate Colbert (1969–74)	315		Steve Garvey (1983–87)	176
Tony Gwynn (1982–88)	250		Carmelo Martinez (1984–89)	170
Terry Kennedy (1981–86)	241		Kevin McReynolds (1983–86)	166
Garry Templeton (1982–89)	234		Gene Tenace (1977–80)	150
Gene Richards (1977–83)	212			

ALL-TIME BATTING AVERAGE LEADERS
(300 game min.)

Tony Gwynn (1982–89)	.332		Steve Garvey (1983–87)	.275
Gene Richards (1977–83)	.291		Terry Kennedy (1981–86)	.274
Johnny Grubb (1972–76)	.288		Ollie Brown (1969–72)	.272
Dave Winfield (1973–80)	.284		Mike Ivie (1971; 1974–77)	.269
Broderick Perkins (1978–82)	.276		Luis Salazar (1980–84; 1987)	.267

ALL-TIME STOLEN BASE LEADERS

Gene Richards (1977–83)	242		Enzo Hernandez (1971–77)	129
Tony Gwynn (1982–89)	221		Garry Templeton (1982–89)	100
Alan Wiggins (1981–85)	171		Luis Salazar (1980–84; 1987)	92
Ozzie Smith (1978–81)	147		Jerry Mumphrey (1980)	52
Dave Winfield (1973–80)	133		Nate Colbert (1969–74)	48

PITCHING

ALL-TIME GAME LEADERS

Eric Show (1981–89)	270	Gary Ross (1969–74)	219
Rollie Fingers (1977–80)	265	Dave Dravecky (1928–87)	199
Randy Jones (1973–80)	264	Andy Hawkins (1982–88)	199
Craig Lefferts (1984–87)	238	Goose Gossage (1984–87)	197
Gary Lucas (1980–83)	230	Bob Shirley (1977–1980)	197
Lance McCullers (1985–88)	229		

ALL-TIME WIN LEADERS

Eric Show (1981–89)	94	Clay Kirby (1969–73)	52
Randy Jones (1973–80)	92	Bob Shirley (1977–80)	39
Andy Hawkins (1982–88)	60	Tim Lollar (1981–84)	36
Ed Whitson (1983–84; 1986–89)	59	Rollie Fingers (1977–80)	34
Dave Dravecky (1982–87)	53	Gaylord Perry (1978–79)	33

ALL-TIME INNINGS PITCHED LEADERS

Randy Jones (1973–80)	1,766	Dave Dravecky (1982–87)	900
Eric Show (1981–89)	1,497	Steve Arlin (1969–74)	746
Clay Kirby (1969–73)	1,128	Dave Freisleben (1974–78)	731
Andy Hawkins (1982–88)	1,103	Bob Shirley (1977–80)	722
Ed Whitson (1983–84; 1986–89)	1,047	Tim Lollar (1981–84)	682

ALL-TIME LOSS LEADERS

Randy Jones (1973–80)	105	Andy Hawkins (1982–88)	58
Clay Kirby (1969–73)	81	Bob Shirley (1977–80)	57
Eric Show (1981–89)	79	Ed Whitson (1983–84; 1986–89)	57
Steve Arlin (1969–74)	62	Dave Freisleben (1974–78)	53
Bill Greif (1972–76)	61	Dave Dravecky (1982–87)	50

ALL-TIME SHUTOUT LEADERS

Randy Jones (1973–80)	18	Dave Dravekcy (1982–87)	6
Steve Arlin (1969–74)	11	Dave Freisleben (1974–78)	6
Eric Show (1981–89)	11	Fred Norman (1971–73)	6
Andy Hawkins (1982–88)	7	Bill Greif (1972–76)	5
Clay Kirby (1969–73)	7	Eric Rasmussen (1978–80)	5

ALL-TIME STRIKEOUTS LEADERS

Eric Show (1981–89)	896	Dave Dravecky (1982–87)	456
Clay Kirby (1969–73)	802	Tim Lollar (1981–84)	454
Randy Jones (1973–80)	677	Steve Arlin (1969–74)	443
Ed Whitson (1983–84; 1986–89)	600	Bob Shirley (1977–80)	432
Andy Hawkins (1982–88)	489	Bill Greif (1972–76)	391

ALL-TIME WALKS LEADERS

Eric Show (1981–89)	552	Dave Freisleben (1974–78)	346
Clay Kirby (1969–73)	505	Tim Lollar (1981–84)	328
Randy Jones (1973–80)	414	Bob Shirley (1977–80)	274
Andy Hawkins (1982–88)	412	Dave Dravecky (1982–87)	270
Steve Arlin (1969–74)	351	Dan Spillner (1974–78)	255

ALL-TIME ERA LEADERS

Gaylord Perry (1978–79)	2.88	Randy Jones (1973–80)	3.30
Dave Roberts (1969–71)	2.99	Eric Show (1981–89)	3.43
Dave Dravecky (1982–87)	3.12		

ALL-TIME WON-LOST PERCENTAGE LEADERS

Gaylord Perry (1978–79)	.660	Dave Dravecky (1982–87)	.515
LaMarr Hoyt (1985–86)	.558	Craig Lefferts (1984–87)	.512
Goose Gossage (1984–87)	.556	Ed Whitson (1983–84; 1986–89)	.509
Eric Show (1981–89)	.543	Andy Hawkins (1982–88)	.508
Mark Thurmond (1983–86)	.517	Jack Curtis (1980–82)	.500

ALL-TIME SAVE LEADERS

Rollie Fingers (1977–80)	108	Craig Lefferts (1984–87)	18
Goose Gossage (1984–87)	83	Butch Metzger (1975–77)	16
Mark Davis (1987–89)	74	Vicente Romo (1973–74)	16
Gary Lucas (1980–83)	49	John D'Acquisto (1977–80)	13
Lance McCullers (1985–88)	36	Bill Greif (1972–76)	13
Luis DeLeon (1982–85)	31		

PADRES LEAGUE LEADERS

BATTING

BATTING AVERAGE
T. Gwynn, 1984, '87, '88

HITS
T. Gwynn, 1984, '86, '87

RBI
D. Winfield, 1979

RUNS
T. Gwynn, 1986 (Tie)

TRIPLES
G. Richards, 1981 (Tie)

PITCHING

WON-LOST PERCENTAGE
G. Perry, 1978

WINS
R. Jones, 1976
G. Perry, 1978

ERA
R. Jones, 1975

SAVES
R. Fingers, 1977, '78
M. Davis, 1989

MOST VALUABLE PLAYERS
none

ROOKIES OF YEAR
B. Metzger, 1976 (Tie)
B. Santiago, 1987

CY YOUNG WINNERS
R. Jones, 1976
G. Perry, 1978
M. Davis, 1989

SAN FRANCISCO GIANTS (NEW YORK)

BATTING

ALL-TIME GAME LEADERS

Willie Mays (1951–52; 1954–72)	2,857	Larry Doyle (1907–16; 1918–20)	1,615
Mel Ott (1926–47)	2,730	Jim Davenport (1958–70)	1,501
Willie McCovey (1959–74; 1977–80)	2,256	Whitey Lockman (1945; 1947–56; 1957–58)	1,485
Bill Terry (1923–36)	1,721	Mike Tiernan (1887–99)	1,474
Travis Jackson (1922–36)	1,656	George Burns (1911–21)	1,362

ALL-TIME AT BAT LEADERS

Willie Mays (1951–52; 1954–72)	10,477	Larry Doyle (1907–16; 1918–20)	5,995
Mel Ott (1926–47)	9,456	Mike Tiernan (1887–99)	5,910
Willie McCovey (1959–74; 1977–80)	7,214	Whitey Lockman (1945; 1947–56; 1957–58)	5,584
Bill Terry (1923–36)	6,428	Jo-Jo Moore (1930–41)	5,427
Travis Jackson (1922–36)	6,086	George Burns (1911–21)	5,311

ALL-TIME RUN LEADERS

Willie Mays (1951–52; 1954–72)	2,011	George Van Haltren (1894–1903)	982
Mel Ott (1926–47)	1,859	Roger Connor (1883–89; 1891; 1893–94)	939
Mike Tiernan (1887–99)	1,312	Larry Doyle (1907–16; 1918–20)	906
Bill Terry (1923–36)	1,120	George Burns (1911–21)	877
Willie McCovey (1959–74; 1977–80)	1,113	George Davis (1893–1901; 1903)	844

ALL-TIME HIT LEADERS

Willie Mays (1951–52; 1954–72)	3,187	Travis Jackson (1922–36)	1,768
Mel Ott (1926–47)	2,876	Larry Doyle (1907–16; 1918–20)	1,751
Bill Terry (1923–36)	2,193	Jo-Jo Moore (1930–41)	1,615
Willie McCovey (1959–74; 1977–80)	1,974	George Van Haltren (1894–1903)	1,592
Mike Tiernan (1887–99)	1,875	Whitey Lockman (1945; 1947–56; 1957–58)	1,571

ALL-TIME DOUBLE LEADERS

Willie Mays (1951–52; 1954–72)	504	Larry Doyle (1907–16; 1918–20)	275
Mel Ott (1926–47)	488	George Burns (1911–21)	267
Bill Terry (1923–36)	374	Jo-Jo Moore (1930–41)	258
Willie McCovey (1959–74; 1977–80)	308	Mike Tiernan (1887–99)	248
Travis Jackson (1922–36)	291	Roger Connor (1883–89; 1891; 1893–94)	240

ALL-TIME TRIPLE LEADERS

Mike Tiernan (1887–99)	159	Buck Ewing (1883–89; 1891–92)	108
Willie Mays (1951–52; 1954–72)	139	George Davis (1893–1901; 1903)	97
Roger Connor (1883–89; 1891; 1893–94)	129	Ross Youngs (1917–26)	93
Larry Doyle (1907–16; 1918–20)	117	George Van Haltren (1894–1903)	90
Bill Terry (1923–36)	112	Travis Jackson (1922–36)	86

ALL-TIME HOME RUN LEADERS

Willie Mays (1951–52; 1954–72)	646	Bobby Bonds (1968–74)	186
Mel Ott (1926–47)	511	Jack Clark (1975–84)	163
Willie McCovey (1959–74; 1977–80)	469	Jim Ray Hart (1963–73)	157
Orlando Cepeda (1958–66)	226	Johnny Mize (1942; 1946–49)	157
Bobby Thomson (1946–53; 1957)	189	Bill Terry (1923–36)	154

ALL-TIME TOTAL BASE LEADERS

Willie Mays (1951–52; 1954–72)	5,907	Travis Jackson (1922–36)	2,636
Mel Ott (1926–47)	5,041	Larry Doyle (1907–16; 1918–20)	2,461
Willie McCovey (1959–74; 1977–80)	3,779	Orlando Cepeda (1958–66)	2,234
Bill Terry (1923–36)	3,253	Whitey Lockman (1945; 1947–56; 1957–58)	2,216
Mike Tiernan (1887–99)	2,765	Jo-Jo Moore (1930–41)	2,216

ALL-TIME RBI LEADERS

Mel Ott (1926–47)	1,860	Mike Tiernan (1887–99)	852
Willie Mays (1951–52; 1954–72)	1,859	George Davis (1893–1901; 1903)	805
Willie McCovey (1959–74; 1977–80)	1,388	Orlando Cepeda (1958–66)	767
Bill Terry (1923–36)	1,078	George "Highpockets" Kelly (1915–17; 1919–26)	761
Travis Jackson (1922–36)	929	Larry Doyle (1907–16; 1918–20)	728

ALL-TIME EXTRA BASE HIT LEADERS

Willie Mays (1951–52; 1954–72)	1,289	Travis Jackson (1922–36)	512
Mel Ott (1926–47)	1,071	Orlando Cepeda (1958–66)	474
Willie McCovey (1959–74; 1977–80)	822	Larry Doyle (1907–16; 1918–20)	459
Bill Terry (1923–36)	640	Roger Connor (1883–89; 1891; 1893–94)	445
Mike Tiernan (1887–99)	515	Bobby Thomson (1946–53; 1957)	437

ALL-TIME BATTING AVERAGE LEADERS
(500 or more games)

Bill Terry (1923–36)	.341	Frankie Frisch (1919–26)	.321
George Davis (1893–1901; 1903)	.335	Freddie Lindstrom (1924–32)	.318
Roger Connor (1883–89; 1891; 1893–94)	.334	Mike Tiernan (1887–99)	.317
George Van Haltren (1894–1903)	.323	Buck Ewing (1883–89; 1891–92)	.315
Ross Youngs (1917–26)	.322	Irish Meusel (1921–26)	.314

ALL-TIME STOLEN BASE LEADERS

George Burns (1911–21)	334	Red Murray (1909–15; 1917)	231
Willie Mays (1951–52; 1954–72)	332	Frankie Frisch (1919–26)	224
Larry Doyle (1907–16; 1918–20)	271	Fred Merkle (1907–16)	192
Art Devlin (1904–11)	264	Fred Snodgrass (1908–15)	190
Bobby Bonds (1968–74)	263	Ross Youngs (1917–26)	153

PITCHING

ALL-TIME GAME LEADERS

Gary Lavelle (1974–84)	647	Juan Marichal (1960–73)	458
Christy Mathewson (1900–16)	634	Freddie Fitzsimmons (1925–37)	403
Greg Minton (1975–87)	552	Jim Barr (1971–78; 1982–83)	394
Carl Hubbell (1928–43)	535	Hal Schumacher (1931–42; 1946)	391
Randy Moffitt (1972–81)	459	Gaylord Perry (1962–71)	367

ALL-TIME WIN LEADERS

Christy Mathewson (1900–16)	372	Joe McGinnity (1902–08)	151
Carl Hubbell (1928–43)	253	Hooks Wiltse (1904–14)	136
Juan Marichal (1960–73)	238	Gaylord Perry (1962–71)	134
Freddie Fitzsimmons (1925–37)	170	Larry Jansen (1947–54)	120
Hal Schumacher (1931–42; 1946)	158	Jeff Tesreau (1912–18)	115

ALL-TIME INNINGS PITCHED LEADERS

Christy Mathewson (1900–16)	4,772	Gaylord Perry (1962–71)	2,295
Carl Hubbell (1928–43)	3,591	Joe McGinnity (1902–08)	2,151
Juan Marichal (1960–73)	3,443	Hooks Wiltse (1904–14)	2,050
Freddie Fitzsimmons (1925–37)	2,515	Red Ames (1903–13)	1,944
Hal Schumacher (1931–42; 1946)	2,483	Dummy Taylor (1900–02; 1903–08)	1,853

ALL-TIME LOSS LEADERS

Christy Mathewson (1900–16)	187		Hal Schumacher (1931–42; 1946)	121
Amos Rusie (1890–98)	163		Freddie Fitzsimmons (1925–37)	114
Carl Hubbell (1928–43)	154		Gaylord Perry (1962–71)	109
Mickey Welch (1883–92)	145		Dave Koslo (1941–42; 1946–53)	104
Juan Marichal (1960–73)	140		Dummy Taylor (1900–02; 1903–08)	103

ALL-TIME SHUTOUT LEADERS

Christy Mathewson (1900–16)	83		Joe McGinnity (1902–08)	26
Juan Marichal (1960–73)	52		Johnny Antonelli (1954–60)	21
Carl Hubbell (1928–43)	36		Freddie Fitzsimmons (1925–37)	21
Hal Schumacher (1931–42; 1946)	29		Gaylord Perry (1962–71)	21
Hooks Wiltse (1904–14)	29		Dummy Taylor (1900–02; 1903–08)	21
Jeff Tesreau (1912–18)	27			

ALL-TIME STRIKEOUT LEADERS

Christy Mathewson (1900–16)	2,502		Mike McCormick (1956–62; 1967–70)	1,030
Juan Marichal (1960–73)	2,281		Bobby Bolin (1961–69)	977
Carl Hubbell (1928–43)	1,677		Hooks Wiltse (1904–14)	948
Gaylord Perry (1962–71)	1,606		Johnny Antonelli (1954–60)	919
Red Ames (1903–13)	1,118		Hal Schumacher (1931–42; 1946)	906

ALL-TIME WALK LEADERS

Hal Schumacher (1931–42; 1946)	902		Red Ames (1903–13)	620
Christy Mathewson (1900–16)	839		Gaylord Perry (1962–71)	581
Carl Hubbell (1928–43)	725		Jeff Tesreau (1912–18)	572
Juan Marichal (1960–73)	690		Johnny Antonelli (1954–60)	548
Freddie Fitzsimmons (1925–37)	670		Dummy Taylor (1900–02; 1903–08)	535

ALL-TIME WON-LOST PERCENTAGE LEADERS

Sal Maglie (1945; 1950–55)	.693		Art Nehf (1919–26)	.641
Tim Keefe (1885–89; 1891)	.680		Fred Toney (1918–22)	.636
Christy Mathewson (1900–16)	.665		Joe McGinnity (1902–08)	.632
Jess Barnes (1918–23)	.656		Juan Marichal (1960–73)	.630
Doc Crandall (1908–13)	.650		Carl Hubbell (1928–43)	.622

ALL-TIME SAVE LEADERS

Gary Lavelle (1974–84)	127	Stu Miller (1958–62)	46
Greg Minton (1975–87)	125	Don McMahon (1969–74)	36
Randy Moffitt (1972–81)	83	Jerry Johnson (1970–72)	27
Frank Linzy (1963; 1965–70)	77	Elias Sosa (1972–74)	27
Scott Garrelts (1982–88)	48	Bobby Bolin (1961–69)	21

GIANTS LEAGUE LEADERS

BATTING

BATTING AVERAGE
L. Doyle, 1915
B. Terry, 1930
W. Mays, 1954

HOME RUNS
R. Murray, 1909
D. Robertson, 1916, '17 (Tie)
G. Kelly, 1921
M. Ott, 1932 (Tie), 1934 (Tie), '36, '37 (Tie), '38, '42
J. Mize, 1947 (Tie), '48 (Tie)
W. Mays, 1955, '62, '64, '65
O. Cepeda, 1961
W. McCovey, 1963 (Tie), '68, '69
K. Mitchell, 1989

HITS
L. Doyle, 1909, '15
F. Frisch, 1923
F. Lindstrom, 1928
B. Terry, 1930
D. Mueller, 1954
R. Schoendienst, 1957 (Also with Milwaulkee)
W. Mays, 1960

RBI
S. Mertes, 1903
B. Dahlen, 1904
H. Zimmerman, 1916 (Also with Chicago), '17
G. Kelly, 1920 (Tie)
I. Meusel, 1923, '24
M. Ott, 1934
J. Mize, 1942, '47
M. Irvin, 1951
O. Cepeda, 1961
W. McCovey, 1968, '69
K. Mitchell, 1989

RUNS SCORED
G. Browne, 1904
M. Donlin, 1905
S. Shannon, 1907
F. Tenney, 1908
G. Burns, 1914, '16, '17, '19, '20
R. Youngs, 1923
F. Frisch, 1924 (Tie)
B. Terry, 1930 (Tie)
M. Ott, 1938, '42
J. Mize, 1947
W. Mays, 1958, '61
B. Bonds, 1969 (Tie), '73
W. Clark, 1989 (Tie)

DOUBLES
S. Mertes, 1903 (Tie)
L. Doyle, 1915
R. Youngs, 1919
A. Dark, 1951
O. Cepeda, 1958

TRIPLES
L. Doyle, 1911
B. Terry, 1931
B. Thomson, 1952
W. Mays, 1954, '55 (Tie), '57
R. Thompson, 1989

STOLEN BASES
G. Van Haltren, 1900 (Tie)
A. Devlin, 1905 (Tie)
G. Burns, 1914, '19
F. Frisch, 1921
W. Mays, 1956, '57, '58, '59

PITCHING
(Post-1900)

WON-LOST PERCENTAGE
J. McGinnity, 1904
C. Mathewson, 1905, 1909
R. Marquard, 1911
F. Schupp, 1917
L. Benton, 1927 (Also Boston), 1928
F. Fitzsimmons, 1930
C. Hubbell, 1936, 1937
L. Jansen, 1947
S. Maglie, 1950
H. Wilhelm, 1952
J. Antonelli, 1954
J. Marichal, 1966
S. Garrelts, 1989 (Tie)

WINS
J. McGinnity, 1903, 1904, 1906
C. Mathewson, 1905, 1907, 1908, 1910
R. Marquard, 1912
J. Barnes, 1919
L. Benton, 1928
C. Hubbell, 1933, 1936, 1937
S. Maglie, 1951 (Tie)
L. Jansen, 1951 (Tie)
S. Jones, 1959 (Tie)
J. Marichal, 1960, 1968
M. McCormick, 1967
G. Perry, 1970
R. Bryant, 1973

STRIKEOUTS
C. Mathewson, 1903, 1904, 1905, 1907, 1908,
R. Marquard, 1911
W. Voiselle, 1944

ERA
J. McGinnity, 1904
C. Mathewson, 1905, 1908, 1909, 1911, 1913
J. Tesreau, 1912
R. Ryan, 1922
W. Walker, 1929, 1931
C. Hubbell, 1933, 1934, 1936
D. Koslo, 1949

J. Hearn, 1950 (Also St. Louis)
H. Wilhelm, 1952
J. Antonelli, 1954
S. Jones, 1959
M. McCormick, 1960
J. Marichal, 1969
A. Hammaker, 1983
S. Garrelts, 1989

R. Miller, 1903 (Tie)
J. McGinnity, 1904, '07
C. Elliott, 1905
G. Ferguson, 1906
C. Mathewson, 1908 (Tie)
R. Benton, 1915 (Tie) (Also with Cincinnati)
H. Sallee, 1917
F. Anderson, 1918 (Tie)
F. Toney, 1918 (Tie) (Also with Cincinnati)
C. Jonnard, 1922, '23
C. Davies, 1926
C. Hubbell, 1934
C. Melton, 1937 (Tie)

R. Coffman, 1938
W. Brown, 1940 (Tie), '41
A. Adams, 1944, '45 (Tie)
S. Miller, 1961 (Tie)

MOST VALUABLE PLAYERS
L. Doyle, 1912
C. Hubbell, 1933, '36
W. Mays, 1954, '65
W. McCovey, 1969

ROOKIES OF YEAR
W. Mays, 1951
O. Cepeda, 1958
W. McCovey, 1959
G. Matthews, 1973
J. Montefusco, 1975

CY YOUNG WINNER
M. McCormick, 1967

AMERICAN LEAGUE

BALTIMORE ORIOLES

BATTING

ALL-TIME GAME LEADERS

Brooks Robinson (1955–77)	2,896	Ken Singleton (1975–84)	1,446
Mark Belanger (1965–81)	1,962	Al Bumbry (1972–84)	1,428
Eddie Murray (1977–88)	1,820	Cal Ripkin (1981–89)	1,315
Boog Powell (1961–74)	1,763	Rick Dempsey (1976–86)	1,237
Paul Blair (1964–76)	1,700	Rich Dauer (1976–85)	1,140

ALL-TIME AT BAT LEADERS

Brooks Robinson (1955–77)	10,654	Ken Singleton (1975–84)	5,115
Eddie Murray (1977–88)	6,845	Cal Ripken (1981–89)	5,055
Boog Powell (1961–74)	5,912	Al Bumbry (1972–84)	4,958
Mark Belanger (1965–81)	5,734	Rich Dauer (1976–85)	3,829
Paul Blair (1964–76)	5,606	Rick Dempsey (1976–86)	3,576

ALL-TIME RUN LEADERS

Brooks Robinson (1955–77)	1,232	Paul Blair (1964–76)	737
Eddie Murray (1977–88)	1,048	Ken Singleton (1975–84)	684
Boog Powell (1961–74)	796	Mark Belanger (1965–81)	670
Cal Ripken (1981–89)	793	Frank Robinson (1966–71)	555
Al Bumbry (1972–84)	772	Rich Dauer (1976–85)	448

ALL-TIME HIT LEADERS

Brooks Robinson (1955–77)	2,848	Al Bumbry (1972–84)	1,403
Eddie Murray (1977–88)	2,021	Cal Ripken (1981–89)	1,402
Boog Powell (1961–74)	1,574	Mark Belanger (1965–81)	1,304
Ken Singleton (1975–84)	1,455	Rich Dauer (1976–85)	984
Paul Blair (1964–76)	1,426	Davey Johnson (1965–72)	904

ALL-TIME DOUBLE LEADERS

Brooks Robinson (1955–77)	482	Ken Singleton (1975–84)	235
Eddie Murray (1977–88)	351	Al Bumbry (1972–84)	217
Paul Blair (1964–76)	269	Rich Dauer (1976–85)	193
Cal Ripken (1981–89)	266	Davey Johnson (1965–72)	186
Boog Powell (1961–74)	243	Mark Belanger (1965–81)	174

ALL-TIME TRIPLE LEADERS

Brooks Robinson (1955–77)	68	Eddie Murray (1977–88)	25
Al Bumbry (1972–84)	52	Cal Ripken (1981–89)	24
Paul Blair (1964–76)	51	Jackie Brandt (1960–65)	22
Luis Aparicio (1963–67)	34	Russ Snyder (1961–67)	20
Mark Belanger (1965–81)	33	Bob Boyd (1956–60)	20
Bobby Grich (1970–76)	27		

ALL-TIME HOME RUN LEADERS

Eddie Murray (1977–88)	333	Frank Robinson (1966–71)	179
Boog Powell (1961–74)	303	Gus Triandos (1955–62)	142
Brooks Robinson (1955–77)	268	Paul Blair (1964–76)	126
Cal Ripken (1981–89)	204	Jim Gentile (1960–63)	124
Ken Singleton (1975–84)	182	Lee May (1975–80)	123

ALL-TIME TOTAL BASE LEADERS

Brooks Robinson (1955–77)	4,270	Paul Blair (1964–76)	2,175
Eddie Murray (1977–88)	3,421	Al Bumbry (1972–84)	1,883
Boog Powell (1961–74)	2,748	Mark Belanger (1965–81)	1,604
Cal Ripken (1981–89)	2,328	Frank Robinson (1966–71)	1,598
Ken Singleton (1975–84)	2,274	Gus Triandos (1955–62)	1,351

ALL-TIME RBI LEADERS

Brooks Robinson (1955–77)	1,357	Paul Blair (1964–76)	567
Eddie Murray (1977–88)	1,190	Frank Robinson (1966–71)	545
Boog Powell (1961–74)	1,063	Gus Triandos (1955–62)	517
Ken Singleton (1975–84)	766	Lee May (1975–80)	487
Cal Ripken (1981–89)	744	Jim Gentile (1960–63)	398

ALL-TIME EXTRA BASE HIT LEADERS

Brooks Robinson (1955–77)	818	Ken Singleton (1975–84)	436
Eddie Murray (1977–88)	709	Frank Robinson (1966–71)	340
Boog Powell (1961–74)	557	Al Bumbry (1972–84)	322
Cal Ripken (1981–89)	494	Doug DeCinces (1973–81)	282
Paul Blair (1964–76)	446	Davey Johnson (1965–72)	268

ALL-TIME BATTING AVERAGE LEADERS
(500 game minimum)

Bob Boyd (1956–60)	.301	Al Bumbry (1972–84)	.283
Frank Robinson (1966–71)	.300	Russ Snyder (1961–67)	.280
Eddie Murray (1977–88)	.295	Cal Ripken (1981–89)	.277
Marv Rettenmund (1968–73)	.284	Don Baylor (1970–75)	.274
Ken Singleton (1975–84)	.284	John Lowenstein (1979–85)	.274

ALL-TIME STOLEN BASE LEADERS

Al Bumbry (1972–84)	252	Don Buford (1968–72)	85
Paul Blair (1964–76)	167	Alan Wiggins (1985–87)	71
Luis Aparicio (1963–67)	166	Eddie Murray (1977–88)	61
Mark Belanger (1965–81)	166	Marv Rettenmund (1968–73)	52
Don Baylor (1970–75)	118	John Shelby (1981–87)	52

PITCHING

ALL-TIME GAME LEADERS

Jim Palmer (1965–84)	558	Mike Flanagan (1975–87)	344
Tippy Martinez (1976–86)	499	Dick Hall (1961–66)	342
Dave McNally (1962–74)	412	Dennis Martinez (1976–86)	319
Eddie Watt (1966–73)	363	Sammy Stewart (1978–85)	307
Scott McGregor (1976–87)	352	Stu Miller (1963–67)	297

ALL-TIME WIN LEADERS

Jim Palmer (1965–84)	268	Milt Pappas (1957–65)	110
Dave McNally (1962–74)	181	Dennis Martinez (1976–86)	108
Mike Cuellar (1969–76)	143	Steve Barber (1960–67)	95
Mike Flanagan (1975–87)	139	Mike Boddicker (1980–87)	73
Scott McGregor (1976–87)	138	Dick Hall (1961–66)	65

ALL-TIME INNINGS PITCHED LEADERS

Jim Palmer (1965–84)	3,948	Dennis Martinez (1976–86)	1,776
Dave McNally (1962–74)	2,653	Milt Pappas (1957–65)	1,632
Mike Flanagan (1975–87)	2,185	Steve Barber (1960–67)	1,415
Scott McGregor (1976–87)	2,124	Mike Boddicker (1980–87)	1,126
Mike Cuellar (1969–76)	2,028	Hal Brown (1955–62)	1,032

ALL-TIME LOSS LEADERS

Jim Palmer (1965–84)	152	Steve Barber (1960–67)	75
Dave McNally (1962–74)	113	Milt Pappas (1957–65)	74
Mike Flanagan (1975–87)	109	Mike Boddicker (1980–87)	61
Dennis Martinez (1976–86)	93	Hal Brown (1955–62)	48
Mike Cuellar (1969–76)	88		

ALL-TIME SHUTOUT LEADERS

Jim Palmer (1965–84)	53	Steve Barber (1960–67)	19
Dave McNally (1962–74)	33	Mike Flanagan (1975–87)	17
Mike Cuellar (1969–76)	30	Mike Boddicker (1980–87)	13
Milt Pappas (1957–65)	26	Tom Phoebus (1966–70)	11
Scott McGregor (1976–87)	23	Dennis Martinez (1976–86)	10

ALL-TIME STRIKEOUT LEADERS

Jim Palmer (1965–84)	2,212	Steve Barber (1960–67)	918
Dave McNally (1962–74)	1,476	Scott McGregor (1976–87)	894
Mike Flanagan (1975–87)	1,225	Dennis Martinez (1976–86)	858
Mike Cuellar (1969–76)	1,011	Mike Boddicker (1980–87)	736
Milt Pappas (1957–65)	944	Tippy Martinez (1976–86)	585

ALL-TIME WALK LEADERS

Jim Palmer (1965–84)	1,311	Dennis Martinez (1976–86)	583
Dave McNally (1962–74)	790	Milt Pappas (1957–65)	531
Mike Flanagan (1975–87)	692	Scott McGregor (1976–87)	511
Steve Barber (1960–67)	668	Sammy Stewart (1978–85)	433
Mike Cuellar (1969–76)	601	Chuck Estrada (1960–64)	394

ALL-TIME ERA LEADERS

Jim Palmer (1965–84)	2.86	Mike Cuellar (1969–76)	3.18
Dick Hall (1961–66; 1969–71)	2.89	Dave McNally (1962–74)	3.18
Tom Phoebus (1966–70)	3.06	Milt Pappas (1957–65)	3.24
Robin Roberts (1962–65)	3.09	Wally Bunker (1963–68)	3.40
Steve Barber (1960–67)	3.12	Tippy Martinez (1976–86)	3.45

ALL-TIME WON-LOST PERCENTAGE LEADERS

Steve Stone (1979–81)	.656	Dave McNally (1962–74)	.616
Jim Palmer (1965–84)	.638	Milt Pappas (1957–65)	.598
Wally Bunker (1963–68)	.620	Pat Dobson (1971–72)	.581
Mike Cuellar (1969–76)	.619	Jim Hardin (1967–71)	.576
Dick Hall (1961–66)	.619	Tom Phoebus (1966–70)	.574

ALL-TIME SAVE LEADERS

Tippy Martinez (1976–86)	105
Stu Miller (1963–67)	100
Eddie Watt (1966–73)	74
Dick Hall (1961–66)	58
Tim Stoddard (1978–83)	57

Don Aase (1985–87)	50
Don Stanhouse (1978–79)	45
Sammy Stewart (1978–85)	42
Hoyt Wilhelm (1958–62)	40
Grant Jackson (1971–76)	39

ORIOLES LEAGUE LEADERS

BATTING

BATTING
F. Robinson, 1966

HOME RUNS
F. Robinson, 1966
E. Murray, 1981 (Tie)

HITS
C. Ripken, 1983

RBI
B. Robinson, 1964
F. Robinson, 1966
L. May, 1976
E. Murray, 1981

RUNS
F. Robinson, 1966
D. Buford, 1971
C. Ripken, 1983

DOUBLES
B. Gardner, 1957 (Tie)

TRIPLES
P. Blair, 1967
A. Bumbry, 1973 (Tie)

STOLEN BASES
L. Aparicio, 1963, 1964

PITCHING

WON-LOST PERCENTAGE
W. Bunker, 1964
M. Cuellar, 1970, 1974
D. McNally, 1971
M. Torrez, 1975
M. Flanagan, 1979
S. Stone, 1980
J. Palmer, 1982 (Tie)

WINS
C. Estrada, 1960 (Tie)
D. McNally, 1970 (Tie)
M. Cuellar, 1970 (Tie)
J. Palmer, 1975 (Tie), 1976, 1977 (Tie)
S. Stone, 1980
D. Martinez, 1981 (Tie)
M. Boddicker, 1984

STRIKEOUTS
B. Turley, 1954
J. Palmer, 1969

ERA
H. Wilhelm, 1959
J. Palmer, 1973, 1975
M. Boddicker, 1984

SAVES
G. Zuverink, 1956
S. Miller, 1963

BOSTON RED SOX

BATTING

ALL-TIME GAME LEADERS

Carl Yastrzemski (1961–83)	3,308	Harry Hooper (1909–20)	1,646
Dwight Evans (1972–89)	2,382	Rico Petrocelli (1963–76)	1,553
Ted Williams (1939–42; 1946–60)	2,292	Dom DiMaggio (1940–42; 1946–53)	1,399
Jim Rice (1974–89)	2,089	Frank Malzone (1955–65)	1,359
Bobby Doerr (1937–44; 1946–51)	1,865	George Scott (1966–71; 1977–79)	1,192

ALL-TIME AT BAT LEADERS

Carl Yastrzemski (1961–83)	11,988	Harry Hooper (1909–20)	6,269
Dwight Evans (1972–89)	8,281	Dom DiMaggio (1940–42; 1946–53)	5,640
Jim Rice (1974–89)	8,225	Rico Petrocelli (1963–76)	5,390
Ted Williams (1939–42; 1946–60)	7,706	Frank Malzone (1955–65)	5,273
Bobby Doerr (1937–44; 1946–51)	7,093	Billy Goodman (1947–57)	4,399

ALL-TIME RUN LEADERS

Carl Yastrzemski (1961–83)	1,816	Dom DiMaggio (1940–42; 1946–53)	1,046
Ted Williams (1939–42; 1946–60)	1,798	Harry Hooper (1909–20)	988
Dwight Evans (1972–89)	1,369	Johnny Pesky (1942; 1946–52)	776
Jim Rice (1974–89)	1,249	Jimmie Foxx (1936–42)	721
Bobby Doerr (1937–44; 1946–51)	1,094	Tris Speaker (1907–15)	703

ALL-TIME HIT LEADERS

Carl Yastrzemski (1961–83)	3,419	Harry Hooper (1909–20)	1,707
Ted Williams (1939–42; 1946–60)	2,654	Dom DiMaggio (1940–42; 1946–53)	1,680
Jim Rice (1974–89)	2,452	Wade Boggs (1982–89)	1,597
Dwight Evans (1972–89)	2,098	Frank Malzone (1955–65)	1,454
Bobby Doerr (1937–44; 1946–51)	2,042	Rico Petrocelli (1963–76)	1,352

ALL-TIME DOUBLE LEADERS

Carl Yastrzemski (1961–83)	646	Dom DiMaggio (1940–42; 1946–53)	308
Ted Williams (1939–42; 1946–60)	525	Joe Cronin (1935–45)	270
Dwight Evans (1972–88)	429	Wade Boggs (1982–88)	263
Bobby Doerr (1937–44; 1946–51)	381	Duffy Lewis (1910–18)	254
Jim Rice (1974–88)	363	Billy Goodman (1947–57)	248

ALL-TIME TRIPLE LEADERS

Harry Hooper (1909–20)	130	Hobe Ferris (1901–07)	77
Tris Speaker (1907–15)	106	Jim Rice (1974–89)	76
Buck Freeman (1901–07)	90	Ted Williams (1939–42; 1946–60)	71
Bobby Doerr (1937–44; 1946–51)	89	Jimmy Collins (1901–07)	65
Larry Gardner (1908–17)	87	Freddy Parent (1901–07)	63

ALL-TIME HOME RUN LEADERS

Ted Williams (1939–42; 1946–60)	521	Jimmie Foxx (1936–42)	222
Carl Yastrzemski (1961–83)	452	Rico Petrocelli (1963–76)	210
Jim Rice (1974–89)	382	Jackie Jensen (1954–61)	170
Dwight Evans (1972–89)	366	Carlton Fisk (1969–80)	162
Bobby Doerr (1937–44; 1946–51)	223	Tony Conigliaro (1964–67; 1969–70; 1975)	162

ALL-TIME TOTAL BASE LEADERS

Carl Yastrzemski (1961–83)	5,539	Dom DiMaggio (1940–42; 1946–53)	2,363
Ted Williams (1939–42; 1946–60)	4,884	Harry Hooper (1909–20)	2,303
Jim Rice (1974–89)	4,129	Rico Petrocelli (1963–76)	2,263
Dwight Evans (1972–89)	3,954	Wade Boggs (1982–89)	2,175
Bobby Doerr (1937–44; 1946–51)	3,270	Frank Malzone (1955–65)	2,123

ALL-TIME RBI LEADERS

Carl Yastrzemski (1961–83)	1,844	Jimmie Foxx (1936–42)	788
Ted Williams (1939–42; 1946–60)	1,839	Rico Petrocelli (1963–76)	773
Jim Rice (1974–89)	1,451	Joe Cronin (1935–45)	737
Dwight Evans (1972–89)	1,283	Jackie Jensen (1954–61)	733
Bobby Doerr (1937–44; 1946–51)	1,247	Frank Malzone (1955–65)	716

ALL-TIME EXTRA BASE HIT LEADERS

Carl Yastrzemski (1961–83)	1,157	Rico Petrocelli (1963–76)	469
Ted Williams (1939–42; 1946–60)	1,117	Dom DiMaggio (1940–42; 1946–53)	452
Dwight Evans (1972–89)	891	Jimmie Foxx (1936–42)	448
Jim Rice (1974–89)	834	Joe Cronin (1935–45)	433
Bobby Doerr (1937–44; 1946–51)	693	Wade Boggs (1982–89)	414

ALL-TIME BATTING AVERAGE LEADERS
(500 games minimum)

Wade Boggs (1982–89)	.352	Roy Johnson (1932–35)	.313
Ted Williams (1939–42; 1946–60)	.344	Johnny Pesky (1942; 1946–52)	.313
Tris Speaker (1907–15)	.337	Fred Lynn (1974–80)	.308
Pete Runnels (1958–62)	.320	Billy Goodman (1947–57)	.306
Jimmie Foxx (1936–42)	.320	Doc Cramer (1936–40)	.302

ALL-TIME STOLEN BASE LEADERS

Harry Hooper (1909–20)	300	Freddy Parent (1901–07)	129
Tris Speaker (1907–15)	266	Tommy Harper (1972–75)	107
Carl Yastrzemski (1961–83)	168	Bill Werber (1933–36)	107
Heinie Wagner (1906–16; 1918)	141	Jimmy Collins (1901–07)	102
Larry Gardner (1908–17)	134	Duffy Lewis (1910–17)	102

PITCHING

ALL-TIME GAME LEADERS

Bob Stanley (1977–89)   637
Ellis Kinder (1948–55)   365
Cy Young (1901–08)   327
Ike Delock (1952–63)   322
Bill Lee (1969–78)   321

Mike Fornieles (1957–63)   286
Dick Radatz (1962–66)   286
Luis Tiant (1971–78)   274
Sparky Lyle (1967–71)   260

ALL-TIME WIN LEADERS

Cy Young (1901–08)   193
Mel Parnell (1947–56)   123
Luis Tiant (1971–78)   122
Smoky Joe Wood (1908–15)   116
Bob Stanley (1977–89)   115

Joe Dobson (1941–43; 1946–50)   106
Lefty Grove (1934–41)   105
Tex Hughson (1941–44; 1946–49)   96
Bill Monbouquette (1958–65)   96
Roger Clemens (1984–89)   95

ALL-TIME INNINGS PITCHED LEADERS

Cy Young (1901–08)   2,728
Luis Tiant (1971–78)   1,774
Mel Parnell (1947–56)   1,752
Bob Stanley (1977–89)   1,707
Bill Monbouquette (1958–65)   1,622

George Winter (1901–08)   1,600
Bruce Hurst (1980–88)   1,559
Joe Dobson (1941–43; 1946–50)   1,544
Lefty Grove (1934–41)   1,540
Tom Brewer (1954–61)   1,509

ALL-TIME LOSS LEADERS

Cy Young (1901–08)   112
Bob Stanley (1977–89)   97
Red Ruffing (1924–30)   96
George Winter (1901–08)   96
Jack Russell (1926–32; 1936)   94

Bill Monbouquette (1958–65)   91
Bill Dineen (1902–07)   86
Tom Brewer (1954–61)   82
Luis Tiant (1971–78)   81
Frank Sullivan (1953–60)   80

ALL-TIME SHUTOUT LEADERS

Cy Young (1901–08)	38	Ray Collins (1909–15)	19
Smoky Joe Wood (1908–15)	28	Tex Hughson (1941–44; 1946–49)	19
Luis Tiant (1971–78)	26	Sad Sam Jones (1916–21)	18
Hubert "Dutch" Leonard (1913–18)	25	Joe Dobson (1941–43; 1946–50)	17
Roger Clemens (1984–89)	21	Babe Ruth (1914–19)	17
Mel Parnell (1947–56)	20		

ALL-TIME STRIKEOUT LEADERS

Cy Young (1901–08)	1,341	Bill Monbouquette (1958–65)	969
Roger Clemens (1984–89)	1,215	Frank Sullivan (1953–60)	821
Luis Tiant (1971–78)	1,075	Ray Culp (1968–73)	794
Bruce Hurst (1980–88)	1,043	Jim Lonborg (1965–71)	784
Smoky Joe Wood (1908–15)	990	Hubert "Dutch" Leonard (1913–18)	771

ALL-TIME WALK LEADERS

Mel Parnell (1947–56)	758	Ike Delock (1952–63)	514
Tom Brewer (1954–61)	669	Mickey McDermott (1948–53)	504
Joe Dobson (1941–43; 1946–50)	604	Luis Tiant (1971–78)	501
Jack Wilson (1935–41)	564	Fritz Ostermueller (1934–40)	491
Willard Nixon (1950–58)	530	Earl Wilson (1959–66)	481

ALL-TIME ERA LEADERS

Smoky Joe Wood (1908–15)	1.99	Ray Collins (1909–15)	2.51
Cy Young (1901–08)	2.00	Bill Dineen (1902–07)	2.81
Hubert "Dutch" Leonard (1913–18)	2.11	George Winter (1901–08)	2.91
Babe Ruth (1914–19)	2.19	Tex Hughson (1941–44; 1946–49)	2.94
Carl Mays (1915–19)	2.21	Roger Clemens (1984–89)	3.07

ALL-TIME WON-LOST PERCENTAGE LEADERS

Roger Clemens (1984–89)	.679	Rube Foster (1913–17)	.630
Smoky Joe Wood (1908–15)	.674	Lefty Grove (1934–41)	.629
Babe Ruth (1914–19)	.659	Ellis Kinder (1948–55)	.623
Tex Hughson (1941–44; 1946–49)	.640	Mel Parnell (1947–56)	.621
Cy Young (1901–08)	.633	Jesse Tannehill (1904–08)	.620

ALL-TIME SAVE LEADERS

Bob Stanley (1977–89)	132	Bill Campbell (1977–81)	51
Dick Radatz (1962–66)	104	Mike Fornieles (1957–63)	48
Ellis Kinder (1948–55)	91	Dick Drago (1974–75; 1978–80)	41
Sparky Lyle (1967–71)	69	Tom Burgmeier (1978–82)	40
Lee Smith (1987–89)	54	Mark Clear (1981–85)	38

RED SOX LEAGUE LEADERS

BATTING

BATTING
D. Alexander, 1932 (Also with Detroit)
J. Foxx, 1938
T. Williams, 1941, '42, '47, '48, '57, '58
B. Goodman, 1950
P. Runnels, 1960, '62
C. Yastrzemski, 1963, '67, '68
F. Lynn, 1979
C. Lansford, 1981
W. Boggs, 1983, '85, '86, '87, '88

HOME RUNS
B. Freeman, 1903
J. Stahl, 1910
T. Speaker, 1912 (Tie)
B. Ruth, 1918 (Tie), '19
J. Foxx, 1939
T. Williams, 1941, '42, '47, '49
T. Conigliaro, 1965
C. Yastrzemski, 1967 (Tie)
J. Rice, 1977, '78, '83
T. Armas, 1984

HITS
P. Hickman, 1902 (Also with Cleveland)
P. Dougherty, 1903
T. Speaker, 1914
J. Vosmik, 1938
D. Cramer, 1940 (Tie)
J. Pesky, 1942, '46, '47
C. Yastrzemski, 1963, '67
J. Rice, 1978
W. Boggs, 1985

RBI
B. Freeman, 1902, '03
B. Ruth, 1919
J. Foxx, 1938
T. Williams, 1939, '42, '47, '49 (Tie)
V. Stephens, 1949 (Tie), '50 (Tie)
W. Dropo, 1950 (Tie)
J. Jensen, 1955 (Tie), '58, '59
D. Stuart, 1963
C. Yastrzemski, 1967
K. Harrelson, 1968
J. Rice, 1978, '83 (Tie)
T. Armas, 1984

RUNS
P. Dougherty, 1903, '04 (Also with New York)
B. Ruth, 1919
T. Williams, 1940, '41, '42, '46, '47, '49
D. DiMaggio, 1950, '51
C. Yastrzemski, 1967, '70, '74
F. Lynn, 1975
D. Evans, 1984
W. Boggs, 1988

DOUBLES
T. Speaker, 1912, '14

E. Webb, 1931
J. Cronin, 1938
T. Williams, 1948, '49
J. Piersall, 1956
C. Yastrzemski, 1963, '65 (Tie), '66
R. Smith, 1968, '71
F. Lynn, 1975
W. Boggs, 1988

TRIPLES
C. Stahl, 1904 (Tie)
B. Freeman, 1904 (Tie)
D. DiMaggio, 1950 (Tie)
B. Doerr, 1950 (Tie)
J. Jensen, 1956 (Tie)
C. Fisk, 1972 (Tie)
J. Rice, 1978

STOLEN BASES
B. Myer, 1928
B. Werber, 1934, '35
B. Chapman, 1937 (Also with Washington)
D. DiMaggio, 1950
J. Jensen, 1954
T. Harper, 1973

PITCHING

WON-LOST PERCENTAGE
C. Young, 1903
J. Wood, 1912, 1915
S. Jones, 1918
L. Grove, 1939
T. Hughson, 1944
B. Ferriss, 1946
J. Kramer, 1948
E. Kinder, 1949
R. Clemens, 1986, 1987

WINS
C. Young, 1901, 1902, 1903
J. Wood, 1912
W. Ferrell, 1935
T. Hughson, 1942
M. Parnell, 1949
F. Sullivan, 1954 (Tie)
J. Lonberg, 1967 (Tie)
R. Clemens, 1986, 1987 (Tie)

STRIKEOUTS
C. Young, 1901
T. Hughson, 1942 (Tie)
J. Lonberg, 1967
R. Clemens, 1988

ERA
C. Young, 1901
D. Leonard, 1914
J. Wood, 1915
B. Ruth, 1916

R. Grove, 1935, 1936, 1938, 1939
M. Parnell, 1949
L. Tiant, 1972
R. Clemens, 1986

SAVES
B. Dineen, 1903 (Tie), 1907 (Also with St. Louis)
C. Young, 1903 (Tie)
F. Arellanes, 1909
C. Hall, 1910 (Tie)

D. Leonard, 1914 (Tie)
C. Mays, 1915
A. Russell, 1919 (Also with New York)
W. Moore, 1931
B. Klinger, 1946
E. Kinder, 1951, '53
M. Fornieles, 1960 (Tie)
D. Radatz, 1962, '64
B. Campbell, 1977

CALIFORNIA ANGELS

BATTING

ALL-TIME GAME LEADERS

Brian Downing (1978–89) 1,565
Jim Fregosi (1961–71) 1,429
Bobby Grich (1977–86) 1,222
Bob Boone (1982–88) 968
Buck Rodgers (1961–69) 932

Rod Carew (1979–85) 834
Don Baylor (1977–82) 824
Bobby Knoop (1964–69) 803
Sandy Alomar (1969–74) 795
Doug DeCinces (1982–87) 787

ALL-TIME AT BAT LEADERS

Brian Downing (1978–89) 5,524
Jim Fregosi (1961–71) 5,244
Bobby Grich (1977–86) 4,100
Don Baylor (1977–82) 3,105
Rod Carew (1979–85) 3,080

Sandy Alomar (1969–74) 3,054
Bob Boone (1982–88) 3,033
Buck Rodgers (1961–69) 3,033
Doug DeCinces (1982–87) 2,884
Bobby Knoop (1964–69) 2,617

ALL-TIME RUN LEADERS

Brian Downing (1978–89) 842
Jim Fregosi (1961–71) 691
Bobby Grich (1977–86) 601
Don Baylor (1977–82) 481
Rod Carew (1979–85) 474

Doug DeCinces (1982–87) 404
Albie Pearson (1961–66) 374
Sandy Alomar (1969–74) 341
Reggie Jackson (1982–86) 331
Gary Pettis (1982–87) 296

ALL-TIME HIT LEADERS

Brian Downing (1978–89)   1,498
Jim Fregosi (1961–71)   1,408
Bobby Grich (1977–86)   1,103
Rod Carew (1979–85)   968
Don Baylor (1977–82)   813

Doug DeCinces (1982–87)   765
Sandy Alomar (1969–74)   758
Bob Boone (1982–88)   742
Buck Rodgers (1961–69)   704
Dave Chalk (1973–78)   631

ALL-TIME DOUBLE LEADERS

Brian Downing (1978–89)   264
Jim Fregosi (1961–71)   219
Bobby Grich (1977–86)   183
Doug DeCinces (1982–87)   149
Rod Carew (1979–85)   140

Don Baylor (1977–82)   140
Bob Boone (1982–88)   115
Buck Rodgers (1961–69)   114
Albie Pearson (1961–66)   98
Fred Lynn (1981–84)   94

ALL-TIME TRIPLE LEADERS

Jim Fregosi (1961–71)   70
Mickey Rivers (1970–75)   32
Bobby Knoop (1964–69)   25
Gary Pettis (1982–87)   23
Rod Carew (1979–85)   22

Bobby Grich (1977–86)   20
Buck Rodgers (1961–69)   18
Jerry Remy (1975–77)   18
Willie Smith (1964–66)   17
Albie Pearson (1961–66)   17

ALL-TIME HOME RUN LEADERS

Brian Downing (1978–89)   208
Bobby Grich (1977–86)   154
Don Baylor (1977–82)   141
Doug DeCinces (1982–87)   130
Reggie Jackson (1982–86)   123

Jim Fregosi (1961–71)   115
Leon Wagner (1961–63)   91
Fred Lynn (1981–84)   71
Rick Reichardt (1964–70)   68
Lee Thomas (1961–64)   61

ALL-TIME TOTAL BASE LEADERS

Brian Downing (1978–89)   2,426
Jim Fregosi (1961–71)   2,112
Bobby Grich (1977–86)   1,788
Don Baylor (1977–82)   1,390
Doug DeCinces (1982–87)   1,334

Rod Carew (1979–85)   1,206
Reggie Jackson (1982–86)   1,025
Buck Rodgers (1961–69)   947
Bobby Knoop (1964–69)   900
Sandy Alomar (1969–74)   885

ALL-TIME RBI LEADERS

Brian Downing (1978–89)	795	Reggie Jackson (1982–86)	374
Bobby Grich (1977–86)	557	Bob Boone (1982–88)	318
Jim Fregosi (1961–71)	546	Buck Rodgers (1961–69)	288
Don Baylor (1977–82)	523	Rod Carew (1979–85)	282
Doug DeCinces (1982–87)	481	Leon Wagner (1961–63)	276

ALL-TIME EXTRA BASE HIT LEADERS

Brian Downing (1978–89)	492	Reggie Jackson (1982–86)	216
Jim Fregosi (1961–71)	404	Rod Carew (1979–85)	180
Bobby Grich (1977–86)	357	Fred Lynn (1981–84)	174
Doug DeCinces (1982–87)	294	Buck Rodgers (1961–69)	163
Don Baylor (1977–82)	288	Bobby Knoop (1964–69)	158

ALL-TIME BATTING AVERAGE LEADERS
(Minimum 500 games)

Rod Carew (1979–85)	.314	Jim Fregosi (1961–71)	.268
Juan Beniquez (1981–85)	.293	Doug DeCinces (1982–87)	.265
Albie Pearson (1961–66)	.275	Don Baylor (1977–82)	.262
Brian Downing (1978–89)	.271	Rick Reichardt (1964–70)	.261
Bobby Grich (1977–86)	.269	Dave Chalk (1973–78)	.255

ALL-TIME STOLEN BASE LEADERS

Gary Pettis (1982–87)	186	Dick Schofield (1983–89)	86
Sandy Alomar (1969–74)	139	Rod Carew (1979–85)	72
Mickey Rivers (1970–75)	126	Bobby Bonds (1976–77)	71
Jerry Remy (1975–77)	110	Jose Cardenal (1965–67)	71
Don Baylor (1977–82)	89	Jim Fregosi (1961–71)	71

PITCHING

ALL-TIME GAME LEADERS

Dave LaRoche (1970–71; 1977–80)	304	Frank Tanana (1973–80)	225
Mike Witt (1981–89)	304	Dean Chance (1961–66)	223
Nolan Ryan (1972–79)	291	Eddie Fisher (1969–72)	219
Clyde Wright (1966–73)	266	Luis Sanchez (1981–85)	194
Andy Hassler (1971–76; 1981–83)	259	George Brunet (1964–69)	194
Rudy May (1965–74)	230	Bob Lee (1964–66)	194

ALL-TIME WIN LEADERS

Nolan Ryan (1972–79)	138	Andy Messersmith (1968–72)	59
Mike Witt (1981–89)	109	George Brunet (1964–69)	54
Frank Tanana (1973–80)	102	Geoff Zahn (1981–85)	52
Clyde Wright (1966–73)	87	Rudy May (1965–74)	51
Dean Chance (1961–66)	74	Ken McBride (1961–65)	40

ALL-TIME INNINGS PITCHED LEADERS

Nolan Ryan (1972–79)	2,182	Rudy May (1965–74)	1,138
Mike Witt (1981–89)	1,945	George Brunet (1964–69)	1,047
Frank Tanana (1973–80)	1,614	Andy Messersmith (1968–72)	973
Clyde Wright (1966–73)	1,404	Geoff Zahn (1981–85)	829
Dean Chance (1961–66)	1,237	Tom Murphy (1968–72)	795

ALL-TIME LOSS LEADERS

Nolan Ryan (1972–79)	121	George Brunet (1964–69)	69
Mike Witt (1981–89)	104	Dean Chance (1961–66)	66
Clyde Wright (1966–73)	85	Tom Murphy (1968–72)	52
Frank Tanana (1973–80)	78	Ken McBride (1961–65)	48
Rudy May (1965–74)	76	Andy Messersmith (1968–72)	47

ALL-TIME SHUTOUT LEADERS

Nolan Ryan (1972–79)	40	Rudy May (1965–74)	12
Frank Tanana (1973–80)	24	Andy Messersmith (1968–72)	11
Dean Chance (1961–66)	21	Mike Witt (1981–87)	10
George Brunet (1964–69)	14	Ken Forsch (1981–84; 1986)	9
Geoff Zahn (1981–85)	13	Clyde Wright (1966–73)	9

ALL-TIME STRIKEOUT LEADERS

Nolan Ryan (1972–79)	2,416	Andy Messersmith (1968–72)	768
Mike Witt (1981–89)	1,269	George Brunet (1964–69)	678
Frank Tanana (1973–80)	1,233	Clyde Wright (1966–73)	571
Dean Chance (1961–66)	857	Ken McBride (1961–65)	487
Rudy May (1965–74)	844	Jim McGlothlin (1965–69)	418

ALL-TIME WALK LEADERS

Nolan Ryan (1972–79)	1,302	Frank Tanana (1973–80)	422
Mike Witt (1981–89)	643	Andy Messersmith (1968–72)	402
Rudy May (1965–74)	484	George Brunet (1964–69)	397
Dean Chance (1961–66)	462	Ken McBride (1961–65)	343
Clyde Wright (1966–73)	449	Andy Hassler (1971–76)	310

ALL-TIME ERA LEADERS

Andy Messersmith (1968–72)	2.77	Paul Hartzell (1976–78)	3.27
Dean Chance (1961–66)	2.83	Clyde Wright (1966–73)	3.28
Nolan Ryan (1972–79)	3.06	Jim McGlothlin (1965–69)	3.37
Frank Tanana (1973–80)	3.08	Fred Newman (1962–67)	3.41
George Brunet (1964–69)	3.13	Mike Witt (1981–89)	3.78

ALL-TIME WON-LOST PERCENTAGE LEADERS

John Candelaria (1985–87)	.694	Geoff Zahn (1981–85)	.553
Luis Sanchez (1981–85)	.571	Kirk McCaskill (1985–87)	.547
Bruce Kison (1980–84)	.569	Don Sutton (1985–87)	.538
Frank Tanana (1973–80)	.567	Nolan Ryan (1972–79)	.533
Andy Messersmith (1968–72)	.557	Mike Witt (1981–89)	.512

ALL-TIME SAVE LEADERS

Dave LaRoche (1970–71; 1977–80)   65
Bob Lee (1964–66)   58
Donnie Moore (1985–87)   57
Minnie Rojas (1966–68)   43
Ken Tatum (1969–70)   39

Luis Sanchez (1981–85)   27
Don Aase (1978–82; 1984)   27
Art Fowler (1961–64)   27
Andy Hassler (1971–76; 1981–83)   24
Mark Clear (1979–80)   23

ANGELS LEAGUE LEADERS

BATTING

BATTING
A. Johnson, 1970

HOME RUNS
B. Grich, 1981 (Tie)
R. Jackson, 1982 (Tie)

RBI
D. Baylor, 1979

RUNS
A. Pearson, 1962
D. Baylor, 1979

TRIPLES
B. Knoop, 1966
J. Fregosi, 1968
M. Rivers, 1974, '75 (Tie)

STOLEN BASES
M. Rivers, 1975

PITCHING

SAVES
M. Rojas, 1967

CHICAGO WHITE SOX

BATTING

ALL-TIME GAME LEADERS

Luke Appling (1930–50)	2,422	Minnie Minoso (1951–57; 1960–61; 1964; 1976; 1980)	1,373
Nellie Fox (1950–63)	2,115	Sherm Lollar (1952–63)	1,358
Ray Schalk (1912–28)	1,755	Shano Collins (1910–20)	1,335
Eddie Collins (1915–26)	1,670	Buck Weaver (1912–20)	1,254
Luis Aparicio (1956–62; 1968–70)	1,511	Willie Kamm (1923–31)	1,170

ALL-TIME AT BAT LEADERS

Luke Appling (1930–50)	8,857	Harold Baines (1980–89)	5,191
Nellie Fox (1950–63)	8,486	Minnie Minoso (1951–57; 1960–61; 1964; 1976; 1980)	5,011
Eddie Collins (1915–26)	6,064	Buck Weaver (1912–20)	4,810
Luis Aparicio (1956–62; 1968–70)	5,856	Shano Collins (1910–20)	4,791
Ray Schalk (1912–28)	5,304	Fielder Jones (1901–08)	4,248

ALL-TIME RUN LEADERS

Luke Appling (1930–50)	1,319	Fielder Jones (1901–08)	692
Nellie Fox (1950–63)	1,187	Harold Baines (1980–89)	661
Eddie Collins (1915–26)	1,063	Buck Weaver (1912–20)	625
Minnie Minoso (1951–57; 1960–61; 1964; 1976; 1980)	893	Johnny Mostil (1918; 1921–29)	618
Luis Aparicio (1956–62; 1968–70)	791	Ray Schalk (1912–28)	579

ALL-TIME HIT LEADERS

Luke Appling (1930–50)	2,749	Minnie Minoso (1951–57; 1960–61; 1964; 1976; 1980)		1,523
Nellie Fox (1950–63)	2,470	Ray Schalk (1912–28)		1,345
Eddie Collins (1915–26)	2,005	Buck Weaver (1912–20)		1,310
Luis Aparicio (1956–62; 1968–70)	1,576	Shano Collins (1910–20)		1,254
Harold Baines (1980–89)	1,528	Bibb Falk (1920–28)		1,219

ALL-TIME DOUBLE LEADERS

Luke Appling (1930–50)	440	Bibb Falk (1920–28)	245
Nellie Fox (1950–63)	335	Willie Kamm (1923–31)	243
Eddie Collins (1915–26)	265	Shano Collins (1910–20)	230
Minnie Minoso (1951–57; 1960–61; 1964; 1976; 1980)	260	Luis Aparicio (1956–62; 1968–70)	223
Harold Baines (1980–88)	247	Johnny Mostil (1918; 1921–29)	209

ALL-TIME TRIPLE LEADERS

Shano Collins (1910–20)	104	Joe Jackson (1915–20)	79
Nellie Fox (1950–63)	104	Minnie Minoso (1951–57; 1960–61; 1964; 1976; 1980)	79
Luke Appling (1930–50)	102	Buck Weaver (1912–20)	69
Eddie Collins (1915–26)	102	Willie Kamm (1923–31)	67
Johnny Mostil (1918; 1921–29)	82	Mike Kreevich (1935–41)	65

ALL-TIME HOME RUN LEADERS

Harold Baines (1980–89)	186	Greg Walker (1982–88)	108
Carlton Fisk (1981–89)	174	Pete Ward (1963–69)	97
Bill Melton (1968–75)	154	Richie Allen (1972–74)	85
Minnie Minoso (1951–57; 1960–61; 1964; 1976; 1980)	135	Carlos May (1968–76)	85
Sherm Lollar (1952–63)	124	Al Smith (1958–62)	85
Ron Kittle (1982–86)	111		

ALL-TIME TOTAL BASE LEADERS

Luke Appling (1930–50)	3,528	Luis Aparicio (1956–62; 1968–70)	2,036
Nellie Fox (1950–63)	3,118	Carlton Fisk (1981–89)	2,029
Eddie Collins (1915–26)	2,567	Shano Collins (1910–20)	1,743
Harold Baines (1980–89)	2,411	Buck Weaver (1912–20)	1,710
Minnie Minoso (1951–57; 1960–61; 1964; 1976; 1980)	2,346	Sherm Lollar (1952–63)	1,698

ALL-TIME RBI LEADERS

Luke Appling (1930–50)	1,116	Nellie Fox (1950–63)	740
Harold Baines (1980–89)	819	Sherm Lollar (1952–63)	631
Minnie Minoso (1951–57; 1960–61; 1964; 1976; 1980)	808	Ray Schalk (1912–28)	596
Eddie Collins (1915–26)	803	Willie Kamm (1923–31)	587
Carlton Fisk (1981–89)	745	Earl Sheely (1921–27)	582

ALL-TIME EXTRA BASE HIT LEADERS

Luke Appling (1930–50)	587	Carlton Fisk (1981–89)	351
Minnie Minoso (1951–57; 1960–61; 1964; 1976; 1980)	474	Bibb Falk (1920–28)	345
Nellie Fox (1950–63)	474	Willie Kamm (1923–31)	335
Harold Baines (1980–89)	499	Luis Aparicio (1956–62; 1968–70)	320
Eddie Collins (1915–26)	398	Sherm Lollar (1952–63)	319
Shano Collins (1910–20)	351		

ALL-TIME BATTING AVERAGE LEADERS (500 Games Min.)

Joe Jackson (1915–20)	.340	Luke Appling (1930–50)	.310
Eddie Collins (1915–26)	.331	Rip Radcliff (1934–39)	.310
Zeke Bonura (1934–37)	.317	Earl Sheely (1921–27)	.305
Bibb Falk (1920–28)	.315	Minnie Minoso (1951–57; 1960–61; 1964; 1976; 1980)	.304
Taffy Wright (1940–42; 1946–48)	.312	Harry Hooper (1921–25)	.302

ALL-TIME STOLEN BASE LEADERS

Eddie Collins (1915–26)	366	Johnny Mostil (1918; 1921–29)	176
Luis Aparicio (1956–62; 1968–70)	318	Ray Schalk (1912–28)	176
Frank Isbell (1901–09)	250	Buck Weaver (1912–20)	172
Fielder Jones (1901–08)	206	Rudy Law (1982–85)	171
Shano Collins (1910–20)	192	Minnie Minoso (1951–57; 1960–61; 1964; 1976; 1980)	171
Luke Appling (1930–50)	179		

PITCHING

ALL-TIME GAME LEADERS

Red Faber (1914–33)	669		Doc White (1902–13)	361
Ted Lyons (1923–42; 1946)	594		Hoyt Wilhelm (1963–68)	361
Wilbur Wood (1967–78)	578		Eddie Cicotte (1912–20)	353
Billy Pierce (1949–61)	456		Joel Horlen (1961–71)	329
Ed Walsh (1904–16)	426		Jim Scott (1909–17)	317

ALL-TIME WIN LEADERS

Ted Lyons (1923–42; 1946)	260		Doc White (1902–13)	159
Red Faber (1914–33)	254		Eddie Cicotte (1912–20)	158
Ed Walsh (1904–16)	194		Joel Horlen (1961–71)	113
Billy Pierce (1949–61)	186		Jim Scott (1909–17)	111
Wilbur Wood (1967–78)	163		Frank Smith (1904–10)	108

ALL-TIME INNINGS PITCHED LEADERS

Ted Lyons (1923–42; 1946)	4,161		Doc White (1902–13)	2,516
Red Faber (1914–33)	4,087		Eddie Cicotte (1912–20)	2,322
Ed Walsh (1904–16)	2,946		Joel Horlen (1961–71)	1,919
Billy Pierce (1949–61)	2,930		Thornton Lee (1937–47)	1,888
Wilbur Wood (1967–78)	2,524		Jim Scott (1909–17)	1,872

ALL-TIME LOSS LEADERS

Ted Lyons (1923–42; 1946)	230		Doc White (1902–13)	123
Red Faber (1914–33)	212		Joel Horlen (1961–71)	113
Billy Pierce (1949–61)	152		Jim Scott (1909–17)	113
Wilbur Wood (1967–78)	148		Thornton Lee (1937–47)	104
Ed Walsh (1904–16)	125		Eddie Cicotte (1912–20)	102

ALL-TIME SHUTOUT LEADERS

Ed Walsh (1904–16)	58		Ted Lyons (1923–42; 1946)	27
Doc White (1902–13)	43		Jim Scott (1909–17)	26
Billy Pierce (1949–61)	35		Frank Smith (1904–10)	25
Red Faber (1914–33)	30		Reb Russell (1913–19)	24
Eddie Cicotte (1912–20)	28		Wilbur Wood (1967–78)	24

ALL-TIME STRIKEOUT LEADERS

Billy Pierce (1949–61)	1,796		Doc White (1902–13)	1,095
Ed Walsh (1904–16)	1,732		Ted Lyons (1923–42; 1946)	1,073
Red Faber (1914–33)	1,471		Joel Horlen (1961–71)	1,007
Wilbur Wood (1967–78)	1,332		Eddie Cicotte (1912–20)	961
Gary Peters (1959–69)	1,098		Jim Scott (1909–17)	945

ALL-TIME WALK LEADERS

Red Faber (1914–33)	1,213		Jim Scott (1909–17)	609
Ted Lyons (1923–42; 1946)	1,121		Ed Walsh (1904–16)	608
Billy Pierce (1949–61)	1,052		Rich Dotson (1979–89)	654
Wilbur Wood (1967–78)	671		Bill Dietrich (1936–46)	561
Thornton Lee (1937–47)	633		Eddie Smith (1939–43; 1946–47)	545

ALL-TIME ERA LEADERS

Ed Walsh (1904–16)	1.81		Reb Russell (1913–19)	2.34
Frank Smith (1904–10)	2.18		Nick Altrock (1903–09)	2.40
Eddie Cicotte (1912–20)	2.24		Joe Benz (1911–19)	2.42
Doc White (1902–13)	2.31		Frank Owen (1903–09)	2.48
Jim Scott (1909–17)	2.32		Roy Patterson (1901–07)	2.75

ALL-TIME WON-LOST PERCENTAGE LEADERS

Lefty Williams (1916–20)	.648		LaMarr Hoyt (1979–84)	.602
Juan Pizarro (1961–66)	.615		Dick Donovan (1955–60)	.593
Dickie Kerr (1919–21; 1925)	.609		Reb Russell (1913–19)	.579
Eddie Cicotte (1912–20)	.608		Frank Smith (1904–10)	.569
Ed Walsh (1904–16)	.608		Doc White (1902–13)	.564

ALL-TIME SAVE LEADERS

Hoyt Wilhelm (1963–68) 98
Bobby Thigpen (1986–89) 91
Terry Forster (1971–76) 75
Wilbur Wood (1967–78) 57
Bob James (1985–87) 56
Ed Farmer (1979–81) 54

Clint Brown (1936–40) 53
Bob Locker (1965–69) 48
Turk Lown (1958–62) 45
Eddie Fisher (1962–66; 1972–73) 44
Lerrin LaGrow (1977–79) 42

WHITE SOX LEAGUE LEADERS

BATTING

BATTING
L. Appling, 1936, '43

HOME RUNS
B. Roth, 1915 (Also with Cleveland)
G. Zernial, 1951 (Also with Philadelphia)
B. Melton, 1971
R. Allen, 1972, '74

HITS
N. Fox, 1952, '54 (Tie), '57, '58
M. Minoso, 1960

RBI
G. Zernial, 1951 (Also with Philadelphia)
R. Allen, 1972

RUNS
J. Mostil, 1925

DOUBLES
D. Kolloway, 1942
W. Moses, 1945
M. Minoso, 1957 (Tie)
F. Robinson, 1962
C. Lemon, 1979 (Tie)

TRIPLES
J. Jackson, 1916, '20
D. Walker, 1937 (Tie)
M. Kreevich, 1937 (Tie)
W. Moses, 1943 (Tie)
M. Minoso, 1951 (Also with Cleveland), '54, '56
J. Rivera, 1953
N. Fox, 1960

STOLEN BASES
F. Isbell, 1901
P. Dougherty, 1908
E. Collins, 1919, '23, '24
J. Mostil, 1925, '26
M. Minoso, 1951 (Also with Cleveland), '52, '53
J. Rivera, 1955
L. Aparicio, 1956, '57, '58, '59, '60, '61, '62

PITCHING

WON-LOST PERCENTAGE
C. Griffith, 1901

E. Walsh, 1908
E. Cicotte, 1916, 1917
R. Russell, 1917
S. Consuegra, 1954
D. Donovan, 1957
B. Shaw, 1969
F. Baumann, 1960
R. Herbert, 1962
J. Horlen, 1967

WINS
D. White, 1907 (Tie)
E. Walsh, 1908
E. Cicotte, 1917, 1919
T. Lyons, 1925 (Tie)
B. Pierce, 1957 (Tie)
E. Wynn, 1959
G. Peters, 1964 (Tie)
W. Wood, 1972 (Tie), 1973
L. Hoyt, 1982, 1983

STRIKEOUTS
E. Walsh, 1908, 1911
F. Smith, 1909
B. Pierce, 1953
E. Wynn, 1958
J. Horlen, 1967

ERA
D. White, 1906
E. Walsh, 1907, 1910
E. Cicotte, 1917
R. Faber, 1921, 1922
T. Lee, 1941
T. Lyons, 1942
S. Rogovin, 1951 (Also with Detroit)
B. Pierce, 1955
G. Peters, 1963, 1966

SAVES
E. Walsh, 1907 (Tie), '08, '10 (Tie), '12
R. Faber, 1914 (Tie)
D. Danforth, 1917
D. Kerr, 1920 (Tie)
C. Brown, 1937
G. Maltzberger, 1943, '44 (Tie)
H. Dorish, 1952
T. Lown, 1959
T. Forster, 1974
G. Gossage, 1975

CLEVELAND INDIANS

BATTING

ALL-TIME GAME LEADERS

Terry Turner (1904–18)	1,617	Ken Keltner (1937–44; 1946–49)	1,513
Nap Lajoie (1902–14)	1,615	Joe Sewell (1920–30)	1,513
Lou Boudreau (1938–50)	1,560	Earl Averill (1929–39)	1,510
Jim Hegan (1941–42; 1946–57)	1,526	Charlie Jamieson (1919–32)	1,483
Tris Speaker (1916–26)	1,519	Jack Graney (1908; 1910–22)	1,403

ALL-TIME AT BAT LEADERS

Nap Lajoie (1902–14)	6,037	Joe Sewell (1920–30)	5,621
Earl Averill (1929–39)	5,915	Charlie Jamieson (1919–32)	5,551
Terry Turner (1904–18)	5,786	Tris Speaker (1916–26)	5,547
Lou Boudreau (1938–50)	5,755	Jack Graney (1908; 1910–22)	4,705
Ken Keltner (1937–44; 1946–49)	5,655	Bill Bradley (1901–10)	4,648

ALL-TIME RUN LEADERS

Earl Averill (1929–39)	1,154	Lou Boudreau (1938–50)	823
Tris Speaker (1916–26)	1,079	Larry Doby (1947–55; 1958)	808
Charlie Jamieson (1919–32)	942	Hal Trosky (1933–41)	758
Nap Lajoie (1902–14)	863	Ken Keltner (1937–44; 1946–49)	735
Joe Sewell (1920–30)	857	Jack Graney (1908; 1910–22)	706

ALL-TIME HIT LEADERS

Nap Lajoie (1902–14)	2,051	Lou Boudreau (1938–50)	1,706
Tris Speaker (1916–26)	1,965	Ken Keltner (1937–44; 1946–49)	1,561
Earl Averill (1929–39)	1,904	Terry Turner (1904–18)	1,471
Joe Sewell (1920–30)	1,800	Hal Trosky (1933–41)	1,365
Charlie Jamieson (1919–32)	1,753	Bill Bradley (1901–10)	1,268

ALL-TIME DOUBLE LEADERS

Tris Speaker (1916–26)	486	Ken Keltner (1937–44; 1946–49)	306
Nap Lajoie (1902–14)	427	Charlie Jamieson (1919–32)	296
Earl Averill (1929–39)	377	Hal Trosky (1933–41)	287
Joe Sewell (1920–30)	375	Bill Bradley (1901–10)	236
Lou Boudreau (1938–50)	367	Odell Hale (1931–40)	235

ALL-TIME TRIPLE LEADERS

Earl Averill (1929–39)	121	Jack Graney (1908; 1910–22)	79
Elmer Flick (1902–10)	108	Terry Turner (1904–18)	77
Tris Speaker (1916–26)	108	Bill Bradley (1901–10)	74
Joe Jackson (1910–15)	89	Charlie Jamieson (1919–32)	74
Jeff Heath (1936–45)	83	Nap Lajoie (1902–14)	74
Ray Chapman (1912–20)	81		

ALL-TIME HOME RUN LEADERS

Earl Averill (1929–39)	226	Rocky Colavito (1955–59; 1965–67)	190
Hal Trosky (1933–41)	216	Ken Keltner (1937–44; 1946–49)	163
Larry Doby (1947–55; 1958)	215	Woodie Held (1958–64)	130
Andre Thornton (1977–88)	214	Jeff Heath (1936–45)	122
Al Rosen (1947–56)	192	Max Alvis (1962–69)	108

ALL-TIME TOTAL BASE LEADERS

Earl Averill (1929–39)	3,201	Lou Boudreau (1938–50)	2,392
Tris Speaker (1916–26)	2,883	Joe Sewell (1920–30)	2,391
Nap Lajoie (1902–14)	2,728	Charlie Jamieson (1919–32)	2,251
Ken Keltner (1937–44; 1946–49)	2,494	Larry Doby (1947–55; 1958)	2,159
Hal Trosky (1933–41)	2,406	Andre Thornton (1977–88)	1,954

ALL-TIME RBI LEADERS

Earl Averill (1929–39)	1,085		Ken Keltner (1937–44; 1946–49)	850
Nap Lajoie (1902–14)	959		Larry Doby (1947–55; 1958)	776
Hal Trosky (1933–41)	911		Andre Thornton (1977–88)	749
Tris Speaker (1916–26)	898		Lou Boudreau (1938–50)	740
Joe Sewell (1920–30)	865		Al Rosen (1947–56)	717

ALL-TIME EXTRA BASE HIT LEADERS

Earl Averill (1929–39)	724		Lou Boudreau (1938–50)	495
Tris Speaker (1916–26)	666		Joe Sewell (1920–30)	468
Hal Trosky (1933–41)	556		Larry Doby (1947–55; 1958)	450
Ken Keltner (1937–44; 1946–49)	538		Andre Thornton (1977–88)	419
Nap Lajoie (1902–14)	535		Jeff Heath (1936–45)	399

ALL-TIME BATTING AVERAGE LEADERS
(500 game minimum)

Joe Jackson (1910–15)	.375		Joe Sewell (1920–30)	.320
Tris Speaker (1916–26)	.354		Johnny Hodapp (1925–32)	.318
Nap Lajoie (1902–14)	.340		Charlie Jamieson (1919–32)	.316
George Burns (1920–21; 1924–28)	.327		Joe Vosmik (1930–36)	.313
Ed Morgan (1928–33)	.323		Hal Trosky (1933–41)	.313
Earl Averill (1929–39)	.322			

ALL-TIME STOLEN BASE LEADERS

Terry Turner (1904–18)	254		Brett Butler (1984–87)	164
Nap Lajoie (1902–14)	240		Bill Bradley (1901–10)	157
Ray Chapman (1912–20)	233		Tris Speaker (1916–26)	153
Elmer Flick (1902–10)	207		Jack Graney (1908; 1910–22)	148
Harry Bay (1902–08)	165		Rick Manning (1975–83)	142

PITCHING

ALL-TIME GAME LEADERS

Mel Harder (1928–47)	582	Mike Garcia (1948–59)	397
Bob Feller (1936–41; 1945–56)	570	Stan Coveleski (1916–24)	360
Willis Hudlin (1926–40)	475	George Uhle (1919–28)	357
Bob Lemon (1941–42; 1946–58)	460	Early Wynn (1949–57)	343
Gary Bell (1958–67)	419	Sam McDowell (1961–71)	336

ALL-TIME WIN LEADERS

Bob Feller (1936–41; 1945–56)	266	Addie Joss (1902–10)	160
Mel Harder (1928–47)	223	Willis Hudlin (1926–40)	157
Bob Lemon (1941–42; 1946–58)	207	George Uhle (1919–28)	147
Stan Coveleski (1916–24)	171	Mike Garcia (1948–59)	142
Early Wynn (1949–57)	164	Jim Bagby (1916–22)	124

ALL-TIME INNINGS PITCHED LEADERS

Bob Feller (1936–41; 1945–56)	3,827	Addie Joss (1902–10)	2,336
Mel Harder (1928–47)	3,426	Early Wynn (1949–57)	2,288
Bob Lemon (1941–42; 1946–58)	2,850	George Uhle (1919–28)	2,200
Willis Hudlin (1926–40)	2,558	Mike Garcia (1948–59)	2,139
Stan Coveleski (1916–24)	2,513	Sam McDowell (1961–71)	2,109

ALL-TIME LOSS LEADERS

Mel Harder (1928–47)	186	George Uhle (1919–28)	119
Bob Feller (1936–41; 1945–56)	162	Sam McDowell (1961–71)	109
Willis Hudlin (1926–40)	151	Early Wynn (1949–57)	102
Bob Lemon (1941–42; 1946–58)	128	Addie Joss (1902–10)	97
Stan Coveleski (1916–24)	122	Mike Garcia (1948–59)	96

ALL-TIME SHUTOUT LEADERS

Bob Feller (1936–41; 1945–56)	46	Mel Harder (1928–47)	24
Addie Joss (1902–10)	45	Early Wynn (1949–57)	24
Stan Coveleski (1916–24)	31	Sam McDowell (1961–71)	22
Bob Lemon (1941–42; 1946–58)	31	Luis Tiant (1964–69)	21
Mike Garcia (1948–59)	27	Guy Morton (1914–24)	19

ALL-TIME STRIKEOUT LEADERS

Bob Feller (1936–41; 1945–56)	2,581	Gary Bell (1958–67)	1,104
Sam McDowell (1961–71)	2,159	Mike Garcia (1948–59)	1,095
Bob Lemon (1941–42; 1946–58)	1,277	Luis Tiant (1964–69)	1,041
Early Wynn (1949–57)	1,277	Addie Joss (1902–10)	926
Mel Harder (1928–47)	1,160	Stan Coveleski (1916–24)	856

ALL-TIME WALK LEADERS

Bob Feller (1936–41; 1945–56)	1,764	Willis Hudlin (1926–40)	832
Bob Lemon (1941–42; 1946–58)	1,251	George Uhle (1919–28)	708
Mel Harder (1928–47)	1,118	Mike Garcia (1948–59)	696
Sam McDowell (1961–71)	1,072	Gary Bell (1958–67)	670
Early Wynn (1949–57)	877	Stan Coveleski (1916–24)	616

ALL-TIME ERA LEADERS

Addie Joss (1902–10)	1.88	Stan Coveleski (1916–24)	2.79
Bob Rhoads (1903–09)	2.39	Willie Mitchell (1909–16)	2.79
Bill Bernhard (1902–07)	2.45	Luis Tiant (1964–69)	2.84
Earl Moore (1901–07)	2.59	Jim Bagby (1916–22)	3.00
Gaylord Perry (1972–75)	2.71	Sam McDowell (1961–71)	3.00

ALL-TIME WON-LOST PERCENTAGE LEADERS

Addie Joss (1902–10)	.623	Mike Garcia (1948–59)	.597
Wes Ferrell (1927–33)	.622	Jim Bagby (1916–22)	.590
Bob Feller (1936–41; 1945–56)	.621	Stan Coveleski (1916–24)	.584
Bob Lemon (1941–42; 1946–58)	.618	Bill Bernhard (1902–07)	.579
Early Wynn (1949–57)	.617	Bob Rhoads (1903–09)	.575

ALL-TIME SAVE LEADERS

Ray Narleski (1954–58)	53	Dave LaRoche (1975–77)	42
Jim Kern (1974–78; 1986)	46	Dan Spillner (1978–84)	41
Sid Monge (1977–81)	46	Joe Heving (1937–38; 1941–44)	32
Gary Bell (1958–67)	45	Don Mossi (1954–58)	32
Ernie Camacho (1983–87)	44	Willis Hudlin (1926–40)	31

INDIANS LEAGUE LEADERS

BATTING

BATTING
N. Lajoie, 1903, '04
E. Flick, 1905
T. Speaker, 1916
L. Fonseca, 1929
L. Boudreau, 1944
B. Avila, 1954

HOME RUNS
B. Roth, 1915 (Also with Chic.)
A. Rosen, 1950, '53
L. Doby, 1952, '54
R. Colavito, 1959 (Tie)

HITS
P. Hickman, 1902 (Also with Bost.)
N. Lajoie, 1904, '06, '10
J. Jackson, 1913
T. Speaker, 1916
C. Jamieson, 1923
G. Burns, 1926 (Tie)
J. Hodapp, 1930
J. Vosmik, 1935
E. Averill, 1936
D. Mitchell, 1949

RBI
N. Lajoie, 1904
T. Speaker, 1923 (Tie)
H. Trosky, 1936
A. Rosen, 1952, '53
L. Doby, 1954
R. Colavito, 1965
J. Carter, 1986

RUNS
E. Flick, 1906
R. Chapman, 1918
L. Doby, 1952
A. Rosen, 1953
A. Smith, 1955

DOUBLES
N. Lajoie, 1904, '06, '10
J. Jackson, 1913
T. Speaker, 1916 (Tie), '18, '20, '21, '22, '23
J. Graney, 1916 (Tie)
J. Sewell, 1924 (Tie)
G. Burns, 1926
J. Hodapp, 1930
J. Vosmik, 1935
L. Boudreau, 1941, '44, '47
T. Francona, 1960

TRIPLES
E. Flick, 1905, '06, '07
J. Jackson, 1912
J. Vosmik, 1935
E. Averill, 1936 (Tie)

J. Heath, 1938, '41
H. Edwards, 1946
D. Mitchell, 1949
M. Minoso, 1951 (Also with Chic.)
B. Avila, 1952
V. Power, 1958 (Tie) (Also with KC)
B. Butler, 1986

STOLEN BASES
H. Bay, 1903
E. Flick, 1904, '06 (Tie)
G. Case, 1946
M. Minoso, 1951 (Also with Chic.)

PITCHING

WON-LOST PERCENTAGE
B. Bernhard, 1902 (Also with Phila.)
E. Moore, 1903
J. Bagby, Sr., 1920
G. Uhle, 1926
J. Allen, 1937
B. Feller, 1951
J. Perry, 1960
S. Siebert, 1966

WINS
A. Joss, 1907 (Tie)
J. Bagby, Sr., 1920
G. Uhle, 1923, 1926
B. Feller, 1939, 1940, 1941, 1946 (Tie), 1947, 1951
B. Lemon, 1950, 1954 (Tie), 1955
E. Wynn, 1954 (Tie)
J. Perry, 1960 (Tie), 1970 (Tie)

STRIKEOUTS
S. Coveleski, 1920
B. Feller, 1938, 1939, 1940, 1941, 1946, 1947, 1948
A. Reynolds, 1943
B. Lemon, 1950
H. Score, 1955, 1956
E. Wynn, 1957
S. McDowell, 1965, 1966, 1968, 1969, 1970
L. Barker, 1980, 1981
B. Blyleven, 1985 (Also with MN)

ERA
A. Joss, 1904, 1908
V. Gregg, 1911
S. Coveleski, 1923
M. Pearson, 1933
G. Bearden, 1948
E. Wynn, 1950
M. Garcia, 1954
S. McDowell, 1965
L. Tiant, 1968
R. Sutcliffe, 1982

SAVES
B. Hoffer, 1901 (Tie)

O. Hess, 1906 (Tie)
E. Klieman, 1947 (Tie)
R. Christopher, 1948

R. Narleski, 1955
J. Klippstein, 1960 (Tie)

DETROIT TIGERS

BATTING

ALL-TIME GAME LEADERS

Al Kaline (1953–74)	2,834	Harry Heilmann (1914–29)	1,989
Ty Cobb (1905–26)	2,806	Donie Bush (1908–1921)	1,872
Charlie Gehringer (1924–42)	2,323	Bill Freehan (1961; 1963–76)	1,774
Sam Crawford (1903–17)	2,114	Dick McAuliffe (1960–73)	1,656
Norm Cash (1960–74)	2,018	Bobby Veach (1912–23)	1,605

ALL-TIME AT BAT LEADERS

Ty Cobb (1905–26)	10,594	Donie Bush (1908–21)	6,970
Al Kaline (1953–74)	10,116	Norm Cash (1960–74)	6,593
Charlie Gehringer (1924–42)	8,860	Bill Freehan (1961; 1963–76)	6,073
Sam Crawford (1903–17)	7,993	Bobby Veach (1912–23)	5,982
Harry Heilmann (1914–29)	7,297	Dick McAuliffe (1960–73)	5,898

ALL-TIME RUN LEADERS

Ty Cobb (1905–26)	2,087	Sam Crawford (1903–17)	1,115
Charlie Gehringer (1924–42)	1,773	Norm Cash (1960–74)	1,028
Al Kaline (1953–74)	1,622	Hank Greenberg (1930; 1933–41; 1945–46)	980
Donie Bush (1908–21)	1,242	Bobby Veach (1912–23)	860
Harry Heilmann (1914–29)	1,209	Dick McAuliffe (1960–73)	856

ALL-TIME HIT LEADERS

Ty Cobb (1905–26)	3,903	Bobby Veach (1912–23)	1,860
Al Kaline (1953–74)	3,007	Norm Cash (1960–74)	1,793
Charlie Gehringer (1924–42)	2,839	Donie Bush (1908–21)	1,745
Harry Heilmann (1914–29)	2,499	Bill Freehan (1916; 1963–76)	1,591
Sam Crawford (1903–17)	2,466	Hank Greenberg (1930; 1933–41; 1945–46)	1,528

ALL-TIME DOUBLE LEADERS

Ty Cobb (1905–26)	665	Bobby Veach (1912–23)	345
Charlie Gehringer (1924–42)	574	Alan Trammell (1977–89)	292
Al Kaline (1953–74)	498	Harvey Kuenn (1952–59)	244
Harry Heilmann (1914–29)	497	Bill Freehan (1961; 1963–76)	241
Sam Crawford (1903–17)	403	Norm Cash (1960–74)	241
Hank Greenberg (1930; 1933–41; 1945–46)	366		

ALL-TIME TRIPLE LEADERS

Ty Cobb (1905–26)	286	Al Kaline (1953–74)	75
Sam Crawford (1903–17)	250	Donie Bush (1908–21)	73
Charlie Gehringer (1924–42)	146	Dick McAuliffe (1960–73)	70
Harry Heilmann (1914–29)	145	Hank Greenberg (1930; 1933–41; 1945–46)	69
Bobby Veach (1912–23)	136	Lu Blue (1921–27)	66

ALL-TIME HOME RUN LEADERS

Al Kaline (1953–74)	399	Lance Parrish (1977–86)	212
Norm Cash (1960–74)	373	Bill Freehan (1961; 1963–76)	200
Hank Greenberg (1930; 1933–41; 1945–46)	306	Dick McAuliffe (1960–73)	192
Willie Horton (1963–77)	262	Charlie Gehringer (1924–42)	184
Rudy York (1934; 1937–45)	239	Harry Heilmann (1914–29)	164

ALL-TIME TOTAL BASE LEADERS

Ty Cobb (1905–26)	5,476	Norm Cash (1960–74)	3,233
Al Kaline (1953–74)	4,852	Hank Greenberg (1930; 1933–41; 1945–46)	2,950
Charlie Gehringer (1924–42)	4,257	Bobby Veach (1912–23)	2,654
Harry Heilmann (1914–29)	3,778	Willie Horton (1963–77)	2,549
Sam Crawford (1903–17)	3,579	Bill Freehan (1961; 1963–76)	2,502

ALL-TIME RBI LEADERS

Ty Cobb (1905–26)	1,821	Hank Greenberg (1930; 1933–41; 1945–46)	1,202
Al Kaline (1953–74)	1,583	Norm Cash (1960–74)	1,087
Harry Heilmann (1914–29)	1,456	Bobby Veach (1912–23)	1,046
Charlie Gehringer (1924–42)	1,427	Rudy York (1934; 1937–45)	936
Sam Crawford (1903–17)	1,264	Willie Horton (1963–77)	886

ALL-TIME EXTRA BASE HIT LEADERS

Ty Cobb (1905–26)	1,063	Sam Crawford (1903–17)	723
Al Kaline (1953–74)	972	Norm Cash (1960–74)	654
Charlie Gehringer (1924–42)	904	Bobby Veach (1912–23)	540
Harry Heilmann (1914–29)	806	Rudy York (1934; 1937–45)	517
Hank Greenberg (1930; 1933–41; 1945–46)	741	Willie Horton (1963–77)	504

ALL-TIME BATTING AVERAGE LEADERS (500 games minimum)

Ty Cobb (1905–26)	.368	Charlie Gehringer (1924–42)	.320
Harry Heilmann (1914–29)	.342	Hank Greenberg (1930; 1933–41; 1945–46)	.319
Bob Fothergill (1922–30)	.337	Gee Walker (1931–37)	.317
George Kell (1946–52)	.325	Harvey Kuenn (1952–59)	.314
Heinie Manush (1923–27)	.321	Barney McCosky (1939–42; 1946)	.312

ALL-TIME STOLEN BASE LEADERS

Ty Cobb (1905–26)	865	Bobby Veach (1912–23)	189
Donie Bush (1908–21)	400	Alan Trammell (1977–89)	187
Sam Crawford (1903–17)	317	Charlie Gehringer (1924–42)	182
Ron LeFlore (1974–79)	294	Kirk Gibson (1979–87)	166
George Moriarty (1909–15)	190	Davy Jones (1906–12)	140

PITCHING

ALL-TIME GAME LEADERS

John Hiller (1965–70; 1972–80)	545	George Mullin (1902–13)	435
Hooks Dauss (1912–26)	538	Tommy Bridges (1930–43; 1945–46)	424
Mickey Lolich (1963–75)	508	Jack Morris (1977–89)	394
Dizzy Trout (1939–52)	493	Aurelio Lopez (1979–85)	355
Hal Newhouser (1939–53)	460	Hank Aguirre (1958–67)	334

ALL-TIME WIN LEADERS

Hooks Dauss (1912–26)	221	Jack Morris (1977–89)	183
George Mullin (1902–13)	209	Dizzy Trout (1939–52)	161
Mickey Lolich (1963–75)	207	Wild Bill Donovan (1903–12)	141
Hal Newhouser (1939–53)	200	Earl Whitehill (1923–32)	133
Tommy Bridges (1930–43; 1945–46)	194	Frank Lary (1954–64)	123

ALL-TIME INNINGS PITCHED LEADERS

George Mullin (1902–13)	3,394	Jack Morris (1977–89)	2,794
Hooks Dauss (1912–26)	3,391	Dizzy Trout (1939–52)	2,591
Mickey Lolich (1963–75)	3,363	Earl Whitehill (1923–32)	2,172
Hal Newhouser (1939–53)	2,944	Wild Bill Donovan (1903–12)	2,139
Tommy Bridges (1930–43; 1945–46)	2,826	Frank Lary (1954–64)	2,008

ALL-TIME LOSS LEADERS

Hooks Dauss (1912–26)	182	Tommy Bridges (1930–43; 1945–46)	138
George Mullin (1902–13)	179	Jack Morris (1977–89)	132
Mickey Lolich (1963–75)	175	Earl Whitehill (1923–32)	119
Dizzy Trout (1939–52)	153	Frank Lary (1954–64)	110
Hal Newhouser (1939–53)	148	Vic Sorrell (1928–37)	101

ALL-TIME SHUTOUT LEADERS

Mickey Lolich (1963–75)	39	Dizzy Trout (1939–52)	28
George Mullin (1902–13)	34	Denny McLain (1963–70)	26
Tommy Bridges (1930–43; 1945–46)	33	Virgil Trucks (1941–43; 1945–52)	22
Hal Newhouser (1939–53)	33	Hooks Dauss (1912–26)	21
Wild Bill Donovan (1903–12)	29	Jack Morris (1977–89)	21

ALL-TIME STRIKEOUT LEADERS

Mickey Lolich (1963–75)	2,679	George Mullin (1902–13)	1,380
Jack Morris (1977–89)	1,819	Hooks Dauss (1912–26)	1,201
Hal Newhouser (1939–53)	1,770	Dizzy Trout (1939–52)	1,199
Tommy Bridges (1930–43; 1945–46)	1,674	Denny McLain (1963–70)	1,150
Jim Bunning (1955–63)	1,406	Wild Bill Donovan (1903–12)	1,079

ALL-TIME WALK LEADERS

Hal Newhouser (1939–53)	1,227	Jack Morris (1977–89)	989
Tommy Bridges (1930–43; 1945–46)	1,192	Dizzy Trout (1939–52)	978
George Mullin (1902–13)	1,106	Earl Whitehill (1923–32)	831
Hooks Dauss (1912–26)	1,067	Virgil Trucks (1941–43; 1945–52)	732
Mickey Lolich (1963–75)	1,014	Vic Sorrell (1928–37)	706

ALL-TIME ERA LEADERS

Harry Coveleski (1914–18)	2.33	John Hiller (1965–70; 1972–80)	2.83
Ed Killian (1904–10)	2.38	Ed Willett (1906–13)	3.05
Wild Bill Donovan (1903–12)	2.49	Jean Dubuc (1912–16)	3.06
Ed Siever (1901–02; 1906–08)	2.61	Hal Newhouser (1939–53)	3.07
George Mullin (1902–13)	2.76	Bernie Boland (1915–20)	3.09

ALL-TIME WON-LOST PERCENTAGE LEADERS

Denny McLain (1963–70)	.654	Eldon Auker (1933–38)	.597
Aurelio Lopez (1979–85)	.639	Wild Bill Donovan (1903–12)	.595
Schoolboy Rowe (1933–42)	.629	Earl Wilson (1966–70)	.587
Harry Coveleski (1914–18)	.616	Tommy Bridges (1930–43; 1945–46)	.584
Ed Summers (1908–12)	.602	Jack Morris (1977–89)	.581

ALL-TIME SAVE LEADERS

John Hiller (1965–70; 1972–80)	125	Larry Sherry (1964–67)	37
Willie Hernandez (1984–89)	120	Fred Scherman (1969–73)	34
Aurelio Lopez (1979–85)	85	Dizzy Trout (1939–52)	34
Terry Fox (1961–66)	55	Tom Timmerman (1969–73)	33
Al Benton (1938–42; 1945–48)	45	Fred Gladding (1961–67)	33
Hooks Dauss (1912–26)	39		

TIGERS LEAGUE LEADERS

BATTING

BATTING
T. Cobb, 1907, '08, '09, '10, '11, '12, '13, '14, '15, '17, '18, '19
H. Heilmann, 1921, '23, '25, '27
H. Manush, 1926
D. Alexander, 1932 (Also with Bost.)
C. Gehringer, 1937
G. Kell, 1949
A. Kaline, 1955
H. Kuenn, 1959
N. Cash, 1961

HOME RUNS
S. Crawford, 1908
T. Cobb, 1909
H. Greenberg, 1935 (Tie), '38, '40, '46
R. York, 1943
D. Evans, 1985

HITS
T. Cobb, 1907, '08, '09, '11, '12, '15, '17, '19 (Tie)
B. Veach, 1919 (Tie)
H. Heilmann, 1921
D. Alexander, 1929 (Tie)
C. Gehringer, 1929 (Tie), '34
D. Wakefield, 1943
G. Kell, 1950, '51
H. Kuenn, 1953, '54 (Tie), '56, '59
A. Kaline, 1955
N. Cash, 1961

RBI
T. Cobb, 1907, '08, '09, '11
S. Crawford, 1910, '14
B. Veach, 1915, '17, '18
H. Greenberg, 1935, '37, '40, '46
R. York, 1943
R. Boone, 1955 (Tie)

RUNS
S. Crawford, 1907
M. McIntyre, 1908
T. Cobb, 1909, '10, '11, '15, '16
D. Bush, 1917
C. Gehringer, 1929, '34
H. Greenberg, 1938
E. Yost, 1959
D. McAuliffe, 1968
R. LeFlore, 1978

DOUBLES
T. Cobb, 1908, '11, '17
S. Crawford, 1909
B. Veach, 1915, '19
H. Heilmann, 1924 (Tie)
R. Johnson, 1929 (Tie)
C. Gehringer, 1929 (Tie), '36
H. Greenberg, 1934, '40
D. Wakefield, 1943

G. Kell, 1950, '51 (Tie)
H. Kuenn, 1955, '58, '59
A. Kaline, 1961

TRIPLES
S. Crawford, 1903, '10, '13, '14, '15
T. Cobb, 1908, '11, '17, '18
B. Veach, 1919
C. Gehringer, 1929
R. Johnson, 1931
B. McCosky, 1940
J. Wood, 1961

STOLEN BASES
T. Cobb, 1907, '09, '11, '15, '16, '17
C. Gehringer, 1929
M. McManus, 1930
R. LeFlore, 1978

PITCHING

WON-LOST PERCENTAGE
B. Donovan, 1907
G. Mullin, 1909
E. Auker, 1935
L. Rowe, 1940
H. Newhouser, 1945
D. McLain, 1968

WINS
G. Mullin, 1909
T. Bridges, 1935, 1936
P. Trout, 1943 (Tie)
H. Newhouser, 1944, 1945, 1946 (Tie), 1948
J. Bunning, 1957 (Tie)
E. Wilson, 1967 (Tie)
D. McLain, 1968, 1969
M. Lolich, 1971

STRIKEOUTS
T. Bridges, 1936
H. Newhouser, 1944, 1945
V. Trucks, 1949
J. Bunning, 1959, 1960
M. Lolich, 1971
J. Morris, 1983

ERA
E. Siever, 1902
P. Trout, 1944
H. Newhouser, 1945, 1946
S. Rogovin, 1951 (Also with Chic.)
H. Aguirre, 1962
M. Fidrych, 1976

SAVES
G. Mullin, 1903 (Tie)
H. Dauss, 1914 (Tie)
J. Middleton, 1921 (Tie)
A. Benton, 1940
J. Hiller, 1973

KANSAS CITY ROYALS

BATTING

ALL-TIME GAME LEADERS

Frank White (1973–89)	2,242		Freddie Patek (1971–79)	1,245
George Brett (1973–89)	2,137		John Mayberry (1972–77)	897
Amos Otis (1970–83)	1,891		Cookie Rojas (1970–77)	880
Hal McRae (1973–87)	1,837		John Wathan (1976–85)	860
Willie Wilson (1976–89)	1,672		Al Cowens (1974–79)	812

ALL-TIME AT BAT LEADERS

George Brett (1973–89)	8,148		Freddie Patek (1971–79)	4,305
Frank White (1973–89)	7,618		John Mayberry (1972–77)	3,131
Amos Otis (1970–83)	7,050		Cookie Rojas (1970–77)	3,072
Hal McRae (1973–87)	6,568		Al Cowens (1974–79)	2,785
Willie Wilson (1976–89)	6,492		Lou Piniella (1969–73)	2,570

ALL-TIME RUNS LEADERS

George Brett (1973–89)	1,300		Freddie Patek (1971–79)	571
Amos Otis (1970–83)	1,074		John Mayberry (1972–77)	459
Willie Wilson (1976–89)	1,011		Al Cowens (1974–79)	373
Frank White (1973–89)	892		Cookie Rojas (1970–77)	324
Hal McRae (1973–87)	873		U. L. Washington (1977–84)	319

ALL-TIME HIT LEADERS

George Brett (1973–89)	2,528		Freddie Patek (1971–79)	1,036
Amos Otis (1970–83)	1,977		Cookie Rojas (1970–77)	824
Frank White (1973–89)	1,954		John Mayberry (1972–77)	816
Hal McRae (1973–87)	1,924		Al Cowens (1974–79)	784
Willie Wilson (1976–89)	1,879		Lou Piniella (1969–73)	734

ALL-TIME DOUBLE LEADERS

George Brett (1973–89)	514		Freddie Patek (1971–79)	182
Hal McRae (1973–87)	449		Cookie Rojas (1970–77)	139
Frank White (1973–89)	393		John Mayberry (1972–77)	139
Amos Otis (1970–83)	365		Lou Piniella (1969–73)	127
Willie Wilson (1976–89)	228		Al Cowens (1974–79)	117

ALL-TIME TRIPLE LEADERS

Willie Wilson (1976–89)	130		Freddie Patek (1971–79)	41
George Brett (1973–89)	120		U. L. Washington (1977–84)	28
Amos Otis (1970–83)	65		John Wathan (1976–85)	25
Hal McRae (1973–87)	63		Darrell Porter (1977–80)	21
Frank White (1973–89)	57		Lou Piniella (1969–73)	21
Al Cowens (1974–79)	44			

ALL-TIME HOME RUN LEADERS

George Brett (1973–89)	267		Steve Balboni (1984–87)	117
Amos Otis (1970–83)	193		Willie Aikens (1980–83)	77
Hal McRae (1973–87)	169		Darrell Porter (1977–80)	61
Frank White (1973–89)	158		Ed Kirkpatrick (1969–73)	56
John Mayberry (1972–77)	143		Bob Oliver (1969–72)	49

ALL-TIME TOTAL BASE LEADERS

George Brett (1973–89)	4,083		John Mayberry (1972–77)	1,404
Amos Otis (1970–83)	3,051		Freddie Patek (1971–79)	1,384
Hal McRae (1973–87)	3,006		Al Cowens (1974–79)	1,124
Frank White (1973–89)	2,935		Cookie Rojas (1970–77)	1,062
Willie Wilson (1976–89)	2,481		Lou Piniella (1969–73)	1,038

ALL-TIME RBI LEADERS

George Brett (1973–89)	1,311	Willie Wilson (1976–89)	467
Hal McRae (1973–87)	1,012	Freddie Patek (1971–79)	382
Amos Otis (1970–83)	992	Al Cowens (1974–79)	374
Frank White (1973–89)	865	Lou Piniella (1969–73)	348
John Mayberry (1972–77)	552	Cookie Rojas (1970–77)	332

ALL-TIME EXTRA BASE HIT LEADERS

George Brett (1973–89)	901	John Mayberry (1972–77)	292
Hal McRae (1973–87)	681	Freddie Patek (1971–79)	251
Amos Otis (1970–83)	623	Steve Balboni (1984–87)	210
Frank White (1973–89)	608	Al Cowens (1974–79)	206
Willie Wilson (1976–89)	396	Lou Piniella (1969–73)	193

ALL-TIME BATTING AVERAGE LEADERS (300 game minimum)

George Brett (1973–89)	.310	Willie Aikens (1980–83)	.282
Hal McRae (1973–87)	.293	Amos Otis (1970–83)	.280
Willie Wilson (1976–89)	.289	Pete LaCock (1977–80)	.277
Lou Piniella (1969–73)	.286	Darrell Porter (1977–80)	.271
Al Cowens (1974–79)	.282	Cookie Rojas (1970–77)	.268

ALL-TIME STOLEN BASE LEADERS

Willie Wilson (1976–89)	588	U. L. Washington (1977–84)	121
Amos Otis (1970–83)	340	Hal McRae (1973–87)	105
Freddie Patek (1971–79)	336	John Wathan (1976–85)	105
Frank White (1973–89)	177	Al Cowens (1974–79)	80
George Brett (1973–89)	175	Pat Kelly (1969–70)	74

PITCHING

ALL-TIME GAME LEADERS

Dan Quisenberry (1979–87)	553		Steve Mingori (1973–79)	264
Paul Splittorff (1970–84)	429		Marty Pattin (1974–80)	244
Dennis Leonard (1974–86)	312		Al Fitzmorris (1969–76)	243
Larry Gura (1976–85)	310		Bud Black (1982–87)	199
Doug Bird (1973–78)	292		Tom Burgmeier (1969–73)	196

ALL-TIME WIN LEADERS

Paul Splittorff (1970–84)	166		Charlie Leibrandt (1984–89)	76
Dennis Leonard (1974–86)	144		Steve Busby (1972–80)	70
Larry Gura (1976–85)	111		Al Fitzmorris (1969–87)	70
Bret Saberhagen (1984–89)	92		Dick Drago (1969–73)	61
Mark Gubicza (1984–89)	84		Bud Black (1982–87)	54

ALL-TIME INNINGS PITCHED LEADERS

Paul Splittorff (1970–84)	2,555		Charlie Leibrandt (1984–89)	1,257
Dennis Leonard (1974–86)	2,188		Dick Drago (1969–73)	1,134
Larry Gura (1976–85)	1,701		Al Fitzmorris (1969–76)	1,098
Bret Saberhagen (1984–89)	1,329		Steve Busby (1972–80)	1,059
Mark Gubicza (1984–89)	1,314		Bud Black (1982–87)	955

ALL-TIME LOSS LEADERS

Paul Splittorff (1970–84)	143		Bret Saberhagen (1984–89)	61
Dennis Leonard (1974–86)	106		Bud Black (1982–87)	56
Larry Gura (1976–85)	78		Steve Busby (1972–80)	54
Dick Drago (1969–73)	70		Danny Jackson (1983–87)	49
Mark Gubicza (1984–89)	67		Al Fitzmorris (1969–76)	48
Charlie Leibrandt (1984–89)	61			

ALL-TIME SHUTOUT LEADERS

Dennis Leonard (1974–86)	23	Dick Drago (1969–73)	10
Paul Splittorff (1970–84)	17	Charlie Leibrandt (1984–89)	10
Larry Gura (1976–85)	14	Steve Busby (1972–80)	7
Mark Gubicza (1984–89)	12	Roger Nelson (1969–72)	7
Bret Saberhagen (1984–89)	12	Jim Rooker (1969–72)	7
Al Fitzmorris (1969–76)	11		

ALL-TIME STRIKEOUT LEADERS

Dennis Leonard (1974–86)	1,323	Larry Gura (1976–85)	633
Paul Splittorff (1970–84)	1,057	Charlie Leibrant (1984–89)	618
Bret Saberhagen (1984–89)	870	Dick Drago (1969–73)	577
Mark Gubicza (1984–89)	850	Bud Black (1982–87)	489
Steve Busby (1972–80)	659	Doug Bird (1973–78)	464

ALL-TIME WALK LEADERS

Paul Splittorff (1970–84)	780	Al Fitzmorris (1969–76)	359
Dennis Leonard (1974–86)	622	Rich Gale (1978–81)	315
Larry Gura (1976–85)	503	Dick Drago (1969–73)	310
Mark Gubicza (1984–89)	502	Danny Jackson (1983–87)	305
Steve Busby (1972–80)	433	Charlie Leibrandt (1984–88)	305

ALL-TIME ERA LEADERS

Dan Quisenberry (1979–87)	2.53	Al Fitzmorris (1969–76)	3.46
Steve Mingori (1973–79)	3.06	Marty Pattin (1974–80)	3.48
Roger Nelson (1969–72)	3.08	Mark Gubicza (1984–89)	3.51
Bret Saberhagen (1984–89)	3.23	Mike Hedlund (1969–72)	3.51
Dick Drago (1969–73)	3.42	Doug Bird (1973–78)	3.57

ALL-TIME WON-LOSS PERCENTAGE LEADERS

Bret Saberhagen (1984–89)	.601	Dennis Leonard (1974–86)	.576
Tom Burgmeier (1969–73)	.600	Steve Busby (1972–80)	.565
Al Fitzmorris (1969–76)	.593	Rich Gale (1978–81)	.560
Larry Gura (1976–85)	.587	Mark Gubicza (1984–89)	.556
Doug Bird (1973–78)	.576	Charlie Leibrandt (1984–89)	.555

ALL-TIME SAVE LEADERS

Dan Quisenberry (1979–87)	237
Doug Bird (1973–78)	58
Steve Farr (1985–89)	48
Ted Abernathy (1970–72)	40
Al Hrabosky (1978–79)	31

Tom Burgmeier (1969–73)	28
Mark Littell (1973–77)	28
Steve Mingori (1973–79)	27
Marty Pattin (1974–80)	21
Gene Garber (1973–74; 1987)	20

ROYALS LEAGUE LEADERS

BATTING

BATTING
G. Brett, 1976, '80
W. Wilson, 1982

HITS
G. Brett, 1975, '76, '79
W. Wilson, 1980
K. Seitzer, 1987 (Tie)

RBI
H. McRae, 1982

RUNS
W. Wilson, 1980

DOUBLES
A. Otis, 1970 (Tie), '76
L. Piniella, 1972
H. McRae, 1977, '82 (Tie)
G. Brett, 1978

TRIPLES
F. Patek, 1971
G. Brett, 1975 (Tie), '76, '79
W. Wilson, 1980 (Tie), '82, '85, '87, '88 (Tie)

STOLEN BASES
A. Otis, 1971
F. Patek, 1977
W. Wilson, 1979

PITCHING

WON-LOST PERCENTAGE
P. Splitorff, 1977

SAVES
D. Quisenberry, 1980 (Tie), '82, '83, '84, '85

MILWAUKEE BREWERS

BATTING

ALL-TIME GAME LEADERS

Robin Yount (1974–89)   2,271
Cecil Cooper (1977–87)   1,490
Jim Gantner (1976–89)   1,472
Paul Molitar (1978–89)   1,437
Charlie Moore (1973–86)   1,283

Don Money (1973–83)   1,196
Ben Oglivie (1978–86)   1,149
Gorman Thomas (1973–83)   1,102
Sixto Lezcano (1974–80)   785
George Scott (1972–76)   782

ALL-TIME AT BAT LEADERS

Robin Yount (1974–89)   8,907
Cecil Cooper (1977–87)   6,019
Paul Molitar (1978–89)   5,828
Jim Gantner (1976–89)   5,084
Don Money (1973–83)   4,330

Ben Oglivie (1978–86)   4,136
Charlie Moore (1973–86)   3,926
Gorman Thomas (1973–83)   3,544
George Scott (1972–76)   3,009
Sixto Lezcano (1974–80)   2,722

ALL-TIME RUN LEADERS

Robin Yount (1974–89)   1,335
Paul Molitor (1978–89)   989
Cecil Cooper (1977–87)   821
Jim Gantner (1976–89)   605
Don Money (1973–83)   596

Ben Oglivie (1978–86)   567
Gorman Thomas (1973–83)   524
Charlie Moore (1973–86)   441
George Scott (1972–76)   402
Sixto Lezcano (1974–80)   360

ALL-TIME HIT LEADERS

Robin Yount (1974–89)	2,602		Ben Oglivie (1978–86)	1,144
Cecil Cooper (1977–87)	1,815		Charlie Moore (1973–86)	1,029
Paul Molitor (1978–89)	1,751		George Scott (1972–76)	851
Jim Gantner (1976–89)	1,399		Gorman Thomas (1973–83)	815
Don Money (1973–83)	1,168		Sixto Lezcano (1974–80)	749

ALL-TIME DOUBLE LEADERS

Robin Yount (1974–89)	481		Ben Oglivie (1978–86)	194
Cecil Cooper (1977–87)	345		Charlie Moore (1973–86)	177
Paul Molitor (1978–89)	310		Gorman Thomas (1973–83)	172
Jim Gantner (1976–89)	215		George Scott (1972–76)	137
Don Money (1973–83)	215		Ted Simmons (1981–85)	132

ALL-TIME TRIPLE LEADERS

Robin Yount (1974–89)	111		Sixto Lezcano (1974–80)	22
Paul Molitor (1978–89)	60		Ben Oglivie (1978–86)	21
Charlie Moore (1973–86)	42		Don Money (1973–83)	20
Cecil Cooper (1977–87)	33		George Scott (1972–76)	19
Jim Gantner (1976–89)	28		John Briggs (1971–75)	17

ALL-TIME HOME RUN LEADERS

Gorman Thomas (1973–83)	208		Paul Molitor (1978–89)	119
Cecil Cooper (1977–87)	201		George Scott (1972–76)	115
Robin Yount (1974–89)	195		Sixto Lezcano (1974–80)	102
Ben Oglivie (1978–86)	176		John Briggs (1971–75)	80
Don Money (1973–83)	134		Dave May (1970–74)	69

ALL-TIME TOTAL BASE LEADERS

Robin Yount (1974–89)	3,929		Jim Gantner (1976–89)	1,802
Cecil Cooper (1977–87)	2,829		Gorman Thomas (1973–83)	1,635
Paul Molitor (1978–89)	2,538		Charlie Moore (1973–86)	1,395
Ben Oglivie (1978–86)	1,908		George Scott (1972–76)	1,371
Don Money (1973–83)	1,825		Sixto Lezcano (1974–80)	1,229

ALL-TIME RBI LEADERS

Robin Yount (1974–89)	1,124	Don Money (1973–83)	529
Cecil Cooper (1977–87)	944	Jim Gantner (1976–89)	478
Ben Oglivie (1978–86)	685	George Scott (1972–76)	463
Gorman Thomas (1973–83)	605	Charlie Moore (1973–86)	401
Paul Molitor (1978–89)	581	Ted Simmons (1981–85)	394

ALL-TIME EXTRA BASE HIT LEADERS

Robin Yount (1974–89)	800	Don Money (1973–83)	369
Cecil Cooper (1977–87)	579	Jim Gantner (1976–89)	287
Paul Molitor (1978–89)	489	George Scott (1972–76)	271
Gorman Thomas (1973–83)	392	Charlie Moore (1973–86)	254
Ben Oglivie (1978–86)	391	Sixto Lezcano (1974–80)	254

ALL-TIME BATTING AVERAGE LEADERS
(300 game minimum)

Cecil Cooper (1977–87)	.302	Jim Gantner (1976–89)	.275
Paul Molitor (1978–89)	.300	Don Money (1973–83)	.270
Robin Yount (1974–89)	.292	Tommy Harper (1970–71)	.264
George Scott (1972–76)	.283	Ted Simmons (1981–85)	.262
Ben Oglivie (1978–86)	.277	Charlie Moore (1973–86)	.262
Sixto Lezcano (1974–80)	.275		

ALL-TIME STOLEN BASES LEADERS

Paul Molitor (1978–89)	344	Don Money (1973–83)	66
Robin Yount (1974–89)	226	Tommy Harper (1970–71)	63
Jim Gantner (1976–89)	109	Charlie Moore (1973–86)	51
Mike Felder (1985–89)	88	Dave May (1970–74)	44
Cecil Cooper (1977–87)	77	Ben Oglivie (1978–86)	44

PITCHING

ALL-TIME GAME LEADERS

Jim Slaton (1971–77)	364	Mike Caldwell (1978–84)	239
Bob McClure (1977–86)	352	Ed Rodriguez (1973–78)	235
Jerry Augustine (1975–84)	279	Ken Sanders (1970–72)	195
Bill Castro (1974–80)	253	Bill Travers (1974–80)	191
Moose Haas (1976–85)	245	Jim Colborn (1972–76)	183

ALL-TIME WIN LEADERS

Jim Slaton (1971–77)	117	Jim Colborn (1972–76)	57
Mike Caldwell (1978–84)	102	Jerry Augustine (1975–84)	55
Moose Haas (1976–85)	79	Larry Sorenson (1977–80)	52
Ted Higuera (1985–88)	69	Bob McClure (1977–86)	45
Bill Travers (1974–80)	65	Pete Vuckovich (1981–86)	40

ALL-TIME INNINGS PITCHED LEADERS

Jim Slaton (1971–77)	2,025	Bill Travers (1974–80)	1,068
Mike Caldwell (1978–84)	1,603	Jerry Augustine (1975–84)	944
Moose Haas (1976–85)	1,542	Larry Sorenson (1977–80)	854
Jim Colborn (1972–76)	1,118	Bob McClure (1977–86)	843
Ted Higuera (1985–89)	1,084	Skip Lockwood (1970–73)	730

ALL-TIME SHUTOUT LEADERS

Jim Slaton (1971–77)	19	Larry Sorenson (1977–80)	7
Mike Caldwell (1978–84)	18	Jim Colborn (1972–76)	7
Ted Higuera (1985–89)	11	Bill Parsons (1971–73)	6
Bill Travers (1974–80)	10	Jerry Augustine (1975–84)	6
Moose Haas (1976–85)	8	Marty Pattin (1970–71)	5

ALL-TIME STRIKEOUT LEADERS

Jim Slaton (1971–77)	929		Jim Colborn (1972–76)	495
Ted Higuera (1985–89)	857		Bill Travers (1974–80)	459
Moose Haas (1976–85)	800		Skip Lockwood (1970–73)	411
Mike Caldwell (1978–84)	540		Ed Rodriguez (1973–78)	404
Bob McClure (1977–86)	497		Marty Pattin (1970–71)	330

ALL-TIME WALKS LEADERS

Jim Slaton (1971–77)	760		Jerry Augustine (1975–84)	340
Moose Haas (1976–85)	408		Ted Higuera (1985–89)	331
Bill Travers (1974–80)	392		Jim Colborn (1972–76)	309
Bob McClure (1977–86)	363		Skip Lockwood (1970–73)	306
Mike Caldwell (1978–84)	353		Ed Rodriguez (1973–78)	289

ALL-TIME ERA LEADERS (400 Inns. Min.)

Bill Castro (1974–80)	2.96		Skip Lockwood (1970–73)	3.75
Ted Higuera (1985–89)	3.28		Ed Rodriguez (1973–78)	3.78
Jim Colborn (1972–76)	3.65		Marty Pattin (1970–71)	3.82
Larry Sorenson (1977–80)	3.72		Don Sutton (1982–84)	3.85
Mike Caldwell (1978–84)	3.74		Jim Slaton (1971–77)	3.86

ALL-TIME WON-LOST PERCENTAGE LEADERS (Min. 20 wins)

Ted Higuera (1985–89)	.639		Moose Haas (1976–85)	.535
Pete Vuckovich (1981–86)	.606		Larry Sorenson (1977–80)	.531
Juan Nieves (1986–88)	.561		Bill Castro (1974–80)	.521
Mike Caldwell (1978–84)	.560		Ed Rodriguez (1973–78)	.521
Billy Champion (1973–76)	.537		Bob McClure (1977–86)	.511

ALL-TIME LOSS LEADERS

Jim Slaton (1971–77)	121	Skip Lockwood (1970–73)	55
Mike Caldwell (1978–84)	80	Larry Sorenson (1977–80)	46
Moose Haas (1976–85)	79	Ted Higuera (1985–89)	44
Bill Travers (1974–80)	67	Bob McClure (1977–86)	43
Jim Colborn (1972–76)	60	Marty Pattin (1970–71)	38
Jerry Augustine (1975–84)	59		

ALL-TIME SAVE LEADERS

Dan Plesac (1986–89)	100	Bob McClure (1977–86)	34
Rollie Fingers (1981–82; 1984–85)	97	Pete Ladd (1982–85)	33
Ken Sanders (1970–72)	61	Ed Rodriguez (1973–78)	30
Bill Castro (1974–80)	44	Frank Linzy (1972–73)	25
Tom Murphy (1974–76)	41	Mark Clear (1986–87)	22

BREWERS LEAGUE LEADERS

BATTING

HOME RUNS
G. Scott, 1975 (Tie)
G. Thomas, 1979, '82 (Tie)
B. Oglivie, 1980 (Tie)

HITS
R. Yount, 1982

RBI
G. Scott, 1975
C. Cooper, 1980, '83 (Tie)

RUNS
P. Molitor, 1982, '87

DOUBLES
P. Garcia, 1973 (Tie)
C. Cooper, 1979 (Tie), '81
R. Yount, 1980, '82 (Tie)
P. Molitor, 1987

TRIPLES
R. Yount, 1983, '88 (Tie)

PITCHING

SAVES
K. Sanders, 1971
R. Fingers, 1981

MINNESOTA TWINS

BATTING

ALL-TIME GAME LEADERS

Harmon Killebrew (1961–74)	1,939	Kent Hrbek (1981–89)	1,152
Tony Oliva (1962–76)	1,676	Roy Smalley (1976–82; 1985–87)	1,148
Rod Carew (1967–78)	1,635	Cesar Tovar (1965–72)	1,090
Bob Allison (1961–70)	1,236	Zoilo Versalles (1961–67)	1,065
Gary Gaetti (1981–89)	1,207	Kirby Puckett (1984–89)	924

ALL-TIME AT BAT LEADERS

Harmon Killebrew (1961–74)	6,593	Zoilo Versalles (1961–67)	4,148
Tony Oliva (1962–76)	6,301	Cesar Tovar (1965–72)	4,142
Rod Carew (1967–78)	6,235	Roy Smalley (1976–82; 1985–87)	3,997
Gary Gaetti (1981–89)	4,412	Bob Allison (1961–70)	3,926
Kent Hrbek (1981–89)	4,178	Kirby Puckett (1984–89)	3,844

ALL-TIME RUN LEADERS

Harmon Killebrew (1961–74)	1,047	Gary Gaetti (1981–89)	585
Rod Carew (1967–78)	950	Zoilo Versalles (1961–67)	564
Tony Oliva (1962–76)	870	Roy Smalley (1976–82; 1985–87)	551
Bob Allison (1961–70)	648	Kirby Puckett (1984–89)	542
Cesar Tovar (1965–72)	646	Tom Brunansky (1982–87)	445
Kent Hrbek (1981–89)	624		

ALL-TIME HIT LEADERS

Rod Carew (1967–78)	2,085	Gary Gaetti (1981–89)	1,144
Tony Oliva (1962–78)	1,917	Roy Smalley (1985–87)	1,046
Harmon Killebrew (1961–74)	1,713	Zoilo Versalles (1961–67)	1,046
Kirby Puckett (1984–89)	1,243	Bob Allison (1961–70)	999
Kent Hrbek (1981–89)	1,212	Tom Brunansky (1982–87)	824

ALL-TIME DOUBLE LEADERS

Tony Oliva (1962–76)	329	Kirby Puckett (1984–89)	197
Rod Carew (1967–78)	305	Cesar Tovar (1965–72)	193
Harmon Killebrew (1961–74)	232	Zoilo Versalles (1961–67)	188
Gary Gaetti (1981–89)	225	Roy Smalley (1976–82; 1985–87)	184
Kent Hrbek (1981–89)	224	Bob Allison (1961–70)	167

ALL-TIME TRIPLE LEADERS

Rod Carew (1967–78)	90	Kirby Puckett (1984–89)	38
Zoilo Versalles (1961–67)	56	John Castino (1979–84)	34
Tony Oliva (1962–76)	48	Lyman Bostock (1975–77)	26
Cesar Tovar (1965–72)	45	Dan Ford (1975–78)	25
Bob Allison (1961–70)	41	Larry Hisle (1973–77)	23

ALL-TIME HOME RUN LEADERS

Harmon Killebrew (1961–74)	475	Tom Brunansky (1982–87)	162
Tony Oliva (1962–76)	220	Roy Smalley (1976–82; 1985–87)	110
Bob Allison (1961–70)	211	Jimmie Hall (1963–66)	98
Kent Hrbek (1981–89)	201	Kirby Puckett (1984–89)	96
Gary Gaetti (1981–89)	185	Don Mincher (1961–66)	90

ALL-TIME TOTAL BASE LEADERS

Harmon Killebrew (1961–74)	3,412	Bob Allison (1961–70)	1,881
Tony Oliva (1962–76)	3,002	Kirby Puckett (1984–89)	1,804
Rod Carew (1967–78)	2,792	Zoilo Versalles (1961–67)	1,604
Kent Hrbek (1981–89)	1,971	Roy Smalley (1976–82; 1985–87)	1,602
Gary Gaetti (1981–89)	1,964	Cesar Tovar (1965–72)	1,561

ALL-TIME RBI LEADERS

Harmon Killebrew (1961–74)	1,325	Gary Gaetti (1981–89)	585
Tony Oliva (1962–76)	947	Kirby Puckett (1984–89)	506
Rod Carew (1967–78)	733	Roy Smalley (1976–82; 1985–87)	485
Kent Hrbek (1981–89)	724	Tom Brunansky (1982–87)	463
Bob Allison (1961–70)	642	Larry Hisle (1973–77)	409

ALL-TIME EXTRA BASE HIT LEADERS

Harmon Killebrew (1961–74)	728	Kirby Puckett (1984–89)	331
Tony Oliva (1962–76)	597	Zoilo Versalles (1961–67)	330
Rod Carew (1967–78)	469	Tom Brunansky (1982–87)	328
Kent Hrbek (1981–89)	441	Roy Smalley (1976–82; 1985–87)	315
Gary Gaetti (1981–89)	430	Cesar Tovar (1965–72)	276
Bob Allison (1961–70)	419		

ALL-TIME BATTING AVERAGE LEADERS (Min. 500 games)

Rod Carew (1967–78)	.334	Steve Braun (1971–76)	.284
Kirby Puckett (1984–89)	.323	Cesar Tovar (1965–72)	.281
Tony Oliva (1962–76)	.304	Glenn Adams (1977–81)	.281
Kent Hrbek (1981–88)	.292	John Castino (1979–84)	.278
Larry Hisle (1973–77)	.286	Earl Battey (1961–67)	.278
Mickey Hatcher (1981–86)	.284		

ALL-TIME STOLEN BASE LEADERS

Rod Carew (1967–78)	271	Zoilo Versalles (1961–67)	84
Cesar Tovar (1965–72)	186	Dan Gladden (1987–89)	76
Larry Hisle (1973–77)	92	Gary Gaetti (1981–89)	68
Tony Oliva (1962–76)	86	Bob Allison (1961–70)	60
Kirby Puckett (1984–89)	84	Ted Uhlaender (1965–69)	46

PITCHING

ALL-TIME GAME LEADERS

Jim Kaat (1961–73)	468	Frank Viola (1982–89)	260
Jim Perry (1963–72)	376	Dave Goltz (1972–79)	247
Bert Blyleven (1970–76; 1985–88)	348	Ron Perranoski (1968–71)	244
Al Worthington (1964–69)	327	Bill Campbell (1973–76)	216
Ron Davis (1982–86)	286	Tom Burgmeier (1974–77)	214

ALL-TIME WIN LEADERS

Jim Kaat (1961–73)	189	Camilio Pascual (1961–66)	88
Bert Blyleven (1970–76; 1985–88)	149	Dave Boswell (1964–70)	67
Jim Perry (1963–72)	128	Geoff Zahn (1977–80)	53
Frank Viola (1982–89)	112	"Mudcat" Grant (1964–67)	50
Dave Goltz (1972–79)	96	Mike Smithson (1984–87)	47

ALL-TIME INNINGS PITCHED LEADERS

Jim Kaat (1961–73)	2,958	Camilio Pascual (1961–66)	1,284
Bert Blyleven (1970–76; 1985–88)	2,566	Dave Boswell (1964–70)	1,036
Jim Perry (1963–72)	1,884	Geoff Zahn (1977–80)	852
Frank Viola (1982–89)	1,771	Mike Smithson (1984–87)	816
Dave Goltz (1972–79)	1,637	"Mudcat" Grant (1964–67)	780

ALL-TIME LOSS LEADERS

Jim Kaat (1961–73)	152	Camilio Pascual (1961–66)	57
Bert Blyleven (1970–76; 1985–88)	138	Dave Boswell (1964–70)	54
Frank Viola (1982–89)	93	Geoff Zahn (1977–80)	53
Jim Perry (1963–72)	90	Pete Redfern (1976–82)	48
Dave Goltz (1972–79)	79	Mike Smithson (1984–88)	48

ALL-TIME SHUTOUT LEADERS

Bert Blyleven (1970–79; 1985–88)	29		"Mudcat" Grant (1964–67)	10
Jim Kaat (1961–73)	23		Frank Viola (1982–89)	10
Camilio Pascual (1961–66)	18		Geoff Zahn (1977–80)	7
Jim Perry (1963–72)	17		Jim Merritt (1965–68)	6
Dave Goltz (1972–79)	11		Dave Boswell (1964–70)	6
Dean Chance (1967–69)	11			

ALL-TIME STRIKEOUT LEADERS

Bert Blyleven (1970–76; 1985–88)	2,035		Dave Goltz (1972–79)	887
Jim Kaat (1961–73)	1,824		Dave Boswell (1964–70)	865
Frank Viola (1982–89)	1,214		Dick Stigman (1962–65)	538
Jim Perry (1963–72)	1,025		Jim Merritt (1965–68)	527
Camilio Pascual (1961–66)	994		Dean Chance (1967–69)	504

ALL-TIME WALK LEADERS

Jim Kaat (1961–73)	694		Dave Boswell (1964–70)	460
Bert Blyleven (1970–76; 1985–88)	674		Camilio Pascual (1961–66)	431
Jim Perry (1963–72)	541		Pete Redfern (1976–82)	306
Frank Viola (1982–89)	521		Joe Decker (1973–76)	272
Dave Goltz (1972–79)	493		Ray Corbin (1971–75)	261

ALL-TIME ERA LEADERS (Min. 500 Inns.)

Dean Chance (1967–69)	2.67		Camilio Pascual (1961–66)	3.31
Jim Merritt (1965–68)	3.03		Dick Woodson (1969–74)	3.35
Jim Perry (1963–72)	3.15		"Mudcat" Grant (1964–67)	3.36
Bert Blyleven (1970–76; 1985–88)	3.28		Dave Boswell (1964–70)	3.49
Jim Kaat (1961–73)	3.29		Dave Goltz (1972–79)	3.49

ALL-TIME WON-LOST PERCENTAGE LEADERS (25 wins min.)

Camilio Pascual (1961–66)	.607	Jim Kaat (1961–73)	.554
Bill Campbell (1973–76)	.604	Dave Goltz (1972–79)	.549
"Mudcat" Grant (1964–67)	.588	Dean Chance (1967–69)	.547
Jim Perry (1963–72)	.587	Frank Viola (1982–89)	.546
Dave Boswell (1964–70)	.554	Al Worthington (1964–69)	.544

ALL-TIME SAVE LEADERS

Ron Davis (1982–86)	108	Bill Campbell (1973–76)	51
Jeff Reardon (1987–89)	104	Doug Corbett (1980–82)	43
Al Worthington (1964–69)	88	Ray Moore (1961–63)	25
Ron Perranoski (1968–71)	76	Tom Burgmeier (1974–77)	23
Mike Marshall (1978–80)	54	Tom Johnson (1974–78)	22

TWINS LEAGUE LEADERS

BATTING

BATTING
 T. Oliva, 1964, '65, '71
 R. Carew, 1969, '72, '73, '74, '75, '77, '78

HOME RUNS
 H. Killebrew, 1962, '63, '64, '67 (Tie), '69

HITS
 T. Oliva, 1964, '65, '66, '69, '70
 C. Tovar, 1971
 R. Carew, 1973, '74, '77
 K. Puckett, 1987 (Tie), '88

RBI
 H. Killebrew, 1962, '69, '71
 L. Hisle, 1977

RUNS
 B. Allison, 1963
 T. Oliva, 1964
 Z. Versalles, 1965
 R. Carew, 1977

DOUBLES
 T. Oliva, 1964, '67, '69, '70 (Tie)
 Z. Versalles, 1965 (Tie)
 C. Tovar, 1970 (Tie)

TRIPLES
 Z. Versalles, 1963, '64 (Tie), '65 (Tie)

 R. Rollins, 1964 (Tie)
 C. Tovar, 1970
 R. Carew, 1973 (Tie), '77
 J. Castino, 1981

PITCHING

WON-LOST PERCENTAGE
 J. Grant, 1965
 W. Campbell, 1976

WINS
 J. Grant, 1965
 J. Kaat, 1966
 J. Perry, 1970 (Tie)
 D. Goltz, 1977 (Tie)
 F. Viola, 1988

STRIKEOUTS
 C. Pascual, 1961, 1962, 1963
 B. Blyleven, 1985 (Also with Cleveland)

ERA
 A. Anderson, 1988

SAVES
 A. Worthington, 1968
 R. Perranoski, 1969, '70
 M. Marshall, 1979

NEW YORK YANKEES

BATTING

ALL-TIME GAME LEADERS

Mickey Mantle (1951–68)   2,401
Lou Gehrig (1923–39)   2,164
Yogi Berra (1946–63)   2,116
Babe Ruth (1920–34)   2,084
Roy White (1965–79)   1,881

Bill Dickey (1928–43; 1946)   1,789
Joe DiMaggio (1936–42; 1946–51)   1,736
Willie Randolph (1976–88)   1,694
Frankie Crosetti (1932–48)   1,682
Phil Rizzuto (1941–42; 1946–56)   1,661

ALL-TIME AT BAT LEADERS

Mickey Mantle (1951–68)   8,102
Lou Gehrig (1923–39)   8,001
Yogi Berra (1946–63)   7,546
Babe Ruth (1920–34)   7,217
Joe DiMaggio (1936–42; 1946–51)   6,821

Roy White (1965–79)   6,650
Willie Randolph (1976–88)   6,303
Bill Dickey (1928–43; 1946)   6,300
Frankie Crosetti (1932–48)   6,277
Tony Lazzeri (1926–37)   6,094

ALL-TIME RUN LEADERS

Babe Ruth (1920–34)   1,959
Lou Gehrig (1923–39)   1,888
Mickey Mantle (1951–68)   1,677
Joe DiMaggio (1936–42; 1946–51)   1,390
Earle Combs (1924–35)   1,186

Yogi Berra (1946–63)   1,174
Willie Randolph (1976–88)   1,027
Frankie Crosetti (1932–48)   1,006
Roy White (1965–79)   964
Tony Lazzeri (1926–37)   952

ALL-TIME HIT LEADERS

Lou Gehrig (1923–39)	2,721	Bill Dickey (1928–43; 1946)	1,969
Babe Ruth (1920–34)	2,518	Earle Combs (1924–35)	1,866
Mickey Mantle (1951–68)	2,415	Roy White (1965–79)	1,803
Joe DiMaggio (1936–42; 1946–51)	2,214	Tony Lazzeri (1926–37)	1,784
Yogi Berra (1946–63)	2,148	Willie Randolph (1976–88)	1,731

ALL-TIME DOUBLE LEADERS

Lou Gehrig (1923–39)	535	Bob Meusel (1920–29)	338
Babe Ruth (1920–34)	424	Tony Lazzeri (1926–37)	327
Joe DiMaggio (1936–42; 1946–51)	389	Yogi Berra (1946–63)	321
Mickey Mantle (1951–68)	344	Earle Combs (1924–35)	309
Bill Dickey (1928–43; 1946)	343	Roy White (1965–79)	300

ALL-TIME TRIPLE LEADERS

Lou Gehrig (1923–39)	162	Babe Ruth (1920–34)	106
Earle Combs (1924–35)	154	Bob Meusel (1920–29)	87
Joe DiMaggio (1936–42; 1946–51)	131	Tommy Henrich (1937–42; 1946–50)	73
Wally Pipp (1915–25)	121	Mickey Mantle (1951–68)	72
Tony Lazzeri (1926–37)	115	Bill Dickey (1928–43; 1946)	72

ALL-TIME HOME RUN LEADERS

Babe Ruth (1920–34)	659	Graig Nettles (1973–83)	250
Mickey Mantle (1951–68)	536	Roger Maris (1960–66)	203
Lou Gehrig (1923–39)	493	Dave Winfield (1981–88)	203
Joe DiMaggio (1936–42; 1946–51)	361	Bill Dickey (1928–43; 1946)	202
Yogi Berra (1946–63)	358	Charlie "King Kong" Keller (1939–43; 1945–49)	184

ALL-TIME TOTAL BASE LEADERS

Babe Ruth (1920–34)	5,131	Bill Dickey (1928–43; 1946)	3,062
Lou Gehrig (1923–39)	5,059	Tony Lazzeri (1926–37)	2,848
Mickey Mantle (1951–68)	4,511	Roy White (1965–79)	2,685
Joe DiMaggio (1936–42; 1946–51)	3,948	Earle Combs (1924–35)	2,657
Yogi Berra (1946–63)	3,641	Bob Meusel (1920–29)	2,515

ALL-TIME RBI LEADERS

Lou Gehrig (1923–39)	1,991	Bill Dickey (1928–43; 1946)	1,209
Babe Ruth (1920–34)	1,970	Tony Lazzeri (1926–37)	1,154
Joe DiMaggio (1936–42; 1946–51)	1,537	Bob Meusel (1920–29)	1,005
Mickey Mantle (1951–68)	1,509	Graig Nettles (1973–83)	834
Yogi Berra (1946–63)	1,430	Wally Pipp (1915–25)	825

ALL-TIME EXTRA BASE HIT LEADERS

Lou Gehrig (1923–39)	1,190	Bill Dickey (1928–43; 1946)	617
Babe Ruth (1920–34)	1,189	Tony Lazzeri (1926–37)	611
Mickey Mantle (1951–68)	952	Bob Meusel (1920–29)	571
Joe DiMaggio (1936–42; 1946–51)	881	Tommy Henrich (1937–42; 1946–50)	525
Yogi Berra (1946–63)	728	Earle Combs (1924–35)	521

ALL-TIME BATTING AVERAGE LEADERS

Babe Ruth (1920–34)	.349	Bill Dickey (1928–43; 1946)	.313
Lou Gehrig (1923–39)	.340	Bob Meusel (1920–29)	.311
Don Mattingly (1982–88)	.327	Ben Chapman (1930–36)	.305
Earle Combs (1924–35)	.325	Mickey Mantle (1951–68)	.298
Joe DiMaggio (1936–42; 1946–51)	.325	Wally Schang (1921–25)	.297

ALL-TIME STOLEN BASE LEADERS

Rickey Henderson (1985–89)	326	Wid Conroy (1903–08)	184
Willie Randolph (1976–88)	251	Bob Meusel (1920–29)	183
Hal Chase (1905–13)	248	Mickey Mantle (1951–68)	153
Roy White (1965–79)	233	Horace Clarke (1965–74)	151
Ben Chapman (1930–36)	184	Phil Rizzuto (1941–42; 1946–56)	149

PITCHING

ALL-TIME GAME LEADERS

Whitey Ford (1950–67)	498	Johnny Murphy (1932; 1934–43; 1946)	383
Dave Righetti (1979; 1981–89)	469	Ron Guidry (1975–88)	368
Red Ruffing (1930–42; 1945–46)	426	Lefty Gomez (1930–42)	367
Sparky Lyle (1972–78)	420	Waite Hoyt (1921–30)	365
Bob Shawkey (1915–27)	415	Mel Stottlemyre (1964–74)	360

ALL-TIME WIN LEADERS

Whitey Ford (1950–67)	236	Mel Stottlemyre (1964–74)	164
Red Ruffing (1930–42; 1945–46)	231	Herb Pennock (1923–33)	162
Lefty Gomez (1930–42)	189	Waite Hoyt (1921–30)	157
Ron Guidry (1975–88)	170	Allie Reynolds (1947–54)	131
Bob Shawkey (1915–27)	168	Jack Chesbro (1903–09)	126

ALL-TIME INNINGS PITCHED LEADERS

Whitey Ford (1950–67)	3,171	Ron Guidry (1975–88)	2,393
Red Ruffing (1930–42; 1945–46)	3,169	Waite Hoyt (1921–30)	2,273
Mel Stottlemyre (1964–74)	2,662	Herb Pennock (1923–33)	2,190
Lefty Gomez (1930–42)	2,498	Jack Chesbro (1903–09)	1,953
Bob Shawkey (1915–27)	2,489	Fritz Peterson (1966–74)	1,856

ALL-TIME LOSS LEADERS

Mel Stottlemyre (1964–74)	139	Lefty Gomez (1930–42)	101
Bob Shawkey (1915–27)	131	Ray Caldwell (1910–18)	99
Red Ruffing (1930–42; 1945–46)	124	Waite Hoyt (1921–30)	98
Whitey Ford (1950–67)	106	Jack Warhop (1908–15)	94
Fritz Peterson (1966–74)	106	Jack Chesbro (1903–09)	92

ALL-TIME SHUTOUT LEADERS

Whitey Ford (1950–67)	45	Ron Guidry (1975–88)	26
Red Ruffing (1930–42; 1945–46)	40	Spud Chandler (1937–47)	26
Mel Stottlemyre (1964–74)	40	Bob Shawkey (1915–27)	24
Lefty Gomez (1930–42)	28	Vic Raschi (1946–54)	24
Allie Reynolds (1947–54)	27	Bob Turley (1955–62)	21

ALL-TIME STRIKEOUT LEADERS

Whitey Ford (1950–67)	1,956	Bob Shawkey (1915–27)	1,163
Ron Guidry (1975–88)	1,778	Al Downing (1961–69)	1,028
Red Ruffing (1930–42; 1945–46)	1,526	Allie Reynolds (1947–54)	967
Lefty Gomez (1930–42)	1,468	Jack Chesbro (1903–09)	913
Mel Stottlemyre (1964–74)	1,257	Bob Turley (1955–62)	909

ALL-TIME WALK LEADERS

Lefty Gomez (1930–42)	1,090	Mel Stottlemyre (1964–74)	809
Whitey Ford (1950–67)	1,086	Tommy Byrne (1943; 1946–51; 1954–57)	763
Red Ruffing (1930–42; 1945–46)	1,069	Bob Turley (1955–62)	761
Bob Shawkey (1915–27)	856	Ron Guidry (1975–88)	633
Allie Reynolds (1947–54)	819	Waite Hoyt (1921–30)	631

ALL-TIME ERA LEADERS (Min. 1,000 inns.)

Russell Ford (1909–13)	2.54	Spud Chandler (1937–47)	2.84
Jack Chesbro (1903–09)	2.58	Ray Fisher (1910–17)	2.91
Al Orth (1904–09)	2.72	Mel Stottlemyre (1964–74)	2.97
Ernie Bonham (1940–46)	2.73	Ray Caldwell (1910–18)	2.99
Whitey Ford (1950–67)	2.74	Jack Warhop (1908–15)	3.09

ALL-TIME WON-LOST PERCENTAGE LEADERS (50 Wins min.)

Spud Chandler (1937–47)	.717	Lefty Gomez (1930–42)	.652
Vic Raschi (1946–53)	.706	Ron Guidry (1975–88)	.651
Whitey Ford (1950–67)	.690	Red Ruffing (1930–42; 1945–46)	.651
Allie Reynolds (1947–54)	.686	Herb Pennock (1923–33)	.643
Carl Mays (1919–23)	.669	Tommy Byrne (1943; 1946–51; 1954–57)	.643
Ed Lopat (1948–55)	.657		

ALL-TIME SAVE LEADERS

Dave Righetti (1979; 1981–89)	188	Lindy McDaniel (1968–1973)	58
Goose Gossage (1978–83; 1989)	151	Ryne Duren (1958–61)	43
Sparky Lyle (1972–78)	141	Luis Arroyo (1960–63)	43
Johnny Murphy (1932; 1934–43; 1946)	104	Allie Reynolds (1947–54)	41
Joe Page (1944–50)	76	Hal Reniff (1961–67)	41

YANKEES LEAGUE LEADERS

BATTING

BATTING
B. Ruth, 1924
L. Gehrig, 1934
J. DiMaggio, 1939, '40
S. Stirnweiss, 1945
M. Mantle, 1956
D. Mattingly, 1984

HOME RUNS
W. Pipp, 1916, '17
B. Ruth, 1920, '21, '23, '24, '26, '27, '28, '29, '30, '31 (Tie)
B. Meusel, 1925
L. Gehrig, 1931 (Tie), '34, '36
J. DiMaggio, 1937, '48
N. Etten, 1944
M. Mantle, 1955, '56, '58, '60
R. Maris, 1961
G. Nettles, 1976
R. Jackson, 1980 (Tie)

HITS
E. Combs, 1927
L. Gehrig, 1931
R. Rolfe, 1939
S. Stirnweiss, 1944, '45
B. Richardson, 1962
D. Mattingly, 1984, '86

RBI
B. Ruth, 1920, '21, '23 (Tie), '26, '28 (Tie)
B. Meusel, 1925
L. Gehrig, 1927, '28 (Tie), '30, '31, '34
J. DiMaggio, 1941, '48
N. Etten, 1945
M. Mantle, 1956
R. Maris, 1960, '61

RUNS
P. Dougherty, 1904 (Also with Bost.)
B. Ruth, 1920, '21, '23, '24, '26, '27, '28
L. Gehrig, 1931, '33, '35, '36
J. DiMaggio, 137
R. Rolfe, 1939
S. Stirnweiss, 1944, '45
T. Henrich, 1948
M. Mantle, 1954, '56, '57, '58, '60, '61 (Tie)
R. Maris, 1961 (Tie)
B. Murcer, 1972
R. White, 1976
R. Henderson, 1985, '86

DOUBLES
L. Gehrig, 1927, '28 (Tie)
R. Rolfe, 1939
D. Mattingly, 1984, '85, '86

TRIPLES
W. Pipp, 1924
L. Gehrig, 1926

E. Combs, 1927, '28, '30
B. Chapman, 1934
R. Rolfe, 1936 (Tie)
J. DiMaggio, 1936 (Tie)
J. Lindell, 1943 (Tie), '44
S. Stirnweiss, 1945
T. Henrich, 1947, '48
M. Mantle, 1955 (Tie)
A. Carey, 1955 (Tie)
H. Bauer, 1957 (Tie)
G. McDougald, 1957 (Tie)
H. Simpson, 1957 (Tie) (Also with KC)

STOLEN BASES
F. Maisel, 1914
B. Chapman, 1931, '32, '33
F. Crosetti, 1938
S. Stirnweiss, 1944, '45
R. Henderson, 1985, '86, '88

PITCHING

WON-LOST PERCENTAGE
J. Chesbro, 1904
C. Mays, 1921
J. Bush, 1922
H. Pennock, 1923
W. Hoyt, 1927
J. Allen, 1932
V. Gomez, 1934, 1941
M. Pearson, 1936
C. Ruffing, 1938
E. Bonham, 1942
S. Chandler, 1943
A. Reynolds, 1947
V. Raschi, 1950
E. Lopat, 1953
T. Byrne, 1955
E. Ford, 1956, 1961, 1963
R. Turley, 1957
R. Guidry, 1978, 1985

WINS
J. Chesbro, 1904
A. Orth, 1906
C. Mays, 1921 (Tie)
W. Hoyt, 1927
G. Pipgras, 1928 (Tie)
V. Gomez, 1934, 1941
C. Ruffing, 1938
S. Chandler, 1943 (Tie)
E. Ford, 1955 (Tie), 1961, 1963
R. Turley, 1958
W. Terry, 1962
R. Guidry, 1978, 1985

STRIKEOUTS
C. Ruffing, 1932
V. Gomez, 1933, 1934, 1937
V. Raschi, 1957

A. Reynolds, 1952
A. Downing, 1964

ERA

R. Shawkey, 1920
W. Hoyt, 1927
V. Gomez, 1934, 1937
E. Bonham, 1940
S. Chandler, 1943, 1947
A. Reynolds, 1952
E. Lopat, 1953
E. Ford, 1956, 1958
R. Shantz, 1957
R. Guidry, 1978, 1979
R. May, 1980

SAVES

R. Shawkey, 1916

G. Mogridge, 1918
A. Russell, 1919 (Also with Bost.)
C. Mays, 1921 (Tie)
S. Jones, 1922
W. Moore, 1927 (Tie)
W. Hoyt, 1928
P. Malone, 1936
J. Murphy, 1938, '39, '41, '42
J. Turner, 1945
J. Page, 1947 (Tie), '49
J. Sain, 1954
R. Grim, 1957
R. Duren, 1958
L. Arroyo, 1961
A. Lyle, 1972, '76
R. Gossage, 1978, '80 (Tie)
D. Righetti, 1986

OAKLAND ATHLETICS (KANSAS CITY)

BATTING

ALL-TIME GAME LEADERS

Bert Campaneris (1964–76)	1,795	Joe Rudi (1967–76)	1,107
Sal Bando (1966–76)	1,468	Wayne Gross (1976–83; 1986)	876
Reggie Jackson (1967–75; 1987)	1,346	Gene Tenace (1969–76)	805
Dick Green (1963–74)	1,288	Rickey Henderson (1979–84)	791
Dwayne Murphy (1978–87)	1,213	Mike Davis (1980–87)	788

ALL-TIME AT BAT LEADERS

Bert Campaneris (1964–76)	7,180	Joe Rudi (1967–76)	3,993
Sal Bando (1966–76)	5,145	Rickey Henderson (1979–84)	2,916
Reggie Jackson (1967–75)	4,686	Wayne Gross (1976–83; 1986)	2,566
Dwayne Murphy (1978–87)	4,047	Mike Davis (1980–87)	2,545
Dick Green (1963–74)	4,007	Tony Armas (1977–82)	2,484

ALL-TIME RUN LEADERS

Bert Campaneris (1964–76)	983	Joe Rudi (1967–76)	487
Reggie Jackson (1967–75; 1987)	756	Dick Green (1963–74)	427
Sal Bando (1966–76)	737	Carney Lansford (1983–89)	413
Dwayne Murphy (1978–88)	614	Billy North (1973–78)	379
Rickey Henderson (1979–84)	586	Mike Davis (1980–87)	369

ALL-TIME HIT LEADERS

Bert Campaneris (1964–76)	1,882	Dwayne Murphy (1978–87)	999
Sal Bando (1966–76)	1,311	Dick Green (1963–74)	960
Reggie Jackson (1967–75; 1987)	1,228	Rickey Henderson (1979–84)	850
Joe Rudi (1967–76)	1,087	Mike Davis (1980–87)	680
Carney Lansford (1983–89)	1,050	Billy North (1973–78)	664

ALL-TIME DOUBLE LEADERS

Bert Campaneris (1964–76)	270	Dick Green (1963–74)	145
Reggie Jackson (1967–75; 1987)	234	Mike Davis (1980–87)	143
Joe Rudi (1967–76)	216	Rickey Henderson (1979–84)	129
Sal Bando (1966–76)	212	Dwayne Murphy (1978–87)	129
Carney Lansford (1983–89)	156	Wayne Gross (1976–83; 1986)	109

ALL-TIME TRIPLE LEADERS

Bert Campaneris (1964–76)	70	Sal Bando (1966–76)	25
Joe Rudi (1967–76)	32	Billy North (1973–78)	23
Rickey Henderson (1979–84)	29	Dick Green (1963–74)	23
Rick Monday (1966–71)	28	Mitchell Page (1977–83)	21
Reggie Jackson (1967–75; 1987)	27	Dwayne Murphy (1978–87)	20

ALL-TIME HOME RUN LEADERS

Reggie Jackson (1967–75; 1987)	269	Joe Rudi (1967–76)	116
Sal Bando (1966–76)	192	Tony Armas (1977–82)	111
Dwayne Murphy (1978–87)	153	Dave Kingman (1984–86)	100
Jose Canseco (1985–89)	128	Wayne Gross (1976–83; 1986)	88
Gene Tenace (1969–76)	121	Mike Davis (1980–87)	84
Mark McGwire (1986–89)	117		

ALL-TIME TOTAL BASE LEADERS

Bert Campaneris (1964–76)	2,502	Carney Lansford (1983–89)	1,500
Reggie Jackson (1967–75; 1987)	2,323	Dick Green (1963–74)	1,391
Sal Bando (1966–76)	2,149	Rickey Henderson (1979–84; 1989)	1,324
Joe Rudi (1967–76)	1,715	Mike Davis (1980–87)	1,101
Dwayne Murphy (1978–87)	1,627	Tony Armas (1977–82)	1,077

ALL-TIME RBI LEADERS

Sal Bando (1966–76)	796	Jose Canseco (1985–89)	424
Reggie Jackson (1967–75; 1987)	776	Dick Green (1963–74)	422
Dwayne Murphy (1978–87)	563	Carney Lansford (1983–89)	422
Joe Rudi (1967–76)	540	Gene Tenace (1969–76)	389
Bert Campaneris (1964–76)	529	Tony Armas (1977–82)	374

ALL-TIME EXTRA BASE HIT LEADERS

Reggie Jackson (1967–75; 1987)	530	Dwayne Murphy (1978–87)	302
Sal Bando (1966–76)	429	Carney Lansford (1983–89)	261
Bert Campaneris (1964–76)	410	Dick Green (1963–74)	248
Joe Rudi (1967–76)	364	Mike Davis (1980–87)	240
Jose Canseco (1985–89)	343	Gene Tenace (1969–76)	217

ALL-TIME BATTING AVERAGE LEADERS
(300 game minimum)

Carney Lansford (1983–89)	.296	Joe Rudi (1967–76)	.272
Rickey Henderson (1979–84; 1989)	.292	Bruce Bochte (1984–86)	.272
Dave Revering (1978–81)	.279	Billy North (1973–78)	.271
Danny Cater (1966–69)	.277	Mike Davis (1980–87)	.267
Alfredo Griffin (1985–87)	.273	Mark McGwire (1986–89)	.259

ALL-TIME STOLEN BASE LEADERS

Rickey Henderson (1979–84; 1989)	545	Mike Davis (1980–87)	121
Bert Campaneris (1964–76)	398	Mitchell Page (1977–83)	104
Billy North (1973–78)	232	Dwayne Murphy (1978–87)	99
Reggie Jackson (1967–75; 1987)	144	Claudell Washington (1974–76)	84
Carney Lansford (1983–89)	123	Alfredo Griffin (1985–87)	83

PITCHING

ALL-TIME GAME LEADERS

Rollie Fingers (1968–76)	502	Vida Blue (1969–77)	273
Paul Lindblad (1965–71; 1973–76)	479	"Blue Moon" Odom (1964–75)	269
"Catfish" Hunter (1965–74)	363	Rick Langford (1977–86)	248
Diego Segui (1962–65; 1968; 1970–72)	323	Bob Lacey (1977–80)	227
John Wyatt (1961–66)	296	Steve McCatty (1977–85)	221

ALL-TIME WIN LEADERS

"Catfish" Hunter (1965–74)	161	Chuck Dobson (1968–73)	72
Vida Blue (1969–77)	124	Dave Stewart (1986–89)	71
"Blue Moon" Odom (1964–75)	80	Rollie Fingers (1968–76)	67
Ken Holtzman (1972–76)	77	Steve McCatty (1977–85)	63
Rick Langford (1977–86)	73	Diego Segui (1962–65; 1968; 1970–72)	59

ALL-TIME INNINGS PITCHED LEADERS

"Catfish" Hunter (1965–74)	2,456	Steve McCatty (1977–85)	1,190
Vida Blue (1969–77)	1,946	Diego Segui (1962–65; 1968; 1970–72)	1,148
Rick Langford (1977–86)	1,468	Mike Norris (1975–83)	1,097
"Blue Moon" Odom (1964–75)	1,413	Ken Holtzman (1972–76)	1,083
Chuck Dobson (1968–73)	1,200	Matt Keough (1977–83)	1,060

ALL-TIME LOSS LEADERS

"Catfish" Hunter (1965–74)	113	Diego Segui (1962–65; 1968; 1970–72)	71
Rick Langford (1977–86)	105	Chuck Dobson (1968–73)	64
Vida Blue (1969–77)	86	Steve McCatty (1977–85)	63
"Blue Moon" Odom (1964–75)	76	Rollie Fingers (1968–76)	61
Matt Keough (1977–83)	75	Mike Norris (1975–83)	59

ALL-TIME SHUTOUT LEADERS

"Catfish" Hunter (1965–74)	31	Rick Langford (1977–86)	10
Vida Blue (1969–77)	28	Jim Nash (1966–69)	9
"Blue Moon" Odom (1964–75)	14	Mike Norris (1975–83)	7
Ken Holtzman (1972–76)	13	Steve McCatty (1977–85)	7
Chuck Dobson (1968–73)	11	Matt Keough (1977–83)	7

ALL-TIME STRIKEOUT LEADERS

"Catfish" Hunter (1965–74)	1,520	Chuck Dobson (1968–73)	728
Vida Blue (1969–77)	1,315	Rick Langford (1977–86)	654
"Blue Moon" Odom (1964–75)	799	Dave Stewart (1986–89)	654
Rollie Fingers (1968–76)	784	Mike Norris (1975–83)	620
Diego Segui (1962–65; 1968; 1970–72)	772	Steve McCatty (1977–85)	541

ALL-TIME WALK LEADERS

"Blue Moon" Odom (1964–75)	732	Diego Segui (1962–65; 1968; 1970–72)	481
"Catfish" Hunter (1965–74)	687	Matt Keough (1977–83)	456
Vida Blue (1969–77)	617	Chuck Dobson (1968–73)	450
Steve McCatty (1977–85)	520	Rick Langford (1977–86)	402
Mike Norris (1975–83)	490	Dave Stewart (1986–89)	349

ALL-TIME ERA LEADERS (Min. 400 inns.)

Rollie Fingers (1968–76)	2.91	Paul Lindblad (1965–71; 1973–76)	3.29
Ken Holtzman (1972–76)	2.93	Dave Stewart (1986–89)	3.46
Vida Blue (1969–77)	2.95	"Blue Moon" Odom (1964–75)	3.54
Jim Nash (1966–69)	2.95	Diego Segui (1962–65; 1968; 1970–72)	3.65
"Catfish" Hunter (1965–74)	3.13	Chuck Dobson (1968–73)	3.66

ALL-TIME WON-LOST PERCENTAGE LEADERS
(Min. 20 wins)

Dave Stewart (1986–89)	.645	Curt Young (1983–88)	.582
Tom Underwood (1981–83)	.595	Dave Wickersham (1960–63)	.556
Vida Blue (1969–77)	.590	Jim Nash (1966–69)	.536
"Catfish" Hunter (1965–74)	.588	Paul Lindblad (1965–71; 1973–76)	.536
Ken Holtzman (1972–76)	.583	Chuck Dobson (1968–73)	.529

ALL-TIME SAVE LEADERS

Rollie Fingers (1968–76)	136	Paul Lindblad (1965–71; 1973–76)	41
Dennis Eckersley (1987–89)	94	Bill Caudill (1984; 1987)	37
John Wyatt (1961–66)	73	Darold Knowles (1971–74)	30
Jay Howell (1985–87)	61	"Mudcat" Grant (1970–71)	27
Jack Aker (1964–68)	58	Dave Beard (1980–83)	25

ATHLETICS LEAGUE LEADERS

BATTING

HOME RUNS
R. Jackson, 1973, '75 (Tie)
T. Armas, 1981 (Tie)
M. McGwire, 1987
J. Conseco, 1988

HITS
B. Campaneris, 1968
J. Rudi, 1972
R. Henderson, 1981

RBI
R. Jackson, 1973
J. Conseco, 1988

RUNS
R. Jackson, 1969, '73
R. Henderson, 1981

DOUBLES
S. Bando, 1973 (Tie)
J. Rudi, 1974

TRIPLES
H. Simpson, 1956 (Tie), '57 (Tie) (Also with New York)
V. Power, 1958 (Also with Cleveland)
G. Cimoli, 1962

B. Campaneris, 1965 (Tie)
J. Rudi, 1972 (Tie)

STOLEN BASES
B. Campaneris, 1965, '66, '67, '68, '70, '72
B. North, 1974, '76
R. Henderson, 1980, '81, '82, '83, '84, '89

PITCHING

WON-LOST PERCENTAGE
J. Hunter, 1972, 1973

WINS
J. Hunter, 1974 (Tie), 1975 (Tie)
S. McCatty, 1981 (Tie)
D. Stewart, 1987 (Tie)

ERA
D. Segui, 1970
V. Blue, 1971
J. Hunter, 1974
S. McCatty, 1981

SAVES
J. Aker, 1966
D. Eckersley, 1988

SEATTLE MARINERS

BATTING

ALL-TIME GAME LEADERS

Alvin Davis (1984–89)	881	Dave Henderson (1981–86)	654
Jim Presley (1984–89)	799	Phil Bradley (1983–87)	607
Julio Cruz (1977–83)	742	Al Cowens (1982–86)	545
Harold Reynolds (1983–89)	693	Larry Milbourne (1977–80)	487
Bruce Bochte (1978–82)	681	Ken Phelps (1983–88)	457
Dan Meyer (1977–81)	655		

ALL-TIME AT BAT LEADERS

Alvin Davis (1984–89)	3,180	Phil Bradley (1983–87)	2,159
Jim Presley (1984–89)	2,946	Dave Henderson (1981–86)	2,123
Julio Cruz (1977–83)	2,667	Al Cowens (1982–86)	1,974
Bruce Bochte (1978–82)	2,404	Ruppert Jones (1977–79)	1,691
Harold Reynolds (1983–89)	2,359	Spike Owen (1983–86)	1,590
Dan Meyer (1977–81)	2,334	Ken Phelps (1983–88)	1,209

ALL-TIME RUN LEADERS

Alvin Davis (1984–89)	461	Harold Reynolds (1983–89)	293
Julio Cruz (1977–83)	402	Dave Henderson (1981–86)	277
Jim Presley (1984–89)	351	Dan Meyer (1977–81)	267
Phil Bradley (1983–87)	346	Ruppert Jones (1977–79)	242
Bruce Bochte (1978–82)	298	Al Cowens (1982–86)	235

ALL-TIME HIT LEADERS

Alvin Davis (1984–89)	921	Dan Meyer (1977–81)	618
Jim Presley (1984–89)	736	Dave Henderson (1981–86)	545
Bruce Bochte (1978–82)	697	Al Cowens (1982–86)	504
Phil Bradley (1983–87)	649	Ruppert Jones (1977–79)	434
Julio Cruz (1977–83)	649	Ken Phelps (1983–88)	295
Harold Reynolds (1983–89)	628		

ALL-TIME DOUBLE LEADERS

Alvin Davis (1984–89)	176	Phil Bradley (1983–87)	112
Jim Presley (1984–89)	147	Harold Reynolds (1983–89)	107
Bruce Bochte (1978–82)	134	Dan Meyer (1977–81)	98
Al Cowens (1982–86)	128	Tom Paciorek (1978–81)	90
Dave Henderson (1981–86)	114	Julio Cruz (1977–83)	86

ALL-TIME TRIPLE LEADERS

Harold Reynolds (1983–89)	34	Al Cowens (1982–86)	17
Phil Bradley (1983–87)	26	Leon Roberts (1978–80)	16
Spike Owen (1983–86)	23	Julio Cruz (1977–83)	16
Ruppert Jones (1977–79)	20	Larry Milbourne (1977–80)	13
Dan Meyer (1977–81)	19	Bruce Bochte (1978–82)	13

ALL-TIME HOME RUN LEADERS

Alvin Davis (1984–89)	131	Bruce Bochte (1978–82)	58
Jim Presley (1984–89)	115	Al Cowens (1982–86)	56
Ken Phelps (1983–88)	91	Phil Bradley (1983–87)	52
Dave Henderson (1981–86)	79	Ruppert Jones (1977–79)	51
Dan Meyer (1977–81)	64	Richie Zisk (1981–83)	49

ALL-TIME TOTAL BASE LEADERS

Alvin Davis (1984–89)	1,508	Al Cowens (1982–86)	834
Jim Presley (1984–89)	1,256	Julio Cruz (1977–83)	818
Bruce Bochte (1978–82)	1,031	Ruppert Jones (1977–79)	706
Phil Bradley (1983–87)	969	Tom Paciorek (1978–81)	637
Dan Meyer (1977–81)	946	Ken Phelps (1983–88)	630
Dave Henderson (1981–86)	920		

ALL-TIME RBI LEADERS

Alvin Davis (1984–89)	530	Al Cowens (1982–86)	266
Jim Presley (1984–89)	418	Phil Bradley (1983–87)	234
Bruce Bochte (1978–82)	329	Ken Phelps (1983–88)	223
Dan Meyer (1977–81)	313	Ruppert Jones (1977–79)	200
Dave Henderson (1981–86)	271	Tom Paciorek (1978–81)	197

ALL-TIME EXTRA BASE HIT LEADERS

Alvin Davis (1984–89)	316	Phil Bradley (1983–87)	190
Jim Presley (1984–89)	275	Dan Meyer (1977–81)	181
Dave Henderson (1981–86)	205	Ruppert Jones (1977–79)	150
Bruce Bochte (1978–82)	205	Ken Phelps (1983–88)	142
Al Cowens (1982–86)	201	Tom Paciorek (1978–81)	139

ALL-TIME BATTING AVERAGE LEADERS (300 game minimum)

Phil Bradley (1983–87)	.301	Leon Roberts (1978–80)	.276
Tom Paciorek (1978–81)	.296	Dan Meyer (1977–81)	.265
Bruce Bochte (1978–82)	.290	Bill Stein (1977–80)	.259
Alvin Davis (1984–89)	.290	Ruppert Jones (1977–79)	.257
Richie Zisk (1981–83)	.286	Dave Henderson (1981–86)	.257

ALL-TIME STOLEN BASE LEADERS

Julio Cruz (1977–83)	290	Phil Bradley (1983–87)	107
Harold Reynolds (1983–89)	154	John Moses (1982–87)	70
		Ruppert Jones (1977–79)	68

PITCHING

ALL-TIME GAME LEADERS

Ed Vande Berg (1982–85)	272		Mark Langston (1984–89)	176
Mike Moore (1982–88)	227		Jim Beattie (1980–86)	163
Shane Rawley (1978–81)	205		Matt Young (1983–86)	157
Edwin Nunez (1982–88)	203		Glenn Abbott (1977–83)	155
Mike Stanton (1982–85)	184		Bill Caudill (1982–83)	133

ALL-TIME WIN LEADERS

Mark Langston (1984–89)	74		Matt Young (1983–86)	37
Mike Moore (1982–88)	66		Scott Bankhead (1987–89)	30
Glenn Abbott (1977–83)	44		Rick Honeycutt (1977–80)	26
Jim Beattie (1980–86)	43		Mike Morgan (1985–87)	24
Floyd Bannister (1979–82)	40		Ed Vande Berg (1982–85)	21

ALL-TIME INNINGS PITCHED LEADERS

Mike Moore (1982–88)	1,457		Rick Honeycutt (1977–80)	560
Mark Langston (1984–89)	1,194		Scott Bankhead (1987–89)	494
Jim Beattie (1980–86)	944		Mike Parrott (1978–81)	490
Glenn Abbott (1977–83)	903		Mike Morgan (1985–87)	429
Floyd Bannister (1979–82)	768		Shane Rawley (1978–81)	377
Matt Young (1983–86)	639			

ALL-TIME LOSS LEADERS

Mike Moore (1982–88)	96		Rick Honeycutt (1977–80)	41
Jim Beattie (1980–86)	72		Mike Parrott (1978–81)	39
Mark Langston (1984–89)	67		Mike Morgan (1985–87)	35
Glenn Abbott (1977–83)	62		Bill Swift (1985–86; 1989)	34
Floyd Bannister (1979–82)	50		Shane Rawley (1978–81)	31
Matt Young (1983–86)	48			

ALL-TIME SHUTOUT LEADERS

Mike Moore (1982–88)	9	Glenn Abbott (1977–83)	3
Mark Langston (1984–89)	9	Scott Bankhead (1987–89)	3
Floyd Bannister (1979–82)	7	Mike Morgan (1985–87)	3
Jim Beattie (1980–86)	6	Bob Stoddard (1981–84)	2
Matt Young (1983–86)	4	Mike Parrott (1978–81)	2
Rick Honeycutt (1977–80)	3	Paul Mitchell (1977–79)	2

ALL-TIME STRIKEOUT LEADERS

Mark Langston (1984–89)	1,078	Scott Bankhead (1987–89)	337
Mike Moore (1982–88)	937	Mike Parrott (1978–81)	264
Floyd Bannister (1979–82)	564	Edwin Nunez (1982–88)	247
Jim Beattie (1980–86)	563	Rick Honeycutt (1977–80)	229
Matt Young (1983–86)	421	Shane Rawley (1978–81)	217
Glenn Abbott (1977–83)	343		

ALL-TIME WALK LEADERS

Mark Langston (1984–89)	575	Glenn Abbott (1977–83)	230
Mike Moore (1982–88)	535	Shane Rawley (1978–81)	192
Jim Beattie (1980–86)	369	Mike Parrott (1978–81)	188
Matt Young (1983–86)	258	Rick Honeycutt (1977–80)	187
Floyd Bannister (1979–82)	250	Bryan Clark (1981–83)	185

ALL-TIME ERA LEADERS (Min. 300 inns.)

Bryan Clark (1981–83)	3.67	Bob Stoddard (1981–84)	4.01
Floyd Bannister (1979–82)	3.75	Edwin Nunez (1982–88)	4.13
Ed Vande Berg (1982–85)	3.75	Jim Beattie (1980–86)	4.15
Shane Rawley (1978–81)	3.80	Rick Honeycutt (1977–80)	4.23
Scott Bankhead (1987–89)	3.90	Matt Young (1983–86)	4.35
Mark Langston (1984–89)	4.01		

ALL-TIME WON-LOST PERCENTAGE LEADERS (Min. 15 wins)

Scott Bankhead (1987–89) .566
Enrique Romero (1977–78) .528
Mark Langston (1984–89) .525
Ed Vande Berg (1982–85) .500
Floyd Bannister (1979–82) .444

John Montague (1977–79) .441
Matt Young (1983–86) .435
Edwin Nunez (1982–88) .417
Glenn Abbott (1977–83) .415
Mike Moore (1982–88) .407

ALL-TIME SAVES LEADERS

Bill Claudill (1982–83) 52
Mike Schooler (1988–89) 48
Shane Rawley (1978–81) 36
Edwin Nunez (1982–88) 35
Enrique Romero (1977–78) 26

Mike Stanton (1982–85) 23
Ed Vande Berg (1982–85) 20
Byron McLaughlin (1977–80) 16
Matt Young (1983–86) 14
Bill Wilkinson (1985; 1987) 10

MARINERS LEAGUE LEADERS

BATTING

TRIPLES
H. Reynolds, 1988 (Tie)

STOLEN BASES
T. Harper, 1969 (with Pilots)
H. Reynolds, 1987

PITCHING

TEXAS RANGERS

BATTING

ALL-TIME GAME LEADERS

Jim Sundberg (1974–83)	1,398		Mike Hargrove (1974–78)	726
Toby Harrah (1972–78)	1,220		Bump Wills (1977–81)	703
Pete O'Brien (1982–88)	946		Billy Sample (1978–84)	675
Buddy Bell (1979–85)	924		Jeff Burroughs (1972–76)	635
Larry Parrish (1982–88)	804		Ruben Sierra (1986–89)	589

ALL-TIME AT BAT LEADERS

Jim Sundberg (1974–83)	4,446		Bump Wills (1977–81)	2,611
Toby Harrah (1972–78)	4,188		Mike Hargrove (1974–78)	2,494
Buddy Bell (1979–85)	3,541		Jeff Burroughs (1972–76)	2,334
Pete O'Brien (1982–88)	3,351		Ruben Sierra (1986–89)	2,274
Larry Parrish (1982–88)	2,975		Billy Sample (1978–84)	2,177

ALL-TIME RUN LEADERS

Toby Harrah (1972–78)	582		Larry Parrish (1982–88)	397
Buddy Bell (1979–85)	467		Mike Hargrove (1974–78)	380
Jim Sundberg (1974–83)	456		Billy Sample (1978–84)	330
Pete O'Brien (1982–88)	419		Ruben Sierra (1986–89)	325
Bump Wills (1977–81)	408		Jeff Burroughs (1972–76)	311

ALL-TIME HIT LEADERS

Jim Sundberg (1974–83)	1,125		Mike Hargrove (1974–78)	730
Toby Harrah (1972–78)	1,086		Bump Wills (1977–81)	693
Buddy Bell (1979–85)	1,045		Al Oliver (1978–81)	668
Pete O'Brien (1982–88)	914		Ruben Sierra (1986–89)	620
Larry Parrish (1982–88)	805		Jeff Burroughs (1972–76)	601

ALL-TIME DOUBLE LEADERS

Buddy Bell (1979–85)	193		Al Oliver (1978–81)	135
Jim Sundberg (1974–83)	189		Mike Hargrove (1974–78)	122
Toby Harrah (1972–78)	176		Ruben Sierra (1986–89)	115
Pete O'Brien (1982–88)	161		Billy Sample (1978–84)	111
Larry Parrish (1982–88)	138		Bump Wills (1977–81)	110

ALL-TIME TRIPLE LEADERS

Ruben Sierra (1986–89)	30		Toby Harrah (1972–78)	19
Jim Sundberg (1974–83)	26		Lenny Randle (1972–76)	18
Buddy Bell (1979–85)	21		Pete O'Brien (1982–88)	16
Oddibe McDowell (1985–88)	21		Gary Ward (1984–86)	16
Bump Wills (1977–81)	20		George Wright (1982–86)	16

ALL-TIME HOME RUN LEADERS

Larry Parrish (1982–88)	142		Ruben Sierra (1986–89)	98
Toby Harrah (1972–78)	122		Buddy Bell (1979–85)	87
Pete O'Brien (1982–88)	114		Tom Grieve (1972–77)	60
Jeff Burroughs (1972–76)	103		Richie Zisk (1978–80)	59
Pete Incaviglia (1986–89)	100		Oddibe McDowell (1985–88)	56

ALL-TIME TOTAL BASE LEADERS

Toby Harrah (1972–78)	1,666		Ruben Sierra (1986–89)	1,089
Buddy Bell (1979–85)	1,541		Mike Hargrove (1974–78)	1,021
Jim Sundberg (1974–83)	1,528		Jeff Burroughs (1972–76)	1,013
Pete O'Brien (1982–88)	1,449		Al Oliver (1978–81)	976
Larry Parrish (1982–88)	1,385		Bump Wills (1977–81)	933

ALL-TIME RBI LEADERS

Toby Harrah (1972–78)   546
Buddy Bell (1979–85)   496
Larry Parrish (1982–88) 496
Pete O'Brien (1982–88)   487
Jim Sundberg (1974–83)   459

Jeff Burroughs (1972–76) 386
Ruben Sierra (1986–89)   374
Al Oliver (1978–81)   337
Mike Hargrove (1974–78) 295
Bump Wills (1977–81)   264

ALL-TIME EXTRA BASE HIT LEADERS

Toby Harrah (1972–78)   317
Buddy Bell (1979–85)   301
Pete O'Brien (1982–88)   291
Larry Parrish (1982–88) 288
Jim Sundberg (1974–83)   269
Ruben Sierra (1986–89)   243

Jeff Burroughs (1972–76) 201
Al Oliver (1978–81)   197
Mike Hargrove (1974–78)   183
Bump Wills (1977–81)   160
Oddibe McDowell (1985–88) 160

ALL-TIME BATTING AVERAGE LEADERS
(300 game minimum)

Al Oliver (1978–81)   .319
Mickey Rivers (1979–84) .303
Buddy Bell (1979–85)   .295
Gary Ward (1984–86)   .293
Mike Hargrove (1974–78) .293

Pete O'Brien (1982–88)   .273
Ruben Sierra (1986–89)   .273
Johnny Grubb (1979–82)   .272
Richie Zisk (1978–80)   .271
Larry Parrish (1982–88)   .271

ALL-TIME STOLEN BASE LEADERS

Bump Wills (1977–81)   161
Toby Harrah (1972–78; 1985–86)   141
Dave Nelson (1972–75)   125
Oddibe McDowell (1985–88)   115
Billy Sample (1978–84)   92

Wayne Tolleson (1981–86)   79
Lenny Randle (1972–76)   76
Juan Beniquez (1976–78)   53
Curt Wilkerson (1983–88)   53
Bert Campaneris (1977–79)   50

PITCHING

ALL-TIME GAMES LEADERS

Charlie Hough (1980–89)	312	Dave Schmidt (1981–85)	172
Mitch Williams (1986–88)	232	Jon Matlack (1978–83)	158
Danny Darwin (1978–84)	217	Steve Comer (1978–82)	151
Steve Foucault (1973–76)	206	Jim Kern (1979–81)	132
Ferguson Jenkins (1974–75; 1978–81)	197	Doc Medich (1978–82)	132
Greg Harris (1985–87)	173	Dale Mohorcic (1986–87)	132

ALL-TIME WINS LEADER

Charlie Hough (1980–89)	127	Jon Matlack (1978–83)	43
Ferguson Jenkins (1974–75; 1978–81)	93	Steve Comer (1978–82)	39
Danny Darwin (1978–84)	53	Jose Guzman (1984–88)	37
Doc Medich (1978–82)	50	Frank Tanana (1982–85)	31
Gaylord Perry (1975–77; 1980)	48	Doyle Alexander (1977–79)	31

ALL-TIME INNINGS PITCHED LEADERS

Charlie Hough (1980–89)	2,089	Doc Medich (1978–82)	790
Ferguson Jenkins (1974–75; 1978–81)	1,410	Frank Tanana (1982–85)	677
Jon Matlack (1978–83)	915	Steve Comer (1978–82)	575
Danny Darwin (1978–84)	839	Mike Mason (1982–87)	561
Gaylord Perry (1975–77; 1980)	827	Doyle Alexander (1977–79)	541

ALL-TIME LOSS LEADERS

Charlie Hough (1980–89)	111	Jose Guzman (1985–88)	44
Ferguson Jenkins (1974–75; 1978–81)	72	Doc Medich (1978–82)	43
Danny Darwin (1978–84)	50	Gaylord Perry (1975–77; 1980)	43
Frank Tanana (1982–85)	49	Mike Mason (1982–87)	37
Jon Matlack (1978–83)	45	Jim Bibby (1973–75; 1984)	35

ALL-TIME SHUTOUT LEADERS

Ferguson Jenkins (1974–75; 1978–81)	17	Jim Umbarger (1975–76)	5
Gaylord Perry (1975–77; 1980)	12	Rick Honeycutt (1981–83)	5
Bert Blyleven (1976–77)	11	Danny Darwin (1978–84)	5
Charlie Hough (1980–89)	11	Jon Matlack (1978–83)	4
Jim Bibby (1973–75; 1980)	8	Jackie Brown (1973–75)	4
Doc Medich (1978–82)	7	Steve Hargan (1974–77)	4

ALL-TIME STRIKEOUT LEADERS

Charlie Hough (1980–89)	1,338	Jon Matlack (1978–83)	493
Ferguson Jenkins (1974–75; 1978–81)	895	Frank Tanana (1982–85)	388
Bobby Witt (1986–89)	648	Jim Bibby (1973–75; 1984)	341
Gaylord Perry (1975–77; 1980)	575	Mike Mason (1982–87)	328
Danny Darwin (1978–84)	544	Bert Blyleven (1976–77)	326

ALL-TIME WALK LEADERS

Charlie Hough (1980–89)	846	Doc Medich (1978–82)	251
Bobby Witt (1986–89)	498	Jose Guzman (1985–88)	238
Ferguson Jenkins (1974–75; 1978–81)	315	Doyle Alexander (1977–79)	222
Danny Darwin (1978–84)	291	Jon Matlack (1978–83)	219
Jim Bibby (1973–75; 1984)	257	Mitch Williams (1986–87)	219

ALL-TIME ERA LEADERS (400 inns. min.)

Bert Blyleven (1976–77)	2.74	Charlie Hough (1980–89)	3.64
Gaylord Perry (1975–77; 1980)	3.26	Rick Honeycutt (1981–83)	3.66
Jon Matlack (1978–83)	3.41	Steve Comer (1978–82)	3.80
Ferguson Jenkins (1974–75; 1978–81)	3.56	Frank Tanana (1982–85)	3.82
Danny Darwin (1978–84)	3.57	Doyle Alexander (1977–79)	3.89

ALL-TIME WON-LOST PERCENTAGE LEADERS
(Min. 20 wins)

Steve Comer (1978–82)	.574	Gaylord Perry (1975–77; 1980)	.527
Ferguson Jenkins (1974–75; 1978–81)	.564	Dock Ellis (1977–79)	.526
Doc Medich (1978–82)	.538	Steve Hargan (1974–77)	.526
Jeff Russell (1985–89)	.537	Doyle Alexander (1977–79)	.525
Charlie Hough (1980–89)	.534	Danny Darwin (1978–84)	.515

ALL-TIME SAVE LEADERS

Jeff Russell (1985–89)	43	Dale Mohorcic (1986–87)	23
Jim Kern (1979–81)	37	Sparky Lyle (1979–80)	21
Steve Foucault (1973–76)	35	Horacio Pina (1972)	15
Mitch Williams (1986–88)	32	Paul Lindblad (1972; 1977–78)	15
Greg Harris (1985–87)	31	Adrian Devine (1977; 1980)	15
Dave Schmidt (1981–85)	26	Danny Darwin (1978–84)	15

RANGERS LEAGUE LEADERS

BATTING

RBI
J. Burroughs, 1974
R. Sierra, 1989

TRIPLES
R. Sierra, 1989

PITCHING

SAVES
J. Russell, 1989

STRIKEOUTS
N. Ryan, 1989

TORONTO BLUE JAYS

BATTING

ALL-TIME GAME LEADERS

Lloyd Moseby (1980–89)	1,392	Rance Mulliniks (1982–89)	958
Ernie Whitt (1977–89)	1,218	Garth Iorg (1978–87)	931
Willie Upshaw (1978–87)	1,115	Damaso Garcia (1980–86)	902
George Bell (1981–89)	1,039	Alfredo Griffin (1979–84)	873
Jesse Barfield (1981–89)	1,031	Tony Fernandez (1983–89)	867

ALL-TIME AT BAT LEADERS

Lloyd Moseby (1980–89)	5,124	Jesse Barfield (1981–89)	3,463
George Bell (1981–89)	3,966	Tony Fernandez (1983–89)	3,317
Willie Upshaw (1978–87)	3,710	Alfredo Griffin (1979–84)	3,151
Damaso Garcia (1980–86)	3,572	Rance Mulliniks (1982–89)	2,674
Ernie Whitt (1977–89)	3,514	Garth Iorg (1978–87)	2,450

ALL-TIME RUN LEADERS

Lloyd Moseby (1980–89)	768	Tony Fernandez (1983–89)	426
George Bell (1981–89)	574	Ernie Whitt (1977–89)	424
Willie Upshaw (1978–87)	538	Alfredo Griffin (1979–84)	346
Jesse Barfield (1981–89)	530	Rance Mulliniks (1982–89)	343
Damaso Garcia (1980–86)	453	Garth Iorg (1978–87)	251

ALL-TIME HIT LEADERS

Lloyd Moseby (1980–89)	1,319	Jesse Barfield (1981–89)	919
George Bell (1981–89)	1,145	Ernie Whitt (1977–89)	888
Damaso Garcia (1980–86)	1,028	Alfredo Griffin (1979–84)	789
Willie Upshaw (1978–87)	982	Rance Mulliniks (1982–89)	754
Tony Fernandez (1983–89)	967	Garth Iorg (1978–87)	633

ALL-TIME DOUBLE LEADERS

Lloyd Moseby (1980–89)	242	Tony Fernandez (1983–89)	165
George Bell (1981–89)	212	Ernie Whitt (1977–89)	164
Rance Mulliniks (1982–89)	188	Jesse Barfield (1981–89)	163
Willie Upshaw (1978–87)	177	Garth Iorg (1978–87)	125
Damaso Garcia (1980–86)	172	Alfredo Griffin (1979–84)	117

ALL-TIME TRIPLE LEADERS

Lloyd Moseby (1980–89)	60	Jesse Barfield (1981–89)	27
Alfredo Griffin (1979–84)	50	Damaso Garcia (1980–86)	26
Tony Fernandez (1983–89)	44	Dave Collins (1983–84)	19
Willie Upshaw (1978–87)	42	Bob Bailor (1977–80)	19
George Bell (1981–89)	30	Roy Howell (1977–80)	17

ALL-TIME HOME RUN LEADERS

George Bell (1981–89)	181	John Mayberry (1978–82)	92
Jesse Barfield (1981–89)	179	Fred McGriff (1986–89)	90
Lloyd Moseby (1980–89)	149	Otto Velez (1977–82)	72
Ernie Whitt (1977–89)	131	Rance Mulliniks (1982–89)	64
Willie Upshaw (1978–87)	112	Cliff Johnson (1983–85)	54

ALL-TIME TOTAL BASE LEADERS

Lloyd Moseby (1980–89)	2,128	Damaso Garcia (1980–86)	1,348
George Bell (1981–89)	1,964	Tony Fernandez (1983–89)	1,328
Jesse Barfield (1981–89)	1,712	Rance Mulliniks (1982–89)	1,160
Willie Upshaw (1978–87)	1,579	Alfredo Griffin (1979–84)	1,045
Ernie Whitt (1977–89)	1,475	Garth Iorg (1978–87)	850

ALL-TIME RBI LEADERS

George Bell (1981–89)	654	Rance Mulliniks (1982–89)	349
Lloyd Moseby (1980–89)	651	Tony Fernandez (1983–89)	338
Jesse Barfield (1981–89)	527	Damaso Garcia (1980–86)	296
Ernie Whitt (1977–89)	518	John Mayberry (1978–82)	272
Willie Upshaw (1978–87)	478	Otto Velez (1977–82)	243

ALL-TIME EXTRA BASE HIT LEADERS

Lloyd Moseby (1980–89)	451	Rance Mulliniks (1982–89)	265
George Bell (1981–89)	425	Tony Fernandez (1983–89)	245
Jesse Barfield (1981–89)	368	Damaso Garcia (1980–86)	230
Willie Upshaw (1978–87)	331	Alfredo Griffin (1979–84)	180
Ernie Whitt (1977–89)	310	Roy Howell (1977–80)	161

ALL-TIME BATTING AVERAGE LEADERS (300 game minimum)

Tony Fernandez (1983–89)	.292	Cliff Johnson (1983–85)	.273
George Bell (1981–89)	.289	Roy Howell (1977–80)	.272
Damaso Garcia (1980–86)	.288	Al Woods (1977–82)	.270
Rance Mulliniks (1982–89)	.282	Jesse Barfield (1981–89)	.265
Barry Bonnell (1980–83)	.281	Willie Upshaw (1978–87)	.265

ALL-TIME STOLEN BASE LEADERS

Lloyd Moseby (1980–89)	255	Willie Upshaw (1979–87)	76
Damasco Garcia (1980–86)	194	George Bell (1983–89)	56
Tony Fernandez (1983–89)	112	Jesse Barfield (1981–89)	55
Dave Collins (1983–84)	91	Kelly Gruber (1984–89)	47
Alfredo Griffin (1979–84)	76	Bob Bailor (1977–80)	46

PITCHING

ALL-TIME GAME LEADERS

Dave Stieb (1979–89)	357	Jerry Garvin (1977–82)	196
Jim Clancy (1977–88)	352	Joey McLaughlin (1980–84)	195
Tom Henke (1985–89)	279	Roy Lee Jackson (1981–84)	190
Jimmy Key (1984–89)	224	Luis Leal (1980–85)	165
Mark Eichhorn (1982; 1986–88)	202	Jim Acker (1983–86)	154

ALL-TIME WIN LEADERS

Dave Stieb (1979–89)	148	Dave Lemanczyk (1977–80)	27
Jim Clancy (1977–88)	128	Mark Eichhorn (1982; 1986–87)	24
Jimmy Key (1984–89)	74	Roy Lee Jackson (1981–84)	24
Luis Leal (1980–85)	51	Joey McLaughlin (1980–84)	22
Doyle Alexander (1983–86)	46	Jesse Jefferson (1977–80)	22

ALL-TIME INNINGS PITCHED LEADERS

Dave Stieb (1979–89)	2,457	Jesse Jefferson (1977–80)	667
Jim Clancy (1977–88)	2,205	Jerry Garvin (1977–82)	607
Jimmy Key (1984–89)	1,114	Dave Lemanczyk (1977–80)	575
Luis Leal (1980–85)	946	Tom Underwood (1978–79)	425
Doyle Alexander (1983–86)	751	Jim Gott (1982–84)	423

ALL-TIME LOSS LEADERS

Jim Clancy (1977–88)	140	Dave Lemanczyk (1977–80)	45
Dave Stieb (1979–89)	117	Jerry Garvin (1977–82)	41
Luis Leal (1980–85)	58	Jim Gott (1982–84)	30
Jesse Jefferson (1977–80)	56	Tom Underwood (1978–79)	30
Jimmy Key (1984–89)	49	Doyle Alexander (1983–86)	26

ALL-TIME SHUTOUT LEADERS

Dave Stieb (1979–89)   28   Luis Leal (1980–85)   3
Jim Clancy (1977–88)   11   Jim Gott (1982–84)   3
Jimmy Key (1984–89)   6   Doyle Alexander (1983–86)   3
Jesse Jefferson (1977–80)   4   Tom Underwood (1978–79)   2
Dave Lemanczyk (1977–80)   3

ALL-TIME STRIKEOUT LEADERS

Dave Stieb (1979–89)   1,432   Tom Henke (1985–89)   470
Jim Clancy (1977–88)   1,237   Jerry Garvin (1977–82)   320
Jimmy Key (1984–89)   614   Jesse Jefferson (1977–80)   307
Luis Leal (1980–85)   491   Mark Eichhorn (1982; 1986–88)   306
Doyle Alexander (1983–86) 392   Jim Gott (1982–84)   276

ALL-TIME WALK LEADERS

Dave Stieb (1979–89)   873   Jerry Garvin (1977–82)   219
Jim Clancy (1977–88)   814   Dave Lemanczyk (1977–80)   212
Luis Leal (1980–85)   320   Jim Gott (1982–84)   183
Jimmy Key (1984–89)   279   Tom Underwood (1978–79)   182
Jesse Jefferson (1977–80)   266   Doyle Alexander (1983–86)   172

ALL-TIME ERA LEADERS (Min. 300 inns.)

Mark Eichhorn (1982; 1986–88) 2.98   John Cerutti (1985–89)   3.67
Jimmy Key (1984–89)   3.36   Joey McLaughlin (1980–84)   3.87
Dave Stieb (1979–89)   3.37   Tom Underwood (1978–79)   3.88
Roy Lee Jackson (1981–84)   3.50   Jim Acker (1983–86)   4.04
Doyle Alexander (1983–86)   3.56   Jim Clancy (1977–88)   4.10